Creating the Market University

Creating the Market University

HOW ACADEMIC SCIENCE BECAME AN ECONOMIC ENGINE

Elizabeth Popp Berman

PRINCETON UNIVERSITY PRESS
PRINCETON AND OXFORD

Published by Princeton University Press, 41 William Street, Princeton, New Jersey 08540
In the United Kingdom: Princeton University Press, 6 Oxford Street, Woodstock,
Oxfordshire OX20 1TW

press.princeton.edu

Library of Congress Cataloging-in-Publication Data

Berman, Elizabeth Popp, 1975–
Creating the market university : how academic science became an economic engine / Elizabeth Popp Berman.
p. cm.
Includes bibliographical references and index.
ISBN 978-0-691-14708-6 (hardback)
1. Science—Study and teaching (Higher)—United States. 2. Universities and colleges—Research—Economic aspects—United States. 3. Academic-industrial collaboration—United States. I. Title.
Q183.3.A1B466 2012
507.1'173–dc23 2011035707

British Library Cataloging-in-Publication Data is available

This book has been composed in Minion Pro

Printed on acid-free paper. ∞

Printed in the United States of America

10 9 8 7 6 5 4 3 2 1

For my parents, with love

Contents

Acknowledgments

THIS BOOK WAS A LONG TIME IN THE MAKING, and I have incurred many debts along the way. Neil Fligstein has been a guiding influence since our first cappuccino at Caffe Strada many years ago. He has always given me the freedom to find my own intellectual path, yet has probably shaped my thinking more than anyone else—maybe with the exception of Max Weber, which is not bad company to be in.

Kim Voss was generous with her time and incisive with her questions as she listened to this project develop over the years. Todd LaPorte, who asked, "What is this a case of?" brought his insider's knowledge of research administration at Berkeley as well as his academic expertise. Cathryn Carson taught me how to think like a historian, for which I am deeply grateful, although I still have an unhistorian-like tendency to look for patterns as well as narratives. And David Kirp provided a critical early opportunity to explore these issues when I worked on his book, *Shakespeare, Einstein, and the Bottom Line: The Marketing of Higher Education*.

I owe enormous thanks to my dissertation group, LDG, for endless rounds of intellectual and moral support at Berkeley and beyond. Hwa-Jen Liu, Teresa Sharpe, Lisa Stampnitzky, and Youyenn Teo, I would not have finished this book without you. Among the many people who made the Berkeley sociology department a lively and supportive place to be, I would particularly like to acknowledge Irene Bloemraad, Greggor Mattson, C. J. Pascoe, Jenn Sherman, and Jennifer Utrata.

At Albany, I have had the good fortune to be part of a warm, collegial, and stimulating sociology department. I am particularly grateful for the support of Richard Lachmann and Jim Zetka, both of whom read the entire manuscript, and for helpful conversations with Ron Jacobs and Karyn Loscocco. My junior colleagues (some no longer junior), Angie Chung, Kecia Johnson, Joanne Kaufman, Ryan King, Aaron Major, and Kate Strully, all gave helpful feedback on chapters as well as making the department a fun place to be. I am also deeply appreciative of research assistance from Rakkoo Chung, Josh McCabe, Laura Milanes, Nick Pagnucco, and Myeongjae Yeo.

A larger intellectual community has also shaped this project. Martin Kenney, Daniel Kleinman, Mike Lounsbury, Jason Owen-Smith, and an anonymous reviewer read the whole manuscript and provided trenchant suggestions that I hope made this a better book. Lauren Edelman, Rita Gaber, Elihu Gerson, Ed Hackett, Chris Niedt, Martha Poon, Sergio Sismondo, and Doogab Yi all provided useful and much-appreciated feedback on shorter sections. Conversations at key moments with Jeannette Colyvas, John Douglass, Henry Etzkowitz, and Irwin Feller helped to develop the project, as did responses from audiences at the American Sociological Association; the Society for Social Studies of Science; the sociology departments of McGill University, UCLA, and the University of Missouri; the STS department of Rensselaer Polytechnic Institute; and Arizona State University's Consortium for Science, Policy, and Outcomes. Abby Kinchy, Annalisa Salonius, and David Schleifer all provided friendship as well as intellectual stimulation.

I owe a great debt to the people involved in the changes described in this book who agreed to be interviewed or with whom I had less formal conversations. The late Norman Latker deserves particular gratitude not only for his time, but also for opening up his home and providing access to his personal papers. So does Jeff Reimer, who provided me with an entrée into the world of chemical engineering, which shows up only as background here but shaped my thinking considerably. Archivists at Berkeley, IEEE, MIT, the University of Michigan, and the University of Illinois all provided indispensible help as well. I draw particularly heavily on oral histories conducted by the Bancroft Library's Regional Oral History Office, which is a wonderful and much-appreciated resource. I was also fortunate to receive financial support for this project from the National Science Foundation, the Social Science Research Corporation, the Spencer Foundation, and, at Berkeley, the Center for Studies in Higher Education, the Department of Sociology and the Graduate Division.

I am perhaps the only person ever lured into graduate school as the result of discovering the *Handbook of Economic Sociology* on the shelf at Borders bookstore. So perhaps it is fitting that at last I, too, am publishing a book with Princeton University Press. Eric Schwartz has been a strong advocate of this project and I appreciate his willingness to take a chance on a first-time author. Janie Chan, Kathleen Cioffi, and Jennifer Harris all helped bring the book to final fruition. My thanks to each of you.

Parts of chapter 5 were previously published as "Why Did Universities Start Patenting? Institution-Building and the Road to the Bayh-Dole Act," *Social Studies of Science* 38:835–871. Permission from copyright holder SAGE Publications to use them here is gratefully acknowledged. I also acknowledge permission to reprint material owned or copyrighted by the Bancroft Library of the University of California, Berkeley; and the National Venture Capital Association.

Finally, on a personal level, I am grateful to the extended Moo and Whoodily families for keeping me sane, or close enough, throughout the duration of this project. I benefited greatly from the advice and support of Patricia Contaxis and Dorothy Duff Brown. A special thanks goes to Adam Stone for being an intellectual sounding board as well as a friend. I dedicate this book to my parents, Kathy and David Popp, who have been much more supportive than I deserve. And my gratitude and love go to my husband and partner, Daniel Berman, and our children, Noah and Naomi. Thank you for everything.

Creating the Market University

CHAPTER 1

Academic Science as an Economic Engine

ON 4 OCTOBER 1961, the president of the University of Illinois received a letter from Illinois governor Otto Kerner. In the letter, Governor Kerner asked the flagship institution to study the impact of universities on economic growth, with an eye toward "insur[ing] that Illinois secures a favorable percentage of the highly desirable growth industries that will lead the economy of the future."[1]

In response, the university convened a committee that met for the next eighteen months to discuss the subject. But despite the university's top-ten departments in industrially relevant fields like chemistry, physics, and various kinds of engineering, the committee was somewhat baffled by its mission.[2] How, it asked, could the university contribute to economic growth? Illinois faculty could act as consultants to companies, as they had done for decades. The university could provide additional training for industrial scientists and engineers. Scholars could undertake research on the economy. But, the committee's final report insisted, "certain basic factors are far more important in attracting industry and in plant location decisions, and therefore in stimulating regional economic growth, than the advantages offered by universities."[3] In 1963, the University of Illinois—like almost every university in the United States—had no way of thinking systematically about its role in the economy.

In 1999, thirty-six years later, the university faced a similar request. The Illinois Board of Higher Education declared that its number-one goal was to "help Illinois business and industry sustain strong economic growth."[4] This time, though, the university knew how to respond. It quickly created a Vice President for Economic Development and Corporate Relations and a Board of Trustees Committee on Economic Development.[5] It titled its annual State of the University report "The University of Illinois: Engine of Economic Development."[6] It expanded its program for patenting and licensing faculty inventions, launched IllinoisVENTURES to provide services to startup companies based on university technologies, and substantially enlarged its research parks in Chicago and Urbana-Champaign.[7] It planned to pour tens of millions of dollars into a Post-Genomics Institute and tens more into the National Center for Supercomputing Applications.[8]

What changed during this period that caused the university to react so differently to similar situations? That question is the puzzle driving this book. It has become common knowledge, at least on university campuses, that academic science is much more closely linked with the market today than it was a few decades ago. In the United States, a university research dollar is now twice as likely to come from industry as it was in the early 1970s, and industry funding has increased ninefold in real terms since then.[9] The patenting of university inventions, a practice that was once rare and sometimes banned, has become routine. About 3,000 U.S. patents are issued to universities each year—eight times the number in 1980 and more than thirty times that in the 1960s—and universities now bring in more than $2 billion in licensing revenue annually.[10] In some fields, it has become common for faculty to also be entrepreneurs; in others, it is a lack of consulting ties that is now looked on askance.[11] Universities once self-consciously held themselves apart from the economic world. How and why did they begin to integrate themselves into it?

This book attempts to answer these questions. The conventional wisdom about why universities become more involved in the marketplace emphasizes two factors. First, the move is seen as the predictable result of universities' ongoing search for new resources. After two decades of rapid growth in government funding for academic science, budgets stopped increasing in the late 1960s and stagnated through most of the 1970s.[12] When this happened, universities, which had grown accustomed to constant expansion, turned to the market as a way of acquiring additional resources. A second argument focuses on the role of industry in pulling universities toward the market. During the 1970s, many cash-strapped firms cut back on doing research—particularly basic research—themselves.[13] Industry, it is presumed, looked to universities to replace the basic research it was no longer conducting internally.

I argue that while there are elements of truth to these explanations, the main reason academic science moved toward the market was not a search for new resources or the changing needs of industry. Instead, I make two central claims about why universities' behavior changed. The first is that it was government that encouraged universities to treat academic science as an economically valuable product—though not by reducing resources so that universities were forced to try to make money off their research. The second is that the spread of a new idea, that scientific and technological innovation serve as engines of economic growth, was critical to this process, transforming first the policy arena and eventually universities' own understanding of their mission.

Despite the perception that universities were secluded ivory towers in the 1950s and 1960s, even this period saw regular experiments with practices that tied science to the marketplace, including the creation of research parks, industrial affiliates programs, and industrial extension offices. But in these decades, there were many barriers—financial, legal, and normative—to the spread of such activities. This situation persisted through the mid-1970s. In the late 1970s, however, policy decisions began to change universities' environment in ways that removed many of these barriers and in some cases replaced them with incentives. The result was the rapid growth of activities like patenting, entrepreneurship, and research collaboration with industry, which by the mid-1980s were becoming widespread in academic science.

These government decisions were made because policymakers became enamored with the idea that technological innovation helps drive the economy. Though the idea itself was not new, historically it had had little political impact. But by the late 1970s, the conjunction of a growing body of economic research, the concerns of industry, and a favorable political situation led to its embrace. For years, the United States had faced an extended period of economic stagnation, including high unemployment, high inflation, low productivity growth, and an energy crisis. Policymakers, desperate for a way out, began arguing that this was, at least in part, an innovation problem, and that policies that explicitly connected science and technology with the economy could help close a growing "innovation gap" with countries like Japan. This led to a variety of policy decisions meant to strengthen innovation as a means of achieving economic goals. These decisions came from diverse locations and reflected a whole spectrum of political and economic philosophies. Many of them were not even aimed at universities. Collectively, however, they changed the environment of academic science in a way that stimulated and legitimized the spread of market-focused activities within it.

This policy-driven change in universities' resource and regulatory environment was critical in encouraging their turn toward the market. But the idea behind the decisions mattered, too, as universities, perceiving the political success of arguments about the economic impact of innovation, began to seize upon this new way of thinking about science. Universities had always been more open to taking an active economic role than the ivory-tower stereotype would imply. But, as the University of Illinois example suggests, before the 1970s universities had a different *way* of thinking about their impact on the economic world. They saw universities as providing the fundamental science that firms would draw upon as needed to solve industrial problems and make technical advances. That is, universities saw academic science primarily as an economic *resource*.

By the early 1980s, though, universities were starting to follow policymakers' lead in seeing science as more than just a resource. Increasingly, universities also saw science as having the potential to actively drive economic growth by serving as a fount of innovation that could launch new industries or transform old ones beyond recognition. Science, universities came to believe, could actually serve as an economic *engine*.

The shift from a "science-as-resource" to "science-as-engine" model had a major impact on the university. It changed the calculus through which universities made decisions about what kinds of activities were appropriate to pursue. It gave universities a new mission: to facilitate economic growth by making sure their research reached the marketplace. It encouraged universities to move away from a passive role in which they simply created the knowledge that industry would draw on—or not—as needed. Instead, they would start working actively to turn scientific innovation into economic activity through technology transfer, faculty entrepreneurship, spinoff firms, and research partnerships with industry. The assimilation of new ideas about the impact of innovation on

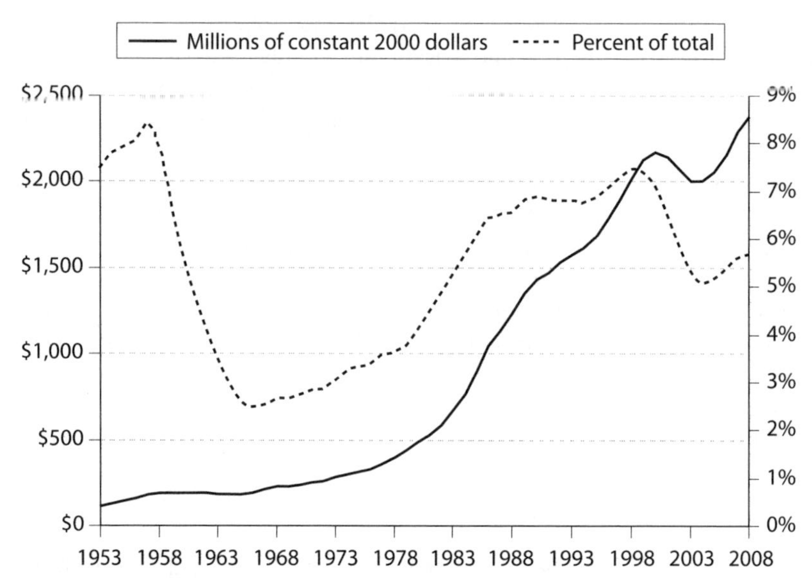

Figure 1.1. University R&D spending provided by industry, 1953–2008 (in millions of constant 2000 dollars and as a percentage of total spending). Adapted from NSB (2010:appendix table 4–3).

the economy led logically enough to other new ideas about what the relationship between academic science and the commercial world should be, and the changed environment policymakers had created made such ideas easier to put into practice. By the time the University of Illinois was asked again how it could help the state's economic growth, it had both a new way of thinking about the question and the surroundings that made it possible to turn those thoughts into action.

The Changing Nature of Academic Science

No single indicator can capture all the ways the relationship between academic science and the market has changed over the decades. But one number at least captures some part of these changes, and helps to highlight when they were taking place: the proportion of academic research and development (R&D) funded by industry, which has risen and fallen over time. Always a small fraction of the total, this number nevertheless tripled between its historical low in 1966 and its 1999 peak (see figure 1.1). (Since then it has declined significantly, a trend returned to in chapter 8.) The total amount of industry funding increased even more dramatically during that period, by an order of magnitude in real terms.

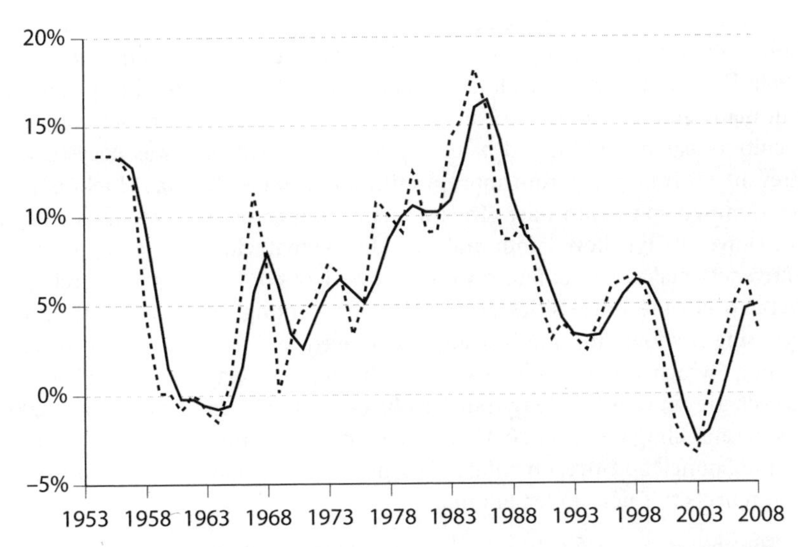

Figure 1.2. University R&D spending provided by industry, percent real change from previous year, 1954–2008. (Dashed line represents annual data; heavy line is three-year moving average.) Adapted from NSB (2010:appendix table 4-3).

The pace of this change shows when the move toward the market was at its fastest. Industry funding plummeted as a *percentage* of total academic R&D spending in the 1950s and early 1960s as the result of a sevenfold increase (in real terms) in federal funding, even though industry support for university research actually rose during this period.[14] But the fraction of funding coming from industry started to increase steadily again during the late 1960s as federal support leveled off. Starting around 1977, increases in industry funding accelerated, and real growth averaged more than 12% a year for the following decade. Between 1985 and 1986, industry funding grew by 18% in inflation-adjusted dollars, the largest jump on record; after that, funding continued to climb but at sharply decelerating rates (see figure 1.2).[15]

Other, more qualitative measures capture some of the flavor of this shift. For example, university attitudes toward patenting evolved dramatically during this time period. Traditionally, universities rarely patented faculty inventions. Most universities felt that since faculty were already being paid to do research, they didn't need additional incentives to invent. And patenting was widely seen as incompatible with the scientific ideals of open communication, disinterestedness, and service of the public good. When Jonas Salk, bacteriology professor at the University of Pittsburgh, invented the vaccine for polio, Edward R. Murrow asked him who owned the patent. Salk replied, famously, "Well, the people, I would say. There is no patent. Could you patent the sun?"[16]

The idea that patents were at odds with the nature of science as well as the public interest can be found in many university patent policies of the 1950s and 1960s.[17] By no means were all universities categorically opposed to patenting. But many emphasized the university's aversion to financially benefiting from faculty research, and limited patenting to cases in which it was necessary to prevent a private party from appropriating an invention.[18] Johns Hopkins' policy summed up this attitude: "The ownership and administration of patents by the University is believed undesirable. . . . Consistent with its general policy, the University makes no claim to royalties growing out of University research."[19]

But over time, universities' perspective on patenting changed. Patenting and licensing are now almost universally encouraged, and seen as a key mechanism through which scientific advances reach the public. Today, more than 150 U.S. universities have technology transfer offices, or TTOs, employing some 2,000 people and filing well over 10,000 new patent applications a year.[20] A statement by the Council on Governmental Relations, an association of research universities, reflects this new understanding:

> The ability to retain title to and license their inventions has been a healthy incentive for universities. . . . It is important to recognize that without such incentives, many inventions may not get carried through the necessary steps and a commercial opportunity will be wasted. This wasting of ideas is a drain on the economy, irrespective of whether it was public or private funding which led to the initial invention.[21]

As the Association of University Technology Managers emphasizes, "These activities can be pursued without disrupting the core values of publication and sharing of information, research results, materials, and know-how."[22]

This change in belief may have aligned with what universities saw as their financial self-interest, but that makes it no less sincere. It goes hand in hand with the idea of science as an economic engine, a source of innovation that can create new products, firms, or even industries. From this point of view, the market is the best way of getting university breakthroughs into the hands of the public, and patents create the incentive that makes this happen. As a university administrator interviewed by Leland Glenna and his colleagues stated, "The truth of the matter is that if things get created at the university and they never get pushed out into the industry sector and turned into a product, they really don't benefit the public good other than for the knowledge of their having existed."[23]

As the university itself has come to focus on the commercial impact of science, so have individual scientists. In the 1950s, academic scientists were supposed to be indifferent to worldly goods. As Steven Shapin has pointed out, in 1953 a letter-writer to *Science* was able to argue that the American scientist

> is not properly concerned with hours of work, wages, fame or fortune. For him an adequate salary is one that provides decent living without frills or

> furbelows. No true scientist wants more, for possessions distract him from doing his beloved work. He is content with an Austin instead of a Packard; with a table model TV set instead of a console; with factory- rather than tailor-made suits, with dollar rather than hand-painted neckties, etc., etc. To boil it down, he is primarily interested in what he can do for science, not in what science can do for him.[24]

While it seems certain that such asceticism was never completely the norm, the fact that such a claim could even be seriously made suggests that a change in ideals has taken place. Ever since Genentech's 1980 initial public offering (IPO) made University of California, San Francisco (UCSF) biochemist Herbert Boyer worth $65 million overnight, the possibility of owning the Packard—or a garage full of them—has not been lost on ambitious scientists.[25] Academic scientists still hold a range of attitudes toward the appropriate role of commercial activity in the university. But a large number join the belief that science has value because it expands human knowledge with the belief that the market is key to maximizing the impact of that knowledge—and that financial rewards are completely appropriate for those who facilitate that process.[26] As one entrepreneurial academic has said, "If there is some gold in the hills, and you happen to get a chunk, well, there is no point in leaving it in the ground if somebody is going to pay you for it."[27]

All these changes have been a part of a gradual shift in values and beliefs, not a wholesale transformation. But they have led to tensions within the university about its proper role in society and where, or if, a boundary between university and industry should be drawn. Critics of this move toward the market see it as posing a threat to science in service of goals that should be secondary, at least for universities, to the pursuit of knowledge. One prominent biochemist expressed concern about "almost a get-rich-quick attitude that is contrary to everything that science and the university stand for, which is knowledge for its own sake, not knowledge that is lucrative."[28] Others worry that these developments distort research agendas, create problematic conflicts of interest, and encourage a secrecy that is detrimental to the progress of science.[29]

Proponents, on the other hand, emphasize the benefits of these changes, pointing to the role of the market in getting science into broader use, the contribution of university inventions to economic development, and the importance of rewarding scientists whose work has a real-world impact.[30] As one academic-turned-entrepreneur said of scientists who criticize patenting, "They don't understand what it takes. They get their money from public funds. They owe it to the public or to the government or to wherever they get their money from, to try to capitalize on that investment as well as they can."[31] From this perspective, the positive effects of this shift far outweigh any new problems it might create.[32]

While universities themselves have moved decisively toward the market, debate between these points of view persists. A few years ago, Berkeley found itself under fire for accepting a $500 million grant from energy firm BP to pursue research on biofuels and other alternative energy sources.[33] Many saw the deal as win-win, leveraging public and private resources to launch a major research effort in a vitally important field.[34] But it was also criticized precisely *because* the research was so socially relevant: critical new technologies developed with public resources might be controlled by a private firm, and research might focus on areas most likely to be commercially viable, not necessarily those with the largest potential impact on climate change.

The nature of such debates has changed remarkably little over time. In 1974, Harvard and chemical firm Monsanto formed a large-scale university-industry research partnership—a then-unheard-of $23 million collaboration to study a substance thought to regulate tumor development. Headlines about the Harvard-Monsanto deal emphasized the project's potential to fight cancer. But concerns came up as well. "Would it undermine peer review? Would it lock the university into business deals it ultimately might not like? If one such arrangement is acceptable, would many subtly work against academic freedom in ways no public interest committee could fully guard against?"[35] These issues have been raised many times since then, and the very same questions continue to be asked today.

Studying the Changes in Academic Science

The purpose of this book, however, is not to resolve such debates, but to explain *why* these changes took place. I do that by comparing the historical development of three different practices closely associated with this shift: faculty entrepreneurship in the biosciences, the patenting of university inventions, and the creation of university-industry research centers (UIRCs). Each of these activities is frequently referred to in discussions of how academic science has changed, and based on their scale and divergence from past practice, they are among the most significant reflections of this trend.[36] But in order to explain why I chose this particular approach and how I came to my conclusions, I will first take a step back and briefly introduce a concept that grounds the larger argument.

The changes in academic science can be seen as one instance of a more general pattern. In the last thirty years, the logic of the marketplace—of property rights and free exchange as the best way to maximize both the individual and collective good—has expanded in a number of fields where it once played a minor role. Domains as diverse as healthcare, the military, water systems, highways and ports, and K–12 education have all been reorganized to some extent around market ideals.

Scholars who study organizations have developed a concept that is useful for thinking about these moves toward the market: that of the *institutional logic*.

An institutional logic is a set of organizing principles for a major social order, such as the market, the state, the family, religion, or science.[37] These principles explain the purpose of social action and serve as a basis for making decisions about how to behave. Different institutional logics frequently conflict with one another. The institutional logic of the family, for example, emphasizes community, loyalty, and support for its members. It would prescribe actions in the interest of the family as a whole, even if they come at a personal cost. The logic of religion, by contrast, suggests action in accordance with a transcendental set of principles. The biblical story of Abraham's anguish over God's demand that he sacrifice his son, Isaac, can be seen as a case of intense conflict between these two logics.

More mundanely, the new practices in academic science that I examine are consistent with the logic of the market, or capitalism. This logic views science as a useful tool for affecting the world. Its success is ultimately measured by whether its results have value in the marketplace, a metric that is the norm in the world of business. But in the field of academic science, another institutional logic has also traditionally been strong: the logic of science.[38] This other logic sees the search for truth as having intrinsic value. Science is fundamentally the pursuit of knowledge, in which practical results are an agreeable but secondary benefit. The ivory-tower stereotype, in which isolated scholars pursue their intellectual agendas without regard to "real-world" relevance, is compatible with this logic.

The story of academic science over the past several decades, then, can be recast as one in which market logic has gained strength relative to the logic of science. Of course these two logics are not the only grounds upon which scientists can act. Science has also been driven by the desire to achieve other goals, like improving human health or contributing to the nation's defense, that do not map neatly onto these two logics. But even these other goals have often been seen through the lens of science or market logic. While scientists once argued that the best way to achieve medical breakthroughs was by following the internal logic of science, they now emphasize the role of the market in getting medical breakthroughs into use. As a shorthand for talking about what has changed, the idea of a shift from science logic to market logic captures a lot.

But how does an institutional logic gain strength in a particular field? Here, organization theory gives us fewer tools to work with.[39] On the one hand, a particular logic may become stronger across a field as a whole. The new logic starts to seem more appropriate and legitimate to people within the field, it more frequently occurs to those people to deploy it, and action based on it becomes more likely to succeed. Some of the changes in academic science have been of this relatively diffuse nature, as people within universities have developed a greater familiarity and comfort with the idea that science's value is realized through the marketplace.

These diffuse changes, however, are difficult to pinpoint and thus to explain. I suggest that in addition to such distributed change, the strength of a new logic also becomes visible because it grounds particular practices that become widespread. In academic science, while there has certainly been a shift in the typical attitude toward the economic role of science, a lot of what has changed is that specific practices grounded in market logic have become more common. The practices I examine here, biotech entrepreneurship, university patenting, and university-industry research centers, each reflect the idea that science matters, and has an impact, because people are willing to pay for its results.

Examining the emergence of specific market-logic practices has two advantages. One is that it provides a focal point that is not available when looking at changes in academic science as a whole. The other, and more important, advantage is that it provides comparative leverage. The trajectories of the three practices I look at are very different. The practices emerged from a variety of disciplines and were initiated by a variety of actors. If they all developed in response to reduced resources, or were all the outcome of industry efforts, or if upper-level administrators championed each one, that should tell us something about why market logic gained strength in the field as a whole.

This approach has limitations, too, of course. It does not examine every market-logic practice that has emerged in academic science. Other practices may have had different causes. It assumes that an explanation of why these particular practices spread tells us something about why market logic gained strength across academic science as a whole, even in other parts of the field. And in its effort to explain the emergence of these specific practices, it cannot account for the possibility that similar factors may have been present and yet not led to the spread of market-logic practices in other parts of academic science. Nevertheless, if these limitations are kept in mind, I believe this research strategy can contribute to our understanding of how academic science moved toward the market.

The initial phase of research, then, involved developing histories of these three practices. To do this, I drew on a variety of sources, ranging from archival records and Congressional hearings, to oral histories and interviews, to contemporary media accounts and published statistics. In each case, I tried to identify reasons each practice spread, looking for evidence along the way that would support or disconfirm any emerging explanations, and to evaluate the relative importance of these reasons. While I tried to remain open to a variety of possible causes, I paid particular attention to the roles of the university itself (including those played by both faculty and administrators), of government, and of industry in encouraging the spread of these practices.

This led to a deeper understanding of each practice, but not to any easy answers about why universities moved toward the market. The practices had very different origins and reasons for their spread, to the extent that their differences initially seemed to outweigh their similarities.

Two commonalities, however, stood out. First, government, more than universities or industry, played an important role in promoting the growth of each practice. While all three practices were initiated in universities prior to and independent of government action, each encountered a variety of barriers that limited its spread until specific policy decisions had been made. Second, all but one of these critical policy decisions were made within a relatively narrow time window in the late 1970s and early 1980s.

The problem, though, was that while government action seemed to be key, the actual policy decisions that contributed to the practices' growth initially appeared to have little in common. The decisions had different supporters with different political philosophies and a variety of goals. A number of them were not even targeted at universities. So simply attributing the shift to government action was not, by itself, a very satisfying answer.

But the temporal overlap of these policy decisions suggested that they might have something in common despite their superficial dissimilarity. This observation led to a second round of research focused specifically on the politics behind ten significant policy decisions. Here, a pattern quickly jumped out. While the important decisions were not initiated by the same groups or for the same reasons, in every case but one new arguments about the economic impact of scientific and technological innovation were very visible as they were being made. During the late 1970s, in the context of a stagnating economy and growing pessimism about the nation's future, arguments that innovation was key to economic growth and that government needed to strengthen innovation became newly popular among policymakers. These arguments gave a political boost to policy proposals that could be framed as improving innovation, whether that was the proposals' original intent or not.

In six of the ten policy decisions I examined, the deployment of such arguments seemed crucial to the decision's being made. In one, these arguments played a role but were probably not decisive, and in two more innovation arguments were visible, but I did not find enough evidence to draw conclusions about how important their role was. The final decision took place before the innovation frame became prominent, and innovation arguments were not visible in that decision. The fact that in nine of ten cases innovation arguments were very visible, and that in six of those they appeared to be critical, suggested that claims about the economic impact of innovation, newly salient in the political sphere, significantly reshaped the environment surrounding academic science.

At this point, then, I had a working argument about why market logic had gained strength in academic science. Universities had already been experimenting with market-logic practices, but until the late 1970s those experiments remained limited in scope because the cultural, resource, and regulatory environment was unfavorable to them. In the late 1970s and early 1980s, however, policy decisions—driven by the idea that innovation spurs economic growth—changed that environment in ways that removed regulatory barriers to such practices and provided new resources for them. In this new environment, market-logic practices grew and spread, and market logic became stronger throughout the field.

A final comparative strategy helped test this argument. Here, the insights of institutional theory were again useful. Friedland and Alford emphasized that the major institutional logics—market, family, state, religion, science, and so on—are available for individuals to use and elaborate across various fields, even though some fields may be dominated by one particular logic.[40] So the idea that people in universities were experimenting with market logic even before it became common is compatible with their conception.

If this is the case, one should expect to find experiments with market logic in the 1950s and 1960s, during the peak years of science logic, as well as in the 1970s, just before the shift began. If the changed policy environment of the late 1970s was critical to the takeoff of contemporaneous market-logic experiments, one would make two predictions about earlier market-logic experiments. First, one should see earlier experiments running into barriers similar to those initially encountered by the practices of the 1970s. Second, one should be able to argue plausibly that earlier experiments also could have grown and spread, had they encountered a policy environment similar to that of the late 1970s.

This turned out to be the case. Three experiments with market logic were initiated during the 1950s and 1960s and experienced some modest success but did not become widespread at the time: industrial affiliates programs, industrial extension offices, and research parks. A look at their development suggested that they ran into barriers quite similar to those initially encountered by the 1970s practices. Furthermore, in each case it seemed plausible that a policy environment focused on encouraging innovation for economic reasons could have led to policies that would have encouraged them. In fact, research parks actually did eventually take off in the 1980s with the intervention of government, after enduring a bust during the 1970s. This last round of comparison reinforced the core argument, which I will now present as a chronological narrative.

Explaining the Rise of Market Logic in Academic Science

The central question this book is trying to answer is why, over a period of several decades, market logic became more influential in academic science. Empirically, I argue that market logic gained strength for two reasons. First, government policies encouraged the growth of small-scale market-logic activities. Second, the reason those government policies changed was because policymakers embraced a new idea: that scientific and technological innovation drive the economy.

Theoretically, I propose a new way of thinking about how an institutional logic can gain influence in a particular field. Individual actors in a field are continually experimenting with innovative activities, most—but not all—of which will draw on the field's dominant logic. Some of these experiments will eventually spread and become institutionalized. But for such practices to thrive and grow, they must be reproducible. That is, those carrying them out must be able to secure whatever resources they need to continue to enact them.

Most of the time, local innovations based on the dominant logic will find it easier to acquire the resources needed to perpetuate themselves than will practices based on other institutional logics. A restaurant based on family loyalty rather than commitment to the bottom line will on average be outcompeted by restaurants focused primarily on profit. But sometimes the broader environment may change in ways that start to favor innovations based on an alternative logic. As these alternative-logic practices themselves start to spread and become institutionalized, the alternative logic gains strength in the field as a whole.

This is what happened in academic science. Multiple logics have always been at play in academic science. But in the decades following World War II, the logic of science—that scientific knowledge should be pursued for its own sake, and that scientists should be free to direct that pursuit—was especially strong. During that period, some people did experiment with practices grounded in market logic—that is, that saw science in terms of its economic value—initiating activities like research parks, industrial affiliates programs, and industrial extension offices. But while such activities spread to a modest extent, they also encountered barriers that limited their growth. In particular, a university-industry culture gap made them difficult to sustain, and they had trouble securing the financial resources they needed to reproduce themselves more broadly.

In the late 1970s, a shift began in the policy realm that changed the environment of academic science in ways that encouraged the growth of market-logic practices. That shift took place because policymakers seized upon a new theory. Economists had explored the idea that technological innovation was a crucial source of economic growth for several decades. But until the 1970s, few policymakers focused on the economic impact of science and technology. As the stagflation of the 1970s dragged on, however, policymakers were looking for new solutions to the nation's economic problems, and by about 1977 they were reaching consensus that encouraging innovation was one such solution. For the next few years, this "innovation economy" frame was particularly strong, and policies that could be argued to strengthen innovation received a political boost.

The result was a variety of policy decisions made claiming to help innovation. Some were new policies created specifically to pursue that goal. Others had long been on the agenda, but were now reframed in innovation terms. The policies were diverse, and represented a range of economic philosophies. Some were free-market-oriented, while others aligned with industrial policy. They were promoted by a variety of individuals and groups with very different interests, and did not reflect a coherent political project. Collectively, however, they would change the environment of academic science in ways that had long-term consequences.

In universities, the 1970s saw several new experiments with market-logic activities, including faculty entrepreneurship in the biosciences, increased patenting efforts, and the creation of university-industry research centers. In many ways, these experiments were no different from the market-logic experiments of the 1950s and 1960s, which had such limited success. In fact, these new experiments ran into very similar difficulties to those the older ones had, and as late as 1977 it seemed unlikely that any of them was on the verge of takeoff. But the new political environment changed in ways that removed limits to the spread of these new practices and created new resources to sustain them. By the end of the decade, all were growing rapidly and were on their way to broader institutionalization.

The modern era of biotech entrepreneurship began in 1976 with the founding of Genentech by an academic and a venture capitalist. The invention of recombinant DNA (rDNA) technology in 1973 had opened new doors for the practical application of biology, and Genentech hoped to capitalize on it. In the next few years, a handful of other biotech firms were started. But there were significant drags on the spread of biotech entrepreneurship. In addition to disapproval within the academic community, there were fears about the hazards of rDNA, and the availability of venture capital was extremely low. Between 1977 and 1979, though, three policy decisions were made that changed that situation.

First, though Congressional regulation of rDNA research looked inevitable as late as August 1977, by the end of the year the tide had turned, and by the spring of 1978 legislation restricting rDNA was permanently off the table. Second, though a few other startups had been created on the Genentech model by 1978, the limited availability of venture capital made funding them a struggle. This was particularly critical since even optimists believed the startups were years away from having rDNA products to sell. In 1978, however, two policy decisions were set into motion that changed the venture capital situation dramatically. The Revenue Act of 1978 was signed into law in November, reducing the top tax rate on capital gains from 49% to 28%. And around the same time, the Department of Labor initiated a regulatory clarification that would allow pension funds, with their massive holdings, to invest some of their money in venture capital. These two actions helped set off a rush of venture capital investment and dramatically changed the resource environment for biotech startups. As a result, not only did more money become available for the handful of firms that had already been founded, but incentives to start new firms also increased dramatically. This was followed by a 1980 Supreme Court decision, *Diamond v. Chakrabarty*, that affirmed that microorganisms could be patented and reassured investors that it would be possible to realize profits on the products of biotechnology. By the early 1980s, over a hundred biotech startups, typically founded by academics and venture capitalists, had been established, and entrepreneurship was becoming common in the bioscience disciplines.

University patenting had taken place on a small scale for many decades. Federal patent policy, however, effectively limited the extent of university patenting, as many agencies restricted it or made it hard to do. But starting in the late 1960s, as the scale of research funding grew, the number of patents being issued to universities gradually began to increase. One important reason for this was that in the late 1960s the National Institutes of Health (NIH) began using institutional patent agreements (IPAs), which made it somewhat easier for universities to patent research supported by the agency. By the early 1970s, the National Science Foundation (NSF) was signing IPAs as well. But an abrupt reversal of this policy at NIH in 1977 suddenly halted the patenting of NIH-funded research and made it clear that the practice was on shaky legal foundations.

Three policy decisions made in the early 1980s changed the resource and regulatory environment in ways that encouraged the growth and spread of university patenting. The most important was the 1980 passage of the Bayh-Dole Act, which gave universities the clear right to patent all government-funded inventions and the obligation to encourage the commercialization of such research. The 1980 *Chakrabarty* decision also helped by expanding the scope of patentability in an area that was particularly significant to universities. And the 1982 creation of the Court of Appeals for the Federal Circuit, a specialized patent court that is widely attributed with having strengthened intellectual property rights in the United States, also played an important role by making patents more valuable to universities as well as other patent holders. The legitimation of university patenting provided by Bayh-Dole, in conjunction with this general fortification of the patent system, helped increase the frequency of university patenting.

University-industry research centers, modeled on the organizational research units that became widespread on campuses in the 1960s, were a new way of organizing ongoing university-industry partnerships. A few schools experimented with them in the 1970s, but they did not spread quickly, in part because they encountered familiar barriers: a university-industry culture gap, and trouble convincing industry that they were worth supporting at levels of ongoing sustainability.

Between about 1978 and 1984, however, federal and state policy decisions changed the environment for UIRCs as well, making them viable by subsidizing them heavily. In 1978, NSF initiated the Industry/University Cooperative Research Centers (I/UCRC) program, a modest effort to support UIRCs. Then in 1983, it established a related—but much larger—Engineering Research Centers (ERC) program that would provide further support. Collectively, NSF programs invested more than $100 million in UIRCs by the end of the 1980s.

At the same time, individual states were also becoming interested in UIRCs. While states had played a major role in funding higher education, historically they had not focused their efforts on scientific research, and they certainly had not tried to leverage science for the purposes of economic development. Beginning around 1979, however, a handful of states began to do just that, and one of the most common forms their efforts took was support for UIRCs. In the early 1980s, such policies spread rapidly across state governments, and during that decade states invested hundreds of millions of dollars in such programs. Thus the spread of UIRCs was facilitated not by making university research more valuable and easier to sell on the market, as the changes in patent policy and in the venture capital environment did, but by actively subsidizing activities that focused on the economic value of science. The UIRC programs supported the spread of market-logic practices even though they were interventionist, not free-market, in nature.

The policy decisions that facilitated the growth of market-logic practices superficially had little in common. They were not promoted by a single group of people working to transform the innovation landscape in the United States. Instead, they resulted from a variety of political projects undertaken by a variety of political actors holding a variety of political and economic philosophies. But in almost every case, policymakers' level of concern with the economic impact of innovation was an important factor in the decision. The way that concern had its effects varied considerably. In some cases, like the passage of Bayh-Dole, policy entrepreneurs reframed a preexisting political effort in innovation terms. In others, the frame was used strategically to defend an agency's autonomy, as when NSF created its I/UCRC program so that Congress did not force it to start supporting industry research directly. In yet others, policy proposals were made politically unviable by being portrayed as stifling innovation, as happened during debates over the regulation of rDNA research. But in each case, the increased political salience of innovation as an economic issue gave a boost to a policy that aligned well with the goal of improving innovation.

Despite the diversity of these policies, and despite the fact that a number of them did not even target universities, collectively they had a consistent effect on academic science. They tended to encourage activities that treated science as an economic input, which effectively meant that they promoted the growth of market-logic practices. While this did not mean that all new efforts to capitalize on the economic value of science would succeed, it did allow a variety of market-logic activities to grow, spread, and begin to institutionalize throughout universities by the mid-1980s.

The practices of biotech entrepreneurship, university patenting, and university-industry research centers did not originate with university leaders, but with faculty and mid-level administrators. But as these activities became visibly successful, others within the university, including upper-level administrators, also became more oriented toward realizing the economic value of science. New experiments with market logic were initiated, like a wave of large-scale biotech research partnerships announced in the early 1980s, and older activities that had not been on a growth trajectory, like research parks, suddenly took off. And increasingly, as the political effectiveness of innovation arguments became visible, representatives of the university began framing both existing activities and new ones in terms of their economic impact, even if they had originally been conceived of in terms other than those of market logic.

These developments all led market logic to gain further strength across academic science. It did not replace the logic of science, though the latter certainly ceded some ground. But by the mid-1980s, market logic had become much better established in universities, and since then it has remained a central way of thinking about the value of science and the best path to realizing that value. The uneasy coexistence of market logic and the logic of science continues to be at the root of some of our most serious debates about the purpose and future of science in the university.

Overview of the Book

The rest of this book is divided into three parts. Chapters 2 and 3 provide background, looking at the state of academic science, and market logic within it, up to the late 1970s. Chapter 4, 5, and 6 contain case studies of the emergence and growth of three market-logic practices in the 1970s and 1980s. And chapters 7 and 8 explore the consolidation of market logic in the 1980s and beyond, and examine its broader implications for the university.

I will begin in chapter 2 with a survey of the postwar golden era, when the logic of science was strong and increases in federal funding were large and steady. Yet even in this period, market logic was present. I look at records from the early 1960s that suggest that universities were not as unfriendly to market logic as one might assume, and describe several experiments made with market-logic practices during this era. But while such activities were not unheard of, sustaining them was difficult, and they did not have a large impact on the university at the time. By the late 1960s, however, changes were starting to undermine the system of federal funding that had supported the logic of science, and these would eventually open the door to other ways of thinking.

Chapter 3 begins by introducing another round of market-logic experiments, this time ones being undertaken in the mid-1970s. Like earlier efforts, these practices encountered limitations and did not, at the time, look poised to take off. But this time, things would be different, as a new idea started to gain influence in the policy realm. While economists had been looking seriously at the impact of innovation since the 1950s, policymakers' attention to the issue was limited before 1970. A spurt of interest in innovation in the early 1970s fizzled out when the economy rebounded briefly, but as the economy lost steam mid-decade, industry leaders, concerned with indicators suggesting that the United States was losing its technological leadership, began to push the idea that government needed to act to strengthen innovation. In the latter part of the decade, the innovation issue would become politically salient and influential, and would shape a variety of policies meant to strengthen the U.S. economy.

Chapters 4, 5, and 6 are the empirical heart of the book. Each looks at the development of a specific new market-logic practice in academic science: faculty entrepreneurship in the biosciences, the patenting of university inventions, and the creation of university-industry research centers. The chapters begin by reviewing the origins of one of these practices, then track its early development as well as limits to its growth and spread. They go on to examine policy decisions that removed these limits and replaced them with incentives, and consider how political concern with the economic impact of innovation contributed to these decisions. The chapters conclude with a look at the subsequent takeoff of each practice, followed by a discussion of the conditions that appear to have been necessary for this takeoff to occur.

Chapter 7 returns the focus to the university as a whole. It asks how the spread of these three practices contributed to a larger shift toward market logic in academic science during the 1980s. This chapter shows how the success of biotech entrepreneurship, university patenting, and university-industry research centers encouraged additional experiments with and expansions of market-logic activity, as well as pushing university leaders to recast much of what academic science did in terms of its economic impact.

The book's conclusion develops two points. First, it reviews how the evidence presented in earlier chapters supports my overall argument, as well as evaluating other possible explanations for the changes that have taken place in academic science. Second, it considers what the story told here has to say to larger conversations—about how institutional logics gain strength, about the role of the state in creating markets, and about how thinking about activities in terms of their economic role can eventually change them.

CHAPTER 2

Market Logic in the Era of Pure Science

It is hard to overstate how much World War II changed the landscape of academic science in the United States. University research was a modest, small-scale endeavor until the Manhattan Project demonstrated the power of science and, in the process, transformed the way it was organized. Building the bomb that ended the war gave scientists a great deal of public respect and influence that, in the postwar years, they would leverage into a massive new system for the support of academic science. This system would be predicated on large and growing levels of federal funding and a great deal of autonomy for scientists in deciding how that funding would be spent. It was this foundation that made it possible for the logic of science—the idea that the pursuit of knowledge is valuable for its own sake—to flourish in universities in the 1950s and 1960s. During this period, market logic would, by comparison, play a fairly minor role.

Before the war, the scope of academic science was relatively small. In 1938, it was estimated that a total of $50 million was spent nationally on research at universities.[1] When Ernest Lawrence began in 1939 to plan his 184-inch cyclotron, which would require a several-thousand-ton, 30-foot-tall magnet and be housed in a dedicated building, it was the biggest of big science projects, with a projected budget of $1.4 million.[2] By contrast, six years later the Manhattan Project had spent $1.89 *billion* dollars, reducing Lawrence's cyclotron to a rounding error.[3]

What science funding there was before the war came from a variety of sources, and federal money did not dominate as it would afterward.[4] The entire budget of the National Institutes of Health (NIH) was under half a million dollars in 1939, and the National Science Foundation (NSF) did not yet exist.[5] Private foundations, like the Rockefeller Foundation and the Carnegie Corporation, played a more significant role than they would later.[6] The limited availability of funding meant that on the one hand, scientists were relatively independent, and those devoted to the pure pursuit of knowledge were free to focus on that. On the other, it also meant that scientists were attuned to multiple ways of supporting research, not just to government funds. MIT, for example, was actively seeking to develop its industry relationships in the early decades of the twentieth century, and at Berkeley Frederick Cottrell was turning his invention of the electrostatic precipitator into a sizable revenue stream.[7] In this smaller world, the logic of science and the logic of the market could both be found.

The mobilization of science for war had two long-term impacts on academic research. First, it was scaled up tremendously. While the Manhattan Project was huge, even that was only a fraction of total wartime spending on R&D. Daniel Kevles has estimated that "the combined bill for radar, proximity fuzes, and rockets far exceeded the $2 billion spent on the atom bomb."[8] The nine universities that held significant wartime contracts with the federal Office of Scientific Research and Development collectively conducted more than $300 million of research during the war, with MIT leading the pack with a whopping $117 million in contracts.[9] By contrast, in 1938 MIT had been estimated to spend a mere $1 to $1.5 million a year on research.[10]

Second, this influx of government dollars made academic science dependent on federal funding to a much greater extent than ever before. While government spending on R&D was exploding, voluntary support of universities remained roughly constant.[11] Though federal spending would not stay at wartime levels after 1945, it would never again account for less than a majority of university R&D support.[12] These changed realities would set the stage for a new, if finite, era in academic science. The postwar decades would see generous government support for university research, including much that was done with little regard for its practical outcome. In this environment, the institutional logic of science would thrive.

Yet even in this period, experiments with market logic were not uncommon on university campuses. The rest of this chapter will look at the roles played by both science and market logics in universities during the decades after the war. First, I sketch a picture of the federal funding system that developed in the years following World War II, and show how it supported the pursuit of science for its own sake. Second, I look at the state of market logic during the same time period. While the ideal of pure science was strong in the 1950s and 1960s, evidence suggests that even then universities were surprisingly willing to consider market-oriented activities when they came with the promise of new resources. Individual institutions experimented with market-logic practices with some modest degree of success. But during this era, their innovations tended to remain local, and the extent to which they were adopted by other universities was limited. There were at least two reasons for this. On the one hand, universities had a different way of thinking about the way science affected the economy—they saw it as a resource for industry, rather than an economic engine—and this tended to encourage a relatively passive role. On the other, local experiments with market-logic were limited because they could not support themselves at a level that would allow them to spread widely. Finally, the chapter ends by looking at late-1960s developments that started to undermine the system of federal support that had helped to keep science logic strong, and that would open the door to new policies that would encourage the spread of market-logic practices instead.

Federal Funding and the Support of Science Logic

The atomic bomb and other wartime science advances were the successful outcome of the largest applied science effort ever made, conducted in pursuit of utterly practical ends. Ironically, scientists would use the legitimacy conferred by these successes to help create a federal funding system that emphasized "pure science" and serendipitous applications, not applied problem-solving. Initial proposals for the establishment of a federal agency to coordinate science focused on the centralization of research, democratic control of the scientific enterprise, and practical results. But the leaders of the science establishment opposed solutions that took so much control out of the hands of scientists. Vannevar Bush, a former MIT dean of engineering and director of the wartime Office of Scientific Research and Development, presented an alternative proposal in his 1945 report, *Science—The Endless Frontier.*[13]

While, as David Hart has pointed out, one can overestimate the role *Science—The Endless Frontier* played as a blueprint for postwar science policy, it certainly can be read as a manifesto for the institutional logic of science.[14] Bush's report argued strongly for the support of basic research, which he defined as being "performed without thought of practical ends."[15] Pure science, he suggested, would lead naturally to technological applications, but must be shielded from any pressure for practical results. Such pressure would harm the progress of basic science, and in the long run be detrimental to the development of useful applications: "*Applied research invariably drives out pure.*"[16] To implement this agenda, Bush called for the creation of a single coordinating agency for science policy, a National Research Foundation. It would be run by a scientist, not a political appointee, since Bush believed that funding decisions should be made on the basis of scientific, not political or practical, criteria. And it would emphasize basic science and deemphasize practical applications.[17]

But Bush's National Research Foundation was never established. Congress's inability to reach political compromise on what such a foundation should look like meant that no single agency came to administer federal science policy. By the time NSF was created in 1950, both the Atomic Energy Commission (AEC) and the Office of Naval Research (ONR) had also been established, and NIH had been budgeted money for handling research contracts.[18] Each of these agencies would claim dominion over a significant piece of science turf, leaving less space for a centralized agency of the sort Bush had imagined.

The NSF that was actually established was smaller than the National Research Foundation proposed by Bush, since it essentially filled in the cracks between other science funding sources that were set up after the war.[19] But it still incorporated many of Bush's ideals. The agency was explicitly designed to support basic science, not applied science. While the director was presidentially appointed, he shared power with the scientist-run National Science Board

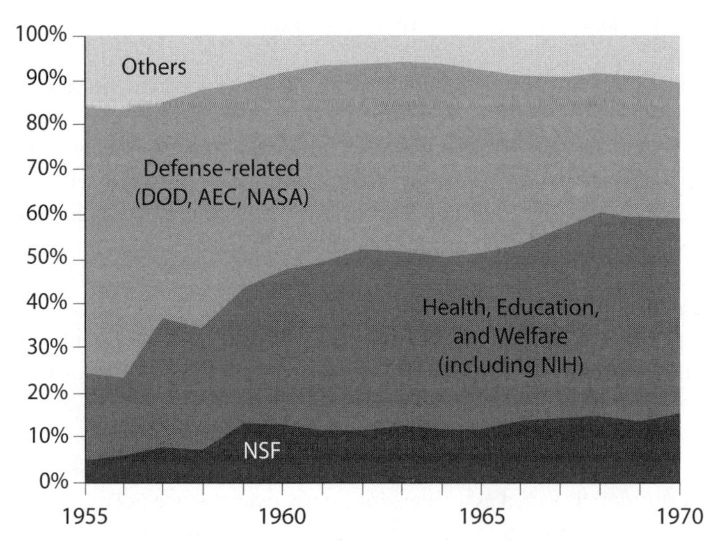

Figure 2.1. Federal obligations for university R&D by type of agency, 1955–1970. Adapted from NSF (2003:table B).

(NSB), and in reality the agency was from the outset oriented toward the concerns of academic scientists.[20] And while peer review was not mentioned in the legislation that created NSF, it was from the beginning a formal part of the grant review process, which meant that scientists themselves had significant control over the direction the research agenda took.[21] The funding provided to academic science by NSF tended to support an orientation to science logic.

But NSF provided a relatively small fraction of the research funding universities received from the federal government—under 15% in the 1950s and 1960s (see figure 2.1).[22] The rest came from agencies that had applied goals for the research they funded. Yet these, too, tended to be surprisingly favorable to the logic of pure science. Defense-related funding, for example, was clearly provided with practical ends in mind. But after the war, the money available for research outstripped the number of scientists available to perform it. Moreover, the Army and the Navy were in competition with one another to maintain the strongest research program.[23] So defense funders were quite generous in their support of basic research, and allowed scientists to determine much of the research agenda. Indeed, according to Roger Geiger, the Office of Naval Research "even claimed unabashedly [in the late 1940s] that it was sustaining basic research in the universities until the Congress could agree to establish a national science foundation."[24] And while military funding did not remain as supportive of "blue-sky" research as it was in the few years immediately following the war, the relative importance of defense funding to universities gradually began to decline anyway as other federal agencies expanded in size. While the

Department of Defense (DOD), AEC, and NASA accounted for a full 60% of federal obligations for university R&D in 1955, they represented only 30% of the total by 1970.[25]

The National Institutes of Health, on the other hand, was rapidly growing in significance. The fraction of university R&D provided by the Department of Health, Education, and Welfare, which contained NIH, increased from 19% in 1955 to 41% in 1962.[26] Like the defense agencies, NIH was very friendly to the logic of science despite its programmatic mission. The agency had introduced peer review as a basis for awarding grants as early as 1946.[27] And it, too, tended to pursue its mission by allowing science to follow its own internal trajectory, a view reflected in a 1953 statement by representatives of the agency's Division of Research Grants:

> Those who established the [research grants] program believed that maximum progress can be achieved only if the scientists enjoy freedom to experiment without direction or interference. . . . The investigator works on problems of his own choosing and is not obliged to adhere to a preconceived plan. He is free to publish as he sees fit and to change his research without clearance if he finds new and more promising leads. He has almost complete budget freedom as long as he uses the funds for research purposes and expends them in accordance with local institutional rules.[28]

As a whole, then, the "social contract for science" (to borrow David Guston's phrase) that emerged during the postwar decades provided substantial resources for academic science while letting scientists control their distribution to a considerable extent.[29] This they tended to do according to the internal criteria of science, not those of agency mission nor certainly those of the market. At the same time, the sheer scale of federal R&D funding for universities had exploded, increasing almost eightfold in real terms between 1953 and 1968 (see figure 2.2), and by 1963 the federal government was providing more than 70% of all university R&D expenditures.[30] In an atmosphere of such generosity, institutional logics other than the logic of science tended to atrophy, as there was no particular need to deploy them in a search for resources to support science. Even Stanford, which had once actively preferred industrial support to that of government, recognized these opportunities and began to advocate the "untempered exploitation of postwar federal patronage."[31] While other logics did not disappear, by the 1960s the logic of science was very strong in academic science.

Using Market Logic in the 1950s and 1960s

As chapter 1 suggested, though, the major institutional logics are available for individuals to draw on and use regardless of which logic currently dominates a given field. It is just that in some times and places, it will be harder for action

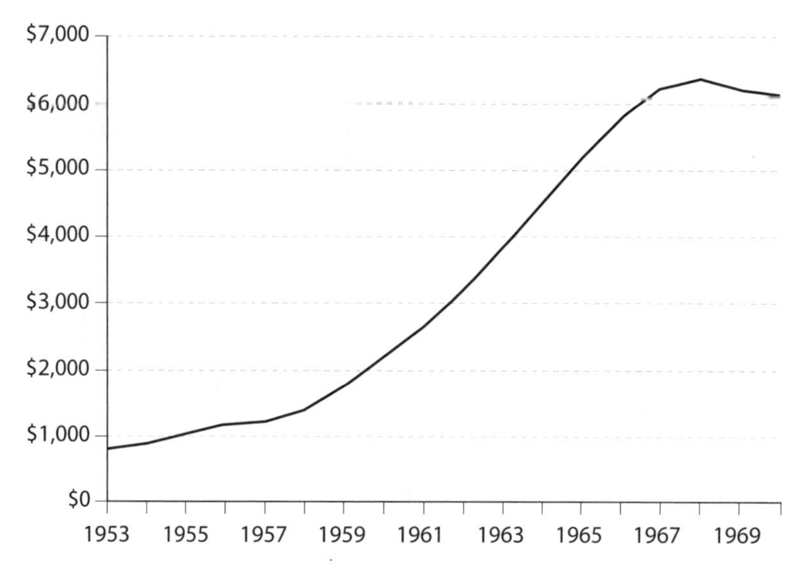

Figure 2.2. Federal R&D expenditures in U.S. universities, 1953–1970 (in millions of constant 2000 dollars). Adapted from NSB (2010:appendix table 4-3).

based on a nondominant logic to succeed, or to serve as a model that others will copy, than in others. This was the situation with market logic in academic science during the 1950s and 1960s. It did not disappear entirely, but it was quiescent, and attempts to use it as the basis for new practices were only modestly successful.

There is often a presumption that universities were actively antagonistic to commercial activity before the 1980s, and there are certainly elements of truth to that assumption. As a 1972 *Science* article on university-industry interactions suggested, "innovators [with university-industry relationships] are few and far between, since the person who can survive in a hostile environment from both camps is extremely rare."[32]

But it is also possible to overestimate the extent of resistance to thinking about the commercial importance of the university. Kleinman, Habinek, and Vallas, for example, looked for market language in higher education publications and found it present as early as 1960, when their data began.[33] Similarly, a 1962 survey of university research park efforts found that "a trend toward closer university-industry relations has been prevalent for some time now," and that "the fact that relatively few dissenters have been heard indicates that this new philosophy has been accepted widely by universities."[34]

An informal survey conducted by the University of Illinois in 1962 reinforces these observations. The Committee on the Role of Universities in Economic Growth, which I described briefly at the beginning of chapter 1 of this book, sent a letter from an imaginary small electronics firm to eighty-one universities across the country in order to see how they would respond. The firm expressed particular interest in the "possibility of locating in a university-connected research park or facility," and also mentioned the potential for establishing research contracts, arranging consulting, hiring undergraduates, and working with graduate students on thesis topics of mutual concern.[35] To its surprise, the committee received seventy-eight overwhelmingly positive responses:[36]

> Over 95 per cent of the universities contacted must be classified as at least "interested". . . . Actually most were strongly favorable and evidenced this with brochures, follow-ups, leads to other agencies, and even a handful of telephone calls. . . . Universities gave the distinct impression in most cases of considerable comfort in the role of a partner with industry, belying any impression that academic attitudes would be negative and adamant.[37]

Writers were described as "effusive." While most universities did not own research parks, consulting was almost always agreeable, several schools specified their encouragement (and sometimes limitation) of faculty consulting to the extent of one day per week, and at least thirty explicitly stated their interest in "contract awards." Schools also mentioned graduate programs available to employees and the possibility of graduate student collaboration, though in the latter case more restrictions were noted.[38]

This suggests that universities were fairly open to market-oriented activities, at least ones that were initiated from the outside and would be self-supporting or could even bring in new resources. But the Illinois committee also noted that while universities seemed to welcome closer relationships with industry, few organized resources were available to assist the imaginary electronics firm. "The rather cumbersome and involuted paths of decision and action," it wrote, "strongly suggest . . . that this relatively novel function of aiding industrial growth through research and development is neither familiar nor well-integrated in the university scheme."[39]

If academic science did not unilaterally reject market logic, though, and if some people were drawing on it here and there, why did market-logic practices not spread more broadly during this period? One answer, as suggested earlier, is that there were so many resources available to support science-logic activities. Market logic simply wasn't necessary. But some experiments with market logic had at least moderate success in the 1950s and 1960s. Looking briefly at three of the more visible practices highlights the factors that limited their spread and serves as a useful backdrop to the more successful market-logic practices of the 1970s.

Industrial Affiliates Programs

One market-focused practice that emerged at a number of universities by the end of the 1960s was the *industrial affiliates program*, sometimes known as *industrial liaison* or *associates programs*. The core of the industrial affiliates idea was that firms would provide annual financial support to a particular department, laboratory, or research group in exchange for privileged access to faculty and their research through both formal (e.g., annual symposia, distribution of preprints) and informal channels. MIT appears to have been the first to formalize these kinds of relationships, when in 1947 the institute approached "several industrial organizations" about the possibility of support. A group of oil companies was the most receptive, and six firms agreed to make a one-time donation of $600,000 in support of the new Laboratory for Nuclear Science and Engineering in exchange for access to the research being done there.[40] The following year, the university created a centralized Industrial Liaison Program (ILP) to manage such relationships, and other labs and departments quickly developed liaison efforts of their own. By 1955, MIT's ILP had more than seventy participating companies contributing over $800,000 a year in membership fees.[41]

A few other universities borrowed the concept in the 1950s. Around 1954, Stanford adapted the idea for its own use when John Linvill, an MIT PhD who had been recruited to build a program in solid-state electronics, started an affiliates program in microelectronics research. In exchange for a modest annual contribution of $5,000, a relationship would be established between the new Solid State Electronics Lab and the affiliate company.[42] By 1959, the microelectronics program was up and running successfully, and Stanford's aeronautical engineering department was circulating plans to copy it.[43] Caltech also had an early program, reporting twenty-three member firms in 1952 and forty-one in 1957, at which point the annual membership fee was $10,000.[44] Other schools with early industrial affiliates programs included Mount Holyoke, the University of Buffalo, and the University of Pennsylvania.[45]

The practice continued to spread to a modest extent during the 1960s. MIT's program sustained its position as the most successful, bringing in $1.6 million from 105 affiliated firms, 43% of which were from the aerospace or electronics industries, by the end of the decade.[46] Stanford also saw affiliates programs established in other research areas, including the chemistry and chemical engineering department and construction engineering.[47] Lehigh University created an affiliates program in materials research in 1963, and the University of Texas had one by 1967.[48] By 1969, MIT claimed that its ILP "ha[d] served as a model for over fifty programs of this type sponsored by the nation's major universities."[49]

Yet despite the widespread awareness that this claim would suggest, most such programs appear to have been small-scale and ephemeral. When universities responded to the fake electronics firm letter sent by the Illinois committee in 1962, industrial affiliates personnel were rarely mentioned as a point of contact, suggesting either that they did not exist, or that the people receiving the letters were not aware of them.[50] Though ninety brochures were sent in return, not one was about a "university-industry liaison program," even though electronics was a field in which one might expect such programs to be found.[51] Similarly, a 1972 article on university-industry relations in *Science* cited MIT and Stanford's programs as "among the best known and most highly developed," and mentioned "fully developed versions" in materials science at Penn State, Lehigh and Case Western, but said ultimately that "this kind of arrangement . . . is still relatively rare on U.S. campuses."[52]

Research Parks

A second innovation that gained some popularity in the postwar decades was the university *research park*, which provided a physical space on or near a university campus in which research-oriented firms could locate. Stanford Industrial Park, possibly the first, was established in 1951 out of economic necessity. In the rapidly growing San Francisco Peninsula, Stanford's large expanses of open land were subject to an increasingly high tax burden, and a high-technology industrial park seemed to administrators like a way of developing the land that was in keeping with the university's larger goals.[53] Cornell University Research Park, the University of Oklahoma Research Park, and Research Triangle Park in North Carolina were also founded during the 1950s, and other universities actively began to consider the idea as well.[54] By 1962, research parks—both university-affiliated and independent—were seen as a "mushrooming" trend, and surveys found ten university research parks already established and another fourteen in the planning stage.[55]

Universities were attracted to the research park idea for a number of reasons. They saw the parks as having the potential to provide financial support for research and academic programs, access to scientific equipment, and consulting opportunities for faculty, while remaining consistent with their educational mission.[56] That is, they appear to have appealed primarily as a way to bring new resources to the university. Yet one also gets the impression in reading material from this era that many universities were unthinkingly jumping on a bandwagon in deciding to establish research parks, since such parks were not easy to make work. In 1962, only one (Stanford's) clearly had more than a 30% occupancy rate, and even Research Triangle Park, which would later become an exemplar, struggled until the mid-1960s.[57]

By about 1965, the research park mini-boom was reaching its peak. That year, an article in *Industrial Research* found seventeen research parks associated with one or more universities, and described the period since 1962 as one of "accelerated development."[58] While it discussed conflict of interest as a potential problem area, recruiting tenants was not mentioned as a particular challenge. But this critical activity *was* a challenge, and by the early 1970s many parks found themselves struggling. A 1971 review counted nineteen university-affiliated parks, but while it cited Stanford, Research Triangle, and MIT's Technology Square (founded in 1963) as successes, it estimated that three-quarters of parks were either "hurting badly or experiencing slow growth."[59] It noted that seven planned parks had been abandoned, and another four had been retooled to focus on universities and government "after they failed to attract industrial interest." "It is doubtful," the author went on to posit, "if the research park movement ever will duplicate the rapid growth experienced in the early 1960s."[60] While that statement turned out to be false, it would not be until the 1980s that new research parks would again be established in significant numbers.

Industrial Extension Offices

A third market-oriented innovation that could be found on university campuses by the late 1960s had much different origins from the first two. *Industrial extension offices*, modeled on the successful tradition of agricultural extension in the land-grant universities, were started primarily because of federal legislation that provided funding for them, not local experimentation and problem-solving. Their goal was to help regional industry, especially small business, solve scientific and technical problems by connecting them with relevant resources, like those of the university. Industrial extension efforts could take a variety of forms, including the dissemination of technical information and the provision of educational programs, but at their heart was field service: active, in-person outreach to individual businesses.

A few activities taking place prior to the mid-1960s might be classified as industrial extension, particularly engineering extension programs, which had a long history at a small handful of state institutions.[61] But the real growth of industrial extension took place in response to the passage of the State Technical Services Act in 1965.[62] The pet project of Assistant Secretary of Commerce for Science and Technology Herbert Hollomon, its goal was "to place the findings of science usefully in the hands of American enterprise" by providing grants to individual states, which could propose to execute that mission in a variety of ways.[63]

Most of them did so by placing a university in charge of outreach efforts to industry, through offices with names like the Industrial Research and Extension Center, Technology and Business Services, the Office of Technical Services, and the Center for Industrial Research and Service.[64] By 1968, twenty-eight states had a university or university system managing their state's technical services effort. While there was variation from state to state in terms of both program organization and effectiveness, a 1969 evaluation by consultants Arthur D. Little found the State Technical Services program, and particularly its field service efforts, both useful and economical.[65]

The problem, however, was that political support for the State Technical Services program was weak from the outset. The program was authorized for only three years, and received less than $15 million in funds over its lifetime, a far cry from the $140 million the Johnson administration had originally envisioned for it.[66] The Arthur D. Little program evaluation identified a number of instances where local extension offices had helped solve specific industrial problems, with measurable and significant economic impacts.[67] But, as one university administrator described implementation of the program in Massachusetts, it could "be divided into two nearly equal phases: about one-and-a-half years to phase in and implement the effort, about one-and-a-half years to phase out the effort, the meanwhile operating on a survival basis against the possibility that the need . . . would generate a revitalized and more vigorous program, more adequately and dependably funded."[68] In 1969, Congress "cut [the program] off without a cent of grant money," and without continued federal funding, few universities had the resources to continue extension efforts, which certainly did not pay for themselves.[69] Industrial extension never became part of the standard repertoire of practices in academic science.

Limits to the Spread of Market Logic

Each of these practices—industrial affiliates programs, research parks, and industrial extension offices—represented an experiment with market logic, in that its focus was on the specifically economic value of science, as opposed to its knowledge value or some other noneconomic purpose, like its contribution to national defense. Market logic was clearly available to universities during this era, and people at least occasionally experimented with practices based on it. And universities did not demonstrate high levels of hostility to market logic, although it certainly deviated from the norms upon which most academic activity was based.

Yet during these postwar years, market logic nevertheless remained limited in scope. At least two factors helped to keep market logic from being used more than occasionally during this period. First, universities had a particular conception of the role that academic science played in the economy—what I call a "science-as-resource" model—that tended to limit aggressive experimentation with market-logic practices. Second, market-logic practices did not spread widely because they had trouble garnering the resources—either from the market itself or from government—they would have needed in order to do so.

The Science-as-Resource Model and Its Implications

Today, the prevalent understanding of the relationship between academic science and economy is closely tied to a particular metaphor: that of the university as an economic engine. This "science-as-engine" model suggests that the knowledge that universities produce is a source of innovation that can lead to new products, jobs, and even industries. This metaphor implies an entrepreneurial role for the university—it should actively work to make this innovation happen—and a focus on transferring the technology it develops to both startup and established firms. It suggests that academic science is a fundamental driver of economic growth, and that the university has a certain responsibility for making sure that the knowledge it creates is leveraged in this way.

Before the late 1970s, however, this was not a common way for universities to think about their economic role. While universities saw science as having a contribution to make to the world of commerce, they had a different understanding of how that contribution could be made. They drew on a "science-as-resource" model that saw universities not as a source of new economic development, but as a collection of resources that could attract industry and help it solve problems. Universities could work to make their knowledge as accessible as possible, by assisting industry when requested, for example, or offering classes to update the technical skills of employees. Their main economic contribution was not to serve as an engine for the creation of new businesses, however, but as an attraction for already-existing businesses that might need or want to take advantage of resources the university could provide. This science-as-resource model implied a relatively passive role for the university.[70]

The early-1960s experience of the University of Illinois in trying to understand its own economic role illustrates this older way of thinking. The university's interest in the topic could be traced back to a provocative speech given in Chicago to the National Electronics Conference by Stanford provost Frederick Terman in October 1960. Until World War II, Chicago had led the national electronics industry, but after the war, the Midwest had returned to making radios and television sets while the coasts moved on to more forward-looking fields. As Terman put it, "To be brutally blunt and frank the major path of electronics took off in a new direction in the decade 1940–50, but too little of the electronics industry of the midwest followed the turn." He placed part of the blame on the doorstep of universities, "who have had it in their power to take much more initiative than they have taken."[71] While New-York-based IBM employed more PhDs from the University of Illinois than from anywhere else, a survey of the largest Midwestern departments of electrical engineering and physics found that of 439 recent PhDs produced, more than 200 had taken jobs in industry, but only three had gone into the Chicago-area electronics industry.[72]

Terman's speech led to general concern in the Midwest that the region was not keeping up with the coasts in developing cutting-edge industries like aerospace and electronics.[73] One consequence was Illinois governor Otto Kerner's request that the University of Illinois examine how universities could contribute to local economic growth and development.

Even the governor's initial letter demonstrated certain assumptions about what universities' possible role might be. He suggested that

> some of your people at the University might be able to review the effect of the Stanford Research Center in California and M.I.T. in Massachusetts in attracting important elements of the newer growth industries to locations in their vicinities. At a time when technological development is such a critical component of the new growth industries the importance of the scientific and research capabilities of our universities as a locational asset in the state's efforts to achieve a favorable rate of economic growth is increasingly significant.[74]

Universities here are assumed to have the potential to *attract* growth industries to their areas, serving "as a locational asset," rather than having the potential to create growth themselves. The actions of the committee that the university formed to respond to the governor's request reflected the science-as-resource model even more clearly in several ways.

First, the activities the committee chose to undertake as it considered the university's economic role are telling. It initiated three main projects, each of which was grounded in the assumption that the economic value of academic science lay in its ability to meet the needs of existing companies. One was the letter from the imaginary electronics firm described earlier, sent to a large number of universities as well as Chambers of Commerce and government agencies. Here, the supposition was that a small company might be searching for a site to locate where universities could provide resources like a research park, undergraduates to hire, or collaborations with graduate students.[75] Another activity the committee undertook was a mail survey of more than a thousand firms in technology-intensive industries. The survey asked about the potential attractions universities might have for industry, as a source of employees, consultants, or contract research, for example, and about the factors that affected plant location.[76] Again, the focus was on identifying industry needs to which the university might respond. Finally, the university's provost sent a three-page letter to its academic deans and directors seeking information about activities going on within the university that they thought might be of value to industry—essentially trying to identify resources already present that could be made more accessible.[77]

Second, the *absence* of the science-as-engine model was reflected in the issues the committee did *not* address: any aspect of entrepreneurship (either within or outside the university), small business or business creation in any form, or any part of the technology transfer process. Each of these would be areas of focus suggested by the idea that university science could drive the creation of new products, firms, and industries, but which were missing from the conversation at Illinois.

Third, other language used by the committee also suggested a science-as-resource model rather than a science-as-engine model. For example, the committee's very first order of business was to hold a small "Conference on Industrial Location Factors" designed to uncover the "locational characteristics of space age industries" and to identify local resources that might attract such industries.[78] Its final report focused mostly on factors like labor availability and costs, industrial climate, and cultural attractions for high-tech industries, not on things like new business creation or support for entrepreneurship.[79] And committee members were actively skeptical of the idea that the university could actually drive economic growth. As one said,

> The Governor's original request . . . appeared to start off with the assumption that universities might play a "leadership" or "enterprising" role in stimulating development. Should universities be expected to play such a role as *initiators* of regional development activity [emphasis in original]? University's [*sic*] cannot accept responsibility for success or failure of the regions in which they are located to grow economically.[80]

Each of these examples highlights how this particular committee, at least, had a specific *way* of talking about the university's economic role that differed substantially from the one that dominates today.

While the records of the Illinois committee are unusual in the level of detail they record about a university reflecting upon its economic role, the science-as-resource model was widespread throughout this era, and language drawing on it is easy to find. For example, a consortium of eleven universities in the Midwest was also studying the issue of universities and regional economic development in the early 1960s, and it, too, suggested that "universities should be looked at as 'natural resources' not fully turned to productive uses."[81] Similarly, in a contemporaneous survey of fifty-eight universities' thoughts about research parks, the open-ended responses all involved attracting existing industry and meeting its needs. None indicated that the intellectual products of the university might help create new companies, drive old companies in new directions, or serve as the basis for new products.[82]

The science-as-resource model implied a different understanding of the relationship between academic science and the economy. This understanding did not explicitly discourage experimentation with market-logic practices. Universities still saw an economic role for their research. The model even provided some justification for market-logic practices as part of the university's public service mission. One could argue that universities had a *responsibility* to make their knowledge available through industrial affiliates programs and the like.

What the science-as-resource model did not suggest, however, was a particularly active role for the university in trying to leverage its economic impact.

While the economic engine model would entail a certain obligation to make sure university innovations actually realized their market potential, seeing academic science as a resource implied that universities' responsibility ended with making that resource as accessible as possible. If business did not choose to take advantage of it, so be it; universities "cannot accept responsibility for success or failure of the regions in which they are located to grow economically."[83]

The Challenge of Supporting Market-Logic Practices

While the science-as-resource model may not have especially encouraged universities to take on market-logic activities, the examples of industrial affiliates programs, research parks, and industrial extension offices show that people within universities sometimes did experiment with them nonetheless. Such experiments could be quite successful at the local level, as MIT's Industrial Liaison Program showed. But during this era, they did not spread to the point of becoming common across campuses or very significant at the national level.

There are two obvious ways that market-logic activities might be derailed. First, normative or legal barriers could limit their growth. Serious cultural opposition from within the university would inhibit such practices, as would government restrictions on them. Second, such practices might not be able to muster up enough resources to sustain and reproduce themselves. Such resources could come from the marketplace, from government, or from universities themselves, but they would have to come from somewhere for the activities to persist.

The activities of industrial affiliates programs, research parks, and industrial extension offices, at least, did not encounter real problems with the first potential barriers. While such practices were unusual within the context of 1960s academia, they do not appear to have been strongly opposed by others in universities. Nor were the practices limited or banned by government. They did, however, all have trouble sustaining themselves financially, at least to an extent that would have allowed them to spread widely.

Industrial affiliates programs were meant to support themselves on the basis of the value they provided to industry. As Frederick Terman described Stanford's program in solid-state electronics, support would "be requested on the basis of enlightened self-interest rather than as an educational donation to Stanford."[84] But the gap between academic research and industrial problem-solving, even in engineering, meant that it was challenging for many affiliates programs to provide something of clear financial value to industrial participants. While firms may have been willing to fund such programs for a few years on a semicharitable basis, they were unlikely to finance them indefinitely. The fact that a relative handful of affiliate programs could effectively meet the needs of all firms also tended to limit the spread of the practice. Stanford's rise is often thought of in conjunction with that of Silicon Valley, but its solid-state program was national in scope, not regional. Of its first fourteen affiliates, only four were locally based, and that number decreased over time.[85] This meant that many of the most important firms working in the solid-state area nationally already had formal ties to Stanford by the end of the 1950s. Few firms were willing to maintain such costly relationships with more than one or a very small handful of universities, or even to be able to take advantage of such relationships. So early movers like Stanford and MIT had a significant advantage in establishing affiliates programs, and most schools found it difficult to make affiliates programs self-supporting. Since universities had no particular incentive to subsidize such efforts internally, and government was not offering support for them, these programs spread only to the extent that they could be financially sustained by the market, which meant they remained modest in scope.

Research parks encountered similar issues. Again, there were no regulatory barriers to establishing them and cultural resistance does not appear to have been significant. But universities underestimated the difficulty of raising the resources needed to maintain research parks. The biggest challenge was demonstrating to businesses that locating near a university provided a comparative advantage that justified the expense of doing so. Frequently, the university was not a significant enough lure to draw a critical mass of research park tenants, and in the absence of this critical mass, many of the new parks foundered. Few could create enough value to industry to become self-supporting. Again, since universities had no interest in subsidizing research parks, and government did not step in with financial support, parks did not become widespread during this period, and the mini-boom seen in the mid-1960s went bust by the early 1970s.

Industrial extension offices followed a slightly different trajectory. Like affiliates programs and research parks, they did not encounter major normative barriers, and far from being restricted by government, government actively supported them. But while they too emphasized the specifically economic value of academic science, industrial extension offices did not from the outset try to support themselves by asking businesses to pay for the cost of their services. Instead, they relied on government financial support, and in fact most were formed in direct response to the availability of that support. But political backing for industrial extension efforts was always shaky and disappeared entirely at the end of the 1960s. Universities would not support industrial extension themselves, and businesses would not pay enough for the support to keep it alive. So when government funding evaporated, most industrial extension offices were simply shut down.

Thus the reasons that these three market-logic experiments were not more successful in the 1950s and 1960s are similar. While one can imagine cultural barriers and government restrictions that might have limited them, their biggest problem was simply that of finding the resources needed to sustain themselves. At most schools, these practices could not create something of enough value in the marketplace to pay for themselves, and in the absence of interest from universities or government in financing them, the practices could not spread beyond a limited extent. This was the situation that would need to change before market logic could become more successful in academic science.

The Pillars of the Postwar System Begin to Crumble

So at the end of the 1960s, the place of market logic in academic science was still modest at best. By the end of the 1970s, however, that situation would be changing. The market value of the products of academic science would be increasing, which in turn would make market-logic practices easier to support. And government would become more interested in promoting market logic, both by making the rules friendlier to it and by subsidizing it directly.

Before that could happen, though, a substantial shift in the policy environment would need to take place. Until the late 1960s, the logic of science had flourished in universities because of two aspects of the postwar system of federal support: generous and increasing levels of funding, and the relatively unrestricted nature of much of that funding. Both of these allowed many scientists to pursue the questions that interested them intellectually regardless of whether they had clear economic or practical implications. While there was certainly much research in universities that was driven by practical concerns, the funding system made possible a lot of activity that pursued knowledge for its own sake.

But these high levels of funding and scientist autonomy rested on three assumptions that, late in the decade, began to be put into question. This in turn upset the momentary balance in which science logic flourished and market logic struggled in academic science.

The first assumption was that economic conditions would permit federal science funding to continue to increase at rapid rates. Between 1953 and 1967, federal support for academic R&D increased an average of 15.8% per year in real terms.[86] Until the end of this period, prominent scientists like Harvey Brooks and George Kistiakowsky, apparently ignoring the realities of mathematics, thought that 15% annual budget increases were a reasonable target for the foreseeable future.[87] But such increases were possible only in an environment of flush economic times and limited pressures on the federal budget.

The second was that universities would be cooperative partners in meeting the needs of government. Universities had reconciled themselves to some loss of independence during the war effort, and afterward they continued to accommodate themselves to government demands in exchange for high funding levels. The postwar bargain relied on universities to remain broadly in line with policymakers' expectations about what their behavior should be.

Third, the system rested on the promise of serendipitous applications. Vannevar Bush and others had assured policymakers that if they only kept the fount of pure science refreshed, useful results would naturally—and by implication effortlessly—result.[88] As this view became widely accepted, serendipity became a justification for funding basic science and for allowing scientists a great deal of control over how such funding was spent.

By the late 1960s, all three of these pillars of the postwar system were being undermined. For one thing, a period of great economic expansion was coming to a close.[89] Nagging worries about inflation and the balance of trade were emerging, and by the end of the decade the economy was slipping into its first recession in nine years.[90] At the same time, Lyndon Johnson's "guns and butter" strategy was creating pressures on the federal budget, and on R&D spending, as *Science* noted as early as 1965.[91] The "scramble to save another nickel" continued to define the science policy environment throughout the second half of the decade.[92]

Simultaneously, the anti-Vietnam protests erupting on college campuses were creating a backlash among policymakers who, like most of the public, continued to support the war. This led to a variety of proposals to punish universities who let campus unrest go too far, like a 1969 bill that would have cut off all federal funds to universities that did not maintain discipline on campus.[93] The Senate tried to limit NASA grants to universities that allowed military recruiters on campus, and the House proposed denying Defense Department funds to universities that did not maintain "academic freedom," a state it defined as including the absence of student disruptions.[94] As cultural cleavages between universities and the larger public became more visible, some policymakers began to reevaluate their past generosity to science.

Finally, the promise that science done for its own sake would serendipitously lead to practical results was increasingly being called into question. Criticism started with NASA, required by statute to encourage broader use of its research, in the early 1960s.[95] Though the agency justified its arcane mission by claiming that its research also led to civilian applications, many challenged whether this was actually happening.[96] By mid-decade, such critiques were being expanded to other agencies. In 1966, President Johnson called for more emphasis on the utilization of NIH research:

> A great deal of basic research has been done. . . . But I think the time has now come to zero in on the targets by trying to get our knowledge fully applied. There are hundreds of millions of dollars spent on laboratory research. . . . Now Presidents, in my judgment, need to show more interest in what the specific results of medical research are during their lifetime and during their administration. I am going to show an interest in the results.[97]

The speech "generated shock waves" among NIH administrators and led to a "year of agitation" in the scientific community, which feared that basic science would be cut back in favor of the large-scale patient trials the president seemed to prefer.[98] Such calls for greater attention to the utilization of scientific research grew even louder as the decade progressed, and forced federal agencies into the unprecedented position of trying to prove the importance of basic research to technological innovation.[99]

The Effects of the Dissolving Federal Consensus

As these pillars of the postwar consensus—rapid funding growth, cooperative universities, and the promise of serendipity—began to dissolve, government science policy shifted in ways that would stop favoring the logic of science so strongly. The most significant change was a dramatic flattening of federal R&D expenditures for academic research. After years of double-digit growth, the real increase plummeted to 2% in 1968. Budgets actually declined slightly in 1969, 1970, and 1971 (see figure 2.2), and would remain stagnant until the second half of the 1970s.[100]

At the same time, policymakers' focus on bang for the federal buck as well as the practical outcomes of basic research meant that research dollars increasingly came with strings attached. A growing focus on mission-oriented research had particular effects at DOD, which had historically funded a great deal of blue-sky research with only indirect implications for defense. In 1969, though, the Mansfield amendment declared that defense funds could be used only for research with "a direct and apparent relationship to a specific military function or operation."[101] One director of the Advanced Research Projects Agency (ARPA, DOD's basic research arm), was highly critical of the amendment's effects, despite being generally quite sympathetic to mission-relevant research: "It made every one of those guys [decision-makers at ARPA] *extremely* conservative [emphasis in original]. They wouldn't put money out to a university for anything, unless it was an obvious need to protect a tank."[102] While the language of the Mansfield amendment was dropped by 1971, the amendment "is generally regarded as having much broader effects on Federal research than its short legal lifetime would suggest."[103]

At NSF, the impact was felt in 1968, when the Daddario-Kennedy amendment authorized the agency to fund applied science for the first time, as well as giving it an explicit role in supporting social science.[104] The new RANN program—Research Applied to National Needs—aimed to address directly social problems in areas like energy, pollution, transportation, and cities by funding relevant research, and by 1973 it made up over 10% of NSF's budget, to the dismay of some scientists.[105] And at NIH, the War on Cancer launched an even larger effort to harness science to solve a specific problem. Public response to the initiative, announced by President Nixon in 1971, was extremely positive, and after Ann Landers wrote a column encouraging readers to write their legislators in support of the effort, one senator received 25,000 pieces of mail.[106] The Cancer Act of 1971 authorized $1.59 billion in spending on cancer research over the next three years, an unprecedented amount to focus on a single disease.[107]

This combination of budget cuts and new restrictions on federal funding led to a dark mood among academic scientists. While federal funding for academic R&D decreased only 4.3% in real terms between its 1968 peak and its 1971 nadir, this relatively modest dip was perceived as extremely painful.[108] As Roger Geiger has pointed out, "The research universities had acquired a growth mentality during the fat years of the 1960s which was not easily eradicated."[109] By 1968, the first year of a level budget, scientists were already "screaming that deep budget cuts ha[d] undermined their ability to do effective research," and by 1970, university presidents were warning that "we fear an unprecedented financial crisis," and that "in a decade we will pay dearly for the economies made now."[110] Nor did scientists like having strings attached to their funding. They complained that "expenditures for applied research would quickly outpace available knowledge and would result in expensive, useless projects that would drain away funds from the necessary basic research."[111]

For the most part, the outraged responses of academics were based on little hard evidence about real impact. Negative outcomes were either anecdotal or promised in the future, and when Smith and Karlesky surveyed the state of academic science a few years later, as cutbacks were ending, they found that "nothing resembling a collapse of the research climate has occurred at the major research-intensive universities," though they did find the scientific enterprise to be somewhat fragile.[112]

The bleak perceptions did have some basis in reality, however. By the end of the 1960s, universities were having other fiscal troubles that made it particularly hard for them to absorb cutbacks in research funding.[113] And in certain fields, like mathematics, engineering, and parts of chemistry, the impact of cuts resulting from the Mansfield amendment was substantial.[114] Federal funding for services that *supported* research, like those subsidizing fellowships, equipment, and facilities, also declined particularly rapidly, from $1 billion in 1967 to less than 30% of that (in constant dollars) in 1976.[115] Some negative outcomes were also difficult to quantify, like a recurrent concern that "'the exciting new gambles' [would] not be taken because of the budget squeeze."[116]

Yet while universities' response to the shifts in science policy was vociferous, in some ways the academic community was slow to perceive just how much had really changed. The dominant reaction was a clamor for a return to the status quo ante of ever-increasing, relatively unrestricted funds for basic research. This often involved reasserting the logic of science: that science needed to follow its own internal compass, and only then would valuable by-products ensue. As Stanford geneticist Joshua Lederberg testified to Congress in 1967,

> It is fair to say that society exploits the poetic fascination that motivates many academic scientists, eventually capitalizing on applications that no one could have foreseen. It may even be an undesirable distraction to its rigor

and sharpness of focus for the research worker himself to be too sensitive to the unpredictable implications of his own work.

It is important, however, that such utilities be discovered as soon as they can be useful: but this is a function of a whole community of basic and applied scientific effort. To place the burden of such justification on individual projects would be the surest possible way of stifling the most creative, the least predictable advances in scientific understanding. . . . From my own experience, I do not know any scientific or technical advance of any importance that did not make utterly unexpected demands on knowledge from unpredictable sources.[117]

What this failed to recognize was that such arguments were no longer convincing to policymakers, and the days of low levels of accountability and rapidly increasing funding were not about to return. Universities' reluctance to adapt earned them criticism that "any retardation of the rate of spending for research and development is viewed as no less a sin than the suppression of truth. I am amazed . . . when scientists say that we must embark upon a major technical project on faith—faith that through serendipity . . . it will turn out to be worthwhile after all."[118] As Bruce L. R. Smith observed, "Saying that government has an obligation to do this and that amounts to a failure on the part of the scientific community to recognize what has hit them."[119]

By the early 1970s, then, the relationship between academic science and the federal government, so strong in the postwar era, had been placed under significant strain. These pressures did not themselves cause universities to abandon the logic of science in favor of the logic of the market. If anything, universities' initial reaction was to double down on science logic. But evolving federal priorities did create an opening for the spread of another logic, since it was unrestricted federal dollars that *supported* practices grounded in the logic of science. As those dollars became scarcer, science logic became harder to reproduce.

But it would take another change in policy preferences before market-logic practices would start to displace science logic, even a little. Policymakers' broad concern with the practical applications of science would, in the late 1970s, shift toward a more focused view of the usefulness of science: that it could be used to solve the nation's growing *economic* problems. As the idea that technological innovation was a key driver of economic growth—and thus that supporting science had important implications for the nation's economy—took hold, the mood of policymakers would shift once again. Again, the environment of academic science would change, this time in ways that would allow practices rooted in the logic of the market, not the logic of science, to grow and thrive. The next chapter tells the story of how this idea became influential in the policy domain, with results that would transform the way science was done at universities.

CHAPTER 3

Innovation Drives the Economy—an Old Idea with New Implications

> Innovation generates economic momentum and helps guarantee American preeminence in a world where power and progress are often measured in terms of technological achievement. Partly as a result, innovation has become the engine that drives many companies to the forefront of their industries: IBM, Dow Chemical, Texas Instruments, Pfizer, General Dynamics, Eastman Kodak, Polaroid, Raytheon, and Xerox—to name only a few. Yet from boardroom to research lab, there is a growing sense that something has happened to American innovation. . . . The country's genius for invention is not what it used to be.
>
> —"The Breakdown of U.S. Innovation,"
> *Business Week*, 16 February 1976

JUST AS PEOPLE IN ACADEMIC SCIENCE sometimes drew on market logic in the 1950s and 1960s, their counterparts in the 1970s also experimented with market logic from time to time, becoming scientist-entrepreneurs, patenting and licensing their research, or creating novel partnerships with industry. But for most of the decade, this new round of experiments ran into difficulties very similar to those encountered by its predecessors. There was always a culture gap between universities and industry to manage, and some practices, like patenting, were explicitly limited by government policy. Most of all, though, these activities were hard to sustain financially on a widespread basis, just as industrial extension programs, research parks, and industrial extension efforts had been in the past.

But in the late 1970s, the environment of academic science would change in a way that would help some of these new efforts to take off. Though several developments shaped that change, the most important reason that market logic practices started to grow and spread at the end of the decade was a significant shift in public policy. That shift would remove limits to universities' ability to treat science as having economic value, make the products of science themselves more valuable, and subsidize activities that saw science in terms of its economic impact. All these things happened because of the growing political impact of an idea: that technological innovation drives the economy.

Today, we take it for granted that science and technology drive economic growth. We see the importance of science-based industries like biotech, computing, pharmaceuticals, and telecommunications, and assume that the country whose innovations launch the next such field will thrive in the twenty-first century. We are used to hearing discussions of the need to stay technologically competitive, to invest in our innovation infrastructure, and to improve the way we move inventions from the lab to the marketplace.

From this perspective, it is hard to realize how little attention was once paid to the role of technology in economic growth, by scientists, policymakers, or anyone else. Of course, people appreciated that technology had transformed the world, and the American inventor-genius was a cultural icon. But it was rare to hear a suggestion that the nation needed to encourage science and technology in order to advance industry, nor did policymakers discuss science policy with an eye toward the national economic well-being.

Although economists had intermittently addressed the impact of technology, it was not until the 1960s and 1970s that the question of innovation began to receive serious attention from policymakers, and even then, interest was sporadic. But by the late 1970s, growing problems with innovation in U.S. industry, increased academic interest in the issue, and a widespread concern with the sorry state of the U.S. economy led to an intense political focus on innovation. Discussions of the state of innovation became widespread, and the banner of improving it was raised in policy debates ranging from tax to pension to patent policy.

The goal of strengthening innovation would be decisive for some policy discussions. In others, innovation concerns would be one consideration among many. But collectively, the idea that technological innovation drives the economy would shape political decisions and create a sea change for academic science. Not all, or even most, of the policy decisions affected by the innovation issue were aimed at academic science. But because policymakers concerned with innovation were trying to maximize the economic impact of science and technology, they tended to encourage activities that focused on the specifically economic value of science—that is, activities that drew on market logic. The result was an environment in which practices like entrepreneurship, patenting, and industry collaboration were able to flourish, and the university began to gain a new appreciation of its role as an economic engine.

The rest of this chapter will develop two themes. First, it will describe briefly three of the experiments with market logic that could be found in universities by the mid-1970s and discuss the reasons they, like their earlier counterparts, did not at that time look poised to spread widely. Second, it will tell the story of the idea that innovation drives the economy—its origins, its early and limited impact on public policy in the 1960s and the first half of the 1970s, and how it became a major political concern later in the decade. Chapters 4, 5, and 6 will then look more closely at the development of each of three specific market-logic practices—biotech entrepreneurship, university patenting, and university-industry research centers—showing how the new political environment led to decisions that removed barriers to and provided support for their growth and spread by the early 1980s.

Market-Logic Practices of the 1970s and Their Limits

In the 1950s and 1960s, while most people in academic science were focused on advancing pure science or solving national problems of defense and health, a handful of innovators were trying to leverage the economic value of science by starting industrial affiliates programs, research parks, and industrial extension offices. As a group, they had some modest, but limited, success. In the 1970s, other innovators once again drew on market logic as they tried to solve local problems and take advantage of new opportunities. Three of these experiments—with faculty entrepreneurship in the biosciences, university patenting, and university-industry research centers—would ultimately be quite successful. Yet although all three of these practices were spreading rapidly by the early 1980s, as late as 1978 each one appeared as if it would remain limited, despite considerable early promise.

Faculty entrepreneurship in the biosciences was almost unheard of before the mid-1970s. But after breakthroughs in biochemistry and molecular biology made it possible for scientists to manipulate genetic material at the molecular level, a handful of academics became involved in efforts to commercialize their research through startup companies. Genentech, founded in 1976 by a university scientist and a venture capitalist, was the first company formed to take advantage of recombinant DNA (rDNA) technology, and in the next two years a few other firms copied the Genentech model. But despite widespread excitement about the biotechnology's potential for practical impact, there were some real limitations on the spread of faculty entrepreneurship at this point. Many in academia considered it inappropriate for their peers to be starting companies. Fears of the potential dangers of recombinant DNA created an uncertain regulatory environment, and as late as mid-1977 it appeared inevitable that legislation would restrict rDNA research. Most importantly, the venture capital environment was awful. Biotechnology would require many further years of research and development before it would result in any marketable products. Although biotech was extremely promising, it could not be developed in small firms run by scientist-entrepreneurs without a large supply of capital, and that capital simply was not available at the time.

Universities had occasionally patented and licensed their research since the early twentieth century, but the practice was relatively uncommon and not at all systematic. By the mid-1970s, though, a loose network of government officials was working to change the rules that limited universities' ability to patent federally funded research. But while rates of university patenting were starting to rise, federal restrictions on patenting were still a barrier. When in 1977 the National Institutes of Health (NIH) made the seemingly arbitrary decision to reverse its previously liberal patent policy, it became clear that without comprehensive legislation, university patenting would remain limited in scale. At the same time, recent advances in biotechnology were leading to many new inventions in universities that were potentially, but not definitely, patentable. Universities' incentives to become involved in patenting would rest partially on government decisions about what constituted a patentable invention—in biotechnology as well as other fields—and about what rights accrued to the holders of patents. In the late 1970s, these incentives were not as strong as they would later become.

University-industry research centers (UIRCs) are organized research units working on problems of interest to both universities and industry that are at least partially supported by industry contributions. In the 1970s, faculty and administrators established a handful of such centers across the country, mostly at engineering-oriented schools like MIT, Rensselaer Polytechnic Institute (RPI), Caltech, and Carnegie Mellon. But the cultural gap between the two parties was difficult to manage. And while there were no regulatory barriers that limited the establishment of UIRCs, they were difficult to maintain financially. As had been the case with affiliates programs, it proved difficult for universities to provide something of enough value that industry would be willing to support such centers at levels of long-term sustainability. While people on both sides were calling for closer university-industry relations by the late 1970s, actual UIRCs were often struggling, and while experimentation continued, it did not appear that this type of organization was about to become widely emulated.

Thus while each of the market-logic practices of the 1970s had some potential, none was on a clear path to institutionalization by 1978. Like the practices of the 1950s and 1960s, they had trouble garnering the resources needed to keep themselves going or to spread widely. Even more than those earlier practices, two of them, biotech entrepreneurship and university patenting, faced the possibility of being actively limited by government. And as had always been the case, bridging the university-industry culture gap was a challenge, if not a deal-breaker. It would take a substantial shift in the policy environment to remove enough of these limitations that the practices would start to spread more widely. But as concern with the economic impact of technological innovation became increasingly strong in the second half of the decade, that is just what would happen. By the early 1980s, each of these activities would be spreading and flourishing in American universities.

The Political Power of an Economic Idea

The idea itself—that technological innovation plays a key role in driving economic growth—is simple, and far from new. While the classical political economists saw labor, land, and capital as the main factors of production, they also recognized the importance of technological innovation in increasing productivity.[1] Yet by the late nineteenth century, economists increasingly ignored the role of technological advance as a productive force, seeing it as an exogenous factor—something to be assumed, not explained.[2] Though an interest in innovation resurfaced occasionally among economists in the first half of the twentieth century—the work of Joseph Schumpeter being the most obvious example—as late as the 1950s, technological innovation was not an issue mainstream economists paid much attention to.[3]

The economic impact of technology rarely came up within science policy, either. In the 1950s and into the 1960s, U.S. science policy was heavily oriented toward defense and defense needs, like the space program. While many policymakers were concerned about the nation's investment in R&D, in the Sputnik years their focus was winning the Cold War, not spurring economic growth. Although universities received most of their federal R&D funding from nondefense-related agencies after 1958, the defense-related agencies accounted for roughly 90% of *total* federal R&D spending in the first half of the 1960s.[4] While of course all this R&D spending represented jobs to legislators, few saw it as having any special economic significance beyond that. As one senator, beating a lonely drum, observed in 1963, "The direct relationship between science and technology on the one hand and our military capability and effort in space exploration on the other is spectacular and obvious. Not nearly so obvious is the dependence of our general economic and social well-being on science and technology."[5]

Nor, on the flip side, did economic policy frequently deal with science or technology. Economic policy meant taxes, or interest rates, or government spending.[6] While policymakers of course knew that the nation's technological infrastructure was part of what made it productive, it was not singled out as an area requiring particular attention from government. As the 1947 *Economic Report of the President* noted, "Our productive capacity has grown not only through technological developments, but also through a steady stream of additions to plant and equipment. . . . The whole history of America indicates that this progress can be entrusted mainly to the initiative and inventiveness within our business system."[7] It was not until 1962 that an *Economic Report* specifically addressed any government role in encouraging technological development.[8]

By the end of the 1970s, though, technological innovation would be seen as a very important economic issue, and one where action clearly needed to be taken. Major magazines and newspapers were writing articles with titles like "Vanishing Innovation," "The 'Innovation Recession,'" and "Something's Happened to Yankee Ingenuity," and the Carter administration was conducting a twenty-eight-agency Domestic Policy Review (DPR) on Industrial Innovation.[9] Members of Congress were considering several dozen bills affecting innovation, and an industrial innovation task force had been formed within Congress as well.[10] In the *Congressional Record*, the phrase "technological innovation" was used eighteen times as often in the 1979 to 1981 period as it was in the first half of the 1960s, and the word *innovation* was used near *economy* or *economic* nine times as often.[11] While innovation policy never quite became a distinct field of its own, concern with technological innovation became salient across a broad range of policy areas.

This shift in the policy environment, which would prove very significant for academic science, took place for a variety of reasons, four of which are particularly noteworthy. First, starting in the 1950s and continuing in the following decades, economists began studying the economic role of technology and building knowledge about its contribution to growth and productivity. Second, in the late 1960s indicators started to emerge that innovation was perhaps no longer thriving in the United States. Third, at about the same time industrialists, particularly those from large, R&D-intensive firms, became increasingly worried about innovation and began pushing government to do something to strengthen it. And finally, the larger U.S. economy deteriorated during the 1970s, causing a broader political concern with trying to fix it. In this context, encouraging technological innovation became a politically appealing solution to the nation's economic woes.

The innovation issue did not originate with academic scientists (if one excludes economists) or with universities, nor did either of these groups play a significant role in promoting it. Relatively little of the innovation debate even addressed university science. Most of it focused on industrial innovation, and only a handful of the many policy recommendations that were made targeted universities. Nevertheless, in the long run the rise of the innovation issue and its salience as a policy frame created an environment that would transform academic science. The rest of this chapter will explain how and why that frame gradually emerged and describe its effects on policymaking by the end of the 1970s.

Technological Innovation in Washington in the 1960s

In the 1950s, economists had gradually begun to explore the role of technology within the new mathematical framework that was beginning to unify the discipline. As data on the national economy improved, it became uncomfortably clear that conventional economic inputs explained relatively little of observed economic growth. In response, scholars began trying to identify the sources of this "residual" growth.[12] The initial approach was to assume that all growth that did not come from known inputs must be attributable to technological change, with the earliest estimates suggesting it was the source of as much as 87.5% of U.S. economic growth in the first half of the twentieth century.[13] During the 1960s, economists worked to specify various components of the residual and to explore the ways in which, left to itself, the market might underinvest in the scientific research that led to technical advances.[14] But while the economists studying technological change were themselves mainstream academics, the subfield remained a relatively marginal one being developed by just a handful of scholars.[15]

Their ideas, however, began filtering into policymaking in the early 1960s, though in a somewhat limited fashion. The Kennedy administration was notable both for its obsession with economic growth and its faith in technocratic expertise, as well as marking the high point of economists' influence in the White House.[16] Thus when economist John Kenneth Galbraith and science adviser Jerome Wiesner wrote to Kennedy in 1961 recommending he create a committee to encourage the development of technology in industries that underused it, they found a receptive audience.[17] The result was the White House Panel on Civilian Technology, led by Wiesner, Council of Economic Advisers (CEA) chairman Walter Heller, and Commerce Secretary Luther Hodges.[18] The CEA was also well aware of the economic importance of technology, with Robert Solow, Richard Nelson, and Kenneth Arrow, pioneers in the economics of innovation, all serving on its staff at various points in the early 1960s.[19] The annual reports of the CEA during this era highlighted the idea that technological advance was central to productivity growth, and that government had a role to play in promoting it, in language that reads as surprisingly contemporary.

The actual impact of the Kennedy administration's interest in the economic effects of technology, however, was modest. The administration did initiate the creation of a new office, the Assistant Secretary of Commerce for Science and Technology, in 1962, and Kennedy appointed General Electric manager Herbert Hollomon to fill it.[20] Hollomon, working along lines congruent with those of the civilian technology panel and the CEA, promoted a Civilian Industrial Technology Program to encourage and better apply existing R&D in technologically lagging industries, but Congress shot down his proposal, largely for political reasons.[21] It was eventually transmuted into the modest State Technical Services Act, mentioned in the previous chapter as the impetus for universities' industrial extension efforts, which became law in 1965 but was defunded in 1969.[22] Although the civilian technology effort was originally seen as having the potential to lead to a program the size of the National Science Foundation (NSF), by the end of the decade the assistant secretary's office itself was the only visible result of the Kennedy administration's interest in innovation.[23]

Hollomon himself returned to civilian life in 1967, but before he did, he initiated two other activities that would be of more lasting importance in advancing the innovation agenda.[24] First, he created an ad hoc Panel on Invention and Innovation that would be tasked with exploring opportunities to "improve the *climate* for technological change [emphasis in original]," focusing particularly on antitrust, taxation, and regulatory policy.[25] Second, he would set a Commerce staff economist, Michael Boretsky, at work analyzing the "economic consequences of technological innovation," a job that would take "several years of hard labor to complete."[26]

In 1967, the Panel on Invention and Innovation published its findings in a report titled "Technological Innovation: Its Environment and Management." Often referred to as the Charpie report, after committee chair Robert Charpie, it was noteworthy for two reasons.[27] One, it was the first study of the government role in innovation to reflect primarily the views of the business community. Eleven of its sixteen members represented industry or law firms, including companies like Xerox, CBS, Western Electric, and Union Carbide. Only one, Dan Throop Smith, was an academic economist, and only one currently held a government position.[28] Several members would go on to be influential in the innovation debate over the next decade, including Peter G. Peterson, who would become commerce secretary under President Nixon, and Richard S. Morse, an inventor and entrepreneur who would coauthor an influential study on the economic importance of small high-tech firms.[29]

Two, the panel presented a distinctive perspective on innovation, and one that would anticipate much of the innovation debate that took place a decade later. While both Hollomon and Kennedy's CEA had assumed that government could and should actively intervene to encourage innovation, the Charpie report, in accordance with its charter, focused on the environment for innovation created by government. Its starting point was the innovative process within the firm, and the report stressed the critical roles of small business and entrepreneurs and of venture capital, themes rarely touched on in this era. It emphasized that R&D expenditures made up a relatively small fraction of the cost of innovation, and criticized the lack of awareness—across both business and government—of the importance of innovation. Its policy suggestions were modest, but its view of the government role—to create a climate in which private innovation could flourish, but not to promote it directly—would prove influential in the long run, particularly as the environment for innovation became perceived as increasingly hostile in the 1970s.[30]

Innovation Policy during the Nixon Years

But in the late 1960s, it was hard to get a lot of attention for innovation issues. While the Kennedy administration had had the luxury of focusing on investments that might increase the nation's long-term rate of economic growth, the Johnson administration, embroiled in a distant war and struggling with an increasingly tight budget, had a shorter-term focus. The economy was not the most pressing political issue, as it had been expanding continuously since 1961, and the nation seemed on the surface to be doing just fine when it came to technological innovation. Indeed, although mentions of a "technology gap" were frequent, the concern was that other nations were trailing the United States, not the reverse.[31] In this environment, strengthening U.S. innovation was relatively low on the list of priorities.

But within a few years, that situation would change. The economic environment was shifting by the end of the decade, with the economy slipping into recession in December 1969. Inflation, which had been under 2% for most of the 1960s, rose to a naggingly high 6% by 1970, and productivity growth, which had been close to 3% for most of the decade, dropped to a mere 0.2% in 1969.[32] Suddenly, the economy was back on the front pages.

At just about the same time, Michael Boretsky, the Commerce Department economist studying technological innovation, began to publicize the results of his research. One of the many economic issues of emergent concern was the trade balance, which by the end of the decade was nearing zero.[33] Boretsky argued that the United States had been experiencing trade deficits for years in raw materials and low-tech manufactured products, and that its positive trade balance had depended largely on high-technology products. By the mid-1960s, however, the balance in the high-tech sector had leveled off as other countries began to catch up technologically, and the growing deficits in the other sectors were pointing toward an overall trade deficit.[34]

Boretsky was not an academic, and his analysis was criticized by some economists. Others, however, believed he was on the right track. Richard Nelson, already a leading scholar in the economics of innovation, said at the time, "I'm basically with Boretsky. . . . I think the argument is almost unassailable."[35] Boretsky's work was completed at just the right moment, and became quite influential, finding "its way into key administration officials' testimony to Congress . . . to a greater extent than his small, two-man office . . . would imply."[36]

By 1970, then, the economy was in decline and Boretsky was circulating evidence that one, the nation's technological lead was the only thing preventing a trade deficit, and two, it was losing that lead. But while concern about the state of industrial technology was on the rise, actual industry investment in R&D was no longer increasing. Government, which funded the majority of industrial R&D in the late 1950s and early 1960s, began to steadily cut its spending on industry R&D after 1967, with the result that total industry R&D expenditures were flat for the 1967 to 1975 period.[37] In an environment of concern about U.S. technological leadership, this was a troublesome sign.

It was this combination of events that led to another serious, if brief, consideration of innovation issues under the Nixon administration. Between mid-1971 and early 1972, an internal debate over how to stimulate technological innovation led to the tantalizing (to some) possibility that a major new government program to encourage it might be initiated. As Nixon was announcing his "new economic policy" in August, in which he implemented wage and price controls, a 10% tax on imports, and temporary suspension of the convertibility of the dollar to gold, his administration was arguing over how to fulfill a simultaneous promise to encourage industrial R&D.[38] Interest in the question had already been percolating, with a National Academy of Engineering symposium addressing it, a high-powered panel of the President's Science Advisory Committee studying it, and Commerce Secretary Maurice Stans, stimulated by Boretsky's work, pushing the issue.[39]

But opinions on how to help maintain the United States' technological lead were far from unified, ranging from the promotion of R&D subsidy through tax breaks and direct loans to the creation of an industrial counterpart of NSF to government support for cooperative industry-wide research associations.[40] To sort out the options, Nixon appointed William Magruder, an aerospace industry executive, to lead a massive study on the topic. The New Technology Opportunities Program (NTOP) that Magruder headed was a grand initiative, drawing together 300 people in fourteen federal agencies to evaluate "virtually every technical proposal made by the government."[41] NTOP had the ambitious but somewhat vague intent of examining all proposed options to address issues of "productivity, balance of trade, unemployment, and the use of technology to solve civilian problems," and its magnitude gave scientists "dreams of billions."[42]

But despite the fanfare with which it was announced, NTOP foundered, due to some combination of its own overambition, Nixon's fickleness regarding science, a rebounding of the economy, and decreasing public support for new government initiatives. Its results were to be included in the first-ever Presidential message to Congress on science and technology in March 1972, but by January it was becoming clear that any resulting program would be much more modest than scientists had hoped.[43] When the outcome was announced, the new program turned out to be something of a phantom. *Science* called it "a sad contrast to the optimistic hints that emanated from the Administration last summer and fall," and wrote that the "Office of Management and Budget, possibly with some cues from the White House inner circle, decided to tighten the purse strings around the throat of a $2-billion list of technical programs that Magruder had drawn up."[44] Only two modest new initiatives, the Experimental Technology Incentives Program at the National Bureau of Standards and the Experimental R&D Incentives Program at NSF, survived, and both were gone before the end of the decade.[45] The effort to marshal support for innovation in service of the economy had once again fizzled out.

Why Interest in Innovation Increased in the Mid-1970s

By 1973, the nation was embroiled in Watergate and the innovation issue had once again lost political visibility. Attention would remain relatively limited during the Ford administration as well. But over the next few years, interest in innovation would continue to simmer within policy circles, and by 1976 the issue was once again becoming politically visible. This rebound of interest in technological innovation would prove to be more intense and more durable than the brief attention the issue received from the Nixon administration, and between about 1978 and 1983 innovation became an issue of widespread political concern, as well as a popular political frame. The new wave of interest was once again driven by the convergence of several factors: the growing body of economic research on the role of technological innovation, a decline in some actual indicators of industrial innovation, the efforts of segments of industry to promote government action to encourage innovation, and, most importantly, the continuing stagnation of the U.S. economy.

While economists did not drive the innovation debate, the knowledge they continued to build during the 1970s helped maintain ongoing political concern with the issue. Academics like Kenneth Arrow, Edwin Mansfield, and Richard Nelson were called to testify before Congress about the economic role of technology in the first half of the 1970s, and by 1976 such economists were "being increasingly consulted and courted by legislators and policy-makers."[46] Government-sponsored analyses continued to have influence as well, such as a frequently mentioned 1975 report to the Department of Commerce on the importance of "new technical enterprises" to the U.S. economy.[47] But while economists agreed that innovation, broadly defined, was very important economically, they were generally reluctant to provide policy prescriptions. As Mansfield wrote in 1976, "There sometimes is a tendency to slur over—or perhaps not recognize—the fact that very little really is known concerning the effects of many of these policy alternatives, or concerning the desirability of their effects. (Indeed, in some areas, no one really knows how to study these questions effectively, let alone provide answers here and now.)"[48] Nevertheless, scholars' continued emphasis on the economic centrality of innovation provided intellectual support for reemerging political concerns.

At the same time, while not all signs were negative, some worrying trends in innovation-related indicators were becoming evident by the mid-1970s. The Boretsky argument that the U.S. was losing its positive trade balance in high-tech industries had become weaker, as critiques had been made of his analysis and even Boretsky's own data showed the U.S. gaining ground after 1972.[49] But developments in other areas did not look as good. After adjusting for inflation, U.S. industry R&D expenditures were 11% lower in 1974 than they had been in 1968–1969.[50] And R&D as a percentage of U.S. gross domestic product (GDP) declined by nearly a quarter between 1964 and 1974. While the United States had once spent a larger fraction of its GDP on R&D than any other country, it had now been surpassed by the Soviet Union and West Germany.[51] Efforts to look at innovation more specifically showed similar trends. A study of 500 major technological innovations introduced commercially between 1953 and 1973, for example, found that while the United States had produced 82% of innovations in the mid-1950s, by the mid-1960s that fraction had decreased to 55%, about the level at which it remained in the mid-1970s.[52]

While some of these developments could be attributed to things other than a decline in U.S. inventiveness—the rebuilding of Western Europe after World War II and the rise of Japan as an economic power, a decline in military R&D funding that may not have been stimulating much commercial innovation anyway—media coverage reflected the perception that the United States had lost something when it came to innovation. As *Time* wrote in 1976, "From corporate boardrooms to garret laboratories, there is a widespread concern that the U.S. genius for invention is going the way of the passenger pigeon."[53] *Chemical Week* claimed, "it seems clear that the [chemical] industry has entered a conservative period during which it will tend to be less venturesome, more defensive (in its research and development programs, for example)."[54] And an influential *Business Week* piece titled "The Breakdown of U.S. Innovation" warned of the results of this change: "less economic growth, fewer jobs, a loss of foreign markets, greater import competition in domestic markets, and finally, of course, a potentially devastating rise in trade deficits."[55]

These perceptions reflected the views of many within the business community, which was itself starting to take a more active role in putting innovation on the political agenda. When the Charpie report was published in 1967, it was somewhat anomalous in representing the industry perspective on innovation. Industry was better represented in the Nixon innovation debate, with Bell Labs' Ed David serving as science adviser.[56] But though industry had a voice, it made little difference since Nixon was not particularly interested in science policy and was actively hostile to the science policy establishment.[57]

Between 1972, when the NTOP effort ended, and 1975, the industry perspective on innovation—along with the issue itself—was not very visible. The Industrial Research Institute (IRI), an industry association of long standing, did publish a 1973 report on *Barriers to Innovation in Industry: Opportunities for Public Policy Changes*.[58] But while a little activity could be seen—a *Science* article by the chairman of Texas Instruments on science policy and the economy, a dinner hosted by the chair of IBM meant to emphasize the need for closer collaboration between universities and industry, the Congressional testimony of a couple of industry leaders on the importance of technological innovation—it was relatively low on the radar.[59]

In 1975 and 1976, though, industry efforts to put innovation back on the political agenda were stepping up. In early 1975, the National Academy of Engineering held a seminar on U.S. technology and international trade, in which representatives of firms like IBM, Hewlett-Packard, Varian Associates, and Halcon International participated.[60] This seminar helped to coalesce interest in the issue and led to a major ten-day workshop on technology, trade, and the economy, at which business was heavily represented, in August 1976.[61] IRI, too, was increasingly involved. Its president (General Electric's Arthur Bueche, who had been involved with the issue since at least the Nixon administration) testified to Congress in early 1976 about the effects of federal policy on industrial innovation, as well as serving on a new advisory group on technology and economic strength appointed by President Ford.[62] *Business Week* started covering innovation heavily in 1976, writing several articles on it and conducting its own survey of R&D activity at 730 firms.[63] As more discussion of the topic developed, industry voices were increasingly well-represented, from Ford's new panel (led by Simon Ramo, founder of aerospace firm TRW) to NSF, where a special industry panel came together to examine NSF-industry relations in the context of innovation needs.[64]

Finally, while economists, innovation trends, and industrialists all played a role in helping to put innovation firmly on the political agenda, their efforts might not have mattered had the economy not become such a nagging problem during the 1970s. The tailing off of the Nixon innovation debate had been closely tied to the short-lived improvement in the economy that took place in 1972 and early 1973.[65] But the first oil crisis, which started in October 1973, pushed the economy back into recession. By 1975, the U.S. economy was still shrinking, unemployment had broken eight percent, and inflation was hovering near ten percent.[66] While the balance of trade in high-tech products may have been improving, the overall trade balance was not, and worker productivity actually turned negative in 1974.[67] In this environment, the political audience was increasingly interested in new diagnoses—and cures—for the nation's economic problems. The idea that the United States needed to strengthen technological innovation because it drove the economy found a positive reception.

The Rise of Innovation as a Policy Frame in the Late 1970s

The conjunction of all these factors meant that by 1976 innovation was reemerging as a significant political issue. As late as 1975, *Science* was editorializing that while in 1972 it had "looked as if government had caught on to the need for explicit public policies toward technological vitality," now government had returned to "muddling through" when it came to technology policy, despite the nation's "deep economic trouble."[68] Yet by 1976, a year that saw Congressional hearings on the economic role of R&D; a presidential advisory panel on technology and economic strength; the ten-day National Academy of Engineering (NAE) workshop on technology, trade, and the economy; and the workshop on NSF-industry relations, perceptions had changed.[69] By September, *Science* was suggesting that "a serious renewal of interest in Washington" in the economic role of R&D was about to occur and that concern was "percolating briskly at the levels where policy is made" on science and technology.[70]

Yet while attention to innovation was growing, concern was not yet widespread. Neither the State of the Union address, the Economic Report of the President, nor the Budget Message of the President touched on the economic importance of innovation in 1976, and neither Ford nor Jimmy Carter campaigned on the issue that fall.[71] In June 1977, *Science* was still complaining that (now President) Carter was not paying enough attention to the role of R&D in economic growth. It even quoted him, damningly, as having said on the campaign trail that "R&D is a microeconomic factor."[72]

But the momentum that had been building got the final push it needed in late 1977. After heavy lobbying by industry executives like Bueche and subsequent IRI president (and Bell Labs executive) N. Bruce Hannay, the Carter administration began discussing its plans for "a Cabinet-level analysis" of "the link between industrial R&D and innovation" in the fall.[73] Innovation *was* mentioned in the 1978 State of the Union address, and in May 1978 Carter officially announced a Domestic Policy Review on Industrial Innovation—the highest level of policy review a president can command.[74] Led by Jordan Baruch, assistant secretary of commerce for science and technology, the Domestic Policy Review extended to twenty-eight federal agencies, involved more than 100 senior industry executives, and resulted in over 200 initial recommendations, which were eventually winnowed down to nine proposals announced in October 1979.[75] The direct effects of the review were modest. *Business Week* called its proposals "a dud" and "a disappointment," particularly due to the lack of any tax incentives, and in mid-1980 reported that "the administration has taken few concrete steps based on those recommendations."[76] Yet the initiation of the Domestic Policy Review had a great deal of indirect influence. It pushed innovation to the next level as a political issue, and helped crystallize the industrial innovation agenda in ways that would be quite influential in the following years.

The year 1978 saw the highest level of media attention to innovation yet, with a *Business Week* piece titled "Vanishing Innovation: A Hostile Climate for New Ideas and Products Is Threatening the Technological Superiority of the U.S." capturing a common tone:

> A grim mood prevails today among industrial research managers. America's vaunted technological superiority of the 1950s and 1960s is vanishing, they fear, the victim of wrongheaded federal policy, neglect, uncertain business conditions, and shortsighted corporate management. . . . Some researchers are bitter about their own companies' lax attitudes toward innovation, but as a group they tend to blame Washington for most of their troubles. "[Government officials] keep asking us, 'Where are the golden eggs?' " explains Sam W. Tinsley, director of corporate technology at Union Carbide Corp., "while the other part of their apparatus is beating hell out of the goose that lays them."[77]

While industry was not so happy with the specific recommendations of the DPR, its representatives generally acknowledged that it had created a new level of political awareness in Washington.[78] By 1979, American Cyanamid Company's Jason Salsbury (that year's IRI president) noted that "Congress seems really to have gotten the picture," and Hannay observed that "there is no question about it: Washington is much more aware."[79] As a result, Congress was considering "a spate of bills affecting innovation," with "seventy-five or eighty" counted in late 1979, and seventy-five again in mid-1980.[80] On the floor of Congress, innovation and the economy came up more than twice as often in 1976 as 1973, nearly four times as often in 1979, and more than six times as often in 1981, the year discussion of the issue peaked.[81] And in contrast to the issue's absence from the 1976 presidential campaign, by 1980 "all the major Presidential candidates . . . had something to say about innovation's plight."[82] The idea that technological innovation played a critical role in economic growth, and its corollary, that improving the innovative process could help the U.S. economy, had become a widespread and powerful theme in American politics.

But while innovation had become a useful policy frame by the late 1970s, it was also a malleable one. What one should actually *do* to improve innovation was an open question. Economists had no clear prescriptions, and were actually "quite cautious about assigning R&D a central role in innovation."[83] Policy entrepreneurs, however, were much less hesitant. The beauty of the innovation frame was that so many issues could be recast in its terms. Much of the business community used innovation as an argument for deregulation and tax cuts. Chrysler's Lee Iacocca claimed, "I never invent anything anymore. Everything I do is to meet a law," and the IRI produced evidence showing that industry R&D efforts devoted to the requirements of the Occupational Safety and Health Administration (OSHA) and proposed legislation were growing by 16.0% to 19.3% a year, while overall R&D spending was increasing by only 9.3% a year.[84] Republican representative Jack Kemp claimed that a big capital gains tax cut would "provide a shot in the arm to our high risk, high technology, capital starved industries."[85]

On the other hand, proponents of industrial policy used innovation as an argument for large-scale government support for research into "generic" industrial technologies—technologies that would be of use to an entire industry.[86] Since the innovation frame only argued that innovation was an important economic problem but did not point to a particular solution, it could be (and was) deployed on behalf of many different kinds of policy proposals. And innovation was a challenging problem to solve. As one journalist observed, "While the legislators may be as alarmed as anyone over the signs of lagging innovation . . . the subject's complexity leaves many of them nonplussed. [According to a Congressional staffer,] 'When you start to mention innovation [to legislators], they sort of draw a blank.' "[87]

The flexibility of the innovation issue could be seen not only in the variety of policies that could ally themselves with it, but also in how those with diametrically opposed viewpoints could lay equal claim to it. When the Reagan administration came to power in 1981, it quickly killed funding for the centers for general industrial technology that Carter had supported. But that did not mean it did not drape itself in the mantle of innovation. It was simply "scornful of the idea that direct federal action can improve the innovation process in industry" and instead argued that innovation was stimulated by a favorable economic climate, to be created through "reductions in federal expenditures, regulatory reform, stable monetary policy, and tax policies that provide incentives for investment in plant and in more research."[88]

Yet the adaptability of the frame to various political philosophies did not mean that some policy proposals were not better positioned than others to take advantage of it. While innovation arguments could be made in support of industrial policy proposals, it was harder to trot them out in favor of increased funding for research aimed at solving social problems, a favorite goal of liberals in the late 1960s and early 1970s. While it worked as an argument for capital gains tax cuts, it was less effective if you wanted to rein in federal science spending. And by the same token, alignment with the innovation frame alone was certainly not enough to guarantee political success. Only a small handful of those seventy-five bills floating around Washington ever became law, and many were directly opposed to one another.

What the broad acceptance of arguments about innovation and the economy did do, however, was provide a political boost to a diverse variety of proposals that happened to fit well with those arguments. Some proposals were realized, and some were not. Other factors almost always came into play. Often a policy's supporters had been pushing it for years for reasons that had nothing to do with innovation, but reframed the policy to take advantage of a political opportunity. Yet by about 1983, one could point to dozens of policy decisions, large and small, that had been made with the justification of supporting innovation. They had little else in common. But as a group, these policies would change the environment in which universities did science. And they would do so in ways that would encourage the spread of practices rooted in the logic of the market.

The Innovation Frame and the University

Universities themselves were not active in putting innovation on the policy agenda. While economists were studying innovation and the occasional university scientist could be found writing about the economic importance of academic research, fundamentally the innovation issue was about American industry—how more innovation would increase its productivity and drive economic growth.[89] University leaders and university associations were not heavily represented in this conversation prior to 1978.[90]

Nor, conversely, was the industrial innovation conversation particularly focused on the university role in the innovative process. Policy recommendations from across the political spectrum focused mostly on improving the R&D process within industry, whether that was by government supporting industry innovation directly (through an R&D tax credit, or a government program to stimulate innovation at the industry level) or by creating a friendlier economic environment for industrial innovation (through tax cuts, deregulation, or a variety of tweaks to antitrust or patent policy). While there were regular acknowledgements by all parties that the basic research done in universities was very important and should continue to be fully funded, as well as frequent statements that the university-industry relationship needed to be improved, these were secondary themes. Even a panel of industry consultants reporting specifically on NSF-industry relations did not emphasize the university role in innovation, noting that "the main problems of R&D incentives and disincentives and the fruitful coupling between industry and academic institutions are ones in which NSF cannot play a direct role."[91] Their suggestions to improve innovation included "Changes in tax rules and accounting practices to permit creation of contingent reserves for R&D," and "Moderate the effect of disincentives such as complex paper work, antitrust laws, property rights, patent regulations," areas far beyond NSF's purview.[92]

Not only were universities neither driving the innovation conversation nor the main subject of it, but of the ten policy decisions I found to be important in stimulating the growth of a market-logic practice, four—a large cut in the capital gains tax, a regulatory clarification allowing pension funds to invest in venture capital, the Supreme Court decision that microorganisms were patentable, and the creation of a federal patent court—had almost nothing to do with universities. Even in decisions like the Bayh-Dole Act, which directly affected universities, the legislation's potential effects on universities were a relatively minor part of the political debate. And yet in each of the three university practices I studied, policy decisions were critical in allowing the practice to grow. In nine of the ten decisions, the innovation frame was used, and in six of those nine, it played a key role in the decision's being made. Arguments neither driven by nor primarily targeted at universities, used in many different ways and political contexts, nevertheless ended up pushing universities in a consistent direction.

This unobvious outcome happened because the innovation frame, regardless of whether it was focused on universities or not, *saw* the value of science and technology in its potential to make an economic contribution. Thus the policies it gave an advantage to also to tended to encourage activities that treated science in terms of its economic value, whether that was in universities or elsewhere. This could mean strengthening the patent system (which tended to increase the value of scientific inventions, thereby giving universities more incentive to patent), or funding university-industry research centers directly (thus supporting research that was oriented toward the specifically economic value of science), or any of a number of other things.

The consequences were not always consistent with the preferences of those who had first raised the innovation alarm. But they *were* consistent with creating an environment that was more favorable to market-logic practices in academic science. And while universities were not the source of the innovation frame, once its success became evident they increasingly started to take the initiative in using it themselves, portraying academic science as a fountainhead of the technological innovation that would make the economy grow. The next three chapters will return the focus to the university, looking at the growth of three specific market-logic practices—biotech entrepreneurship, university patenting, and university-industry research centers—both before and after the turn toward innovation policy. I begin in chapter 4 with the emergence and spread of entrepreneurship among academic bioscientists.

CHAPTER 4

Faculty Entrepreneurship in the Biosciences

In November 1973, a scientific paper was published that would transform university-industry relations in the biosciences. "Construction of Biologically Functional Bacterial Plasmids *In Vitro*" described how two different plasmids—extrachromosomal rings of DNA capable of self-replication—could be split apart and then rejoined to one another to create a completely new plasmid, one with characteristics of both parent molecules and capable of reproducing on its own.[1] This technique for recombining DNA from two different sources to form novel DNA sequences would provide the basis for the growth of a $360-billion industry, one that academics, to a large extent, created.[2]

Academic scientists have played a role in the world of industry since the nineteenth century, in fields from chemicals to electronics to agriculture.[3] Yet academics' role in the birth of the biotechnology industry during the late 1970s and early 1980s was fundamentally different from any part they had taken before. In the past, professors had acted as consultants, inventors, and even founders of firms. But they did so while acknowledging a fairly clear boundary between the university and industry.

Formally or informally, most universities have long adhered to the "one-day-a-week" rule regarding faculty consulting.[4] Faculty are permitted and even encouraged to work with outside organizations for the equivalent of one day a week, in the belief that such engagement with the "real world" is good for both parties. At the same time, the limit reminds any overenthusiastic professors that their primary obligation is to the university that pays their salaries.[5] Historically, when academic scientists became more deeply involved in business activities they would leave their university appointments. Occasionally, a scientist might cycle back and forth between university and industry positions, particularly in engineering fields, but this was uncommon, and it was assumed scientists would not hold two positions simultaneously. The line between the two kinds of work was reasonably well-defined.

Biotechnology changed this. Emerging from disciplines with almost no tradition of industry relations, it ignored the old model entirely in favor of a university-firm relationship that was both better integrated and blurrier. From the earliest years of the biotech industry, university faculty acted not only as consultants but as entrepreneurs. They started firms, served on boards, and announced their advances not only in scientific journals but also at press conferences. Early on, very few people had the knowledge needed to conduct biotech research, and almost all of them were at universities. Most of these scientists had no interest in quitting their academic jobs to become entrepreneurs in an unproven industry. Venture capitalists who wanted to start firms had to find ways to entice academics to participate without asking them to leave their universities.

As a result, academic scientists began founding firms while remaining faculty members, at least until the firms grew too big to manage this way. Fledgling firms also needed scientific legitimacy in order to persuade venture capitalists and multinational corporations—which generally lacked the ability to judge the technical feasibility of a startup's ideas—to invest in them. So scientific advisory boards, filled (ideally) with renowned scientists, were created to signal this legitimacy to potential investors. This tied not just one but many professors to a firm, giving them a personal and financial stake in its success.

Between 1979 and 1982, the biotechnology industry experienced a boom that drew many more faculty into these sorts of entrepreneurial activities. A handful of professors became fabulously wealthy after the initial public offerings (IPOs) of their startups, and by 1980 even faculty who had once professed disinterest were getting involved. While this entrepreneurial spirit drew concern from some quarters, such activities nevertheless spread so rapidly that they had already become common in certain fields by the early 1980s, and they continue to the present day.

The story is often told as if all this were inevitable. The technological breakthrough of recombinant DNA (rDNA) technology was so great that it had to be commercialized, and there was no one to do it but academics. Certainly the scientific advance was a great one, with enormous practical implications. But this chapter will argue that it was not, in fact, inevitable that biotechnology take this particular path of development, one that hybridized academic and industrial science. There were actually substantial barriers to making faculty entrepreneurship a new norm in the biosciences.

These barriers were not, as one might suspect, primarily cultural, though there was definitely criticism of entrepreneurial activities within universities. Instead, the main barrier was the limited quantity of capital interested in investing in the fledgling industry, in which the path from academic invention to marketable product would clearly take years to traverse. The likelihood (as it appeared in 1977) that rDNA research would be heavily regulated for safety reasons was moderately discouraging to potential investors. But the biggest problem was a venture capital market that had almost completely dried up by 1978. Without a change in this situation, the future of biotech startups—and thus of academic entrepreneurship, at least in this particular form—was highly questionable.

Three policy decisions—a decision by Congress not to regulate rDNA research in late 1977, the passage of a large capital gains tax cut in late 1978, and a regulatory clarification by the Department of Labor allowing pension funds to invest in venture capital in 1979—changed the environment of biotech startups in ways that helped them to grow and spread rapidly by the end of the decade. In each of these cases, arguments about the economic role of innovation were important, and they were decisive in the rDNA regulatory decision. The rest of this chapter will tell the story of how biotech entrepreneurship got its start, of how barriers to its growth were broken down by policy decisions shaped by innovation arguments, and of how it ultimately became a common practice at research universities.

Before Biotech

While many academic fields had traditions of industry collaboration before the 1970s, biology was not one of them. Faculty entrepreneurship in the biosciences was nearly nonexistent, as, in fact, were almost any university-industry relationships in those fields. Primarily this was because the major scientific breakthroughs of the postwar decades—most significantly the discovery of the structure of DNA—had not yet created knowledge that anyone could *do* something with. As one early participant in the biotech industry recalled,

> Notwithstanding the fact that a lot of chemical and chemical engineering and physical and electronic developments had turned into companies, that hadn't happened yet in biology. It was like maybe a dam waiting to burst or an egg waiting to hatch, but the fact is, there were a lot of Nobel Prizes in molecular biology, but no practical applications. . . . [Before the development of rDNA in 1973 and monoclonal antibodies in 1975], the Nobel Prizes that had been awarded might as well have been awarded in astronomy. You can look at the stars all you want; you can't move them around.[6]

Similarly, in recalling an abortive attempt by Stanford's biochemistry department to start an industrial affiliates program, the then-department chair pointed out, "You realize that in 1970 our department did not have something it could go out and sell as easily as it did in 1979."[7]

This lack of practical applications went along with a cultural distance between universities and industry that was much larger than in many scientific fields. Another Stanford biochemistry chair described the attitude of academic biologists in the 1960s:

> Chemistry departments traditionally were tightly linked with industry. Their Ph.D. and M.S. graduates invariably went into industry. Very few went into academia. . . . But in biology it was utterly unknown. . . . For one of our graduates to enter industry would have been regarded a disaster, comparable perhaps to the marriage of an orthodox Jew to an orthodox Gentile. . . . It was not acceptable to degrade and prostitute yourself by engaging in activity that was done under such nonscientific, unproductive intellectual circumstances.

> The thinking was that people in the pharmaceutical industry, even if they started off bright, became drudges. Their function was to find ways to avoid an existing patent or to get some new patent based on a trivial thing.[8]

In this environment, consulting was rare, and entrepreneurship was almost unheard of.[9]

The relative plenitude of National Institutes of Health (NIH) funding also contributed to the lack of interest in industry relationships. Between 1956 and 1966, NIH appropriations increased by nearly an order of magnitude and ended above the billion-dollar mark, with the bulk of this money going to university laboratories.[10] There was little reason for biologists to turn to industry when budgets were already growing at this rate.

But in the postwar decades, the biological sciences were undergoing a change. Older disciplines like zoology and botany were being displaced by a reductionist approach to biology that studied life at the molecular level. Applying techniques borrowed from physics and chemistry to biological questions, the molecular study of biology had already led to major advances during the 1940s.[11] Watson and Crick's 1953 breakthrough, made possible by x-ray crystallography, seemed the ultimate validation of this new strategy.[12] By the 1960s, molecular biology and related fields like biochemistry were clearly ascendant, and ambitious universities were increasingly making these fields central to their biology programs.[13]

Some schools, like Berkeley, had trouble reorganizing biology along molecular lines.[14] Others, however, transformed their departments. Stanford's legendary provost, Frederick Terman, wanted the university's solid but individualistic biology department to become more collaborative and cross-disciplinary to take advantage of new funding opportunities created by the growth of NIH.[15] His strategy was to hire a world-class biochemist to shake things up. Terman chose Arthur Kornberg, a young professor and soon-to-be Nobel laureate at Washington University, luring him to Palo Alto with an offer to "hire his entire Biochemistry Department . . . 'down to the last dishwasher'" as well as "unchecked power to reshape the department . . . as he alone saw fit."[16] The gamble paid off, and by the mid-1960s Stanford's biological sciences were among the best in the field.[17] Similarly, the University of California, San Francisco (UCSF) was able to transform itself from a second-rate medical school to a first-rate research institution in part through a massive investment in its biochemistry department, which would go on to produce major breakthroughs.[18]

While these intellectual advances had not led to practical applications by the late 1960s, it was nevertheless becoming increasingly clear that such applications were just over the horizon. In 1967, Arthur Kornberg, postdoc Mehran Goulian, and Caltech biophysics professor Robert Sinsheimer announced the synthesis of self-replicating viral DNA.[19] Newspapers announced that this was a step toward "the time when life can be manufactured in a test tube," and while that overstated the reality, it alarmed Congress enough to call Kornberg and a colleague to testify about the ethical implications of the advance.[20]

The real practical breakthrough, however, did not come until 1973. Stanford biochemist Paul Berg, along with postdoc David Jackson and Robert Symons, a visiting scholar from Australia, had actually created recombinant DNA in 1972.[21] But the method Berg's lab used was so technically challenging that it was not clear it could be replicated without that lab's particular resources and expertise.[22] Since the technique used tumor viruses, there were also fears that it was dangerous, and that it might be possible to put a tumor virus into *E. coli*, for example, and create an easily transmitted bacterium that could cause cancer in humans.[23] This led Stanley Cohen, a Stanford professor of medicine, and Herbert Boyer, a UCSF professor of microbiology, to decide, in a legendary meeting at a Hawaiian delicatessen, to try to "creat[e] hybrid DNA molecules without the help of viruses."[24] The Cohen-Boyer collaboration moved with unexpected speed, facilitated by the atmosphere of intense competition and round-the-clock effort found in UCSF's biochemistry labs.[25] In late 1973, the first major paper from their work, coauthored by Robert Helling, a visiting scientist from Michigan, and UCSF technician Annie Chang, was published.[26]

The new work on recombinant DNA attracted a great deal of attention. Unlike Berg's method, the Cohen-Boyer technique could be performed by almost any lab.[27] But even though it avoided tumor viruses, the method's easy replicability led to a new wave of fears about what sort of dangerous chimeras might be created. For the next several years, the scientific community would exert a great deal of energy trying to deal with those fears.[28]

After the first Cohen-Boyer paper was published, Philip Handler, president of the National Academy of Sciences (NAS), asked Paul Berg to head a committee to propose ways of managing this new technology. In April 1974, by which point it was clear "that anything could be inserted into a plasmid and cloned," Berg organized a meeting at MIT with some of his most prominent colleagues.[29] The MIT meeting decided that the risks of rDNA research, while unknown, were great enough that scientists should observe a temporary moratorium on certain types of experiments, and a letter to this effect, signed by luminaries including Cohen and Boyer, was published in *Science*, *Nature*, and the *Proceedings of the National Academy of Sciences*.[30] The letter also suggested that NIH should form an advisory committee to guide further research, which the agency quickly did.[31] Planning for a conference on potential hazards—to be held at the Asilomar Conference Center, near Santa Cruz, in February 1975—began right away.[32]

The quick move by the scientific community to address the potential risks of rDNA research helped temporarily to keep the issue under the purview of scientists rather than policymakers. The Asilomar conference, a carefully managed event with a restricted guest list, saw scientists argue late into the night before coming to an agreement that the moratorium could be lifted, that research in previously halted areas could proceed under conditions of physical containment, and that voluntary guidelines should continue to be observed.[33]

But the issue proved difficult to contain. As early as April 1975, Senator Edward Kennedy was holding hearings on the risks of genetic engineering and whether scientists could be trusted to manage those risks.[34] As NIH's new Recombinant DNA Advisory Committee prepared to release guidelines for rDNA research in early 1976, controversy began to erupt in the college towns where such research would be taking place. In June, Cambridge placed a three-month moratorium of its own on rDNA research while it evaluated the new NIH controls, and over the next year a string of local and state governments considered similar measures. By the beginning of 1977, bills to regulate rDNA research were being introduced into Congress. The future of rDNA research was in question.[35]

Early Entrepreneurship

The potential risks of recombinant DNA technology gained immediate attention when it was first developed, but so did its potential for practical application. As early as 1974, the *New York Times* was suggesting the new technique might lead to the creation of nitrogen-fixing microbes that could replace fertilizer, new insulin supplies for diabetics, and easier production of the antibiotic streptomycin, and *Fortune* was claiming that "We stand at the threshold of an enormously more sophisticated extension of industrial microbiology through genetic upgrading of organisms."[36] To the scientists involved, the implications—that biology would now be able to "move around the stars"—were apparent.[37]

What was much less clear was *how* that would happen, and what academics' role would be in making it happen. Because the line between academia and industry was so sharp in the biological sciences, there were very few industry scientists who had the skill set needed to build recombinant DNA research programs. The relevant knowledge was all located in universities, so if rDNA was going to be applied commercially, academics would have to be involved. But that could happen in a variety of ways—through faculty consulting with existing firms, for example, or through industry hiring of new PhDs, both of which would have been more traditional routes. Or academics might have become involved in starting companies, but left their faculty positions to do so. A number of paths were conceivable.

But not a lot of movement toward commercialization actually took place before 1976. One small microbiology company, Cetus, did announce in 1975 that it would be moving into the rDNA area.[38] Cetus was that then-rare creature, a bioscience startup actually founded by academics.[39] In 1971, faculty from Berkeley, MIT, and Stanford had established the firm with a plan to produce instrumentation that could screen large microbial colonies for beneficial mutants that might, for example, produce antibodies more rapidly. Cetus's early success was modest, and while by 1974 the company had contracts with pharmaceutical companies Schering-Plough, Upjohn, and Bayer, it was in internal disarray and was frantically seeking to diversify into other areas of research.[40] The next year, Cetus signed Stanley Cohen on as an advisor, and made a grand announcement:

> We propose to do no less than to stitch, into the DNA of industrial microorganisms, the genes to render them capable of producing vast quantities of vitally-needed human proteins. . . . We are proposing to create an entire new industry, with the ambitious aim of manufacturing a vast and important spectrum of wholly new microbial products using industrial microorganisms.[41]

But the firm did not yet have an actual research program to go along with its plans.

Beyond Cohen's signing on as a consultant with Cetus, the most entrepreneurial thing that had happened in academia involved not a scientist but Niels Reimers, director of Stanford's Office of Technology Licensing. Neither Cohen nor Boyer had investigated the possibility of patenting their method of recombining DNA. But Reimers, clued into Cohen's work by an article in the *New York Times*, approached Cohen about the possibility. Cohen initially objected, seeing rDNA technology as inappropriate for patenting.[42] Reimers, however, convinced him that patenting would both benefit Stanford financially and accelerate the technology's path to market. In November 1974, just before the one-year filing deadline, Stanford and the University of California filed to patent the Cohen-Boyer technique.[43]

Nor was much progress toward commercialization happening outside of universities. A handful of multinational pharmaceutical companies had started modest internal research programs on rDNA, and Imperial Chemical Industries (ICI), a British firm, committed £40,000 to a genetic engineering collaboration with the University of Edinburgh.[44] But for the most part, large firms tended to be conservative, and their investments in rDNA research were made defensively, to preserve existing markets.[45] As one ICI scientist explained, "To invest money in [a genetic engineering company] to achieve expression of mammalian genes in *E. coli* would be worthless because the likelihood is that this will first be done by one of the many academics working in this area; then we will all have access to the information."[46] Furthermore, the consensus seemed to be that rDNA technology, while promising, was still a very long distance from applications, and as late as 1977 an estimate that marketable products of genetic engineering would be developed "in less than five years" was called "one of the earliest yet stated."[47]

So at the beginning of 1976, there was very little investment in rDNA by the chemical or pharmaceutical industries. No new firms had been started with the specific purpose of commercializing rDNA technology. And Cetus, the only firm that had announced it would be specifically focusing on the development of rDNA, was not terribly promising, with one investor going so far as to call it "a high-class fraud."[48] But a new company, one that would provide a successful model for academic entrepreneurship in the biosciences, was about to be formed. The impetus for its formation, however, would come not from academia, but from the venture capital community.

The Genentech Model

In 1975, a young venture capitalist named Robert Swanson was about to be let go from his position at Silicon Valley firm Kleiner & Perkins. Swanson was looking for a new job. He had recently learned about rDNA technology and become excited about its prospects, and he was familiar with Cetus because Kleiner & Perkins had invested in the company. Since Cetus did not yet have an active rDNA research program, Swanson proposed that the company hire him to start one. Cetus, however, turned him down. So Swanson began cold-calling academics to talk to them about the new technology.[49]

Most people Swanson spoke with felt that rDNA technology was still too embryonic to try to develop commercially. But when Swanson met with UCSF biochemist Herbert Boyer, Boyer reacted positively.[50] As Boyer later recalled, "I had thought about the technology being ready to be commercialized, and had discussed it with at least one drug company that I can recall, but they weren't very interested in it."[51] In April 1976, Swanson and Boyer founded Genentech with $1,000 of their own cash. Shortly thereafter, Kleiner & Perkins put in $100,000.[52]

Swanson and Boyer had a clear business strategy. Their vision was to produce medically useful compounds by expressing them from genetically engineered bacteria. Their first goal, which would serve as a proof of technological feasibility, was the expression of somatostatin, a human growth-related hormone that was chosen because of its simplicity. The second project would be to produce human insulin, which had a several-hundred-million-dollar market in the United States alone.[53] There was no immediate plan to establish a research facility outside Boyer's UCSF lab. Instead, they would contract with others—initially, Arthur Riggs and Keiichi Itakura at the City of Hope Medical Center—to do whatever research couldn't be done at UCSF.[54]

Genentech's early years were tumultuous. This kind of entrepreneurship—starting a company while remaining a professor—was very rare, and many people looked askance at it. Some scientists' responses were relatively neutral. Riggs and Itakura, for example, had no particular aversion to working with industry, though Itakura expressed some very mild reservations.[55] Nor did they encounter strong negative reactions from their colleagues at City of Hope, possibly because it was a freestanding hospital, not a university, and also, perhaps, because the organization had no endowment and was thus already oriented toward fundraising.[56]

But other relationships that Swanson and Boyer tried to develop were quickly derailed by anti-industry sentiment. Boyer's colleagues William Rutter and Howard Goodrich agreed to consult for Genentech, but, according to Swanson, "backed out because they couldn't stand the peer pressure against being affiliated with an industrial company."[57] Moreover, the boundaries between Genentech, the company, and Boyer's academic lab were blurred to the point of being nonexistent, which led to great tension in Boyer's department, including his being "viciously attacked" by some of his colleagues.[58] Boyer later recalled

> criticisms that there was a big greed factor, that I was compromising my research, a big conflict of interest. . . . It was very difficult for me. I had a lot of anxieties and bouts of depression associated with this. Here I thought I was doing something [laughs] that was valuable to society, and doing something that would make a contribution, and then to have the accusations and criticisms, it was extremely difficult. . . . And the way the attacks went, I felt like I was just a criminal.[59]

Despite the controversy, however, the two labs plugged away with the somatostatin experiments. By mid-1977, it was becoming clear that their approach was going to work—faster than anyone had anticipated. In November 1977, in an unusual move, NAS president Philip Handler and Paul Berg announced at Congressional hearings on rDNA regulation—even before the results were published—that Genentech had successfully produced somatostatin.[60]

Barriers to the Spread of Academic Entrepreneurship

Yet despite Genentech's rapid progress, the initial growth of academic entrepreneurship was far from explosive. By the end of 1977, Genex was the only additional rDNA company that had been formed, and while it had an academic as chair of its scientific advisory board, its founders were a venture capitalist and a physician-businessman.[61] Monoclonal antibodies, another technology upon which many biotech firms would later be built, were also developed in a British research institute in 1975, but no one had begun commercializing them, either.[62] Bioscience entrepreneurship did not appear to be on the verge of rapid spread.

There were several reasons for this. First, entrepreneurship was still quite unusual within the culture of academic biology. Starting a company was not an obvious move for many academics, and as Boyer found out, there were social sanctions against those who tried it. That was doubtless a disincentive for some.

Second, the perception that the technology was still far from practical application limited commercial development efforts. Riggs and Itakura, who worked on the production of somatostatin for Genentech, were actually rejected for an

NIH grant to try the same thing, partly on the grounds that their three-year projected timeframe was unrealistically aggressive.[63] Genentech would, in fact, manage to produce somatostatin in a year and a half, but the belief that the science would take a long time to develop was widespread.

Third, in 1977 the threat that Congress would act to regulate—and perhaps restrict—rDNA research was growing. Between January and April, more than a dozen bills and resolutions on rDNA were introduced to Congress, and in July, a science policy reporter observed that "the legislative process is . . . now well advanced and its momentum is probably unstoppable."[64] In this environment, many scientists' efforts were focused on avoiding or moderating government regulation of their research, not on starting companies with it. Paul Berg later said that he stayed away from commercial activity during this period so as not to appear compromised when he spoke about the safety of rDNA research, and Stanley Cohen suggested that he became a consultant to Cetus rather than founding his own company because he felt that if he started a firm, he would be perceived as having too much at stake to be objective.[65] Even the voluntary NIH safety guidelines then in effect would have been problematic in an industrial setting, and the prospect that such guidelines might be strengthened and made law did not encourage significant investment.[66]

But the fourth factor—the limited availability of capital—may have been most important of all. In the mid-1970s, risk capital was very hard to come by. Small business was caught in a "maddening struggle to survive," with interest rates high and banks reluctant to lend.[67] With the stock market in an extended slump, initial public offerings of small firms dwindled to almost nothing, from 649 in 1969 down to one in the first half of 1975.[68]

The venture capital community was particularly hard hit. Though wealthy individuals had long been investing in new companies, formal venture capital organizations had only begun to flourish in the 1960s.[69] The year 1969 was a record one for venture capital investment, with $171 million in new funds raised. But 1970 marked the beginning of a deep slump, which bottomed out in 1975, a year in which only $10 million in new funds was invested (see figure 4.1). Although investment then increased modestly, to $50 million in 1976 and $39 million in 1977, this was still a very small amount of money on a national scale.[70] As economist Josh Lerner has pointed out, during these years "firms seeking to commercialize many of the personal computing and networking technologies that would prove to have such a revolutionary impact in the 1980s and 1990 . . . struggled to raise the financing necessary to commercialize their ideas."[71] While recombinant DNA was also a promising technology, there was little money seeking high-risk investments of any sort.

This poor climate for investment meant that there was relatively little impetus for the creation of new firms. The earliest biotech startups, including Cetus, Genentech, Genex, and Biogen (created in early 1978), were all initiated by venture capitalists who actively sought to bring academics on board, and not

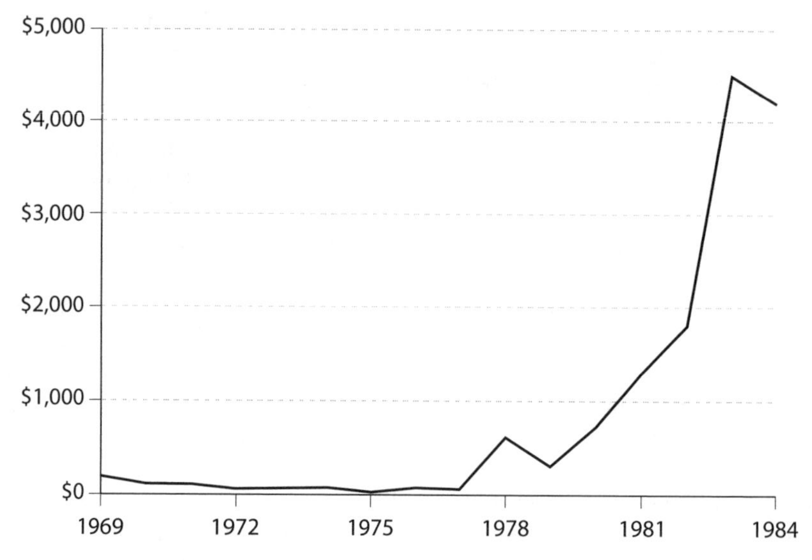

Figure 4.1. New funds raised by venture capital companies, 1969–1984 (in millions of current dollars). Adapted from Perez (1986:30).

the reverse.[72] Fewer venture capitalists looking for deals meant less pull for academics, not already oriented toward business, into entrepreneurship.

The limited availability of capital did not only discourage the formation of new firms. If the financial environment that existed as late as early 1978 had persisted, it is hard to imagine that even already-established biotech startups could have survived for long. While scientific progress was moving faster than some had anticipated, the first rDNA product, insulin, would not hit the market until 1982, six long years after Genentech was formed.[73] As late as 1987, *no* biotechnology firm had "been able to report a profit solely from the sale of biotechnology products."[74] And these firms burned through money. By 1979, Cetus would employ 200, but bring in only $7 million in revenues.[75] As the *Economist* wrote in 1978, "Genentech has run smack up against one feature of biotechnology that may distinguish it from integrated circuits: entry costs in bulk manufacture too high to be hurdled by venture capital."[76]

The other obvious source of capital for startups was investment by large multinationals in industries like pharmaceuticals and chemicals. While Monsanto did take a very modest early stake in Genentech, most companies in relevant industries—particularly the drug companies—were not in a rush to invest.[77] Cetus cofounder Ronald Cape had a psychological theory to explain this reluctance:

> If you're a 45- to 55-year-old decision-maker in a drug company, and you see a new technology that's going to revolutionize your business, you have everything to lose and nothing to gain by making a decision [to invest in it]. . . . If you are wrong in moving with this new technology . . . you're going to suffer for it, you're family's going to suffer for it, your career's going to suffer for it. If you were right, you will have retired by the time it becomes clear that you were right, okay? So you've got everything to lose and nothing to gain.[78]

And cofounder Donald Glaser recalled that when Cetus finally did attract investment from multinationals, it came from unexpected sources:

> They were two oil companies, Chevron and Amoco, which is Standard Oil of Indiana, same thing. Their reason is really peculiar. They were just rolling in money at that time. . . . What they wanted was an investment that looked promising but was guaranteed not to make any money for ten years [laughs]. So we could promise them that. National Distillers, same deal. . . . Whatever it was, that's where we got serious money and none from a drug company, even though we tried.[79]

So while multinationals were not completely uninterested in biotechnology, they certainly were not about to provide a flood of new dollars. In this environment, with so many deterrents to entrepreneurship, the chances that academic bioscience was about to experience an entrepreneurial revolution still appeared remote.

1978: A Turning Point

But in 1978, the larger environment started to change in ways that would indeed help set off such an entrepreneurial revolution. Between November 1977 and June 1979, three policy decisions were made that contributed to the unleashing of a wave of entrepreneurship in the biosciences. The first was the decision *not* to regulate rDNA research through legislation, which removed one disincentive to entrepreneurship and investment in rDNA technology. The second was the passage in November of the Revenue Act of 1978, which sharply cut capital gains taxes. And the third was a change in Department of Labor regulations, proposed in April 1978 and finalized in June 1979, that allowed pension funds to invest in venture capital. These last two moves would unleash a flood of new venture capital that changed the business environment considerably and helped young companies to grow rapidly. In each of these three policy decisions, new arguments about the economic importance of innovation played an important role.

While some academic scientists were categorically opposed to working with industry, more had mildly negative feelings about the possibility but were not militant about their position. Such scientists had never entertained the idea of entrepreneurship—but less because of sharp ideological opposition than because it was a totally foreign path for an academic career to take. But when policy decisions made large new pools of resources available, many academics were lured into entrepreneurship, slowly at first, and then, after a few scientists struck it rich, in a rush. By 1981, entrepreneurship was becoming common in some parts of biology, and in 1982, a *Washington Post* reporter wrote—perhaps hyperbolically—that "there is no notable biologist in this field [molecular biology] anywhere in America who is not working in some way for a business. I interviewed some two dozen of the best molecular biologists in the country and found none."[80] Policy decisions were not the only thing that contributed to this entrepreneurial revolution, and I will consider other factors as well. But they were a necessary condition, and they were shaped by the growing influence of the idea that technological innovation was critical in driving the economy.

Recombinant DNA Legislation

The debate over the safety of recombinant DNA moved from the local to the national stage at the beginning of 1977. The previous year municipalities, unhappy with the voluntary guidelines on rDNA research that NIH had just released, had begun proposing local ordinances that would further restrict it by requiring higher (and very expensive) levels of containment.[81] As the year went on, both policymakers and the public grew increasingly concerned, and early 1977 saw Congress consider a variety of legislative proposals to regulate rDNA, ranging from one that would keep NIH the locus of control to one that would give a presidentially appointed commission with a majority of lay members the power to control rDNA research.[82]

The uproar over genetic engineering was so great that in the first half of 1977 most observers agreed that some sort of legislation was likely to pass.[83] Even opponents of regulation, like NAS president Philip Handler, had "reluctantly concluded that legislation . . . is inevitable," and some industry representatives looked forward to at least having the regulatory uncertainty resolved.[84] "Legislation on this matter has to come. . . . There has to be some government involvement," announced C. Joseph Stetler, president of the Pharmaceutical Manufacturers Association."[85] While many scientists publicly continued to oppose any Congressional intervention, their organized lobbying efforts were aimed mostly at making sure whatever legislation passed would be reasonably acceptable, not at killing it entirely.[86]

The real question was what such legislation would look like. Many academics found scientist-led NIH regulation to be reasonable. But for the commercial development of rDNA, even the voluntary NIH guidelines were problematic.

For example, they stated that labs could create no more than ten liters of recombinant material—a quantity that would have been entirely inadequate for industrial purposes. Similarly, the requirement that rDNA material be available for NIH inspection would have been strongly objectionable in a proprietary environment.[87]

The fact that no legislation actually passed, then, and that serious discussion of the possibility had come to an end by May 1978, was very positive in terms of encouraging commercial development. Regulatory uncertainty was one reason that Biogen, led by Harvard biologist Walter Gilbert, was incorporated in Luxembourg, not Cambridge, in early 1978, and the desire to avoid a P4 level of containment—one that required "spacesuits" and to which no American university even had direct access—led Eli Lilly to set up an rDNA lab in France rather than the United States.[88] What changed between mid-1977 and mid-1978 that turned the tide? One important development was the introduction of arguments about the economic impact of innovation—in this case, the claim that regulation would harm the growth of a very promising new industry.

By late 1977, the issue of innovation was becoming more politically visible, with Jordan Baruch, Carter's secretary of commerce, publicly discussing what would become by November the Domestic Policy Review of Industrial Innovation.[89] But the debate over the safety of recombinant DNA was not initially focused on the economic potential of this new technology. Instead, opponents of regulation tended to emphasize the scientific and medical contributions that would be made by rDNA research, and the likelihood that legislation would slow such advances. At Senate hearings in April 1977, for example, while commercial applications of rDNA were frequently mentioned in passing, no one argued that regulation might pose a threat to their development.[90] But by the fall, the argument that regulation would have specifically *economic* consequences was showing up with increasing regularity.

The real turning point in the debate was another set of Senate hearings that took place in November. These were the hearings at which NAS president Philip Handler took the very unusual step of announcing an unpublished scientific advance: that Genentech's Herbert Boyer had managed to get *E. coli* to produce somatostatin using recombinant methods.[91] This was the first concrete demonstration that rDNA techniques could be used to produce such substances, and it was presented, both at the hearings and in the media, as evidence that commercial applications had become a reality.[92]

The rest of the November hearings focused heavily on the potential threats of rDNA regulation to a nascent industry. Speakers emphasized that regulation could result in "an exodus of industry," have "economic consequences," cause the technology to be "exploited elsewhere," and cause industry to "move elsewhere."[93] Historians have called the somatostatin announcement a "critical event in turning the tide of Congressional opinion" and said that the "argument, and implicit threat, from leaders of industry and science that a new field would be held back and its 'benefits' squandered if legislation was enacted was influential. No legislator wanted to be accused later on of blocking a potentially valuable source of international trade."[94]

While debate over the regulation of rDNA continued into the spring, from this point on, antiregulatory arguments stressed the potential economic impact of legislation. "The advent of commercial prospects for genetic engineering [had] moved questions about control of the field firmly into the context of international competition."[95] The March 1978 report of a House subcommittee, for example, emphasized the rate at which other countries were moving forward with commercial applications of rDNA technology.[96] Proponents of regulation found themselves making little headway, and within a few months, serious discussion of legislation had ended.

The Capital Gains Tax Cut and Regulatory Changes for Pension Funds

The possibility that Congress might regulate rDNA research was a modest disincentive to commercial investment in biotechnology. But even if had there been no chance of regulation, the risk capital environment would have been a problem for developing the technology. While the dearth of venture capital had multiple causes, including a stock market that had been flat for ten years and an economy that had been through two recessions in five years, two factors were particularly important.[97] One was a series of increases in the capital gains tax between 1967 and 1976 that raised the top effective marginal rate from 25% to 49%, thereby discouraging individuals from investing in venture capital.[98] The other was the 1974 passage of ERISA, the Employee Retirement Income Security Act. Created in response to abuse of pension funds, ERISA contained an obscure provision called the "prudent man rule," which stated that fund managers could be held personally liable for the performance of any investments riskier than those a hypothetical prudent man might make.[99] This led pension funds—which controlled a great deal of capital, $297 billion in 1977—to stop putting money in high-risk investments almost entirely, which made the risk capital environment deteriorate further.[100]

The decisions to reduce capital gains taxes sharply and to loosen the prudent man rule emerged from a much different political debate than the one over the safety of recombinant DNA, and it had little direct relevance to universities. But it, too, was shaped by innovation concerns. In the early and mid-1970s, various business interests, increasingly worried about the drift of the country toward greater regulation and higher taxes, started to organize politically. Among a number of such groups, the National Venture Capital Association (NVCA), a small organization representing several dozen venture capital firms, was formed in 1973.[101] The NVCA was very unhappy with the high tax rates on capital gains, but it did not have a high political profile, nor was it easy to gain popular sympathy for the interests of venture capitalists.[102]

But when the Department of Commerce released a report in early 1976 showing that a small group of innovative high-technology companies were creating more jobs than a group of mature companies with forty times the revenues of the small firms, the NVCA decided that this—focusing on the jobs created by the kinds of firms its members funded—was a good strategic approach to build upon.[103] Later that year, it issued a report of its own ("Emerging Innovative Companies—An Endangered Species"), which emphasized that "emerging innovative companies play a far more important role in our economy than is generally understood," and that "in order to flourish, innovative companies require: the availability of capital to fund the formation of new small companies" and "the availability of capital to finance the growth of successful innovative companies themselves."[104] It then recommended policy changes including a reduction in the capital gains tax and clarification of the prudent man rule to encourage such investment.[105]

At the same time, President Jimmy Carter's commitment to tax reform was increasing the salience of the capital gains tax issue. Carter, who entered office in January 1977, hoped to raise the capital gains tax rate further yet, arguing that taxing unearned investment income at lower rates than ordinary income was unfair.[106] The result was that groups that thought the capital gains tax rate was already too high got "galvanized into action in a way that nobody else had ever been galvanized before."[107] For a while, the NVCA had hoped to enlist the much larger American Electronics Association (AEA) to help it work toward a capital gains tax cut, but before this, the AEA had not been very interested.[108] In February 1977, however, the AEA committed to the issue, forming a Task Force on Capital Formation.[109] The two groups allied with the American Council for Capital Formation (ACCF), another relatively new organization representing business interests, to launch a lobbying campaign that would largely be framed around the relationship between the capital gains tax, the health of young, innovative companies, and the economic importance of those companies.[110] By summer, the issue of risk capital for small innovative businesses had become a hot topic on Capitol Hill. While the debate covered a range of issues, both ERISA and the capital gains tax received substantial attention.[111]

The idea of allowing pension funds to invest in venture capital was the less controversial of the two, particularly at a time when inflation was eating up returns on blue-chip stocks. The ERISA legislation had created other unanticipated problems in the three years since its passage, and many in Washington would have supported a broad-based ERISA reform. Though two bills proposed in the summer of 1977 that specifically allowed pension fund investment in venture capital went nowhere, a Carter administration proposal for a larger reorganization of ERISA briefly gained steam before being shelved in early 1978 due to political turf battles.[112]

The Department of Labor (DOL) opposed the legislative proposals, arguing that they would weaken fiduciary standards, that ERISA had not in fact caused pension funds to concentrate their investment in blue-chip stocks, and that pension managers did have legal leeway to invest in smaller, riskier companies in the context of a larger prudent portfolio.[113] But after internal debate, DOL reiterated that "Clearly, we believe the stocks of smaller companies have a place in investment portfolios. When prudently selected to include adequate diversification, these stocks can offer above average potential and will significantly add to the overall diversification and returns on pension assets."[114] In April 1978, the department proposed new rules that would loosen the prudent man requirements in a way that would clearly permit investment in venture capital.[115] The proposed regulations were favorably received by the NVCA and other interested groups, and went quietly into effect in June 1979.[116] Pension funds reacted quickly. The fraction of new venture capital investment being provided by pension funds increased dramatically, from 15% in 1978 to 31%—of a growing base—in 1979.[117]

The debate over the capital gains tax was much more volatile. During 1977, the AEA and the ACCF launched an all-out effort to counter the Carter administration's intent to increase the capital gains tax, speaking at hearings, conducting surveys of small electronics firms, and commissioning studies in support of their arguments.[118] By November, the administration was indicating that it would not try to eliminate the tax preference for capital gains, emphasizing that it understood "the important role that preferential tax rates for capital gains have played in encouraging capital formation—especially for venture capital and new businesses."[119] This eliminated the worst possibility in the eyes of those concerned with capital availability, but as late as February 1978, the *Economist* noted that "few people are convinced that risk capital is going to get a break" in the form of *lower* taxes.[120]

In the spring of 1978, however, events took a surprising turn, as the supporters of this seemingly quixotic campaign gained an important sponsor. On 7 March, Edwin Zschau, chairman of the AEA's Task Force on Capital Formation, was about to testify before the House Ways and Means Committee. He had managed to schedule a half-hour meeting with Representative William Steiger, an up-and-coming young Republican from Wisconsin, before his testimony. Zschau gave his pitch, and, according to one source, "asked Steiger whether he would be willing to introduce legislation to accomplish what they were discussing. Steiger replied, 'I'd be very interested.' Zschau asked, 'What would it take to get you to do it?' Steiger replied, 'Get me a bill.' "[121]

Zschau's testimony, and presumably his conversation with Steiger, emphasized the ways in which a capital gains tax cut would encourage the development of high-technology industries like electronics. A tax cut would increase jobs, exports ("to lessen the trade deficit which reached a new record $26.7 billion in 1977"), tax revenues ("which result from the rapid growth for which small high-technology companies have become famous"), and the development of new technology (which would "improve productivity").[122] He described government as "unwittingly . . . killing this goose laying the golden eggs" with capital gains taxes.[123]

Steiger, apparently inspired by this argument, went on to introduce an amendment to the Carter administration's tax reform package. Far from increasing the capital gains tax rate as Carter would have liked, he proposed to reduce capital gains taxes to 1969 levels.[124] Though few people initially took this radical idea seriously, in late April a *Wall Street Journal* editorial titled "Stupendous Steiger" suddenly pushed it into the public eye, calling the proposal an "intellectual and financial breakthrough" and claiming it would increase tax revenues.[125] Suddenly, Steiger's (and Zschau's) modest proposal became an "overnight sensation," sparking huge support and huge controversy, with liberals painting it as a tax break for the rich and "threaten[ing] to vote to scuttle the entire Carter tax-cut package if the Steiger amendment [was] approved."[126] As the nation took a sharp turn in an anti-tax direction (California's Proposition 13 was passed in early June), a cut in the capital gains tax became an unlikely winner.[127] It gathered a large and eclectic group of supporters, including, by late May, sixty cosponsors in the Democrat-controlled Senate.[128]

But while the national mood may have been anti-tax, a capital gains tax cut was not an obvious populist move, since it would go mostly to the rich. As the Carter administration pointed out, more than 80% of the benefits would accrue to families making more than $100,000—roughly $320,000 in today's dollars—and the family making $15,000 to $20,000 would receive an average tax break of merely twenty-five cents.[129] This meant that the tax cut's core constituency was much different from the California homeowners concerned about their property taxes who supported Proposition 13.

Certainly one cannot attribute the success of the capital gains tax cut primarily to the innovation arguments that were attached to it. The shift in the political climate around taxes resulted from a larger and more complex set of changes. But the arguments made on behalf of the tax cut were closely tied to concerns with technological innovation and U.S. competitiveness, as exemplified by this argument, made by Democratic senator Thomas McIntyre before the Select Committee on Small Business in August 1978:

> The Department of Commerce stated in April 1977 that there were "disquieting trends" in U.S. productivity, the decline of applications for patents, the increasingly adverse balance of payments, and the sharp reduction in the number of technical companies being created. Our Senate committee has since underlined the lack of risk capital available. . . . We have also shown that many of the most advanced of these new companies are being acquired by foreign corporations; and that many of the survivors are short of capital and therefore vulnerable to an economic downturn.
>
> This has brought home to us the necessity of a broad, coordinated approach to improving innovation. We know that small enterprises can have a

> tremendous payoff for the Nation. A classical example has been in miniature electronics where new, small companies backed by venture capital professionals have given the United States worldwide leadership in the multibillion dollar microelectronics field. . . . We can multiply these benefits in many industries if we have the skill to encourage the ideas of small enterprises and help them develop into the marketplace.[130]

In the economic climate of the time, such arguments did have real resonance—even with legislators who might be expected to oppose such a tax cut. As one venture capitalist recalled about the political efforts of the NVCA,

> We had real serious material and evidence from a disinterested third party—MIT and IEEE [that is, the Commerce-commissioned report "The Role of New Technical Enterprises in the U.S. Economy"]—that it was small enterprise that really provided the thrust of new employment opportunities in the country. . . . We started out, one at a time, going in [to legislators' offices] and sitting down and showing what we had and what we're up to. Not all the times were we successful, but many times it was like turning a light on in a barn. These guys would say, What, I don't believe this. This is fantastic. Where have you guys been?[131]

In the right political environment, these arguments were very effective. By late July, the *Washington Post* was calling "Liberal Chances 'Dim'" for less than a sharp cut in the capital gains tax, and by early October it was noting that "Not since the late Sixties has the venture field seen so much activity. The spurt has been encouraged both by the likelihood of a decrease in the capital gains tax and by the revival of the stock markets."[132] On 6 November 1978, President Carter clinched the deal by signing the tax package—including the Steiger amendment—into law, despite his distaste for the capital gains tax cut.[133] In 1978, $600 million in new funds poured into venture capital, an amount greater than all the funds raised since 1970. Most came in the last quarter of the year.[134]

Academic Entrepreneurship: Money Changes Everything

At the beginning of 1978, a little over four years after the Cohen et al. paper was published, Cetus, Genentech, and Genex were the only startups working to commercialize recombinant DNA technology.[135] The tide had just turned on the debate over rDNA legislation, but the possibility that research on recombinant DNA might be further restricted was still on the table. The risk capital situation was poor, and a capital gains tax cut seemed extremely unlikely.

But 1978 was a year of changes. By the end of the year, the climate for biotech entrepreneurship would be substantially different, and over the next few years, a growing number of academics would become involved with startups. This would build up, in 1979 and 1980, to something of a biotech frenzy, culminating with the October 1980 initial public offering of Genentech, which valued the company at $532 million and led one banker to note, "I can't recall any new issue having such a meteoric rise in such a short period of time—not even in the sixties."[136] The year 1981 would be the peak for the formation of new biotech firms, and new investment in the industry would crest in 1983.[137] After that, both excitement and investment would deflate somewhat, but by that point, entrepreneurship had already become relatively mainstream in the academic biosciences. The rest of this chapter will trace these developments, then consider the role of policy decisions—as well as other factors—in shaping them.

1978: Competition and Struggle

As well as being a year of political change, 1978 was also a year of intense scientific competition. After Genentech announced the synthesis of somatostatin in November 1977, insulin was the next big target. But Genentech was not the only group working on recombinant DNA. Right at its heels were the labs of Herbert Boyer's UCSF colleagues William Rutter and Howard Goodman and the Harvard lab of Walter Gilbert.[138] And Gilbert would be the next bioscientist to found a company to commercialize his research.

As had been the case with Boyer, Gilbert did not actively seek to become an entrepreneur. He valued the intellectual independence academia provided, and was not especially interested in the world of commerce.[139] But in early 1978, three venture capitalists would convince him to take the lead in founding the next significant biotech startup, Biogen. Daniel Adams and Raymond Schaefer worked for the small venture capital arm of International Nickel Company (Inco), an early funder of Genentech. The firm was intrigued enough by recombinant DNA to want a larger piece of the action. So Adams and Schaefer teamed up with C. Kevin Landry of Boston's T. A. Associates to recruit a long list of prominent scientists from the United States and Europe to their venture, including MIT's Philip Sharp as well as Gilbert, and Biogen was incorporated in Luxembourg in May.[140] According to Robert Swanson, in fact, Adams initially promised to bring these prominent scientists to Genentech: "And then he set up Biogen, took our business plan, and funded these scientists in starting Biogen who were supposed to be advisors to us."[141] (Adams doubtless has a different perspective.)

Like Genentech—and in contrast with Cetus—at the outset Biogen existed mainly in the labs of universities and research institutes.[142] Gilbert's lab managed to be the first to express rat proinsulin in mid-1978, but a disastrous experiment a few months later set it back in its effort to copy the feat with human insulin.[143] In the meanwhile, by September Genentech had announced the production of human insulin itself, scoring a PR coup and helping the company to secure the support of Eli Lilly in a critical deal to scale up production.[144] At the same time, Cetus, which did all its research in-house rather than in academic labs, was also growing. It employed 150 people by midyear, though only five of these were PhDs working on rDNA.[145] And Bethesda Research Laboratories, which had been started in 1975 (not by academics) to sell restriction enzymes to labs, had just hired a director of genetic engineering and announced its intent to move into the field.[146]

Two other startups founded in 1978 moved in new directions. One was Hybritech, the first firm to use hybridomas to produce monoclonal antibodies, a three-year-old biotechnology distinct from recombinant DNA.[147] In contrast with other biotech startups, Hybritech actually was initiated by an academic. According to Brook Byers of venture capital firm Kleiner & Perkins,

> Around May of 1978, I received a call from a scientist at University of California, San Diego, named Dr. Ivor Royston. He described to me an idea he had to start a new biotechnology company. He, on the phone, drew a parallel with Genentech. The reason he did was that he admired what our firm had done in taking the risk to invest in Genentech, and he proposed the idea of starting a new company to work on monoclonal antibodies and asked if I would meet with him. . . . Well, this was just the thing I had been looking for, because I had been curious about the whole biotechnology industry, had been inspired by Bob Swanson, I was working in a firm that had the nerve and the willingness to take risk to invest in a biotechnology start-up. I felt as though I was, by destiny, in the right place at the right time.[148]

A different sort of new ground was broken with the founding of the International Plant Research Institute (IPRI), which also planned to use rDNA technology but to focus specifically on agricultural products, rather than the pharmaceuticals and chemicals the existing startups were targeting.[149]

Yet despite this sense of ferment, the future of academic entrepreneurship was far from assured. There were still only half-a-dozen or so firms that could plausibly be described as biotech startups (or genetic engineering startups, as the term *biotechnology* was not yet widely used), and they were all quite small.[150] They had a great deal of development left to do before they could possibly bring products to market, and the cost of running them was high. And as Gary Pisano has pointed out, in the mid-1970s "there were simply no viable funding mechanisms available for long-term, high fixed-costs investments. It is no wonder that venture capitalists in the United States during the 1960s and 1970s preferred to focus their attention and capital on electronics companies rather than pharmaceutical companies."[151] Until Genentech would show, in 1980, that "a firm without product revenues could raise money in public equity markets," there was a real question about whether it was even possible for such companies to survive.[152]

In the meanwhile, there was the constant pressure of raising funds at a time when money was scarce. While the startups' founders publicly gushed about the bright future of genetic engineering, behind the scenes the firms were working very hard to bring in new financing. Cetus, the largest and most financially successful, had already sold off about half of its shares to the oil companies that had wanted the "investment that . . . was guaranteed not to make any money for ten years."[153] Genentech had raised several modest rounds of venture capital, but things were touch and go for the company in 1978.[154] Rather than continue to pursue venture capital, Genentech's plan was to convince a large pharmaceutical company to partner with it to help it scale up production, "in part because [it] didn't have enough equity to sell to pay for all the science that had to be done."[155] In September, it would manage to form such a partnership with Eli Lilly, and ultimately this would become a financial model for other firms.[156] But the likelihood of partnership depended on Genentech being the first to produce insulin, and the race was very close.[157] And as Arthur Riggs later put it, "Genentech needed those dollars from Lilly."[158]

1979: The Beginning of the Boom

But a turning point had been reached. Several developments would take place in 1979. Venture capital availability would shoot up dramatically, and much of it would flow to biotechnology. The number of biotech firms would roughly double to about a dozen.[159] New money would pour into existing companies, with the four best-known firms—Cetus, Genentech, Genex, and Biogen—valued at $225 million by the end of the year though none of them had yet brought a product to market.[160] And while there would be scientific advances, a sense of hype would also grow around the promise of biotechnology, with a great deal of breathless media coverage as well as the occasional skeptical voice. By the end of the year, a biotech craze would be in full swing, and it was this craze, as much as anything—the convergence of the science, the money, and whatever mysterious X-factor contributes to such things—that started to pull more and more academics into entrepreneurship. What, they wondered, were they missing out on?

A lot of easy money, for one thing. The capital gains tax cut and the ERISA clarification had a dramatic impact on venture capital. While new investment had averaged about $40 million a year in the mid-1970s, in 1978 that figure skyrocketed to $600 million.[161] Venture capitalists themselves have attributed this influx primarily to the policy changes, saying that "confidence in growth began to return with a vengeance," that they "really opened the floodgates," and that they "opened the doors for the growth in venture capital."[162] Economists, too, have made this claim, arguing that while the promise of biotechnology doubtless encouraged investment, the push factor of policy change rather than the pull of technological developments was more significant in causing the late 1970s explosion of venture capital.[163] The result was a rapid shift from an environment of capital scarcity to one of abundance. By the end of 1979, investors were quoted saying things like, "There's plenty of money around for deals. . . . The biggest complaint I hear is that it's hard to find good deals," and "There's too much money chasing too few good investments."[164]

At the same time, the buzz around biotech was growing. As *Chemical Week* put it in June, "The drive to get aboard the recombinant-DNA bandwagon has intensified."[165] The mainstream media was often gushing in tone, as in a *U.S. News & World Report* article that called gene splicing the "key to miracles in science": "Officials in the new industry estimate the profits will be enormous. 'We are talking about billion-dollar potentials,' says one enthusiastic investor."[166] Experts (many of whom had financial stakes in such companies) were "agree[ing] that it will be only a few years before microbial 'factories' will be competing with conventional processes in markets worth billions of dollars annually."[167] Among the promises made were that biomass conversion of plant matter into alcohols to replace gasoline would be "practical within five years" and one particularly memorable claim that "We are going to make pork chops grow on trees."[168]

In this environment, it is not surprising that firms were being started at an increasing rate. Several, including Monoclonal Antibodies, Centocor, and Clonal Research, were founded to take advantage of hybridoma technology.[169] Other new entrants included Molecular Genetics, which had ties to scientists at the University of Minnesota, and Collaborative Genetics, which was able to recruit a particularly prominent scientific advisory board, including David Baltimore and David Botstein of MIT, Ronald Davis of Stanford, and Gerald Fink of Cornell.[170] These firms were based on a variety of organizational models and incorporated scientists in a variety of roles, but all had relatively close ties to academia. Centocor, for example, was cofounded by an entrepreneur in collaboration with three scientists, two from the Wistar Institute (a nonprofit biomedical research institute) and one who was a postdoc at Harvard and Mass General, and the company was housed at a research park tied to the University of Pennsylvania.[171] In addition to new firms being founded, existing startups were expanding rapidly, too. By the end of 1979 Genentech, which had been just Boyer and Swanson in 1976, employed 50 people, including 25 PhDs, and was valued at $65 million. Cetus employed 200, including 35 PhDs, and was worth $100 million.[172]

Scientific advances continued to be made. Genentech and Howard Goodman's UCSF lab, still in intense competition, independently announced the production of human growth hormone within a day of one another in July 1979.[173] And Hybritech actually became the first company to bring a biotech product to market in December.[174] But to some observers, the rapid expansion of the nascent industry seemed based on hype as much as reality. In November, *Science* noted that despite the large paper valuation of the four main gene-splicing companies, "the first recombinant DNA product, if it be human insulin, is probably at least a year away from the market. . . . Nor is any fermentation process yet known to be proceeding with the help of gene-spliced organisms. . . . At present, the commercial applications of recombinant DNA remain as much shouting as substance."[175] (In fact, human insulin, which would indeed be the first rDNA product, would not hit the market for three more years.)[176] The new practice of publicly announcing experimental results before they were published in scientific journals led to glowing media coverage even when the achievements "were neither novel nor commercially significant." One observer called this "gene cloning by press conference."[177]

And one other issue still loomed over the future of commercial biotechnology: patents. While Stanford and the University of California had applied to patent Cohen and Boyer's recombinant DNA method all the way back in 1974, a decision about the outcome had long been delayed.[178] In 1972, a scientist at General Electric named Ananda Chakrabarty had filed for a patent on a bacterium—one created with conventional breeding methods, not genetic engineering—that could eat oil and thus be useful for, say, cleaning up oil spills. The patent office declined to issue a patent on the grounds that while Congress had passed legislation specifically protecting the property rights of the creators of new plant varieties, there was no evidence it intended other forms of life to be patentable.[179] GE sued, and in the meanwhile, more than a hundred applications for patents on living things—as well as the Cohen-Boyer application—awaited resolution of the case.[180]

Thus in 1979, no one yet knew whether and to what extent the products of recombinant DNA would be patentable, which created significant uncertainty. Some observers argued that biotechnology would develop just fine even without patents. David Baltimore of MIT and Collaborative Genetics claimed, for example, that "there is enough potential in the field that it doesn't need patent protection to stimulate activity."[181] Similarly, speakers at a June 1979 meeting on rDNA in the chemical industry "seemed to feel the patent issue [was] not an overriding one. 'We don't look to patents as a safety valve. . . . We don't lose any sleep over this question.' "[182] More common, however, was the belief that patents were absolutely critical to the development of the new industry. As Dennis Kleid, scientist and patent agent for Genentech, later recalled,

> Kleid: The question was, were we going to be able to have any patents at all? That would have been devastating, because then everything that Genentech worked on would end up being generic immediately. As soon as we did something valuable, everybody would just copy it.
>
> Hughes [interviewer]: That might have killed the industry.
>
> Kleid: Well, yes. It would certainly have killed us, and we were the industry [laughter].[183]

1980: Biotech Takes Off

> 1980 was the best year to start a company . . .
> —*Reid Dennis, venture capital pioneer, 2009*[184]

But while some participants felt that the Patent Office's unwillingness to issue patents on microorganisms "cast somewhat of a pall over the nascent industry, and raised questions in the minds of investors whether the fruits of deep research and investment would be protected," any effects on investment were not very visible in early 1980.[185] Between November 1979 and May 1980, the paper value of the four largest gene splicing companies doubled again, to over $500 million.[186] As one shocked industry observer pointed out, Cetus's paper value of $250 million was now a quarter of that of Upjohn, a large pharmaceutical company of long standing, despite that fact that Cetus had not yet produced anything. "What stream of products will come from Cetus that could justify that investment?"[187]

But the favorable resolution of the patent question in June would turn up the heat on the biotech boom even more. In June, the Supreme Court issued a 5–4 ruling in *Diamond v. Chakrabarty* that living microorganisms could indeed be patented.[188] The Chakrabarty decision was warmly welcomed by both firms and investors. As one scientist-entrepreneur later recalled, "All the early patents were viewed as positive [within the industry], because if you couldn't protect this intellectual property, then people were not going to invest in the field. So it was the fact that patents would issue, even if they were in your way, that gave people confidence that the field would be able to create value."[189]

Once again, innovation arguments figured prominently in the debate. Genentech, the Pharmaceutical Manufacturers Association, the University of California, and the American Society for Microbiology all filed *amicus* briefs in support of Chakrabarty, claiming that "patents encouraged technological innovation, and they should be allowed to encourage it in genetic engineering, since the field was recognized as a richly promising contributor to the nation's high-technology competitiveness."[190] Genentech suggested that had Congress intended to *remove* such a large area of technology from patentability, it would have explicitly done so:

> We stood the argument [that Congress hadn't said life *could* be patented] on its head and told the Supreme Court it was being asked by the Patent Office to legislate in Congress's stead. . . . We thus gave the Court an excuse to pass the buck on to Congress. It did. By the time [the issue] got to Congress, the benefits [of biotechnology] were rolling in and one could say to Congress, "This goose is laying some golden eggs here. Don't mess with it." And to their credit, to this day, they haven't. And eggs abound.[191]

The decision smoothed the way for what was perhaps the biggest moment in the early development of the biotech industry: the initial public offering of Genentech in October 1980, which was made partly on the strength of *Chakrabarty*.[192] Genentech's stock price was set at $35 a share, but it was bid up rapidly to a peak of $89, and closed the first day at $70. That gave Genentech a value—and not just a self-assessed one—of $532 million.[193] "For a company that was unprofitable and going public in the midst of the deepest recession since the Great Depression, the offering was a spectacular success."[194] Amidst all this effervescence, some two dozen new biotech companies were formed in 1980, tripling the total number of firms.[195]

The effects of the boom were beginning to show in academia. For one thing, the *Chakrabarty* decision cleared the way for the issuing of the Cohen-Boyer patents, the first of which was granted to Stanford and UC in December 1980.[196] These patents would eventually bring in more than a quarter of a billion dollars for the two universities.[197]

But beyond that, the excitement around the growing industry was drawing more academics in, and leading those who had not yet become involved in entrepreneurship to feel like they were missing out. Already, in the hybridoma domain, one industry analyst claimed that "most experienced university-based investigators are almost to a person either directly or indirectly involved in commercial hybridoma ventures."[198] And by the end of 1980 Genentech's Herb Boyer was worth $65 million, an astronomical sum.[199] Moreover, those who had remained solely in academia were not only at a financial disadvantage. As William Rutter, chair of UCSF's biochemistry department, recalled, "The best people in my lab were being recruited by other companies. It became obvious that I had to get in or lose out."[200]

The growing temptation of other opportunities led to a shift in the way academics became involved in biotech ventures. As Martin Kenney has explained,

> In the late 1970s the formation of a genetic engineering company nearly always involved an entrepreneur soliciting various professors until he discovered one who was interested in forming a company. This search usually took six months to a year in the 1976–78 period. . . . Understandably, in the gold rush atmosphere that prevailed from 1979 to 1981 many scientists performed the role of entrepreneurs and directly approached venture capitalists with business plans. By 1980 this had become the prevalent pattern as scientists became sensitized to the value of their results.[201]

Amgen, founded as Applied Molecular Genetics in 1980, was created the old way. William Bowes, who had recently left a long career in investment banking to focus on venture capital, later recalled,

> There were a lot of superb scientists who were not associated with any biotech company, so I thought there was room for another good one down

> south, as opposed to the Bay Area. So . . . I thought the first step would be to put together a scientific advisory board, who could point [us in] promising directions, and it'd also be a help in attracting good management to the company."[202]

He and another venture capitalist recruited Winston Salser, a prominent cancer biologist at UCLA, to assemble such a board.[203] As Amgen's founding CEO George Rathmann (himself from the pharmaceutical industry) noted, "That was one approach to building one of these new companies: take a scientific board of real preeminent scientists, and then have that as a kind of lightning rod to attract scientists and investors and to guide your research."[204] Salser then helped to sign up that kind of high-powered board.[205]

But other scientists were starting to make entrepreneurial moves on their own, even some who had been vocally reluctant to commercialize their research themselves. Paul Berg, the Stanford biochemist who had recombined DNA even before Cohen and Boyer, had studiously avoided commercial involvement with biotechnology, in part because of his central role in the rDNA safety debate.[206] Other Stanford faculty also shunned such activity, to the point that one observer has said that in the late 1970s, "the bastion of anti-entrepreneurial activity was temporarily Stanford."[207] Yet in 1980, Berg cofounded DNAX with Stanford colleagues Arthur Kornberg and Charles Yanofsky. Berg and his colleagues had been approached by a chemical engineering professor about becoming involved in a startup, but they became disillusioned after meeting with venture capitalists. After a conversation with investor and entrepreneur Alex Zaffaroni, a longtime friend of Kornberg, they decided to start their own company with him instead.[208] Berg explained that while he was initially skeptical about commercialization, he later adopted the position that "this field of genetic engineering is going to blossom and is going to move ahead. If you participate in it, you have a greater chance of influencing that it does it right and properly and ethically than if you stay out of it."[209]

In other cases, academics who simply hadn't considered entrepreneurship found themselves being drawn into it as friends and colleagues got involved. Edward Penhoet, a biochemistry professor at Berkeley, described how this process worked in his own case:

> Penhoet: George [Rathmann, CEO of Amgen] showed up on my doorstep to discuss with me my interest in becoming the research director of Amgen. . . . I was perfectly happy where I was here on campus. On the other hand, I'd had enough involvement in what was going on in the field to be intrigued. . . . By then I was doing recombinant DNA work, and I knew the players, and I could see what was happening in that field.
>
> Hughes [interviewer]: Had you before this approach from Rathmann considered moving into industry?

> Penhoet: No, not even vaguely. I just didn't have any interest in doing commercial stuff. . . . I wasn't worried about the stigma. I enjoyed what I was doing. I had made the decision some time earlier to go into academics, not into business, so I was perfectly happy with that decision. On the other hand, by then the field was becoming intriguing. By the time George knocked on my door, Amgen had already raised $20 million in venture financing. Genentech had already done a number of things. These friends of mine, Colby and Gelfand, had already gone to Cetus. So I thought, well, it's at least worth talking to George to see what he has in mind.[210]

While Penhoet did not join Amgen, the meeting planted a seed that would lead him to start the firm Chiron a year later.[211]

After 1980: Dénouement

Investment in biotechnology would continue to increase for the first few years of the 1980s. The year 1981 would be the peak for the formation of new firms, with forty-three founded, once again doubling the population of startups.[212] New investment in the industry would continue to increase until 1983, when it would crest at $850 million.[213] And the first genetically engineered product, human insulin from Genentech and Eli Lilly, would go on the market in late 1982, allowing some of biotechnology's commercial promise finally to begin to be realized.[214]

Yet although there was hardly a crash, or the popping of a bubble, some of the giddiness around biotechnology started to dissipate after Genentech went public. While Cetus's March 1981 IPO was "the largest single stock offering by a new corporation in history," its underwriters nevertheless had to repurchase shares in order to maintain the offering price.[215] Startups Collaborative Genetics, Molecular Research, and Genex all had disappointing IPOs in 1982.[216] A rash of new companies were being created, but many of them were jumping on a bandwagon, having little even of intellectual value to offer and lacking the scientific firepower of the earliest startups.

As a result, venture capital was becoming increasingly cautious about further investment.[217] The new funds raised by venture capital companies (for all industries, not just biotech) continued to rise rapidly, from $700 million in 1980 to $1.3 billion in 1981, $1.8 billion in 1982, and $4.5 billion in 1983.[218] But 1981 and 1982 were the years of the greatest venture capital investment in biotechnology, with roughly $400 million taking place.[219] And even by then, venture capital had already become expensive for startups in comparison to 1980. That year, venture capitalists had to invest $5 to $25 million to get 25% equity in a biotech startup. In the 1981 to 1982 period, however, investments were more typically $2 to $4 million in exchange for 40% to 50% of the company.[220]

Already by 1981, many observers were predicting a coming "shakeout" in biotechnology.[221] The formation of new firms did decline sharply, with about half as many founded in 1982 as 1981.[222] And with the slow movement of products to market there was an increasing realization that "the commercialization of biotechnology now may be more time-consuming, more expensive, and less profitable than was initially hoped."[223] In fact, as late as 1988, twelve years and billions of dollars after Genentech was founded, only six biotechnology therapeutics had reached the market: "human insulin, human growth hormone, alpha-2 interferon, a monoclonal antibody for reversing kidney transplant rejection, a hepatitis B subunit vaccine, and tPA [tissue plasminogen activator, given to treat blood clots]."[224]

By 1986, new investment in biotechnology was projected at only $200 million, less than a quarter of its 1983 peak.[225] Clearly the biotech "boom" of 1980 to 1984, as the Office of Technology Assessment described it a few years later, was over.[226] And hindsight was, of course, 20/20. As one industry insider stated with some hubris, "Most investors now recognize that [biotechnology] is nothing but a tool to dissect biology. . . . Anyone who knew anything about it as early as 1976 could have predicted all that has happened."[227] Yet the deflation was relatively gradual, and despite the repeated promises of a shakeout, by 1988 none had yet materialized.[228]

But by the time the rapid growth of the young biotech industry began to slow down around 1982 or 1983, substantial changes were already being felt on university campuses. In the early years of the biotech business, the relevant scientific expertise was still located predominantly on university campuses. New startups generally drew directly on this expertise. They typically involved academic scientists not only as cofounders, but also as members of scientific advisory boards, which were generally made up of about four to ten academic scientists (though Cetus eventually had thirty-one).[229] Startups also hired faculty as consultants—Hybritech, for example, listed seventeen scientific consultants by 1982, all of them academics.[230] Thus one startup might involve from five to several dozen academic scientists in some way, and by 1981 at least eighty biotech startups had been created.[231] Even for the many scientists who were primarily consulting for the new companies, not starting firms themselves, this was a dramatic change from the situation that had formerly existed in biology, where academics had had almost no interaction with industry.

While some observers claimed that academic scientists working on technologies like monoclonal antibodies and recombinant DNA were "almost to a person" involved with commercial ventures—and perhaps this was true of an elite handful—in reality active entrepreneurship was still far from universal.[232] In 1983, Henry Etzkowitz wrote that

> in interviews with molecular biologists in the department of biological sciences at Columbia University, I found that less than one-fourth either had or were actively negotiating to arrange extensive research contracts or the

> formation of private firms, while no scientist who was not a molecular biologist had even undertaken more than occasional consultation for industry in the course of his or her career.[233]

Similarly, the first large-scale survey of faculty at major research universities who were involved with biotechnology, conducted in the winter of 1985, found that only 8% held equity in a company based on their research, while 23% were principal investigators on grants or contracts from industrial sources.[234]

At least as significant as the total numbers of entrepreneurial faculty, however, was that such activity was increasingly being accepted as normal and appropriate by universities and their faculty. In the late 1970s, scientists who started companies had been criticized for their decisions. Venture capitalist Brook Byers recalled that when University of California, San Diego professor of medicine Ivor Royston founded Hybritech in 1978,

> there was suspicion. It was sort of like when Bob Dylan went electric in the sixties. It was controversial. People were wondering, what's up with that, and will bad come of this? Ivor, I remember had to suffer indignation and suspicion from his colleagues on campus. . . . Because remember at that time, this was all new. . . . With Ivor, we were seeing him as a pioneer, but his colleagues in academia were seeing him as a turncoat.[235]

But by the early 1980s, it was faculty critics of what one called the "rising entrepreneurial tide" on campus who were receiving a "less than enthusiastic reaction" from their colleagues.[236] As *Science* noted in 1982, "Scientists who ten years ago would have snubbed their academic noses at industrial money now eagerly seek it out."[237] Universities were still struggling with how best to manage conflicts of interest and the challenges to traditional academic values that resulted from the biotechnology boom.[238] The issue of whether or not they would have to deal with such developments, however, was less and less in question.

Why Did Bioscience Entrepreneurship Take Off?

The goal of this book, once again, is to explain why market logic became more significant in academic science starting in the late 1970s, which I do by comparing the emergence and spread of three specific market-oriented practices. The overarching argument is that policy decisions, shaped by the idea that innovation drives the economy, were necessary to the growth of each practice and were the factor that proved significant across all three cases.

But the three practices did not take off solely because of policy decisions. In each case, a number of developments had to align before the market-oriented practice could become something more than the occasional experiment undertaken by an adventuresome individual. In the last pages of this chapter, I will consider what these developments were in the case of biotech entrepreneurship and how critical each of them was to its rapid expansion. While I include policy decisions among the conditions that were necessary and note the role innovation arguments played in making these decisions, I do not yet focus on making the case that policy decisions and innovation arguments specifically were the most important factor in explaining the takeoff of market logic. That argument will be developed more fully in the chapters that follow, as I present the other two cases and the similarities and differences in their trajectories can be compared directly.

It is unquestionable that the scientific breakthroughs in the biological sciences that took place in the 1950s, 1960s, and especially the 1970s paved the way for biotech entrepreneurship. Without them, there would have been no technological basis for a new industry and no direct impetus to entrepreneurialism. Yet the scientific breakthroughs are not enough to explain why ivory-tower academics ended up starting firms to commercialize their research in significant numbers. The electronics industry, for example, was heavily science-based and had close ties to academia and yet did not take a similar path in the late 1970s.

The fact that expertise in biotechnology could *only* be found in academia certainly played a part. This does distinguish biotechnology from electronics, where breakthroughs like the transistor and the integrated circuit came from industry, not academia. But while academic expertise was necessary for the development of the technology, it still conceivably could have been incorporated into large firms through more traditional means, like consulting or the hiring of new PhDs. The risk-averse nature of big pharmaceutical and chemical firms, along with the sharp line between academia and industry in the biosciences, were clearly obstacles that made that particular path more difficult to take. But identifying those obstacles is not the same as providing a positive explanation for the path biotechnology *did* take—being developed in an independent industrial sector closely integrated with academia. In order for that to happen, starting a company had to look exciting and promising enough that a critical mass of reputable scientists would risk stepping off the traditional academic career path and braving the disapproval of their peers in order to do it. Then their companies had to be successful enough that their example would encourage yet more bioscientists to become entrepreneurial.

In many ways, that seemed an unlikely outcome. Venture capitalists had to lure the first academics into starting companies. While Herbert Boyer appears to have been amenable to entrepreneurship from the outset, Walter Gilbert required months of courting before he would help start Biogen, and even Boyer did not act until he was approached.[239] And once firms were started, their financial viability was still questionable. It took six years for Genentech to get the first recombinant DNA product on the market, during which time the company raised—and spent—hundreds of millions of dollars, and Genentech was hardly alone in its lack of products. Even now, commercializing biotechnology is so challenging that Gary Pisano has suggested that the entire model of the public biotechnology firm may not be sustainable, since public financing leads to pressure for short-term results, a problem for firms with such long horizons for product development. In the mid-1970s, there was simply no mechanism for financing startup companies that were going to take that kind of time and capital before they would have products to sell.[240]

As late as the end of 1977, then, the spread of biotech entrepreneurship seemed far from inevitable. Yet by the end of 1980, after Genentech's wildly successful IPO and the move toward entrepreneurship even by scientists who were once critical of such behavior, the practice was rapidly becoming part of the fabric of life in certain parts of biology. While the young biotech industry certainly could have collapsed after that point—and academic entrepreneurship with it—momentum was in its favor.

Beyond the scientific advances and the academic location of biotech expertise, both of which were necessary but not sufficient conditions for launching academic entrepreneurship, four developments played an important role: the gradual relaxing of restrictions on recombinant DNA research, the successful organizational model provided by Genentech, a dramatic change in the venture capital environment, and the Supreme Court decision that microorganisms could be patented.

The relaxing of rDNA restrictions, and in particular the decision made around the end of 1977 that rDNA would not be regulated via legislation, was helpful, at least in the short run. Recombinant DNA was already a highly risky investment, and the possibility that rDNA would be further regulated had a dampening effect on potential investment for several reasons. It could have made it much harder to do research on an industrial scale by limiting the quantity of rDNA material that could be created and requiring that it be available for inspection. It also could have sharply increased the costs of doing rDNA research and its logistical challenges by requiring higher levels of containment. In 1977, it was estimated that converting an ordinary lab into a P3 lab cost $50,000, and building a P4 lab, the most secure type, cost $200,000.[241] P4 labs, in particular, made conducting research very cumbersome, with their requirements that "spacesuits" be worn inside and that everything entering and leaving be washed with formaldehyde.[242] Presumably as evidence accumulated that recombinant DNA was not especially risky, such restrictions would have been relaxed anyway. But they might have slowed investment for long enough to hinder the particular path to development that biotechnology took.

The successful organizational model of Genentech was another important factor in launching academic entrepreneurship. Genentech, partly through strategy and partly through luck, did two things that would be widely emulated by other young biotech firms. First, it developed a viable financial model that, at least in the context of the generous investment environment that was emerging by the end of 1978, showed how a firm with such high capital requirements and such a long timeline to market could sustain itself. Unlike Cetus, Genentech did not immediately hire employees or rent research facilities, but rather conducted its research in Boyer's lab and in the labs of other researchers with which it contracted.[243] This kept the company's costs down and its research focused, as well as tending to further blur the line between university and industry. Then, by signing a contract to work on insulin in partnership with Eli Lilly in late 1978, the firm showed that development could be funded by contracting with a large pharmaceutical firm, which was historically unusual in the vertically integrated pharmaceutical industry.[244] This and other contracts carried Genentech to its blockbuster IPO in October 1980, which subsequently demonstrated that it was possible to finance publicly a company without products.

Second, Genentech created a unique corporate culture that rewarded scientific excellence and understood scientific values without, as the saying goes, letting the inmates run the asylum. The strong commitment to doing first-rate science was present from the beginning. William K. Bowes, a venture capitalist who had served on Cetus's board and went on to found Amgen, recalled that

> within six months of Genentech being founded, I figured they were doing it the right way [while Cetus, by implication, was not]. . . . I knew the names of the scientists they'd hired. They had great resumes. They weren't spending money on peripheral stuff. It was all science. . . . Herb Boyer worked in the company. He wasn't just an advisor. He had his sleeves rolled up. . . . I just knew they were hiring terrific, terrific people.[245]

But in order to hire such "terrific, terrific people," the startup had to have an environment that would appeal to such people. This meant developing an intense but intellectually open atmosphere which shared many traits with academic life, including, for example, the freedom to publish results. Axel Ullrich, one of Genentech's initial scientists, later said,

> Ullrich: The reason Genentech became such a major power in basic research is because of people like me and Peter [Seeburg, another early scientist]. We were worried that if we started doing commercial research we would have problems returning to academia if things didn't work out. . . . We would be in the streets. So we had to publish. We put pressure on Bob Swanson who didn't like that. We said, "Okay, we have to publish. We have to establish a university-like atmosphere." And that succeeded.
>
> Hughes [interviewer]: That set a precedent, didn't it?
>
> Ullrich: Oh, absolutely. It was a completely new model, which is very, very powerful.[246]

But at the same time, Genentech never gave so much freedom to its scientists that the company lost focus on its bottom line. Biogen, by contrast, was heavily dominated by its scientists, a model that created "coordination costs" for the firm as different scientists pulled it in different directions.[247] The 50-50 partnership between Swanson and Boyer, on the other hand, allowed for a successful balance between business and science. "Bob was always a little more worried than Herb about publications and other people knowing what we were doing. That was probably a healthy tension—Bob at one end, Herb at the other. And somewhere in the middle was how the company worked."[248]

While the decision not to legislate restrictions on rDNA research and the successful organizational model of Genentech were both important, the dramatic change in the venture capital environment in late 1978 was truly transformative for the emerging industry. As late as February of that year, the *Economist* was calling American venture capital "fun no more" and noting that "innovators, who now face demands from venture capitalists of up to 80% ownership at the start-up . . . are selling out to cash-rich industrial giants" rather than continue to struggle for financing.[249]

But over the next few months, this situation changed dramatically. An improvement in the stock market starting in April, and in particular a growing receptivity to initial public offerings, freed up some venture capital as well as providing encouragement to small businesses looking for a way to finance their growth. The official proposal by the Department of Labor to allow pension funds to invest in venture capital in April, followed by the slashing of the capital gains tax in November, accelerated this change, leading to a venture capital environment in the late 1970s and early 1980s that one observer described as "euphoria."[250] While undoubtedly multiple factors led to such a significant change in the investment environment, there is good evidence that the regulatory clarification and the tax cut played a major part. Certainly people experiencing the shift perceived that that was the case. *Newsweek*, in a typical piece, wrote in July 1979 that

> The new boom in venture capital was touched off last year when Congress reduced the maximum tax on capital gains from 49 per cent to 28 per cent. . . . The government also helped attract venture capital with a Labor Department guideline suggesting that pension-fund managers could invest in a certain number of new ventures and still live up to their fiduciary responsibilities.[251]

Venture capitalists, too, have suggested that both factors were important, and even that the two decisions reinforced each other: "Without the tax law change, you wouldn't have gotten the practitioners [i.e., employees at big firms] to come into the industry [i.e., start companies]. . . . Pension funds can't do it by themselves. They need entrepreneurs and professional managers who are good at taking risks, and you don't find them in pension funds or commercial banks."[252] Once pension money did start pouring in, however, it provided additional incentives to potential entrepreneurs. This conventional wisdom has more recently been backed up by economic research. The body of literature on the history of venture capital is modest. But the work of Paul Gompers and Josh Lerner, the most systematic in this area, suggests that both the capital gains tax cut and the ERISA clarification were very important in encouraging venture capital investment, and that policy decisions were more significant than technological advances in driving its increase.[253]

An international comparison reinforces the argument that venture capital availability—as well as a relaxed regulatory environment—helped the biotech sector to take off in the U.S. Britain was on the cutting edge of academic bioscience in the 1970s—the structure of DNA, after all, had been deciphered in a Cambridge lab. British scientists were the first to create antibody-producing hybridomas as well.[254] But Britain had much less success than the United States at turning its capacity for basic science into commercial applications. Notably, it lacked venture capital. Even in 1977, when venture capital was at a low ebb in the United States, the *Economist* was comparing the British situation unfavorably to that across the Atlantic.[255] As a result, the country's investment in commercial biotechnology came primarily through slower-moving multinational firms rather than the lighter-footed biotech startups found in the United States.[256] Britain also took longer to relax regulations on rDNA research than did the United States.[257] So by mid-1979, only two British companies—multinationals or startups—were working on rDNA, compared to perhaps three dozen in the United States, and in 1983 Britain was described as having perhaps a tenth as many biotechnology firms as the United States.[258] Multiple observers saw this as the result of the bleaker venture capital environment. The *Economist* warned that "unless more is done quickly, this will be a variation on a sad old theme: invented in Britain, made abroad."[259] Biogen's Gilbert, too, attributed the U.S. biotech industry as being "due wholly to the effervescence of America's venture capitalists . . . who are the missing link in England."[260] Britain never developed as vibrant a biotech sector as the United States, and its academics did not move decisively toward entrepreneurship till much later.[261]

Finally, while a great deal of entrepreneurial ferment had already developed in U.S. biotechnology by mid-1980, the Supreme Court's *Diamond v. Chakrabarty* decision in June, which said that microorganisms could indeed be patented, certainly helped solidify the position of the young biotech companies. Opinions about how critical *Chakrabarty* was to the survival of individual firms or the industry as a whole vary, and one can argue that biotechnology firms still would have found a way to make money even if the case had been decided the other way. But it is unquestionable that in the short run *Chakrabarty* gave the industry a boost and encouraged investors' confidence that the small firms would indeed find a way to convert their scientific knowledge into profitable products.

Thus at least six factors came together to launch and sustain the practice of academic entrepreneurship in the biosciences successfully in the late 1970s and early 1980s. Four of these—the scientific advances, the academic location of expertise, the organizational model of Genentech, and the changed venture capital environment—were arguably necessary for biotech to develop the way

CHAPTER 5

Patenting University Inventions

THE FIRST OF THE PATENTS on Stanley Cohen and Herbert Boyer's method for recombining DNA was issued to Stanford University and the University of California in December 1980.[1] A few weeks later, President Jimmy Carter signed the University and Small Business Patent Procedures Act, more commonly known as the Bayh-Dole Act, into law. The legislation affirmed universities' right to patent government-funded inventions like Cohen and Boyer's recombinant DNA (rDNA) technology and encouraged them to do so.[2] The Cohen-Boyer patents would become the first blockbusters of the Bayh-Dole era, earning an unprecedented $250 million in revenues over the next seventeen years.[3] During this period, dozens of universities would try to emulate Stanford and UC, launching technology transfer offices and seeking blockbuster patents of their own.

A few would succeed. In the 1980s, two Yale faculty members made breakthroughs that led to the development of the HIV drug Zerit and to a patent that earned more than $250 million for the university.[4] In the early 1990s, a Florida State chemistry professor developed a technique for synthesizing taxol, a breakthrough cancer drug originally found only in the bark of the scarce Pacific yew tree, and a license on his method eventually generated $350 million in revenues for the university.[5] For these and a handful of other universities, patenting and licensing faculty inventions would result in a major new source of revenue.

But such huge financial rewards were rare. While more than 150 universities had technology transfer offices by the year 2007, only thirteen of these reported earning more than $25 million in licensing income. The median revenue from licensing that year was only $1.8 million, even though the median technology transfer office employed seven people full-time.[6] In many respects, the patenting game was like a lottery, in which most tickets would be worth nothing, but a very few would pay off big. Yet no university wanted to be caught without a ticket, and during the 1980s and 1990s universities established technology transfer offices at a rapid clip as they tried to fulfill the mandate of Bayh-Dole while simultaneously building a new income stream.

Traditionally, the patenting of research was seen as a questionable activity for universities. Some patenting had always taken place, and a few schools, including MIT, Wisconsin, Florida, and Indiana, had even brought in significant that it did, and two more—the lack of rDNA regulation and the decision tc allow patents on life—were facilitating, but less clearly decisive. And four polic decisions helped to create these conditions: the decision not to regulate rDN through legislation, the *Chakrabarty* decision of the Supreme Court, the clarifi cation of the prudent man rule, and the capital gains tax cut. In all four of thes policy decisions, innovation arguments were clearly present. In two of ther the ERISA clarification and *Chakrabarty*, it is difficult to know how importa a role they played, though the limited evidence available suggests they matter at least to some extent. In the capital gains tax cut, innovation arguments we clearly significant, though probably not decisive. And in the decision abc rDNA regulation, their introduction appears to have marked a critical tu ing point in the debate. Chapter 8 will return to consider more fully the r of innovation arguments and policy decisions in encouraging market logi the context of not only biotech entrepreneurship, but in other practices in a demic science as well. Next, however, I will turn to the development of ano one of those practices, universities' patenting of faculty inventions.

revenues by licensing patents. But the logic of science implied that the knowledge created by universities should be freely available, and many had a problem with the idea that universities might directly profit from that knowledge. Often patenting was restricted to unusual circumstances, and when universities did pursue patents, they sought to insulate themselves from charges of mercenary behavior by creating independent research foundations or by contracting with an outside organization to manage them.

But by the 1980s, both the attitude and the behavior had started to change. Increasingly, universities were actively seeking to patent research, and they were doing so on the basis of a new argument. Patents, they pointed out, were necessary to encourage companies to invest in developing inventions, so universities had a responsibility to patent in order to prevent publicly funded research from languishing unused. Simply creating knowledge and making it accessible was not enough. Universities also needed to harness the power of the market to make sure that their knowledge got into use.

The foundation for this change was laid as early as the 1960s, when a handful of government employees began working to make it easier for universities to patent their research. By the mid-1970s, a group of university administrators was also organizing in an effort to strengthen universities' capacity for patenting and licensing inventions. Due in part to these dual efforts, the number of patents issued to universities roughly tripled between the mid-1960s and the mid-1970s.[7]

Yet while it was on the rise, the practice of university patenting was also on shaky legal ground. Government supporters were doing what they could to encourage it, but without legislation clearly giving universities the right to patent government-funded inventions, permission to patent could rapidly be retracted, as a 1977 reversal of NIH's generous patent policy made evident. While patenting was becoming more common, its future was nevertheless uncertain.

But the 1980 passage of the Bayh-Dole Act helped assure its continuation. Buttressed by arguments about the role of patents in strengthening innovation and thus in helping the economy, the legislation marked a decisive federal shift toward support for the practice. Other policies, including the Supreme Court's *Chakrabarty* decision earlier that year and the creation of the Court of Appeals for the Federal Circuit in 1982, helped to strengthen patent rights further and to expand their scope, which in turn created additional incentives for universities to pursue patents. During the next two decades, the growth of university patenting accelerated. While fewer than 400 patents were issued to universities in 1980, that number had risen to over 3300 by 1999.[8] The rest of this chapter will recount how the practice of patenting emerged in universities, slowly and haltingly spread, then ultimately went on to become a common and taken-for-granted part of academic science.

University Patenting during the Science-Logic Era

The issuing of patents is one of the handful of activities that is actually reserved for the federal government in the U.S. Constitution, which gives Congress the power "to promote the progress of science and useful arts, by securing for limited times to authors and inventors the exclusive right to their respective writings and discoveries."[9] By giving inventors a temporary monopoly on the use of their inventions, patents aim to create an incentive that rewards such creativity.

But while patenting has a long history in the United States and has generally been embraced as an important means of encouraging "American ingenuity," universities have traditionally questioned whether it was appropriate for *their* inventors to pursue such a monopoly. Those who saw the university as an institution dedicated first and foremost to the pursuit of knowledge often perceived the world of commerce as having a potentially corrupting influence. Even observers with fewer doubts about commercial activity sometimes argued that university faculty were already being paid to invent, and did not need additional rewards to do what was already their job. Many also saw universities as having a responsibility to ensure that the fruits of their research remained in the public domain, accessible to all.[10]

Such arguments date back to the early twentieth century, where they sound surprisingly contemporary. Frederick Cottrell, a chemist at the University of California, created the nonprofit Research Corporation in 1912 to manage the patents on his own work precisely because he was concerned about what participation in patent management might do to universities:

> A danger was involved, especially should the experiment [of having the university manage patents] prove highly profitable to the university and lead to a general emulation of the plan. University trustees are continually seeking for funds and in direct proportion to the success of our experiment its repetition might be expected elsewhere. . . . The danger this suggested was the possibility of growing commercialism and competition between institutions and an accompanying tendency for secrecy in scientific work.[11]

The prominence of this anti-patenting view, however, did not mean that university patenting was nonexistent, or that no one within universities believed patenting could be beneficial. The most conservative position was that patenting might be appropriate for a university to take as a defensive measure, whether because a private entity might otherwise patent the invention itself and prevent it from being more generally used, or as a means of ensuring some level of standardization in products that might otherwise be risky—a particular concern prior to the emergence of a strong Food and Drug Administration. For example, in the 1920s professor Harry Steenbock of the University of Wisconsin invented a process for creating vitamin D. This was a massive public health advance during an era in which rickets, a nutritional deficiency which led to bowed legs, a curved spine, weak bones, and which could eventually be fatal, was widespread.[12] Steenbock moved to patent his invention partly because he was afraid that a "patent pirate" would otherwise claim it and charge exorbitant fees for its use. He was also concerned that only reputable manufacturers be allowed to produce vitamin D and wanted to prevent advertisers from making outrageous claims about its benefits.[13]

But others advanced broader arguments in favor of university patenting. Some believed that professors and universities deserved rewards for their inventions as much as anyone else, particularly since royalties were likely to be plowed back into research. Others emphasized the need to patent so that firms had an incentive to develop, produce, and market the inventions that came out of universities, and argued that without patents, such development would not be pursued, for, as Cottrell put it, "what is everybody's business is nobody's business."[14] As Grischa Metlay notes, the cases for and against university patenting have changed relatively little over the years.[15]

What this diversity of views meant in practice was that universities took a variety of approaches to patenting in the decades leading up to the 1960s. In the 1930s, universities' formal patent policies varied widely, and a number had no explicit policy at all.[16] Of those that did have a policy, several approaches could be found, heavily influenced by the desire to protect the university from charges that it was trying to profit from its research.

The best-known of the early patenters was the University of Wisconsin. In the 1925, the university founded WARF, the Wisconsin Alumni Research Foundation, to handle Steenbock's lucrative patents on the process for making vitamin D.[17] An independent, nonprofit entity, WARF's mission was to manage such patents in the public interest and return any proceeds to the university to further its research. WARF was a successful experiment. The Steenbock patents returned $20 million over their lifetime, and the resulting research funds were vital to the university during the Depression and long after.[18] Other valuable patents—notably on the anticoagulant Warfarin, patented as a rodenticide in 1948—followed, and by 1956 more than fifty universities had copied the WARF model by establishing independent research foundations of their own, though rarely were they so successful.[19] Despite WARF's nominal independence from the university, however, the University of Wisconsin nevertheless came under criticism—and eventually a Department of Justice antitrust investigation—for its unwillingness to license the Steenbock patents to the margarine industry, demonstrating that the research foundation strategy could only go so far to shield universities from the risks of commercial involvement.[20]

A second common approach was for universities to work with a completely independent organization devoted to patent management. The largest such organization was Cottrell's Research Corporation, founded on the basis of his patents on the electrostatic precipitator, a device that used an electrostatic charge to remove particulates from the air. Though it had agreed to manage specific inventions for a handful of universities in the 1920s and early 1930s, Research Corporation began negotiating formal agreements to handle universities' patents in 1937, when it developed such an understanding with MIT.[21] By 1952, the nonprofit had about 50 such arrangements, and by the late 1960s, the number had risen to over 200.[22]

Finally, a number of universities handled patenting internally by establishing a committee that was responsible for making decisions about the management of inventions. The Regents of the University of California, for example, appointed faculty and administrators to a nine-member Board of Patents, and the University of Notre Dame and Oklahoma A&M had similar policies.[23]

By 1962, almost 350 institutions reported having a formal or informal patent policy.[24] Yet the wide prevalence of patent policies is somewhat misleading, since the total number of patents being issued to universities each year was about 100, with another 25 or so going to Research Corporation on their behalf.[25] So while universities had procedures for handling patents, few used these on a regular basis. Only a small handful had what could be called active patenting efforts in the 1960s. Howard Bremer, longtime patent counsel for WARF, recalled being in regular contact with only the University of California, Iowa State University, Research Corporation, and Battelle Development Corporation, a smaller nonprofit research management organization, during this era. While informal networks existed to a certain extent, "there were just not that many people involved" in university patenting at the time.[26]

The Role of Federal Patent Policy

There were several reasons university patenting remained so limited before the 1970s. Before World War II, the small scale of university research meant that there simply weren't very many inventions to patent. But even after the war, as academic science expanded dramatically, patenting remained fairly uncommon. There was skepticism about whether patenting was appropriate in universities. The infrequency of the practice meant that it might never even occur to a faculty member to consider pursuing a patent. And most universities, which might identify only one or two inventions a year, lacked the administrative capacity to apply for and manage patents and licenses.

The single most important factor, however, in discouraging university patenting was government patent policy. During the 1930s, when debate over university patenting was most active, universities were relatively independent from the federal government.[27] What modest external research funding there was came mostly from foundations and corporations, and while these might have their own concerns about the ownership of inventions, federal patent policy had little relevance.[28] But as federal funding of academic science increased during and after World War II, government patent policy became much more significant in outlining what universities could and couldn't patent. And as such funding came to dominate university research—it made up 55% of university R&D spending in 1953, and peaked at 73% in 1966—federal patent policy effectively came to set the parameters for all university patenting.[29]

As federal spending on science and technology—in both universities and industry—rose after 1940, the question of what should be done with resulting inventions emerged as well. Most answers ranged on a continuum between two poles: a "government-title" policy on one end, and a "government-license" policy on the other. Under a government-title policy, government would keep the rights to such inventions, either patenting them itself or putting them in the public domain. If the government chose to patent an invention, it would then license it to interested parties as it saw fit. There might be a waiver process through which the inventor could request rights to the invention, in which case the government would decide whether such a waiver was in the public interest. Under a government-license policy, on the other hand, inventors would keep the rights to their inventions, while government would retain the option of a royalty-free nonexclusive license for public use. The inventor (or the inventor's employer) would decide whether or not to patent and how to handle licensing. There might be specific situations, however, in which government could step in and take over the patent to make sure the public interest was being served.[30]

During the war, most military research gave title to contractors with provisions for a government license.[31] But after the war ended, a political battle developed over what the government role in science would look like, with Vannevar Bush leading the effort to establish a scientist-controlled National Research Foundation and Senator Harley Kilgore fighting for Washington to have more direct oversight of scientific research. The differences between Bush and Kilgore extended to patent policy as well. Bush, who was politically conservative and had close ties to industry, argued that patents were an absolutely necessary incentive to encourage private-sector investment in technology. He supported a government-license policy.[32] Kilgore, on the other hand, was a "true New Dealer with a distrust of monopolies that dated from the days when his father was driven out of business by Standard Oil." He thought that giving contractors patent rights would hinder the free flow of scientific information, especially since industry had a motive to restrict, rather than spread, the dissemination of research.[33] Kilgore's initial proposal gave all patent rights to the government, though a later revision would have allowed the sponsoring agency to assign rights to the inventor under certain conditions.[34]

No quick compromise was reached between Bush's and Kilgore's proposals, on either the organization of science funding or the patent issue. If it had been, the result might have been one strong, centralized agency to oversee the administration of all federally funded science, as both Bush and Kilgore wanted, and such an agency might have had a single clear patent policy. But the political stalemate that resulted meant that the research efforts that had sprung up in many different federal agencies during the war continued to develop on an ad hoc basis and were never brought under the guidance of a single agency. This decentralized and fragmented system of support for science led in turn to a decentralized and fragmented set of policies regarding the patenting of federally funded research.[35]

Since no single law established a uniform patent policy for the various funding agencies, the agencies developed a variety of different policies, some set internally and some by statute. Each had its own concerns when it came to patenting. The Atomic Energy Commission (AEC), for example, with its roots in the Manhattan Project, was very concerned with its ability to control research results, and as a result maintained title to almost everything.[36] The Defense Department, on the other hand, felt it needed only a license, and was generally happy to leave invention rights to contractors or grantees, who were then free to pursue commercial development if they desired.[37] Other funding agencies each had approaches of their own.[38]

What this meant for universities was that if they *were* interested in patenting faculty inventions, they had to negotiate a very complicated set of government policies. Some funding agencies allowed them to patent with little hassle. Others would almost never allow such patenting. Still others would allow universities to patent inventions on a case-by-case basis, but only after a formal request that the government waive its rights to the invention, a bureaucratic and time-consuming procedure. And a great deal of research was funded by more than one federal agency, in which case several policies would have to be negotiated and the strictest would generally apply. There were occasional efforts to simplify the situation, but they went nowhere. In 1965, for example, the Senate Judiciary Committee found itself considering three comprehensive patent policy bills: one proposing a government-title policy, one a government-license policy, and one a policy that would vary from agency to agency.[39] The debate looked just like the one that had taken place twenty years earlier, and the outcome was similar as well. None of the bills became law.

Since so much university research was funded by the federal government, this situation limited the extent to which universities could patent their research even if they wanted to. In many cases, laws or regulations simply prohibited it, but even when it might have been permitted bureaucratic complexity discouraged the practice. Few schools had someone on staff with the expertise to negotiate this minefield, and patenting remained only an occasional practice at universities throughout the 1960s.

An Uptick in University Patenting

But at the end of the 1960s, the number of patents issued to universities began to rise. While fewer than 100 patents were issued to universities most years in the 1950s and 60s, by 1972 the number broke 200 and by 1975 it reached 300. In 1980, the year Bayh-Dole was passed, universities received almost 400 patents.[40] Because patenting has increased so much since the Bayh-Dole Act, it is easy to overlook this earlier rise, but from the perspective of 1980 it was a meaningful increase—roughly fourfold in fifteen years.

Two main factors contributed to this jump. One was simply that universities were doing more inventing as research funding increased. Even if the rate of patenting had remained constant, the growth of the academic research enterprise would have led to a significant increase in the number of patents issued. But the number of university patents per research dollar spent also rose substantially, so the rise in research spending alone does not explain the increase.[41]

Another important reason patenting became more prevalent was that several groups of people began actively encouraging the practice. The Research Corporation started promoting more university involvement in patenting during the 1960s. A small group of government employees began working to simplify the process of patenting federally funded research a few years later. And in the mid-1970s, a professional network of university patent administrators began to emerge and disseminate information about and support for university patenting efforts.

The Research Corporation effort was prompted by a contentious dispute between itself and MIT. MIT alleged that Research Corporation was not acting in its best interests and in 1963 cancelled its invention administration agreement. This move caused a significant rethinking of strategy at Research Corporation, and one result was an effort to improve communications with universities and inventors. The organization made hundreds of outreach visits to schools in the mid-1960s, and in the 1970s initiated a "Patent Awareness Program" that attempted to teach universities to do more early evaluation of their own inventions.

The outreach efforts had no positive effect on Research Corporation's deteriorating financial condition. But they did help train universities to handle inventions, a development that eventually contributed to Research Corporation's demise as a patent management organization. By 1975, a growing number of Research Corporation's university clients were "cherry-picking" inventions, managing the most promising themselves rather than sending them to Research Corporation.[42]

The government effort to encourage university patenting began at the Department of Health, Education, and Welfare (HEW), which housed NIH. In 1963, HEW—already the largest federal funder of university research and still growing rapidly—hired a patent attorney to sort out its incoherent patent policy.[43] HEW was one of the agencies that had a good deal of discretion over how it handled inventions, since its policy was not governed by statute. In the 1950s and early 1960s, the agency's official position was that it would waive title to an invention upon the request of a grantee, provided that the grantee could show it had the capacity to pursue development of the invention. But in the late 1950s, the agency became increasingly reluctant to waive its rights. By 1964, NIH director James Shannon was writing internally that "in practice, [patent rights have not been waived] in approximately five years and proposals which have been advanced for department approval have invariably resulted in decisions to keep title in all reported inventions with the Federal Government."[44]

The patent attorney hired by HEW, Norman Latker, was a strong proponent of inventor's rights. Latker was inherently skeptical of government's ability to manage inventions it knew little about and believed that the closer an invention could be kept to its inventor, the more likely it was that it would someday be used. After arriving and surveying the situation, he made clear that he believed the department's patent policy was too heavy-handed, and that it should generally waive title to universities upon request.[45] Before long, Latker found himself in open conflict with other offices at HEW.[46]

In 1968, public embarrassment turned the tide in Latker's favor within the agency. Two major studies of federal patent policy were published, and both singled out NIH's medicinal chemistry program for negative attention. The medicinal chemistry program supported research that resulted in new compounds with therapeutic potential. But because HEW would not permit exclusive licenses, no pharmaceutical companies were willing to invest in developing the compounds. The costs of bringing a drug to market were so great that without the protection of an exclusive license, they had no incentive to become involved. As a result, the promising compounds were gathering dust.[47]

Both of these reports recommended that HEW modify its patent policy along the lines Latker had been suggesting. The attention they received in Washington defused some of the opposition within HEW, which not only led to more frequent approval of individual waiver requests, but also allowed Latker to revive a more significant innovation, the institutional patent agreement (IPA). IPAs were contracts between HEW and a research institution under which HEW would waive title to all HEW-funded inventions that met certain conditions. They allowed a university to avoid the time-consuming process of applying for individual invention waivers, instead permitting them to apply only once, for an IPA.[48] In December 1968, the first dozen universities formed IPAs with HEW, and by 1971, thirty-seven universities held IPAs.[49] Between 1968 and 1974, universities with IPAs filed 167 patent applications on HEW-sponsored inventions, and HEW granted 162 petitions for waivers of title to universities without IPAs—compared to almost none in the pre-1968 years.[50]

The battle to reform HEW's patent policy strengthened Latker's commitment to keeping government out of the patent management business. After his changes were implemented at HEW, he turned his attention to other federal agencies. The Federal Council for Science and Technology, an office of the executive branch, had a committee on government patent policy made up of representatives of each of the R&D-funding agencies. Here Latker hoped to find counterparts who might be interested in adopting IPAs.

To his disappointment, he learned that most of his peers favored a government-title policy and had little interest in IPAs. One exception, however, was Jesse Lasken, who helped manage patents at NSF. Lasken also believed that universities would be better at handling inventions than government, and the two quickly formed a partnership. In 1973, NSF began signing IPAs of its own, modeled closely on HEW's.[51] This was a significant step. NSF was the second-largest funder of university research. With both HEW and NSF on board, 68% of federal research dollars could potentially be governed by IPAs.[52] Adding in the Defense Department, which had long had a similar mechanism, universities with the capacity to manage patents had the option of pursuing them on inventions resulting from almost 80% of federal funds.[53]

While the outside efforts of Research Corporation and of federal administrators were significant in encouraging university patenting starting in the late 1960s, by the early 1970s another group was starting to promote the practice from within universities. In part, this was an outcome of what Research Corporation was doing—training universities in patent management. IPAs, too, had moved universities in this direction. By requiring that a specific person at a university be responsible for managing inventions, they helped to create a new constituency of administrators who were actually in charge of patenting and licensing university research.[54] But the emerging community of technology transfer professionals would also make its own independent contribution toward the expansion of universities' patenting activities.

A small-scale network among university patent administrators did exist in the 1960s. WARF's Howard Bremer recalled that "about every eighteen months to two years we'd get together and just, in some hotel . . . discuss happenings and see what developments there were."[55] But this was a tiny group representing about half-a-dozen universities and patent management organizations. While "there were phone conversations and mentoring kind of help . . . it was rather limited at that time" because of the small numbers.[56]

But by 1973, the growing interest in university patenting was leading to more formal organization. Betsy Ancker-Johnson, a physicist who was herself an inventor and patent holder, was appointed Assistant Secretary of Commerce for Science and Technology. *Ex officio*, she headed the Federal Council for Science and Technology committee on which Latker had sought allies. She came to the job with strong pro-patent views, and thought opposition to the liberalization of patent policy arose mostly out of ignorance of how patents really worked.[57] Ancker-Johnson quickly allied with Latker and Lasken and lent political clout to their campaign to strengthen university patenting. She also, according to two attendees, was the motivating force behind the first-ever conference on university technology transfer:

> At the 1973 annual meeting of the National Council of University Research Administrators, part of one afternoon was devoted to patents. . . . The truly

> significant part of this meeting was the principal luncheon speaker, Betsy A. Johnson, Ph.D. . . . The theme of her speech was astounding. She said that the government's treatment of the universities' inventions was disgraceful, and why did we not get together and do something about it. That was invitation enough.[58]

The result was an October 1974 meeting at Case Western Reserve University that drew 118 attendees representing over fifty universities.[59]

Participants in the three-day meeting found they had lots to talk about. They shared information about how to organize a technology transfer office, how to improve communication with faculty, how to market university inventions, and how to negotiate government bureaucracy.[60] The conference led directly to the creation of SUPA, the Society of University Patent Administrators, which had its charter meeting in Chicago the following year.[61] As the decade progressed, SUPA became increasingly established, with regular, well-attended meetings.[62]

The creation of a professional association helped stabilize the informal social networks that had already been developing across universities. It facilitated the exchange of know-how from school to school, and helped to create a constituency that would support the expansion of university patenting. Thus by the mid-1970s, the practice of patenting, though still modest in scale, was steadily expanding in universities, supported not only by the growing research base but by the efforts of multiple groups to encourage it.

Barriers to the Expansion of University Patenting

Yet as the 1970s progressed, it was becoming increasingly clear that this grassroots interest in university patenting could expand only so far without legislative change. In the first part of the decade, Latker, Lasken, Ancker-Johnson, and a handful of others continued their efforts in Washington to expand universities' capacity to patent federally funded research. Latker had hoped more agencies might start using institutional patent agreements, but after NSF adopted them in 1973, their spread stalled. Agencies had philosophical differences regarding patent management, and there were practical considerations as well. Some, like NASA, were governed by statutes that allowed them little leeway in the disposition of invention rights.[63] Others, defending their turf, were reluctant to give up control of something, regardless of what it was.[64] And the fact that some agencies' money went primarily to industry contractors, not to universities, gave them a different set of considerations. By 1974, it was clear IPAs would go no further. As one observer noted, "Those of us who are in university patent administration would find our lives quite a bit easier if we could operate under institutional patent agreements across the board. Of course that is really pie in the sky because there are some agencies that are so far from an institutional patent agreement, that I am sure that we, our children, nor our grandchildren will ever see one."[65]

As IPAs reached their limit as a way to facilitate university patenting, patent policy reformers turned their efforts in other directions. For example, the Atomic Energy Commission was being replaced by ERDA, the Energy Research and Development Administration.[66] The AEC had taken title to almost all the inventions it funded, and David Eden, special assistant to Ancker-Johnson, worked—successfully—to make sure that ERDA did not end up with a similar policy.[67] Another project, led by Latker and Lasken, involved rewriting relevant regulations to clearly permit IPAs at agencies for which they were not forbidden by statute.[68] Though it took several years, their proposed changes were made official in 1978.[69]

But it was quickly becoming obvious that university patenting would not be on stable ground without legislative intervention. For one thing, many agencies' policies *were* governed by statute. For another, IPAs were already being challenged in court. Ralph Nader's organization, Public Citizen, sued the federal government in the early 1970s on the grounds that IPAs were "an unconstitutional disposition of property."[70] Though Nader's suit was dismissed due to lack of standing, Latker recognized that Nader had a legitimate legal argument. Proponents of change, Latker later recalled, "knew that we were on relatively weak ground. We tried to make the best arguments we could . . . [but] we knew that there was a weakness, and the only way you could cure it was by legislation."[71]

On top of this, a setback at HEW made it clear how rapidly existing patent practices could be reversed. With Norman Latker in charge of patenting, waivers of government patent rights had become routine at the agency. But with the arrival of the Carter administration in 1977 came a new secretary, Joseph Califano. Califano strongly disapproved of giving universities patent rights, and in August of that year he ordered Latker to start sending all patent waiver requests to the general counsel's office for approval.[72]

The general counsel's office, however, did not actually approve any waivers. Instead, Califano announced that the patent policy was under review, and the requests sat there, neither approved nor denied. The months dragged on, and by September 1978 more than thirty inventions were stuck in bureaucratic limbo.[73] The shift shocked and angered university patent administrators, who had grown used to quick approval of their requests for title, but who now realized how fragile the practice actually was.

Latker had been working on government patent policy legislation as early as 1972, when he contributed to a draft bill published by the Commission on Government Procurement.[74] But in 1976, the Federal Council for Science and Technology proposed a more serious effort at legislative change. This draft bill was sweeping in scope, giving patent rights to all federal contractors and grantees, not just the universities, nonprofits, and small businesses that would eventually be covered by Bayh-Dole.[75] Ray Thornton, chair of the House Subcommittee on Science, Research, and Technology, twice introduced the bill into committee, but it quickly died there since the committee did not have jurisdiction over patents.[76]

Worse for the bill's supporters, this drew the negative attention of Senator Gaylord Nelson, who argued that giving private contractors invention rights would be like government "playing Santa Claus."[77] In December 1977, Nelson brought together some of the longest-standing opponents of a government-license policy to testify at Congressional hearings.[78] The same stalemate that began in 1945 was being played out again between those who believed that inventions would not be developed unless their inventors could patent them and those who believed that allowing inventors to patent government-funded inventions was a misappropriation of taxpayer dollars. In the beginning of 1978, the practice of university patenting was under attack, and it was not looking likely that legislation would be passed to shore it up.

Innovation, the Economy, and Government Patent Policy

At this critical juncture, supporters of a liberalized government patent policy realized that they seriously needed to rethink their tactics. As a result, they made two major changes in strategy. First, they decided to reduce the scope of their proposed legislation so that it would not cover all government contractors and grantees, but only universities, other nonprofits, and small businesses. Second, they reframed the bill as being a piece of the solution to what were increasingly perceived as problems with U.S. economic competitiveness.

The decision to cut large corporations out of the bill defused a lot of potential criticism without raising much new opposition. A big problem with the Thornton bill was that it was perceived as being a "government giveaway." In particular, critics were upset that government would be paying big companies to do R&D for it, and then allowing those companies to patent and profit from the results of that research. Supporters of the bill saw this strategic decision as critical to the bill's success. As Jesse Lasken later said, "I think what happened that turned the tide was that we avoided dealing with big business."[79] Unsurprisingly, big business was not happy about being cut from the proposed legislation. But although business interests actively supported an alternate proposal, they did agree not to oppose the scaled-back bill, perhaps because Latker and his allies explicitly stated that they hoped eventually to extend the bill to include all federal contractors.[80]

Cutting out big business not only reduced opposition, but also directly brought in the support of small business. The small business lobby saw patents as a form of monopoly with which deep-pocketed big businesses could keep small businesses from competing, and thus thought that allowing large corporations to patent government-funded inventions would hurt small business. The Senate Select Committee on Small Business, in fact, had historically been a strong source of opposition to a government-license patent policy.[81] Limiting the scope of the bill turned allies of small business from likely opponents to active supporters.

The decision to reduce the scope of the bill was important, and it is doubtful that legislation could have passed had this choice not been made. Yet the second part of the strategy, reframing the bill around economic issues, was also critical. In the past, the primary argument proponents of a government-license patent policy made was that such a policy would improve the utilization of publicly funded research. Businesses would not be willing to invest in developing government-funded inventions without the reassurance of patent protection, they said, and without such investment, these inventions would never get into use. While this was a fine argument as far as it went, it was not especially emotionally compelling.

But after 1977, supporters of patent reform began to emphasize a different argument with broader political resonance. In light of intense public concern with the economy and the growing consensus that innovation problems were contributing to U.S. economic weakness, the proposed patent legislation was presented as a way to accelerate the process through which inventions reached the market. This was a timely and powerful argument, but not one that had previously been emphasized. As Norman Latker later said, "That was an issue that came up after the fact that we could use to support the bill."[82]

The shift away from arguments about getting inventions into use and toward arguments about economic competitiveness is reflected in a series of Congressional hearings on patent policy that were held in the late 1970s. The first set, in September 1976, was led by Representative Thornton and dominated by those who wanted to give patent rights to federal contractors and grantees. Here, though, there was little emphasis on the economic effects of such a change. Thornton opened the hearings by emphasizing the "significant impact [of patent policy] on the development of inventions and the technological advances of our Nation," but did not tie that to any particular effects on the economy.[83] The nine individuals testifying described how patents would help get government-sponsored inventions into use more effectively, but they did not emphasize the economic impact of their proposal either. Only one, Ancker-Johnson, mentioned economic effects more than in passing, and even in her statement such effects are clearly secondary to the primary goal of improving the utilization of government-funded research.[84]

Twenty months later, in May 1978, an overlapping group testified on institutional patent agreements before a hostile Senator Nelson. These hearings covered a narrower range of questions and focused primarily on universities. The testimony presented still did not make the economy a central issue. However, some of those testifying—particularly those representing the Carter administration—were beginning to make explicit the connection between patent policy and economic development. Assistant Secretary of Commerce for Science and Technology Jordan Baruch, for example, began by noting that "innovation, the development and use of new inventions, is a primary means for achieving noninflationary economic growth, job creation, and a stronger international position for America and for American industry," a position that accorded with his role as leader of Carter's Domestic Policy Review of Industrial Innovation.[85]

In 1978, supporters of patent policy liberalization managed to secure the support of senators Robert Dole and Birch Bayh, a development inadvertently facilitated by Califano's shutdown of the waiver process at HEW. University patent administrators, frustrated with the change in policy, began contacting their members of Congress, and one such meeting brought Senator Bayh on board.[86] Similarly, an aide to Senator Dole who had a background as a scientist and inventor became aware of what was happening at HEW and brought the issue to Dole's attention.[87] In September, the two senators announced that they were introducing legislation that would establish a broad government-license patent policy covering universities, nonprofits, and small businesses.[88]

By the time hearings on this new bill were held in May 1979, the focus of debate had shifted substantially. Instead of simply emphasizing the importance of getting inventions into use, the issue was framed explicitly and repeatedly in terms of the need to reform patent policy in order to regain the U.S. economy's technological edge. From Bayh's opening, in which he expressed his concern about the United States "rapidly losing its preeminent position in the development and production of new technologies," supporters claimed that patent policy should be changed for the sake of the economy:

> The United States has built its prosperity on innovation. That tradition of unsurpassed innovation remains our heritage, but without continued effort it is not necessarily our destiny. There is no engraving in stone from on high that we shall remain No. 1 in international economic competition. In a number of industries we are no longer even No. 2. New incentives and policies are needed to reverse this trend. The [Bayh-Dole Act] will be a step in the direction of encouraging innovation and productivity in the United States.[89]

This bill, unlike the Thornton bill, did not immediately arouse strong opposition. Commentators attributed the shift to the bill's exclusion of big business and to "heightened national concern over the waning of innovation."[90] The legislative process took several more turns before the Bayh-Dole Act was signed into law in December 1980. But from this point on, those on both sides of the debate accepted the new economic framing. Proponents argued that an improved patent policy would help U.S. competitiveness. Among opponents, the claim that the policy was a government giveaway was made less often, replaced by a meeker challenge that it was not the most effective means of speeding technological innovations to the marketplace.[91]

Increasing the Value and Scope of Intellectual Property

The Bayh-Dole Act had a direct effect on universities' decisions about how actively to pursue patenting because it gave them the clear right to patent government-funded inventions and legitimized what had remained, right through the 1970s, a somewhat dubious activity. But after 1980, not only were universities officially permitted to patent and license such inventions, but the incentives to do so gradually increased as intellectual property rights became stronger and the scope of what could be patented was enlarged.[92] This shift, which was facilitated by several policy decisions, was not aimed specifically at universities, but nevertheless changed the environment in which universities as well as for-profit firms made decisions about how to handle inventions.

One of these was the 1980 *Diamond v. Chakrabarty* Supreme Court decision introduced in the previous chapter. *Chakrabarty* made microorganisms patentable, and eventually the protection it afforded was extended to more complex forms of life as well.[93] Universities, with their cutting-edge research in genetic engineering, were particularly well-poised to take advantage of this expansion of property rights, and it was Harvard University that received the first-ever patent on an animal in 1988.[94] As chapter 4 described, innovation arguments were used in the *Chakrabarty* case, with friends of the court like Genentech and the University of California arguing that "adoption of a *per se* [that is, across-the-board] rule excluding all living things from patentability will inhibit commercial development."[95] This general line of argument could be found in other patent policy debates as well. As Bruce Abramson has recently noted, "Between 1980 and 1984, four major legislative changes and two lines of Supreme Court rulings altered the contours of the American patent system almost beyond recognition. Inquiries into the best ways to enhance American competitiveness motivated all six changes."[96]

Particularly important among these was Congress's creation in 1982 of a new appellate court, the Court of Appeals for the Federal Circuit (CAFC), a primary purpose of which was to hear patent appeals. Before CAFC, someone who wanted to challenge a district court's decision on a patent case would appeal to one of the general appellate courts of the regional circuits. The circuit courts, however, differed dramatically in their treatment of patents, with some tending to favor patent holders and others being much less likely to do so.[97] Since the Supreme Court was relatively uninterested in hearing patent cases, this variation remained unresolved and led to the practice of "forum shopping," in which litigators and defendants both tried to get their case heard in a circuit they thought likely to favor themselves.[98] Congress ended this situation by sending all patent appeals to CAFC.

The creation of CAFC is widely seen as having strengthened patent protection. Scholars have argued that it is more likely than prior courts "to affirm [district court] judgments in favor of patent owners," that it is less likely to uphold decisions of patent invalidity, and that by increasing the enforceability of patents it spawned a complementary increase in patent litigation.[99] Evidence on whether the creation of CAFC is partially responsible for the surge in patenting that began in the 1980s is less unified, but leans in that direction as well.[100] While there is considerable debate over the exact nature and extent of CAFC's effects, there is a broad consensus that such effects exist.

As was the case for the effort to pass Bayh-Dole, the emerging focus on innovation policy seemed to mark a turning point in the push to create CAFC. Congress had begun to consider the forum-shopping issue as early as 1972, when Senator Roman Hruska was appointed head of a commission to study reform of the appellate court system.[101] But while the Hruska Commission recommended the creation of a national court of appeals, its proposal gained little traction upon its publication in 1975.[102] In 1978, though, just as "the entire subject seemed in danger of fading from the agenda," the Attorney General's Office for Improvements in the Administration of Justice (OIAJ) began to promote a national patent court.[103] The OIAJ secured the support of Senator Ted Kennedy, who chaired the Senate Judiciary Committee, but had a great deal of trouble gaining the interest of the House Judiciary Committee, which was chaired by Representative Robert Kastenmeier.[104]

As Daniel Meador, assistant attorney general at the time and a key proponent of the proposal later noted, "Representative Kastenmeier's subcommittee seemed more interested in industrial innovations than it did in the idea of the Federal Circuit."[105] He also recalled that

> the [Court of Appeals for the] Federal Circuit was carried forward in the House, at least initially, by its confluence with what was referred to as 'industrial innovations proposals.' . . . It had always been one of our arguments in support of the centralized patent jurisdiction that predictability as to the validity of patents was important in promoting investment in research and production. Thus, the Federal Circuit and proposals for industrial innovations made a natural match.[106]

Others like attorney Donald Dunner began with an interest in innovation policy, not court reform, but found the CAFC idea appealing:

> Not long after the Hruska Commission completed its task and the proposed national court of appeals disappeared from the scene, there developed a great concern over the state of the innovation in the United States. To deal with that concern, in 1978 President Carter convened a Domestic Policy Review on Industrial Innovation, on whose Patent Advisory Committee I served. By that time Messrs. Meador and Rosenberg had given birth to their Federal

Circuit idea, an idea the Patent Advisory Committee and the Carter Domestic Policy Review warmly embraced.[107]

Pauline Newman, an attorney who served on the same patent advisory committee, helped to rally industry—which previously had taken no collective position on the circuit court debate—behind the proposal. "The industries," she later noted, "that were now working to create this court represented three-quarters of the nation's industrial product," and she represented them before the Kastenmeier committee.[108] Supporters of CAFC drew heavily on the innovation frame in the hearings preceding the bill, and Kastenmeier's language emphasized how important the industrial innovation angle was for him.[109] He recapped the testimony by complimenting Newman for

> restat[ing] the case, which I think largely had been lost upon the subcommittee which has been looking at the technical aspects of the case . . . for the creation of this court; she reminded us that it is not merely for the patent lawyers themselves but for the industrial and research organizations of this country upon whom we depend for advances in technology and for economic competitiveness with the world that this was in the first place suggested.[110]

Tying the reform to innovation helped the bill to pass the House and become law in April 1982.

The *Chakrabarty* decision, the creation of CAFC, and other policy changes strengthened and expanded the U.S. intellectual property system during the 1980s. At least partly as a result, patent applications skyrocketed, more than tripling between 1980 and 2000 after decades of very gradual increase.[111] To the best of my knowledge, no one has tried to isolate the impact of the generally strengthened patent system (outside of Bayh-Dole) on university patenting, but it would be surprising if universities had not followed other organizations to some extent in responding to these changed incentives.

University Patenting after 1980

University patenting increased considerably in the years following Bayh-Dole. Yet this increase was an acceleration of an existing trend more than a dramatic shift. While the practice of biotech entrepreneurship was very limited until about 1979 and then exploded over the course of a few years, patenting had already been rising at a steady clip (if from a low base) during the 1970s, and after Bayh-Dole patenting accelerated moderately rather than taking off precipitously. While the number of patents issued to universities had increased by an average of 7.3% a year between 1969 and 1980, that figure rose to 12.7% for the 1981 to 1999 period.[112] (After 1999, the number of university patents being granted leveled off.)

While Bayh-Dole certainly provided an impetus for universities to pursue technology transfer, the long timeline from identifying an invention to applying for a patent on it and then actually receiving that patent meant that the number of patents issued to universities did not immediately shoot up after its passage. Universities were awarded 390 patents in 1980, and that number had only risen to 434 by 1983.[113] The legislation's impact was also not uniform across institutions. David Mowery and his collaborators see Bayh-Dole as having more modest effects at universities that were already pursuing patenting than at those without technology transfer programs. Case studies of Stanford, the University of California, and Columbia lead them to argue that at the first two institutions, which were already active patenters by 1980, "Bayh-Dole was an important, but not a determinative, factor in the growth and changing composition of patenting and licensing activity."[114] At Columbia, however, which had done some patenting but had no formal program, they think that "it is likely that the change in federal policy embodied in Bayh-Dole led to a more dramatic change in policies, procedures, and rules than would otherwise have occurred," such as the establishment of an Office of Science and Technology Development in 1982.[115]

A 1986 survey of research universities supports Mowery et al.'s hypothesis that Bayh-Dole had differential effects. The Association of American Universities asked its members how much the legislation had affected their patenting strategy, and received a mixed response:

> Many respondents . . . credit the new Federal patent law with providing the incentive for the university to establish an aggressive patent and licensing program, including the commercialization of inventions resulting from privately supported research. However, other respondents stated that Federal patent policy had no impact upon their patent and licensing efforts. This latter view was shared both by institutions that are pursuing an active program and those that are not.[116]

Gary Matkin suggests that the "divergence highlights a more basic split in universities' views of patent operations that existed at the beginning of the decade. Institutions that had patent programs . . . saw the act as part of a general trend . . . while those that had not been aggressive saw the act as a causal factor in the development of patent administration."[117]

Nevertheless, while the universities that were already active patenters may have seen the act as not affecting their behavior, and universities that were new to patenting may have had few immediate results because of the long timeline and steep learning curve associated with the activity, more universities did launch technology transfer efforts during the early 1980s. While twenty-three tech transfer offices had been established by 1980, another twenty-six were started between 1981 and 1985.[118] Similarly, the Society of University Patent Administrators saw its membership more than double between 1982 and 1984 as new entrants sought to learn from universities with longer-established patent efforts.[119]

While Bayh-Dole provided one impetus for the increase in patenting activity, there were pull factors as well as the push of legislation. As already noted, in the early 1980s the creation of CAFC and other policy decisions began to strengthen intellectual property rights and expand the scope of the patentable, which gradually increased the incentives to patent for corporations as well as universities. The total number of patents issued in the United States increased substantially during the 1980s—by roughly 50%—so some of the increase in patents awarded to universities likely reflects the same trends affecting non-university patenters.[120]

Since university patents roughly tripled during the same period, however, changes in the larger patent regime probably explain only a modest part of the total increase. The explosion of the biotechnology industry, however, so closely connected to academia and already in progress by 1980, was another more immediate enticement for universities. The *Chakrabarty* decision in June 1980 assured observers that biotech products would indeed be patentable, and the first Cohen-Boyer patent on recombinant DNA technology was at long last granted to Stanford and the University of California in December of that year, the same month Bayh-Dole was signed into law.[121]

Cohen-Boyer would start pulling in revenues right away, with seventy-two companies licensing the patent for $20,000 each by the end of 1981, and as noted in chapter 4, would ultimately bring in more than $250 million.[122] Within a few years, other blockbuster patents would be issued to universities as well. In 1983, for example, Columbia University would be granted the first of several patents on cotransformation, a process for inserting DNA into cells in order to produce proteins, which would eventually earn $790 million.[123] While universities had occasionally had "hit" patents in the past, this was success on a new scale, and the possibility of emulating it must have been tempting to cash-strapped administrators. At the same time, the increased entrepreneurialism of bioscience faculty meant that they were becoming attuned to the commercial value of their work and the possibility of patenting in a way they hadn't been before. This combination of factors provided new incentives for pursuing patents and licenses that went well beyond Bayh-Dole.

By the second half of the decade, the effects of these changes were becoming more visible as the growth in the number of patents being issued to universities accelerated. That growth was at its fastest in the late 1980s. The number of patents granted to universities doubled between 1985 and 1990, from 589 to 1,182, and another thirty-seven technology transfer offices were established during the same period.[124] In keeping with the links between biotechnology and university patenting, a disproportionate and increasing fraction of these patents were biomedical in nature. While in 1965, less than 15% of university patents were in drug and medical classes, by 1988 such patents made up about

35% of the total.[125] And biomedical patents represented a much larger share of universities' patent portfolios than they did of the overall patent population. While four specific classes of biomedical patent made up only 5% of all patent awards, they constituted a full 32% of university patents.[126]

During this period, universities continued to grapple with questions about how to balance their commitment to scientific values with the new imperative to pursue technology transfer via patenting and licensing.[127] A 1988 survey found that 59% of research universities had changed their patent policies in the last three years, and 26% of graduate deans thought that patent issues were among the four most critical issues facing universities.[128] In addition to debating questions about openness and the integrity of science, technology transfer offices were also experimenting with novel ways of managing the licensing process. MIT, for example, began taking equity as part of its licensing agreements for some patents in 1988.[129] While universities also tried other methods of investing in startups, this relatively simple arrangement, in which equity in a startup was accepted in lieu of some or all royalties on a patent license, became the most common. By the mid-1990s, more than 500 such licenses were being issued by universities each year.[130]

While questions remained about how best to manage patenting, the practice itself had become firmly established by the end of the decade. If the passage of Bayh-Dole and the institutionalization of the technology transfer office hadn't clinched the deal, the revenues that were finally starting to be generated by patents would have. While systematic data on licensing revenues were not collected prior to the 1990s, a National Science Board report found that universities had earned $7.3 million in fiscal year (FY) 1980 and $9.2 million in FY 1981.[131] By contrast, when the Association of University Technology Managers began surveying universities in FY 1991, it found that they received $123 million in licensing revenues.[132] This figure would break the billion-dollar mark by the year 2000.[133]

Why Did University Patenting Take Off?

Despite their mutually reinforcing nature, university patenting and bioscience entrepreneurship were fairly distinct practices. The two had different origins, different barriers to their spread, different trajectories, and different reasons for eventually taking off as well. Yet they do share some commonalities. The last section of this chapter will develop two points. First, I will consider the various factors that contributed to the expansion of university patenting as a practice. Second, I will then explore the similarities and differences between those factors and the ones identified in the previous chapter as contributing to the spread of biotech entrepreneurship.

The 1980 passage of Bayh-Dole is often seen as a turning point for both university patenting and the larger shift of academic science toward the market. But while Bayh-Dole was unquestionably important in encouraging the spread of patenting, Bayh-Dole itself would not have been possible without earlier efforts to build a critical mass of interest in the practice. In particular, and in roughly chronological order, Research Corporation's work teaching university administrators about the patent process, the establishment of institutional patent agreements by a loose network of federal employees, and the increasing organization of a professional community of university patent administrators were all significant in expanding patenting activity prior to the Bayh-Dole Act. In addition, they had the secondary effect of helping to create a political base that would, when the time came, fight for the passage of patent policy reform.

But despite the fact that these activities contributed to the increase in university patenting during the 1970s, as of 1978 it was far from clear that the practice was about to accelerate in pace. In fact, there was a serious possibility that more restrictions would be placed on it, as was demonstrated when Califano's Department of Health, Education, and Welfare stopped granting waivers of patent rights for NIH-funded inventions. If HEW had continued down this path and Bayh-Dole had not stopped it, it is hard to imagine that university patent activity would have expanded nearly as much during the 1980s as it actually did.

But the passage of Bayh-Dole did, of course, reverse Califano's action and dramatically change the policy environment for university technology transfer. The rise of biotechnology and the general strengthening of intellectual property rights, both of which began around the same time, further increased the incentives for universities to pursue active patenting programs. Thus there were at least six factors that facilitated the institutionalization of university patenting that could be seen by the end of the 1980s.

It is harder to evaluate the relative importance of each factor that contributed to the increase in patenting than it was to evaluate those that led to the rise of bioscience entrepreneurship. In the latter case, one can reasonably imagine conditions under which the practice simply would not have developed in academia to any significant extent. If biotechnology had not survived as an independent industry, it seems unlikely that bioscience entrepreneurship would have gained much traction at all. So if venture capital availability was a necessary condition for the development of an independent biotech sector, then it was also necessary to the takeoff of bioscience entrepreneurship.

In the case of patenting, however, one can imagine many situations that that might have led to *some* increase in patenting, but a less rapid increase. Even if Bayh-Dole had never become law, university patenting still might have expanded moderately during the 1980s due to all the other factors mentioned earlier. Furthermore, some of the causes of the increase in patenting (like Bayh-Dole) were at least partly effects of earlier causes of the increase in patenting (like the efforts of government officials to establish IPAs and the emergence of a professional community).

Nevertheless, some of these contributors were doubtless more important than others. Three—the activities of the network of government administrators, the passage of Bayh-Dole itself, and the rise of biotech as an academic-industrial field—were particularly significant. The federal officials who developed IPAs mattered because they were instrumental not only in directly encouraging early growth in the practice, but also because they facilitated the development of the professional community, and both they and that professional community were in turn critical to getting Bayh-Dole passed.[134] Bayh-Dole itself, of course, had both practical and legitimating effects that encouraged university patenting. And biotechnology would produce many (though far from all) of the most lucrative university patents of the 1980s and 1990s.

As in the case of bioscience entrepreneurship, several of the factors that contributed to the rise of university patenting involved policy decisions. In addition to Bayh-Dole itself, the development and expansion of IPAs was a policy decision, as were the *Chakrabarty* case and the creation of CAFC, both of which helped strengthen the larger patent system. Once again, innovation arguments were widely used.

While the push to expand IPAs predated the rise of concern with innovation and was not couched in terms of innovation, when the promoters of IPAs ran into limits in trying to expand them and otherwise make it easier for universities to patent, they chose to reframe their political project in innovation language, a decision that both participants and observers credited as being critical in building support for the passage of Bayh-Dole. In the *Chakrabarty* decision, one can see innovation arguments being used, but it is difficult to know whether or how much they influenced the Supreme Court. Finally, innovation concerns were very important in getting appellate court reform and the creation of CAFC on the political agenda. Carter's Domestic Policy Review of Industrial Innovation helped bring together supporters of such a court and to raise industry interest in the issue, and growing concern with innovation in Congress was important for attracting the interest of Kastenmeier's House Judiciary Committee. So the issue of technological innovation was arguably critical to the passage of Bayh-Dole and to the creation of CAFC, and was visible, but of unknown importance, in the *Chakrabarty* decision. Finally, if the development of biotech itself contributed to the growth of university patenting, and biotech was also shaped by innovation arguments, that is another indirect path through which innovation arguments encouraged the practice of patenting.

Bioscience Entrepreneurship versus University Patenting

Recall that in the case of bioscience entrepreneurship, the elements that contributed to growth of the practice included (1) particular scientific breakthroughs, (2) the academic location of relevant expertise, (3) the decision not to restrict rDNA research, (4) the organizational model of Genentech, (5) changes in the venture capital environment, and (6) the *Chakrabarty* decision. If one compares those to the factors that were important to the growth of university patenting—(1) the invention management training of Research Corporation, (2) the efforts of federal administrators to make university patenting easier, (3) the emergence of a professional community, (4) the passage of Bayh-Dole, (5) the rise of biotech, and (6) the strengthening of the patent regime—it is notable that there is not much overlap between the two lists. Biotech entrepreneurship and university patenting fed into one another, to be sure, but they emerged as relatively independent phenomena, and while each contributed to the other's growth, it is possible to imagine scenarios in which one of them became common but not the other. The diversity of the reasons that each was able to grow is also noteworthy. Changes in science, changes in law, collective action, and shifts in resource availability, among other factors, all played a part.

Some potential causes of expansion are also absent from both lists. Industry played little role in encouraging either practice, and what role it did play was indirect. The pharmaceutical industry, for example, was not pushing to have more access to academia. Venture capitalists did seek academics to found biotech companies early on, but this kind of industry impetus differs from the image one might have of large R&D-intensive firms outsourcing their research efforts to universities. And while industry groups did lobby for policies like the capital gains tax cut and the creation of CAFC, these were not policies that were aimed at or expected to affect universities. So while industry is not missing entirely from this picture, its role in encouraging the development of market logic in academic science is clearly secondary.

A second missing factor is universities systematically trying to use their science to make money. Certainly, shifts in financial incentives were crucial in encouraging the development of each practice. But in neither case did the practice emerge because university leaders were looking for opportunities to solve budget problems by making more money off of science. Instead, people within the university—scientists and mid-level administrators—were trying to solve local problems and to take advantage of new opportunities, and only once the practices had begun to take off internally did upper-level administrators start to actively promote them and try to generate revenue from them.

What, then, did the two cases share? In both cases, government played a critical—though certainly not the only—role in creating the environment that encouraged the expansion and eventual institutionalization of each practice. Some interventions were more important than others, but policy decisions seem to have been a necessary condition for the rapid growth of both biotech entrepreneurship and university patenting. But while the significant policy decisions—chronologically, the creation of IPAs, the decision not to regulate rDNA research by statute, the capital gains tax cut, the relaxation of the prudent man rule, the *Chakrabarty* decision, the passage of Bayh-Dole, and the creation of the Federal Circuit—cover a wide territory (and several were not even aimed at academic science), with one exception innovation arguments were visible in the making of those decisions, and in three of them innovation arguments appear to have been decisive. The exception was the effort to create IPAs, and that, too, was eventually tied to innovation concerns as it morphed into the campaign for the passage of Bayh-Dole. While innovation arguments were sometimes more important than others, the consistency with which they were deployed is noteworthy.

Thus despite their diversity, collectively these decisions changed the *environment* in which academic science existed, and in which decisions about its future were made. It was not inevitable that they would lead to the growth of market-oriented practices in academic science. Clearly a number of other factors, some of them essential, also needed to be present. Nor is it clear that none of these decisions would have been taken in the absence of the innovation policy frame. But the preponderance of policies shaped by this frame which then went on to facilitate the growth of market-oriented activities suggests that the innovation leitmotif made a critical contribution to the strengthening of market logic in the university.

The next chapter will consider the emergence of a third and final market-logic practice in academic science: the university-industry research center (UIRC). This case is less closely linked to the first two than they are to each other. University-industry research centers are more common in fields like materials science, chemical engineering, and electronics than they are in the biotech-related fields, and patents play a much less critical part in them. They are also grounded in a different set of ideas about *how* science plays its economic role, one that expects government to take a more active part in encouraging university-industry collaboration, rather than focusing on strengthening of property rights or reducing barriers to investment. Yet here, too, policy decisions turned out to play a critical role—this time at the state level as significantly as the federal—and once again, arguments about the economic impact of innovation were key.

CHAPTER 6

Creating University-Industry Research Centers

In universities all over the United States, faculty and graduate students work in research centers where they interact regularly with industry sponsors. They may actively collaborate with industry scientists who have come to the university for a year to work in an academic environment, sharing equipment and publishing together. Or their relationship may be more arm's length, perhaps involving periodic conversations with distant industry counterparts about ongoing research agendas. Many of the centers in which they conduct their research hold annual meetings for their industry associates. Here, the academics put on a bit of a dog-and-pony show, demonstrating their latest breakthroughs and giving sponsors a chance to meet students who are about to receive their PhDs and start looking for jobs. At such meetings, sponsors not only learn what is going on at the forefront of the field, but may also enjoy the chance to talk science with their competitors, with whom interaction is generally restricted, on the neutral grounds of the university campus. If all goes well, such research centers can achieve the twin goals of advancing fundamental science and creating knowledge that is of direct practical use to industry, while at the same time developing the ongoing revenue stream that makes both objectives possible.

Variations on this scenario are going on in hundreds of places. Yet thirty-five years ago, such formal research collaborations between universities and industry were very uncommon. While some faculty consulted for industry and were paid to bring their expertise to a company's problems, and others conducted contract research, carrying out specific projects that were of interest to a sponsor, the kind of organized, ongoing partnership just described was infrequent. The university-industry research center (UIRC), defined here as an organized research unit working on problems of interest to both universities and industry and at least partly supported by industry contributions, has antecedents throughout the twentieth century. But in their current form, these centers began to spread rapidly only around the year 1980. This chapter attempts to explain how and why the growth of UIRCs occurred.

UIRCs versus Biotech Entrepreneurship and University Patenting

But before telling that story, I want to briefly put UIRCs into perspective by comparing them with the practices of bioscience entrepreneurship and university patenting examined in the last two chapters. In some ways, the UIRC is an odd person out among the three, and it is important to make the logic behind their inclusion as a case explicit. While any choice of cases involves tradeoffs, on balance, I would argue, UIRCs' dissimilarities from the other two practices strengthen the overall argument I present here rather than detracting from it.

First, the differences. UIRCs are a less well-defined phenomenon than biotech entrepreneurship or patenting. It is hard to draw a clear line saying that one set of activities counts as a center and another does not. There is great variation among UIRCs, which range from centers that exist in little more than name to institutes with hundred-million-dollar budgets, all of which can be organized in many different ways. UIRCs also represent a different set of disciplines than the other two practices. The biological sciences are obviously central to biotech entrepreneurship, and while patenting takes place in a variety of scientific fields, the biosciences are disproportionately important to the practice. UIRCs, by contrast, are much less frequently focused on the biosciences. The fields that historically have been most strongly represented in UIRCs include electronics, materials science, and computer-assisted-design and manufacturing—fields that were already engineering-focused and had traditions of industry collaboration.

UIRCs are a less entrepreneurial activity than biotech entrepreneurship and patenting. While both of the latter practices require that someone take the initiative to identify a new idea and figure out how to leverage it in the marketplace, whether by starting a company or by applying for a patent and seeking licensees, UIRCs have more continuity with traditional ways of organizing university research. In some ways, running a UIRC is not so different from running a government-funded research center—one must acquire sponsors and conduct research that those sponsors find valuable enough to continue funding, but one does not necessarily have to produce a product that is more broadly marketable, as a startup company would. In this way, the UIRC is less of a qualitative shift from the kinds of activities academic scientists have historically pursued than are biotech entrepreneurship and patenting.

Finally, one might argue that UIRCs have really been a failed, or at best partially successful, experiment with market logic. Unlike biotech entrepreneurship and patenting, many UIRCs owe their ongoing existence to government funding aimed at encouraging university-industry collaboration. Without such funding, they would not be able to secure enough resources from industry sponsors to sustain themselves. Market logic involves selling the products of science in the marketplace, but UIRCs have often been able to do that only when their product, research, has been subsidized by government.

While some of these differences detract from the desirability of UIRCs as a case, others are actually a strength. The ill-defined nature of the UIRC certainly makes it harder to study: What is in? What is out? Are UIRCs even a coherent phenomenon? While it would be convenient for my purposes if UIRCs demonstrated more isomorphism, their ongoing nature and focus on specific shared research problems nevertheless distinguishes them in important ways from both consulting and contract research as well as industrial affiliates programs. Since I am looking at the origins and development of UIRCs rather than trying to survey them as a body, I view the UIRC as an ideal type that in practice shows considerable variation, rather than as a well-defined organizational form.

UIRCs' disciplinary differences from biotech entrepreneurship and patenting, however, are a plus, not a minus. While the biological sciences are interesting because a market orientation was once rare in them and then rapidly became common, the engineering-related fields many UIRCs focus on have a much longer tradition of industry relations. Yet they, too, have shifted in terms of their orientation toward the market, and a study of changes in academic science as a whole should not ignore that. Similarly, UIRCs' lesser degree of entrepreneurialism does not pose problems given my focus on explaining a shift in institutional logics, not on entrepreneurialism per se. The core contrast I make is between market logic, which measures the success of science in terms of the economic value it produces, and science logic, which sees science's value primarily in the knowledge it creates. UIRCs clearly lean toward the former. One can be oriented toward market logic without being particularly entrepreneurial.

Finally, there is the question of whether UIRCs are actually an example of a successful market-logic practice, given their continued reliance on government subsidy. Here, I would argue that it is exactly this reliance on government subsidy that shows how government action, shaped by innovation arguments, encourages market logic in multiple ways. For market-logic practices to spread widely, they must be able to garner enough resources to sustain themselves. That is, they must be able to sell enough of their product, however that is defined, to reproduce themselves successfully. The case of university patenting highlights two ways government action can facilitate this: by changing the rules so that it is easier to sell the products of science (as Bayh-Dole did), or by making those products more valuable (as strengthening intellectual property rights did).

But there is also a third way that government can help science sell its products: by subsidizing them directly, so that they cost less for the private sector to buy. This is what happened in the case of UIRCs. It is a different kind of intervention, but in all three cases government action is encouraging a market orientation by making it easier and more remunerative for universities to sell the science they produce. Just as we would not say the agriculture industry and the oil industry are not primarily oriented toward the market simply because they are federally subsidized (though we might acknowledge how the subsidy affects their behavior), UIRCs are not a "failed" market-logic practice so long as they remain widespread and focused on the economic value of science.

The Trajectory of University-Industry Research Centers

With all of that in mind, I now turn to review the emergence and spread of the university-industry research center. The antecedents to UIRCs date back as far as the early twentieth century, when a handful of land-grant institutions formed engineering extension offices, and continue through the industrial affiliates programs that began popping up in the postwar decades. It was the conjoining of these kinds of traditional university-industry relationships with the organized research unit, which began to flourish in the 1950s and 1960s as a way of coordinating scholarship on a particular topic that did not fit the boundaries of a conventional academic discipline, that set the stage for the UIRC's further development.

During the 1970s, a handful of attempts were made to create workable, ongoing university-industry research partnerships that took the form of centers. Several of these were initiated independently at a list of engineering-oriented schools that included Carnegie Mellon, Caltech, Rensselaer Polytechnic Institute (RPI), and the University of Delaware. Three centers were also established under the auspices of a small NSF program meant to experiment with ways of creating incentives for technological innovation. While some of these efforts were moderately successful, collectively they struggled with problems similar to those encountered by earlier forms of university-industry collaboration like industrial affiliates programs. In particular, it was hard for academic and industry scientists, with their different goals, reward systems, and cultures, to make common cause, and it was challenging for the centers to provide enough value to industry partners to justify ongoing support at levels of long-term sustainability.

As these challenges were occurring, however, government interest in encouraging technological innovation for economic reasons was also increasing. The Nixon-era focus on innovation that had led to the original small NSF program had waned by the mid-1970s. But in 1978, NSF responded to the renewed wave of concern with innovation by making the most successful of its three experiments the model for a new university-industry research center program. By 1983, the agency was supporting a range of UIRCs on both smaller and larger scales.

At the same time, interest in the economic impact of technological innovation was not limited to the federal level. Beginning around 1980, state governments, too, started to focus on encouraging innovation as an economic development strategy. Frequently, they did this by creating university-industry research centers. California, North Carolina, Pennsylvania, and Arizona were among the early initiators of such programs, and by the middle of the decade, forty-four states were supporting university-based centers.[1]

Such programs helped to provide models of successful university-industry collaboration, but even more importantly, this large influx of government funding at both the state and federal levels changed the resource environment in which UIRCs were created and developed. During the 1980s, the number of UIRCs grew rapidly. While centers were relatively uncommon in the 1970s, by 1990 one survey estimated a national population of UIRCs at over a thousand.[2] Once again, and even more directly than in the cases of biotech entrepreneurship and university patenting, policy decisions shaped by new ideas about the economic importance of technological innovation had helped to launch a new market-logic practice in academic science.

Early Development of University-Industry Research Centers

Relationships between universities and industry did exist in the 1950s and 1960s, and can be seen as setting the stage for the UIRCs that would begin to develop in the 1970s. But these university-industry ties were nevertheless weak in comparison to later decades. In 1972, materials scientist Rustum Roy reviewed "University-Industry Interaction Patterns" for *Science*, noting that "for several decades there have been only two or three universally acceptable mechanisms through which an entire university or a particular department could interact with industry," namely, faculty consulting, contract research projects, and fellowships, which were essentially provided as gifts.[3] Roy also described "two notable classes of experiments in university-industry coupling," including industrial affiliates programs (which I describe in chapter 2), and government-initiated pairings, in which the government acted as a broker to bring the two parties to work together on a specific problem.[4] Roy also observed, however, that "the two golden decades of science funding in the United States, 1948 to 1968, were not notable for inventiveness at the industry-university interface."[5]

Those decades *were* noteworthy, however, for the rise of the organized research unit (ORU) within universities. As the research enterprise grew, ORUs became increasingly common as a way to connect scholars working on a particular topic that crossed departmental lines. By 1970, a wide variety of ORUs were flourishing on university campuses in the form of area studies centers, survey research centers, engineering research institutes, computer labs, and so on. One scholar estimated that year that 5,000 ORUs had been established, though many of these were doubtless ephemeral.[6] But while such units were interdisciplinary, few were oriented toward the world outside of academia. A book-length survey of ORUs published in 1972 barely mentions industry, and of the hundreds of ORUs it describes, only a small handful sound as if they could conceivably be called UIRCs.[7] Even ORUs with clear industrial relevance, like the Advanced Research Projects Agency (ARPA)–funded Materials Research Centers at Cornell, MIT, and elsewhere, had little interaction with industry during the 1960s.[8]

During the 1970s, however, a variety of people within academic science would begin to experiment with marrying the form of the organizational research unit with existing kinds of industry relationships like the industrial affiliates program and contract research. These efforts developed slowly and initially had only moderate success, but the most successful would become models for later UIRCs. Lessons would be learned from the failures as well.

Experimenting with UIRCs at the National Science Foundation

One of these early organizational models could trace its origins to the brief Nixon-era wave of interest in technological innovation in Washington. Chapter 3 described how the Nixon administration, worried about the economy and responding to signs that the United States might be losing its trade advantage in high-technology fields, launched a massive review of policy options for strengthening innovation called the New Technology Opportunities Program. The political timing was bad, however, and what had been proposed as a multibillion-dollar new policy initiative was slashed to almost nothing. What was left at the end was two modest new programs with budgets of about $20 million each that were meant to experiment with the best ways of improving technological innovation. One, the Experimental Technology Incentives Program, was aimed at industry and housed at the National Bureau of Standards.[9] The other, oriented toward universities and located at NSF, was called the Experimental R&D Incentives Program (ERDIP).

NSF's ERDIP officially began in the summer of 1972, a few months after Nixon proposed it, but it got off to a slow start. The Office of Management and Budget was reluctant to disperse funds for the program, it was not entirely apparent what ERDIP was supposed to do, and as *Science* reported in early 1973, "ERDIP so far has no clear idea as to how technological innovation comes about. For this reason, maybe, ERDIP staff have great difficulty in explaining in general terms what their future 'experiments' will 'test.' "[10]

In practice, ERDIP tried to identify the factors that blocked technological innovation, look at the universe of incentives that might remove such blockages, and then initiate experiments to test whether such incentives worked.[11] An initial call for proposals brought in an unexpectedly large 600 by February 1973, but "according to advisers to the program . . . many [were] from money-hungry firms seeking . . . 'to invent a better kind of peanut butter.' "[12] Ultimately, ERDIP initiated ten such experiments in its first two years, ranging from an Office of Legislative Technical Assistance intended to serve Alabama state legislators by connecting them with sources of technical information, to a program in which NSF would fund private laboratories to conduct validation tests of promising technologies.[13]

One of these ten was the University-Industry Cooperative Research Centers Experiment.[14] As the name suggests, the program was meant to support centers where universities and industry would jointly conduct research on problems of mutual relevance. The program began in 1973 by choosing fourteen proposals that would receive a preliminary year of funding. The three most promising were then selected for an additional four-year period of support.[15] The effort was modest in size. Over the experiment's lifespan, NSF spent about $2.4 million on it, and industry groups invested another $3 million or so.[16] The fully funded centers each took a slightly different approach. The Furniture R&D Applications Institute housed North Carolina State University faculty conducting research in response to the needs of a fragmented low-tech industry. The New England Energy Development Systems (NEEDS) Center created a third-party nonprofit organization to serve as a broker between a group of universities and firms and aimed to help electric utilities improve their technological innovation process. And the MIT-Industry Polymer Processing Program (PPP) brought together a number of firms with an interest in polymers to jointly develop an ongoing research agenda with the program's director, the graduate students who conducted most of the research, and other faculty.[17]

Only the last center, the Polymer Processing Program, was considered a success. It was able to become self-supporting by the end of its five-year period of NSF funding and in fact continued to thrive for many more years. The other two experiments encountered familiar problems. The Furniture Institute suffered from leadership turnover that hurt its efforts, but the more central problem seemed to be that the furniture industry, which was struggling anyway, was not accustomed to doing research and development. This made the university-industry gap especially hard to bridge. The broker model of NEEDS was intended to provide such a bridge in its own domain, but instead it added an extra layer of complexity and cost that made it even harder for the two parties to collaborate effectively.[18]

In the PPP, by contrast, although the industry targeted was also fragmented, it did have a preexisting R&D effort, which seemed to be a critical element of success. The program itself not only had a strong director, but also was organized so that he played a particularly strong role. Evaluators drew the lesson that such centers need "champions"—committed individuals who are personally and professionally devoted to them. The center also held "technical review meetings" with industry partners quarterly (and initially bimonthly), so that feedback in both directions was regular and ongoing.[19] And it helped that the program targeted an industry that shared common and relatively fundamental technical concerns, so that it was not solving problems for individual firms, but performing research of value to a whole group of them.[20]

Thus with the creation of the PPP—and through comparison with failed efforts to encourage university-industry partnership—NSF hit upon a new way of organizing such collaboration that appeared to be successful and even self-supporting in the long-run, if one that was workable in a relatively limited set of circumstances. But the ERDIP program itself was short-lived. It had never enjoyed strong or consistent political support, and from its outset, observers had noted that "if the economy recover[ed], 'There would be a tendency to take a lot of the steam out of it,' since the impetus for the program stemmed from economic troubles."[21] And indeed, when the economy temporarily bounced back in 1973, the brief surge of political interest in innovation waned, and funds for ERDIP were cut. Even though the recovery ended with the oil crisis that began in October, ERDIP did not regain momentum. By 1975, though the centers still had three years of funding left, the program was being described as "practically shelved."[22]

Other University Experiments with UIRCs

Just as universities had experimented with industrial affiliates programs and research parks in the 1950s and 1960s, so some were experimenting with university-industry research centers on their own by the 1970s. Such efforts are difficult to track because many were ephemeral and others, even if more durable, gathered little attention. I have identified about a dozen such centers (see table 6.1), and sketch here a picture of a few of them to provide a sense of what these early UIRCs looked like, the successes they achieved, and the challenges they faced.

Outside of the centers created through ERDIP, almost none were established before 1975. One exception to this, however, was Carnegie Mellon's Processing Research Institute (PRI), funded in 1971 by NSF's Research Applied to National Needs (RANN) program. A joint effort between Carnegie Mellon's departments of chemical, mechanical, and materials engineering, PRI was created to develop a master's degree in process manufacturing. In conjunction with this effort, large companies like DuPont, Exxon, and Westinghouse contributed support for specific cooperative research projects conducted by graduate students. In the institute's first three-and-a-half years, twenty-six firms and industrial associations provided $800,000 in support and PRI matched those contributions with $500,000 of money from NSF. PRI appears to have ended around 1977, at about the same time that the RANN program, long under political fire, was eliminated.[23]

More UIRCs began to be established after the mid-1970s, though they were still quite uncommon. One notable example was Caltech's Silicon Structures Project. While Caltech was generally known for its arm's-length approach to industry relations, engineering professor Carver Mead started to build closer ties with industry around 1977 after becoming interested in the automated design of integrated circuits. Because doing such work required access to expensive fabrication facilities, he and Ivan Sutherland, who had been recruited to Caltech to start a computer science department, created the Silicon Structures Project to bring together companies like Xerox and IBM with Caltech scientists to work collaboratively on chip design.[24] Sutherland gained the involvement of Xerox's Palo Alto Research Center (Xerox PARC) through his brother, William "Bert" Sutherland, who managed a Xerox PARC laboratory, and Xerox became

TABLE 6.1.
UIRCs Founded 1970 to 1980

University	*Name of center*	*Year founded*	*Targeted government support*
Carnegie Mellon	Processing Research Institute	1971	NSF (RANN); existed until about 1977
MIT	Polymer Processing Program	1973	NSF (ERDIP); existed well into the 2000s
NC State	Furniture R&D Applications Institute	1973	NSF (ERDIP); ended in late 1970s
Caltech	Silicon Structures Project	1977	Independent; disbanded in early 1980s
RPI	Center for Interactive Computer Graphics	1977	Independent; became NSF I/UCRC in 1979; became state-funded in 1982
Delaware	Center for Composite Materials	Founded in 1974; industry-funded in 1978	Independent; became NSF ERC in 1985
Delaware	Center for Catalytic Science and Technology	1978	Independent; still in existence
Carnegie Mellon	Robotics Institute	1979	Independent; still in existence
Minnesota	Micro-Electronics Information Sciences Center (MEIS)	1979	Independent; became state-funded around 1983
RPI	Center for Manufacturing Productivity	1979	Independent; became state-funded in 1982
Arizona State	Center for Engineering Excellence	1980	State-funded
Case Western	Center for Applied Polymer Research	1980	NSF I/UCRC
Ohio State	Center for Welding Research	1980	NSF I/UCRC
Purdue	Computer Integrated Design, Manufacturing and Automation Center	1980	Independent; became NSF ERC in 1985
Stanford	Center for Integrated Systems	1980	Independent; still in existence
UMass	Center for UMass/Industry Research on Polymers	1980	NSF I/UCRC
UNC/Duke/ NC State	Microelectronics Center of North Carolina (MCNC)	1980	State-funded

an early and important sponsor.[25] By 1980, the Silicon Structures Project had five other sponsors as well, including Hewlett-Packard, Digital Equipment Corporation, and Burroughs, each of which was paying $100,000 to participate.[26] In many ways, the Silicon Structures Project functioned like an industrial affiliates program. But it was differentiated in part by the fact that each sponsor actually sent one of its scientists to Caltech for a year to work on the project.[27] This created a more active and intimate relationship between university scientists and their industry partners than was typically found in affiliates programs.

The Silicon Structures Project was widely seen as a success and helped to launch the field of very-large-scale integration (VLSI), which would transform the production of semiconductor chips. By 1982, its twelve sponsors were bringing Caltech $1.2 million a year.[28] But the project was not without its challenges. Mead found it frustrating to try to bridge the academic and industrial research environments:

> It was really an interesting experience trying to keep an academic program going with that many industry guys, because of course they were used to a project-oriented, very disciplined environment rather than open-ended research. It was very hard to get the students to focus on degrees rather than on doing projects. There was a whole bunch of stuff that looked more like development than research. It was a very hard time. I got very discouraged.[29]

By the time the project was in full swing, the number of sponsors, each of which was sending a company scientist to Caltech, substantially outnumbered the five faculty involved, further tilting the balance toward industrial science. But industry, too, found the relationship frustrating:

> "We thought we could send who we wanted and this person could do what he or she wanted," complained one corporate executive. "Apparently this is not so." "Some industry people came with specific assignments," said [Linda R.] Getting [administrative director of the Silicon Structures Project]. "This was less than desirable because they used resources without increasing knowledge. Some projects could have been done at corporate laboratories."[30]

Within a few years, the project was "winding down . . . because," according to Mead, "we'd done what we could do with these companies."[31] It had ended by 1985 or so.

Another early UIRC also focused on computer science but was organized along different lines than the Silicon Structures Project. Planning for the University of Minnesota's Microelectronics and Information Sciences (MEIS) Center began in 1979 with a $2.3 million challenge grant from Minnesota-based Control Data Corporation.[32] Soon Honeywell also committed $2 million, and 3M and Sperry Univac made contributions of about $1 million each.[33] MEIS was not intended to support a laboratory, but instead acted as a local funding clearinghouse for industrially relevant microelectronics research. The funding was also expected to substantially expand the university's output of computer science PhDs.[34]

From the outset, MEIS intended to leverage industry support "dollar-for-dollar, with funds from the National Science Foundation and the Defense and Energy Departments."[35] A board of eight university representatives and five industry representatives made funding decisions, and they expected grant applicants to bring in matching funds from other sources.[36] By 1983, the Minnesota State Legislature, interested in keeping the local electronics industry competitive, had invested $1.5 million as well.[37] MEIS got off to a slow start in terms of actually distributing funds, and received some criticism for this. By 1983, it was supporting only about $600,000 in research, though director Robert Hexter was stating that its four-year budget target was $10.3 million. One representative of the center justified the pace, however, saying that "the benefits of taking the time to work out an arrangement that suited the needs of the university and the sponsoring industries outweighed the costs of delay."[38]

But despite the care taken in negotiating the details, MEIS was not able to maintain its high level of industry support for long. "The successes of [its] type of research funding were not strong enough to prevent the founding companies from stopping their funding during the electronics crisis of the mid-'80s, which was particularly bad in the Minnesota area."[39] Increasingly, MEIS found itself turning to state support, requesting funds for the construction of a new cleanroom laboratory. When the laboratory was completed in 1990, the center changed its name to the Microelectronics Laboratory for Research and Education to reflect this new direction. By the early 1990s, the state of Minnesota was providing about 80% of the center's funding, though state funds were anticipated to decrease.[40]

A third late-1970s effort to create UIRCs took place at Rensselaer Polytechnic Institute. As a technical institute, RPI, like MIT, had a long tradition of industry relations, but RPI was a lower-profile institution focused primarily on undergraduate education, not sponsored research. When George Low, a NASA administrator known as "the man who put a man on the moon," was recruited to become president of RPI in 1975, he immediately launched an ambitious plan, modeled on Frederick Terman's "steeples of excellence" strategy at Stanford, to transform RPI from a strong regional engineering college into a nationally competitive research university.[41] A key pillar of this plan was the building of interdisciplinary centers that would partner RPI with major regional high-tech firms such as General Electric and IBM. The first such center, the Center for Interactive Computer Graphics, was launched in September 1977, and focused on computer-aided-design and computer-aided-manufacturing (CAD-CAM) research. It offered industrial affiliates memberships starting at $20,000 a year, and quickly signed on two dozen affiliates from the region and across the country.[42] In 1979, it received a grant from a new NSF program aimed specifically at supporting UIRCs.[43]

The second RPI center, the Center for Manufacturing Productivity and Technology Transfer, was started in 1979. Intended to bring high-tech methods to production processes, it was a timely intervention into an area that was of significant concern to firms but that was overlooked by most universities. Since government support for academic research in manufacturing was not available, the center was sponsored solely by industry.[44] Founding members, which provided $300,000 each in seed money, included General Electric, General Motors, Boeing, and Norton. And the third center, founded in 1981, was the Center for

Integrated Electronics. Like the Silicon Structures Project, the Center for Integrated Electronics focused on the manufacturing of VLSI circuits. It convinced IBM to donate the expensive ($2.75 million) electron-beam tool that would make it possible for the center to produce its own chips.[45] General Electric also committed $1.25 million in research support over three years, and center director Andrew Steckl expected to secure another $6 million in industry support in 1982.[46]

RPI's centers were quite successful, especially considering that the university did not have the national stature of Stanford or MIT. The institute quadrupled its sponsored research expenditures between 1976 and 1981, which placed it ninth among all U.S. engineering schools.[47] The next step in Low's plan was to bring the three UIRCs together in a massive Center for Industrial Innovation, and in 1982 he and General Electric CEO Jack Welsh convinced the state of New York to finance a $30 million building project to house the new centers.[48] But in 1984, Low unexpectedly succumbed to cancer at the age of 58, and his death deprived RPI of a charismatic leader and some of its upward momentum.[49]

The decline of New York's industrial base relative to both Japan and the Sun Belt states was also an ongoing challenge for RPI.[50] Nevertheless, substantial state support helped the university's UIRCs to continue to draw contributions from industry and remain resilient during the 1980s. By 1985, the Center for Interactive Computer Graphics had thirty-five companies sponsoring it at the level of $40,000 a year as well as a $3 million equipment grant from IBM, and by 1988 it was up to forty sponsors. The Center for Manufacturing Productivity was being supported by eight founding members and five affiliates in 1985, and was conducting more than $6 million of industry-sponsored research by 1988. The Center for Integrated Electronics, too, was doing well, receiving about $2 million a year in industry funding by the latter date.[51]

The examples of Caltech, the University of Minnesota, and RPI illustrate the range of approaches taken to university-industry research collaboration in the late 1970s. Yet they had some similarities as well. Notably, these experiments did not originate with the biotech-related fields, but instead came primarily from engineering disciplines that had a history of university-industry ties, even if those ties were relatively weak in the 1970s. While these early UIRCs were clearly descendants of the industrial affiliates programs pioneered by MIT and Stanford in the 1950s and 1960s, over time they became more actively collaborative than the industrial affiliates programs had been. Industry scientists were brought in as visiting scholars, as in the Silicon Structures Project. Sponsors were given greater say in how support was distributed, as at MEIS. Or, as at RPI, whole programs were designed around problems of significant industrial interest that academics on their own might never have approached.

Yet despite the moderate level of success these UIRCs seemed to be achieving in the late 1970s, they still faced challenges, and certainly did not appear so successful that one would expect they were about to become widely emulated. The businesses that were putting up the bulk of the funds for these centers did so in anticipation of a clear-cut payoff, whether in terms of R&D advances or well-trained future employees. An old problem, however, persisted. While much academic research was of moderate use to industry, most simply lacked a large enough payoff to justify high levels of ongoing support, particularly at moments when industrial R&D budgets became tight. The UIRCs described here all encountered this problem. Caltech's Silicon Structures Project wound down after about five years, as both university and industry partners became frustrated with the collaboration. MEIS lost funding from its corporate sponsors after a similar length of time, when a downturn in the electronics industry forced them to stop supporting activities that did not clearly pay for themselves. Of the centers just examined, only RPI maintained a high level of industrial sponsorship throughout the 1980s.

Yet the way that RPI managed that successfully is key to explaining why UIRCs became so prevalent during the 1980s and beyond *despite* these obvious barriers to their long-term viability. RPI was successful because it leveraged the sponsorship of industry with the sponsorship of government, beginning with the 1979 NSF grant that helped underwrite the Center for Interactive Computer Graphics and continuing with the $30 million in financing Albany provided for the Center for Industrial Innovation in 1982. This kind of funding differed from the generic research grants from NSF or the Department of Defense (DOD) that other academics were applying for. It represented the leading edge of a new wave of support specifically targeted at encouraging university-industry research collaboration. On their own, UIRCs appeared to be financially viable only under a fairly narrow range of circumstances. But with significant government subsidy, they proved relatively successful at creating more durable university-industry connections. And once again, it turns out that policymakers' decisions to provide this support were strongly shaped by ideas about the critical economic role played by technological innovation.

The Emergence of Federal and State Support for UIRCs

NSF's ERDIP program had been motivated by an early round of concern with the state of innovation in the United States. And it had identified, in the form of MIT's Polymer Processing Program, at least one successful organizational model for UIRCs—one that could even be self-supporting in the long run—as well as examples of less successful approaches.

But when the economy rebounded briefly in 1973, ERDIP lost political support before it had a chance to try to clone its single successful center. And while by the late 1970s universities and industry were showing mild interest in increasing their levels of interaction (as Smith and Karlesky noted cautiously in 1977, "the beginnings of a closer relationship are discernable"), independent experiments with UIRCs had trouble remaining financially viable in the long run.[52]

The renewed concern with innovation that began to emerge in Washington around 1976, however, led directly to new levels of support for UIRCs. Government funding that specifically targeted these kinds of centers would permit companies to leverage modest investments in them and encouraged industry participation. Efforts at NSF to identify the factors that made UIRCs successful and allowed them to become self-supporting over time were a further help. This second wave of innovation-driven government policies began in 1978 with a modest, but successful, NSF program designed specifically to fund centers built on the Polymer Processing Program model. For a while, it looked as if that program might be scaled up dramatically and expanded to other federal agencies, but the Reagan administration ended that possibility when it took office. Instead, individual states, which were also coming to see technological innovation as critical to their economic development strategies, picked up where the feds had left off, and the early 1980s saw a large wave of state-level funding aimed at encouraging university-industry research centers. By the mid-1980s, even Reagan was favoring an expansion of support for centers at NSF, and the rest of the decade saw UIRCs funded generously at both the state and federal levels.

NSF's Industry/University Cooperative Research Centers

From its inception, the National Science Foundation had focused its support on basic research and the academic science community. The late 1960s had seen its mission expand to include social science research as well as to science targeted at solving specific social problems.[53] But NSF's close ties to academia meant that the agency generally opposed the direct funding of industry scientists, since it suspected that such support might come out of the pockets of university researchers. While the National Science Board, which governed the agency, established an NSF-Industry Relations Committee in 1971, as late as 1975 it was reaffirming NSF's policy of providing support to for-profit organizations only in exceptional cases.[54]

In 1976, however, as policymakers started to become more concerned with industrial innovation, Congress requested that NSF report on the pros and cons of allowing industry scientists to apply directly for the agency's grants.[55] While NSF staff prepared a response that was favorable to such a change, the National Science Board, made up mostly of academics, blocked the proposal.[56]

But as industrial innovation continued to gain political salience, the board began to rethink its opposition. Senator Edward Kennedy, historically a strong supporter of NSF, introduced a measure to allow industry "to compete on an equal footing with universities for NSF's basic research funds" into the agency's budget authorization in 1977.[57] Though the measure did not end up in the final bill, the board took notice. While still not enthusiastic about funding industry, the board acknowledged that it was "politically expedient for the Foundation to support basic research in industry and that, if the NSF did not take the initiative in such plans, legislation would be passed to require it."[58]

The board's strategy was to make the best of a bad situation. It would try to address Congress's concern by funding joint university-industry research, thereby avoiding—hopefully—the necessity of allowing industry to compete directly for grants. Representatives of the board began making a new case to Congress: that while basic research in industry was unquestionably important, the best role for NSF was not to fund such research directly, but to encourage university-industry collaboration.[59] In January 1978, NSF director Richard Atkinson, using the prevailing language regarding foreign competition, job creation, and economic growth, officially requested funding for "an expanded effort in the area of university-industry cooperative research programs," emphasizing the "strong base of economic data indicating relationships between research and development activities and the gross national product."[60] While the actual amount was quite small—only $1 million was requested for 1979—Atkinson drew a disproportionate amount of attention to it in budget appropriation hearings.[61]

Atkinson's proposal was received warmly by Congress, and in 1979 NSF began to support university-industry collaboration both through targeted research grants and the new Industry/University Cooperative Research Centers (I/UCRC) program. *Business Week* quoted a "knowledgeable source" on NSF's success at getting these new efforts funded: "One of the [persuasive] arguments was the importance of industrial innovation" [bracketed text in original].[62]

The actual centers were created at a very modest rate, with only four—two focusing on polymers, one on welding research, and one, the pre-existing RPI center, on computer graphics—funded between 1979 and 1981 (see table 6.1).[63] Political reception, however, was very positive. In fact, scaling up support for NSF's centers and copying the program at other agencies was a key recommendation of Carter's Domestic Policy Review of Industrial Innovation when it completed its work in late 1979. The administration proposed that NSF be given $20 million to fund UIRCs in 1981 and in following years. It also wanted NSF to help extend the concept, with the eventual goal a multi-agency program providing $150 million a year of support for UIRCs.[64]

In 1980, this recommendation became part of the Stevenson-Wydler Act, better known for requiring federal laboratories to establish technology transfer offices.[65] But only weeks after Stevenson-Wydler was passed, Carter lost the election to Ronald Reagan, and the political climate changed dramatically. Though the Reagan administration was no less interested in innovation, its approach was different. As one reporter put it in August 1981, "The Carter administration's efforts to promote research collaboration between academe and industry have largely been wiped out by the Reaganite faith in the marketplace attending to whatever is useful in society."[66] The centers proposed by Stevenson-Wydler were never funded, and thus never created.[67]

Yet NSF's I/UCRC program survived. While its budget did not increase by the order of magnitude envisioned by the Carter administration, it continued to grow slowly. In 1982, it funded another four centers—to conduct research in ceramics, robotics, material handling, and communication and signal processing—and gave one-year planning grants to two more proposals.[68] This modest expansion continued throughout the decade, and by 1989 the program had funded thirty-nine centers, all but three of which were still in operation and sixteen of which had become self-supporting.[69]

Thus in terms of sheer numbers, the I/UCRC program was of only moderate importance, given that Cohen, Florida, and Goe estimated a U.S. population of more than a thousand UIRCs in 1990.[70] But its overall impact was disproportionate to its size. First, it helped demonstrate that the model of MIT's Polymer Processing Program was replicable and further refined it. As one analyst suggested in 1980, "A principal question is estimating how many successful university-based centers can be created on the MIT model. Professor Suh's success at MIT may be so unique that few individuals and institutions can emulate it without descending into research mediocrity or creating administrative nightmares."[71] But the I/UCRC program proved that this was not the case. By requiring I/UCRCs to maintain a high level of interaction with the agency as well as incorporating a strong component of program evaluation, NSF used its growing base of experience to provide active support in making university-industry collaboration work.[72]

Second, it also demonstrated how centers could eventually become self-sustaining. While NSF funding was critical in getting centers up and running, I/UCRC funding was always intended to last for a limited period, and after five years centers were expected to have found other means of support. But while independent UIRCs had trouble maintaining industry funding for more than a few years, I/UCRCs were fairly good at solving this problem, perhaps because of their ability to draw on past examples of success. Over the long run, I/UCRCs have had impressive longevity. Of the seventy-seven centers that had "graduated" from the I/UCRC program by 2007—that is, that were no longer receiving I/UCRC support—73% still existed five years post-graduation and 62% were around after ten years.[73]

This in itself was a significant achievement. But the small I/UCRC program played a third role as well by serving as a model for other, larger programs. While Carter's vision of $150 million a year of federal funds to UIRCs never became a reality, the federal role in supporting UIRCs was, as a 1983 General Accounting Office report acknowledged, important in building interest in such efforts.[74] By the mid-1980s, other, larger UIRC programs would be created at NSF and, to a lesser extent, elsewhere within the federal government, partly based on the success of the I/UCRC program. But the most significant factor in the further creation and expansion of UIRCs would not be additional federal programs. Instead, somewhat unexpectedly, it would be state governments that came to play a decisive role in encouraging the development of UIRCs in the early 1980s.

Moving to the States: State Governments and S&T-Driven Economic Development

While individual states had a long history of funding public institutions of higher education, states did not traditionally have much in the way of science policy. Science policy emerged as the domain of federal government, and it was not till the 1960s that states even began to develop science and technology (S&T) efforts of their own. Even then, the stimulus came from Washington, as federal agencies started to encourage the appointment of state-level science advisors and the creation of state science and engineering foundations, small versions of the NSF.[75] In the early 1970s, Nixon's New Federalism, which encouraged the devolution of government to the state and local level, increased this effort.[76] By 1974, every state had an S&T advisor, and in 1977 Congress authorized a new NSF program to help states develop their own S&T plans.[77] Although it was never fully funded, the program issued planning grants to almost every state, further strengthening the modest state-level S&T infrastructure.[78]

For most of this period, however, this infrastructure was oriented toward providing advice to governors and legislators on science and technology issues. To an even greater extent than in the federal government, state S&T policy had almost no economic development component.[79] Beginning in the late 1970s, however, that would change dramatically.

Peter Eisinger has described the transformation of state economic development policy in the 1970s and 1980s as a shift from a supply-side to a demand-side model of development. A supply-side model of economic development assumes that "investment, which in turn generates jobs, would be attracted to those locales where the costs of factors of production—entered on the supply side of the economic-growth equation—are lower."[80] This model leads states to create policies that will induce firms to locate there: tax incentives, government subsidies, and the like. Sometimes derogatorily called "smokestack chasing," this is a zero-sum game, as it does not create new jobs but tries to lure existing jobs to a particular location. The supply-side model was the universal approach to state economic development until the late 1970s, and science and technology played little role in it.[81]

A demand-side model of development, by contrast, "emphasize[s] local resources as the basis for growth rather than competitive engagement with other states for mobile capital."[82] This approach focuses on encouraging the development of small business—often homegrown, often high-tech. It looks for ways to strengthen local entrepreneurship, partly by making more capital available but also through practical support like providing business incubators or help with business plans. Significantly, this approach emphasizes scientific and technological innovation as a primary source of new business creation, so many of its strategies focus on ways to improve the innovative process and its translation into new products, businesses, and markets.

States, like the federal government, were open to a new economic development strategy because of the poor economic environment of the 1970s and early 1980s. The problems were severest in the Rust Belt, and it was governors of states like Pennsylvania, New York, Michigan, and Ohio, all of whom had a lot to lose if things didn't change, who first began to experiment with novel development policies.[83] This group included both Democrats and Republicans, but shared a willingness to look for unconventional solutions in the face of extremely high unemployment—as high as 14% in Ohio and 17% in Michigan.[84]

According to author and policy analyst David Osborne, the ideas behind this new approach originated in Massachusetts, in the mid-1970s gubernatorial administration of Michael Dukakis, and were disseminated through the tiny Washington-based Council of State Planning Agencies (CSPA) beginning around 1978. Drawing heavily on new research by MIT economist David Birch that claimed that most jobs were created by firms less than five years old, CSPA began pushing books driven by the idea that states needed to focus on bottom-up economic development.[85] CSPA's representatives promoted their work "relentlessly" at the National Governors Association, gave seminars to state officials, and consulted with governors and their staffs on economic development issues.[86]

This led to significant new economic development programs in several states and the beginning of a national trend. For the first time, states began actively trying to promote economic growth through technological innovation, and as part of this process to develop S&T policy strategies—ones that were not imposed at the behest of the National Science Foundation or the Department of Commerce, but that came from within.[87]

These innovation-oriented economic development strategies took a variety of forms. Some state programs focused on the industrial side of innovation—for example, state venture capital funds and technical assistance programs for industry.[88] But the largest and most visible efforts tried to encourage innovation-driven economic development by bridging the gap between universities and industry. States did this in a number of ways, but one of the most common was by supporting university-industry research centers.[89] These state-funded centers were typically much larger in scale than the NSF-funded I/UCRCs, with budgets in the millions or even tens of millions of dollars.

A few examples of such efforts can give a sense of their scope and range. One of the earliest took place in Arizona, where in 1978 a group of Phoenix business leaders, many of whom represented high-tech firms like Motorola, Honeywell, and Sperry, began to discuss their concerns with the difficulty of hiring good engineers and the lack of local high-quality graduate education in engineering. With Roland Haden, the new dean of Arizona State University's engineering school, they approached Democratic governor Bruce Babbitt about the need to strengthen local engineering resources as part of a high-tech development strategy. Babbitt issued a challenge to the group, charging them, according to one participant, to "think big. I'm not interested in being behind short-term or small-time budget increases; come back to me with a sweeping multiyear program, and I'll support you."[90]

In response, the group proposed a five-year, $30 million public-private partnership to strengthen engineering at Arizona State, with a third of the money to come from the private sector.[91] At its heart was a large-scale, multidisciplinary Center for Excellence in Engineering, and over the next five years the university built a 120,000-square-foot building, and added more than sixty engineering faculty and $15 million in new equipment.[92] The program was very effective at raising both private funds and the profile of Arizona State. The university secured roughly double its initial goal for industry support, and in 1984 the National Academy of Sciences (NAS) ranked Arizona State's mechanical engineering and electrical engineering departments second and third nationally in terms of improvement over the last five years.[93] In 1985, the state signed on for a second, even larger, five-year plan.[94]

A similar initiative developed in North Carolina, where Democratic governor Jim Hunt championed the Microelectronics Center of North Carolina (MCNC). When General Electric selected Research Triangle Park as the site for its new microelectronics plant in 1979, it funded the Research Triangle Institute to propose a public-private partnership to strengthen research and education in microelectronics, and Governor Hunt reacted with enthusiasm.[95] In 1980, MCNC was established with $1.8 million in funds from the Research Triangle Foundation, GE, and other sources.[96] In 1981, Hunt obtained an additional $24 million from the state legislature, to be supplemented by $6 million in private support, upping the ante considerably.[97]

Intended to bring together at least five universities with GE and other firms, MCNC was established as an independent nonprofit rather than being organizationally located within a university.[98] In the next few years, the center built a $30 million facility, recruited more than thirty new faculty members, and hired more than seventy full-time staff.[99] By early 1982, GE was still the only industry sponsor, and representatives were saying that the center was waiting to hire a president before recruiting more.[100] But an industrial affiliates program got underway shortly thereafter, and by 1985 the center expected to have twenty firms participating.[101] By 1985, the state of North Carolina had put $67 million toward MCNC.[102]

Democratic governor Jerry Brown of California was also a strong early supporter of innovation-driven economic development. In January 1981, he proposed a $23 million reindustrialization program "to 'invest in the future' through cooperative research and aid to small, innovative companies."[103] To pursue this vision, Brown appointed a California Commission on Industrial Innovation made up of representatives of business, academia, and labor.[104] UC San Diego chancellor Richard Atkinson, who had championed I/UCRC programs when he directed NSF, was one notable member.[105]

State politics meant that much of Brown's proposal never became a reality. But one piece that was put into practice was the Microelectronics Innovation and Computer Research Opportunities (MICRO) program at the University of California. Conceived in part by CSPA author Michael Kieschnick, the MICRO program was described as a "model of simplicity and reliance on the marketplace rather than the bureaucracy," and was patterned, by one account, after the University of Minnesota's MEIS center.[106] MICRO was not itself a center, but faculty from any UC campus could bring it proposals for microelectronics research that partnered with California industry, and MICRO would match industry funds. MICRO was not a large program, with a budget of just under $1 million in 1981, but it supported thirty-one projects in its first year and fifty-one in its second.[107] While it did not specifically target UIRCs, much of the kind of research it supported was conducted in centers.

Finally, one of the best-known innovation-focused state economic development programs was sponsored by a Republican governor, not a Democrat. Pennsylvania had a relatively strong state S&T infrastructure, having established both a technical assistance program for small business (PennTAP) and a state science and engineering foundation (PSEF) in the 1960s, but these programs were in some respects legacies of another era.[108] In 1979, Governor Richard Thornburgh appointed Walter Plosila to create a new economic development plan, and Plosila, who had learned about David Birch's work on small business and job creation through the CSPA, developed a strategy based on the "growth of innovative, advanced technology companies."[109] This led to a 1982 proposal to reinvigorate PSEF, which would be renamed the Ben Franklin Partnership in honor of the state's entrepreneurial pioneer.[110]

Like MICRO and MEIS, the Ben Franklin Partnership started as a challenge grants program to be operated through four university-based Advanced Technology Centers spread throughout the state. Each center focused on two to four research areas, including robotics, advanced materials, CAD-CAM, microelectronics, and biotechnology, and the centers competed with one another for state funds, which had to be matched with equivalent support from industry.[111] The state legislature appropriated $1 million to the program in 1983, and industry contributed $3 million in its first year.[112] The Ben Franklin Partnership expanded rapidly, providing $77 million of challenge grants to 1,500 individual projects over its first four years, and eventually adding support for business incubators and seed venture capital to the challenge grants.[113] By fiscal year

(FY) 1986, industry was contributing $54 million to Ben Franklin Partnership–supported research.[114]

The Expansion of State and Federal Support for UIRCs in the 1980s

During the early 1980s, states' move to demand-side, innovation-oriented economic development strategies spread rapidly. Arizona and California excepted, the trend moved generally from the Rust Belt to the Sun Belt, with Ohio, Michigan, and New York among other early sponsors of UIRC programs.[115] Counts of when such programs were implemented vary, but all suggest that the number of states using innovation-driven development strategies increased greatly in the first half of the decade, with one typical survey identifying four states with general programs "for the development of science and technology industries" in 1979, but thirty-three states with such programs in 1984.[116] Irwin Feller reflected a consensus view in 1984 when he wrote that state high-tech development programs had "just passed through the take-off phase in accelerated diffusion."[117]

Not all these programs were designed to support UIRCs, of course, but the UIRC strategy was a common one, with Coburn and Berglund observing that "government-sponsored university-industry technology centers were by far the most prevalent means of providing technology development services for industry" during this period.[118] An analysis of governors' state-of-the-state speeches found that the first two proposals for cooperative university-industry high-tech programs appeared in 1982, with fourteen more announced in 1983, six in 1984, and another four in 1985.[119] By 1985, Herb Brody found forty-four states sponsoring "university-based centers" to improve high-technology education, and in 1988, the state of Minnesota learned from a national survey that 41% of all state S&T funds, totaling more than $225 million, were going to "technology or research centers to promote research and development."[120]

While this massive increase in state funding was probably the most significant factor contributing to the rapid growth in the numbers of UIRCs during the 1980s, support at the federal level also continued to expand in the same period, most notably at NSF, where the success of the modest I/UCRC program helped to spawn other, larger center programs. The first of these was the Engineering Research Center (ERC) program, which was explicitly intended to harness scientific and technological innovation in service of the economy, and particularly to improve U.S. "competitiveness," the latest buzzword. Conceived in 1983, the ERCs tried to bring engineering education more in line with industry needs, with a focus on interdisciplinary questions and hands-on research for students.[121] While the Reagan administration was generally "scornful of the idea that direct federal action [could] improve the innovation process in industry," presidential science adviser George Keyworth was strongly supportive of the ERC concept, arguing that involving industry more directly in engineering education was vital to the nation's economic health.[122] Observers saw Keyworth's commitment as politically critical "in view of considerable skepticism, if not opposition, within the administration."[123]

By early 1984, the new program was approved and a call for proposals made.[124] Many within academic science were critical of the ERC idea, fearing it would take money away from the individual investigator grants that were an NSF mainstay.[125] Nevertheless, NSF received an overwhelming number of proposals—requesting a total of $2 billion for 142 centers, far more than the $10 million allotted for the first year—and in April 1985 the agency announced the five proposed centers that would be funded.[126] In the meanwhile, Nam Suh, director of MIT's Polymer Processing Program, was now overseeing the ERC program as assistant director for engineering.[127]

While Suh's involvement suggests some continuity between the I/UCRCs and the ERCs, in many ways the programs differed. ERCs focused explicitly on education, and they were much larger. While NSF typically spent about $50,000 to $100,000 a year on an I/UCRC, ERCs—which were typically expected to raise about half their support from industry—received about $2 million a year from NSF, with no clear sunset date.[128] Over the next few years, the ERC program steadily expanded, with twenty-nine centers created between 1985 and 1990, representing more than $100 million in investment by NSF.[129]

NSF's move toward centers did not stop with ERCs. As director Erich Bloch announced in 1987, "The idea of centers is central to economic competitiveness. It's also central to what's happening at the agency."[130] At the time, Bloch was involved in planning a new Science and Technology Centers (STCs) program, which President Reagan would announce in his State of the Union address.[131] Similar to ERCs in terms of their emphasis on education and the needs of industry, but focusing on interdisciplinary basic science rather than engineering, NSF funded twenty-five Science and Technology Centers between 1989 and 1991, again at annual levels of about $2 million each.[132] Across its three center programs, then, NSF directly supported at least eighty-three UIRCs by the year 1990 with a total of perhaps $200 million in funding.[133]

Outside NSF, however, federal support for UIRCs remained limited and uncoordinated. The Defense Advanced Research Projects Agency (DARPA) supported joint university-industry research during the 1980s, but it had no program dedicated to centers, instead focusing most of its efforts on precompetitive industry research consortia like SEMATECH, the Semiconductor Manufacturing Technology Consortium.[134] While SEMATECH in turn provided funds to universities for industrially relevant research, it did not focus specifically on centers. NIH, the largest federal funder of university science, had no specific support for centers, and in general did not emphasize university-industry collaboration.[135] NASA started funding UIRCs meant to conduct space-based research in industrially relevant fields in the latter part of the decade, but though it was supporting seventeen such centers by 1992, they were not "successful in attracting a significant amount of non-NASA funding into NASA efforts at space commercialization," and the program was gradually phased out.[136]

Nevertheless, the rapid growth of UIRC programs at the state level and within NSF provided a large influx of resources for new and existing centers during the 1980s. UIRCs had been very uncommon in the early 1970s, when only a handful appear to have existed, and as late as 1977 they were considered unusual and experimental.[137] But by 1983, when the National Science Board published the first detailed survey of university-industry research relationships, and by which point the UIRC phenomenon was clearly beginning to spread, it found seventy-one "university-industry cooperative research centers and institutions" at the thirty-nine research institutions it studied.[138] Since these universities represented about 25% to 30% of all academic R&D spending, that suggested a total UIRC population of about 250.[139] By 1990, when Cohen, Florida, and Goe conducted a comprehensive national survey of UIRCs, they estimated a total population of 1,056.[140] Though the studies do not use identical definitions, they are similar enough to illustrate the large increase in the number of UIRCs that took place during the decade.[141]

Why Did University-Industry Research Centers Spread?

During the 1980s, industry funding of university research tripled in real terms, and by 1990 69% of such funding was being channeled through UIRCs.[142] University-industry research centers went from being a relatively rare type of arrangement on university campuses in the mid-1970s to a common, if internally diverse, way of organizing research activity by the end of the 1980s. Their relatively rapid spread took place for at least four reasons.

First, both universities and industry appear to have been slightly more interested in the possibility of collaborating with one another by the late 1970s, even independent of growing government interest in encouraging such partnerships[143] Such a change is hard to quantify or provide an incontrovertible explanation for, but substantial anecdotal evidence points to it. The chemical industry, for example, was making overtures of its own to academic science by the end of the 1970s. The Dow Chemical Company sponsored the First Midland Conference on Advances in Chemical Science and Technology in 1979, an event that brought together university and industry researchers in a way unusual enough for *Chemical Week* to observe that "no one attending . . . seemed able to recall any other [conference] quite like it."[144] This as well as a handful of other university-industry interactions, like Caltech's Silicon Structures Project and the University of Minnesota's Microelectronics and Information Sciences Center, developed independently of government efforts to promote innovation.

The more constrained resource environment that universities found themselves in during the 1970s probably encouraged this sort of interest, as did industry's increasing concern with the negative trends of innovation indicators. The pendulum of academic R&D may also just have swung as far away from industrial application as was reasonable during the 1960s and early 1970s, and then begun to swing back more or less on its own. But while it is important not to overlook the relatively organic development of interest in university-industry relations, one also should not overemphasize it. The mere fact that universities and industry were becoming more interested in finding common ground did not mean that UIRCs or any other type of collaboration would necessarily be a straightforward and financially sustainable means of finding such ground, as several 1970s UIRC experiments showed.

Instead, it took multiple changes in the policy environment to provide the financial and, secondarily, organizational support that helped such experimentation to become successful and widespread. The creation of the small I/UCRC program at NSF in 1978 helped identify and replicate a successful UIRC model, as well as raising political awareness of and support for this type of activity. The rapid spread of state-level funding for university-industry collaboration beginning around 1980 provided a major influx of resources in support of UIRCs that would allow industry to leverage its investment in such centers and help stabilize their finances. And the scaling up of center programs at the federal level—particularly at NSF—starting around 1983 provided another wave of resources for new and larger UIRCs. These three policy developments collectively provided targeted support for UIRCs that was very important in allowing centers to move from being an activity that seemed like a good idea but that was difficult to keep running to a type of collaboration that, while challenging, could clearly be sustained over time.

What was the relative importance of each of these factors in contributing to the spread of UIRCs? In the case of university patenting, I noted that it was hard to make a strong argument about exactly which developments were most critical to the practice's growth. In looking at biotech entrepreneurship, on the other hand, it was easier to make the claim that certain conditions were necessary for the practice to take off. The UIRC case falls somewhere in between. It seems pretty clear that the massive wave of state funding was important in encouraging the spread of centers. While comprehensive data are not available regarding the total level of state spending on UIRCs, it almost certainly totaled more than $1 billion during the 1980s.[145] In 1990, 69% of UIRCs indicated they had received at least some state funding in the last five years, even though states provided only 8.1% of all academic R&D funding.[146] This money not only directly supported centers, but also, by generally requiring matching support from industry, encouraged significant levels of nongovernmental support as well. The state of Pennsylvania, for example, claimed that the $77 million it invested in the Ben Franklin Partnership between 1983 and 1986 "leveraged $281 million in other investments, the majority of them from private industry."[147]

It also seems likely that NSF's I/UCRC program had a large impact on the development of UIRCs, or at the very least, one disproportionate to its size. The I/UCRC program disseminated the successful organizational model of MIT's Polymer Processing Program by explicitly trying to copy it.[148] It included a major element of program evaluation from very early on, including the publication of historical profiles of all its centers, a "practice manual" for those directing centers, and a steady stream of publications reflecting on lessons learned from the program.[149] All these activities helped NSF to continue to refine the initial model. And NSF's early centers played what a General Accounting Office report called a "convening and catalytic" role in building interest in and support for UIRC programs in Washington and elsewhere.[150] The idea of centers certainly gained visibility when the Carter administration proposed that the I/UCRC program should be scaled up dramatically and when language to that effect was included in the Stevenson-Wydler Act, even though the proposed "generic technology centers" were never in fact funded.[151] So while the growing seed of interest in university-industry collaboration and the later scaling up of centers at NSF were no doubt helpful in encouraging growth of the UIRCs nationally, the state efforts and the initial I/UCRC program were arguably more important in encouraging their spread.

To a greater extent than in the cases of biotech entrepreneurship and university patenting, then, policy decisions played a direct role in causing the number of UIRCs to increase. And once again, arguments about the economic importance of innovation had an integral part in the policymaking process. The I/UCRC program was created defensively by NSF in reaction to a Congressional push, driven by concern with the state of industrial innovation, to extend eligibility for NSF funding to industry as well as academic researchers. Among the state programs, many were directly influenced by the efforts of the Council of State Planning Agencies to promote an innovation-driven model of economic development, while in others where there is no particular evidence of CSPA influence, plans were still clearly rooted in the idea that high-tech innovation drives economic growth.[152] And the impetus for NSF's second wave of centers, the ERCs and STCs, was a new focus on the role of science and engineering in keeping U.S. industry "competitive," an argument explicitly based on the idea that technological innovation could help the nation meet its changing economic needs.[153] It is hard to imagine government support for UIRCs becoming so widespread had innovation not become such a salient political issue.

Comparing All Three Practices

How do the changes that led to the spread of UIRCs compare to those that caused university patenting and biotech entrepreneurship to become relatively common in the same era? Table 6.2 lists the factors that were significant contributors to the development of each of the three practices, breaking them down into ones that appear to have been necessary for the practice to become

Table 6.2.
Factors Contributing to the Spread of Market-Logic Practices in Academic Science

	Biotech	*Patenting*	*UIRCs*
Necessary conditions	Scientific breakthroughs Academic location of expertise Organizational model of Genentech Generous venture capital environment (Driven by **capital gains tax cut**, **ERISA decision**, and promise of new technology)	**Creation of IPAs by network of government administrators** **Passage of the Bayh-Dole Act** Emergence of biotechnology industry	**NSF's I/UCRC programs** **State funding for UIRCs**
Facilitating conditions	**Congressional decision not to regulate rDNA research** ***Diamond v. Chakrabarty***	Efforts of Research Corporation to train universities to patent Increasing organization of professional community of university patent administrators Strengthening of U.S. patent regime **(*Chakrabarty*, CAFC)**	Growing interest of universities and industry in collaborating by late 1970s **Expansion of NSF support for UIRCs in the 1980s**

Note: Policy decisions are in boldface.

widespread and ones that facilitated that process but were probably less decisive. Policy decisions, which played a major role in all three cases, are highlighted in bold.

Several things are worth noting here. First, introducing this third case adds a whole new set of reasons that a market-logic practice might spread. While the three practices did not emerge completely independently of one another, there is not much overlap in the factors that most directly contributed to the development of each practice, and this is particularly the case for UIRCs.

Second, while industry took more early interest in the creation of UIRCs than it did in early biotech entrepreneurship or university patenting, industry still did not play a driving role in launching the practice. While some specific UIRCs, such as the Microelectronics Center of North Carolina or Arizona State's Center for Excellence in Engineering, may have been initiated by industry, for the most part academics and government were the ones who showed the greatest interest in their development. Some academics, like Caltech's Carver Mead and RPI's George Low, began by building direct ties with industry. Others, like MIT's Nam Suh, acted in response to new government funding opportunities. Some state UIRC programs were started by policymakers who were pursuing the demand-side economic development strategies being promoted by the Council of State Planning Agencies. Others were influenced by university lobbying for such programs, particularly after they had started to spread. Their origins were diverse, but they were not industry-dominated.

Third, while universities did eventually begin lobbying for state UIRC programs, the practice still was not propelled primarily by university administrators seeking new resource opportunities. But here there is a distinction to make between UIRCs and the first two practices. Early on, university administrators played little role in promoting government support for UIRCs. However, over time, as such programs became more visible nationally, they increasingly began pushing state governments for this kind of support. In general, the role of university administrations in directly promoting any of the practices I look at was limited until 1981 or so, but became increasingly visible after that—a theme I will return to in the next chapter. Since the first significant period of growth of UIRCs lagged that of patenting and biotech entrepreneurship by a couple of years, active administrative involvement in the practice began at a slightly earlier period in its development. Nevertheless, administrators who were promoting state UIRC programs in the early 1980s were jumping on a bandwagon of support for a practice that had already become politically appealing more than they were trying to make the case for an unheard of approach to economic development, which was the position CSPA had been in a few years earlier.

Finally, while it is notable that some factors did *not* play a major role in encouraging the spread of biotech entrepreneurship, university patenting, or UIRCs, there is of course one that is very visible across all three: policy decisions. Again, the policy decisions that helped support UIRCs were different from those that encouraged the other two practices. And not only were the specific policy decisions different, but they embodied an entirely different economic approach, one essentially interventionist rather than free-market in nature. Nevertheless, innovation arguments played an important role in the making of these policy decisions, just as was the case for the decisions that encouraged biotech entrepreneurship and university patenting. In all three cases, political arguments about the economic impact of technological innovation were critical in creating the conditions that allowed these market-logic practices to spread. In the concluding chapter, I will further discuss why this argument led to policies that looked so different but had similar effects on academic science, at least in terms of encouraging market logic. First, though, chapter 7 will look at how market logic became more influential throughout academic science during the 1980s, so that by the end of the decade it was a significant, legitimate, and very visible alternative to the traditional institutional logic of science.

CHAPTER 7

The Spread of Market Logic

> Fifteen years ago, there were few parts of the academic world where [the] term [intellectual property], if indeed it was known at all, would have been viewed as anything other than alien and unwelcome. Today, the idea that the products of the mind constitute of kind of property—and valuable property at that—is part of common campus discourse."
>
> —Robert M. Rosenzweig, President, Association of American Universities, Spring 1985[1]

As late as 1977, market logic was still relatively weak within academic science. While biotech entrepreneurship, patenting, and university-industry research centers (UIRCs) were all emerging locally, they were still seen as unusual experiments, not the wave of the future. Not only did these activities depart from cultural norms on campuses, but it was difficult to find the financial resources needed to sustain them, and an uncertain regulatory environment held the potential to further limit their development. These practices were predicated on the idea that science had economic value, and policymakers were increasingly interested in trying to leverage that value. Yet it was still relatively uncommon for proponents of such activities to defend or promote them on the basis of their contribution to the nation's economic well-being. Even less frequently did one see university leaders justify the broader worth of academic science in purely economic terms.

Yet by the mid-1980s, all three of these practices had spread widely across American universities and were increasingly regarded as appropriate within them. Their value, and the value of academic science more generally, had come to be identified with their potential to promote innovation and thus economic growth—that is, to allow academic science to serve as an economic engine. The statement that opens this chapter, made by the leader of the organization of major U.S. research universities, reflects the extent to which by 1985 universities had already come to see science's worth in its ability to produce knowledge with value in the marketplace. While Rosenzweig acknowledged that some might take issue with this way of thinking about science, he continued, "It is necessary to face the facts: The chief route to public use in this country is commerce; profit is the engine that drives the machinery of commerce; and ownership, or at least exclusive use, is a critical instrument for the generation of profit. That logic . . . applies to the products of the mind as well as to other forms of property."[2]

The preceding three chapters showed how changes in the policy environment, driven by a newfound political concern with innovation, allowed specific market-oriented practices to grow and spread across universities in the late 1970s and early 1980s. This chapter will examine how the market logic embodied in those practices became increasingly influential throughout academic science during the 1980s. Not only did the three practices themselves continue to expand, but university leaders responded both to their success and to the positive reception innovation arguments were finding with policymakers. The 1980s saw universities initiate a spate of further experiments with market logic, only some of which were successful, as well as a new wave of expansion of older market-oriented activities, like research parks, that had stagnated during the 1970s.

But the strength of market logic did not increase only through the initiation and expansion of specific practices with clear economic relevance. University administrators had been searching since the late 1960s for new ways to persuade legislators that they deserved high levels of financial support. With the argument that academic science could be an economic engine, they finally found a strategy that did not expect the inherent value of science to be as obvious to policymakers as it was to universities. Increasingly, universities began to actively recast their mission in terms of their economic role. Sometimes this was just lip service or political opportunism. But often the adoption of arguments about the economic impact of science served as the fundamental justification for new kinds of activities, and a new way of thinking about the university, that would not have made sense in their absence. By the end of the decade, though the use of market logic was still contentious, it had nevertheless become widespread at all levels of the university. Academic science had become, at least rhetorically, an economic engine.

The Expansion of Biotech Entrepreneurship, Patenting, and UIRCs

Prior to 1980, biotech entrepreneurship, patenting, and UIRCs were usually initiated by individual faculty or mid-level administrators, not by presidents or provosts. By its nature, such activity was focused on the marketplace. But it was not consistently justified to the outside world in terms of its economic impact. One of the important changes of the 1980s was that market-oriented practices that had emerged somewhat organically from the activities of specific scientists and administrators were increasingly embraced by university leaders and framed explicitly in terms of their economic role. So one way that the expansion of these three practices helped to strengthen market logic throughout academic science was by providing very visible examples of how a market orientation could be successful, examples that university leaders would want to emulate.

The spread of biotech entrepreneurship, patenting, and UIRCs, however, also had a more direct role in increasing the influence of market logic—they simply got more people within academic science involved in using it. The rapid growth of the biotech industry, for example, and the extent to which it remained closely tied to academia meant that a large and growing number of academic scientists became involved with commercial biotechnology in some way. While only a handful of biotech firms had been founded by 1979, twenty-six were started in 1980, and in 1981, the peak year for firm formation, forty-three were established.[3] By 1988, there were hundreds of dedicated biotechnology firms.[4] These firms were often founded or cofounded by academics, generally had scientific advisory boards made up of academics, and frequently hired academics as consultants. At least in the elite reaches of the relevant scientific fields, involvement with the biotech industry had become the norm. As early as 1983, a *New York Times* reporter claimed that "it would be difficult to find" even a single top researcher in biotechnology "without a commercial tie . . . so rapid and comprehensive has the entanglement with industry been."[5] The application of biotechnology to additional fields also extended this new model of university-industry relations into other schools and departments. While most of the first biotech firms focused on pharmaceuticals and drew on faculty from departments like molecular biology and biochemistry, other companies were soon created that used biotechnology in industries like agriculture, mining, chemicals, and environmental remediation, which naturally enough led to ties with other parts of the university.[6]

Patenting, too, had an expanding sphere of influence. While only twenty universities had technology transfer offices before 1980, by 1990 eighty-six universities did (see figure 7.1).[7] The number of people actually working in tech transfer offices was relatively tiny. But a central part of their job was to raise awareness of inventions among faculty, encouraging them to disclose such inventions to the university and pursue their commercialization where appropriate. An active technology transfer office could encourage market logic throughout the university even if it never brought in much licensing revenue, since it educated scientists to think explicitly about the economic value of their work. This impact cannot be measured directly, but such efforts must have had some degree of success, since the number of patents issued to universities increased from less than 400 in 1980 to more than 1,100 in 1990 (see also figure 7.1).[8]

Finally, the rapid increase in the number of UIRCs also helped to disseminate market logic. While the fraction of university research dollars provided by industry increased during the 1980s, from 4.1% in 1980 to 6.9% in 1990 (see figure 1.1), direct support from industry still accounted for only a small portion of all research spending.[9] UIRCs, however, were fairly uncommon before the 1980s, numbered roughly 250 by 1983, and by 1990 were estimated at about

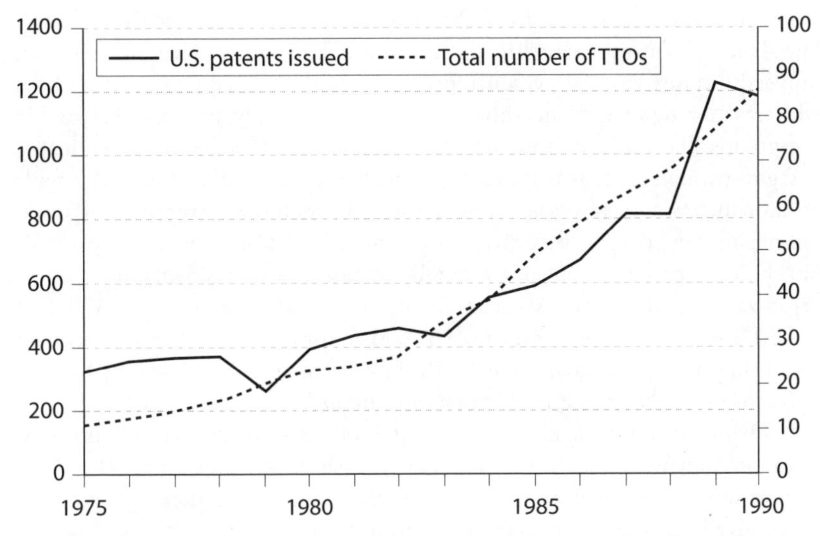

Figure 7.1. Number of U.S. patents issued to and technology transfer offices at U.S. universities and colleges, 1975–1990. Data from AUTM (2004:12); NSB (1996:appendix table 5-42 and 2006:appendix table 5-68).

a thousand, at which point they represented about 15% of all academic R&D spending.[10] Since UIRCs brought university and industry resources together to work on problems of common interest, they necessarily involved an awareness of the economic value of science. But because the whole point of establishing a UIRC was to organize people around problems of industrial, as well as academic, interest, this meant that substantial government and institutional funding became oriented toward such problems as well, since industry itself provided only about 31% of UIRC funding in 1990.[11]

Market Logic Elsewhere in Academic Science

In the late 1970s, policymakers were making decisions that would, intentionally or not, encourage the use of market logic in academic science, and they were doing so based on arguments about the critical economic role played by innovation. But for the most part, it was not university leaders who were making these arguments. There were exceptions to the rule that university presidents did not emphasize the economic impact of science during these years; George Low, president of Rensselaer Polytechnic Institute (RPI), comes immediately to mind. But innovation concerns were put on the national political agenda by R&D-intensive industries and promoted at the state level by groups focused on encouraging economic development, not on academic science.[12] While innovation arguments were critical to the assortment of policy decisions that allowed biotech entrepreneurship, patenting, and UIRCs to become common on university campuses, the evidence presented in the preceding chapters about who was making such claims shows that it was not usually university leadership but groups like venture capitalists, biotech startups, the electronics industry, and government officials who were arguing that certain policies were desirable because they would strengthen innovation. Universities were represented occasionally in these debates by university patent administrators or faculty-turned-biotech-entrepreneurs, but not generally by university presidents or lobbying organizations. The same Association of American Universities (AAU) that Robert Rosenzweig represented in 1985 had, in the late 1970s, been ambivalent about supporting the Bayh-Dole Act, feeling unsure that it was appropriate for universities to be systematically pursuing patents.[13]

But while university leaders were not the source of the new emphasis on innovation, they were hardly unaware that changes were taking place. The 1980s saw university administrations respond to the success of market logic on campus, as well as to policymakers' own responsiveness to innovation concerns, by increasingly moving to deploy market logic on their own, both rhetorically and through the initiation and expansion of additional market-logic practices. Some of these efforts were quite successful, and others much less so. But during the decade, as suggested by Rosenzweig's remarks, the assumption that academic science could and should be working to leverage its value in the marketplace grew much stronger.

One way this happened was that older market-oriented activities, like research parks and industrial affiliates programs, experienced a new phase of development. While many universities had planned or established research parks in the 1960s, by the early 1970s the era of research park expansion was already seen as over.[14] Few parks were established during that decade, and a 1980 study found only eleven university research parks in existence, of a total of twenty-seven founded since 1951.[15] But research parks experienced another boom in the early 1980s. Researcher Douglas Porter counted thirty-one schools either developing or planning to develop research parks in 1983, and in 1985 reported that thirty-one universities were "actively engaged in developing research parks," while another two or three dozen were in earlier stages of discussion and planning.[16] This growth continued throughout the decade, and by 1989 a representative of the Association of University-Related Research Parks stated that "of the 115 parks in existence today, over half have been created since 1985."[17]

As was the case with university-industry research centers, much of this expansion was supported by growing state and local government interest in promoting technology-based economic development. Illinois promised $10 million to purchase a building for a new biomedical research park affiliated with the University of Illinois, and the city of Chicago expected to contribute planning and infrastructure construction.[18] Connecticut spent $2 million on site improvements for a research park being developed at Yale, and New Haven created a $1 million venture capital fund for small businesses located there.[19] North Carolina invested $46 million in the Microelectronics Center of North Carolina, located in Research Triangle Park.[20] Similar investments could be found in many parts of the country.[21]

Though the long-term success of such research parks was only partial, with nearly half of the parks in existence in 1989 failing over the next two decades, Battelle Memorial Institute nonetheless found 174 university-related research parks in existence by 2007, demonstrating that the organizational form had become widespread.[22] The new wave of government support for technology-driven economic development projects doubtless helped make parks more fiscally viable than they had been for most universities in the 1960s. But it is also possible that by the 1980s other changes in university-industry relations made it easier for universities to convince industry they had something worthwhile to offer, and the relative importance of each factor is not easy to untangle.

Similarly, many universities moved to establish new industrial affiliates programs in the 1980s. A 1983 study found that well over half the programs it identified had been started since 1979, and a 1990 study determined that two-thirds of those it surveyed were created during the previous decade.[23] Since industrial affiliates programs are such an internally diverse group, few people have studied them as a specific type of activity, so it is difficult to know how many universities were establishing affiliates programs before the 1980s, or how many of those started in the 1980s survived in the long run.[24] My guess is that many did not last for long. It seems unlikely, however, that the two surveys just mentioned do not reflect an actual uptick in the creation of such programs starting in the early 1980s.

Besides implementing or expanding older market-logic practices, universities also tried creating new ones, though here they generally had less success. Many of these experiments involved biotechnology. While there had been few blockbuster university patents during the 1970s and UIRCs did not start to spread rapidly until after the decade had ended, by 1980 a small frenzy was already building around biotech startups amidst what one observer called "the enjoyable hoopla that surrounds large sums of money being put at risk."[25] After Genentech's initial public offering, UCSF's Herbert Boyer was worth more than $65 million.[26] It would have been surprising had universities *not* wanted to get a piece of this action that had, after all, been generated by university science.

Attempts to do so took two main forms. One focused on somehow trying to insert the university into the entrepreneurial activity of its faculty. The other emphasized large-scale research partnerships with multinationals interested in biotechnology. Harvard was on the cutting edge of both kinds of effort, first with a high-profile attempt to become directly involved in faculty entrepreneurship and then through its involvement in the establishment at Massachusetts General Hospital of an especially large university-industry research partnership.

Administrators at Harvard were particularly aware of the financial potential of biotech, as Biogen, founded by Harvard molecular biologist Walter Gilbert, was already worth $100 million by mid-1980.[27] In October of that year, the university, noting "the possibility of substantial financial return," announced that it was considering helping to start a biotech company itself based on the research of Mark Ptashne, another faculty member.[28] The result was a very public controversy, fanned by cover stories in both the *New York Times* and the *Washington Post*.[29] Questions were raised about pressures for secrecy, distraction from the mission of basic science, competition between the proposed firm and Harvard's departments for the best scientists, and potential favoritism for those involved with the company. As the *Times* noted, "developments [were] being watched with considerable interest at several other major universities, including Stanford, Yale, the Massachusetts Institute of Technology, and the University of California."[30] But a month later, apparently surprised by the extent of the controversy, Harvard withdrew the proposal, citing faculty opposition.[31]

Other initial attempts by universities to become directly involved in faculty entrepreneurship went further, but were not much more successful. Berkeley and Stanford were involved with the creation of Engenics, a company financed with capital from six large corporations and organized in a complex way to shield the universities from real or perceived conflicts of interest, but Engenics itself did not do particularly well.[32] Michigan State set up Neogen, a startup primarily owned by the Michigan State Research Foundation, but while Neogen achieved modest growth it was no Genentech.[33] There was even one notable disaster, as Boston University lost tens of millions of dollars on its investment in faculty-founded biotech firm Seragen.[34] Over the course of the decade, universities did work out ways of taking a limited stake in faculty entrepreneurship, most notably by licensing university-owned patents to faculty-founded startups in exchange for equity, but in general this activity did not live up to universities' initial hopes for capturing some of the returns on the emerging biotech industry.[35]

The second type of effort, involvement with large-scale university-industry research partnerships, was an attempt to connect directly with multinationals that wanted a window on developments in biotechnology. As buying a piece of a biotech startup became a more expensive way for firms to get such a window, connecting directly with academia started to seem like a smart move. Harvard, again, was a leader. In 1981, Harvard-affiliated hospital Mass General announced that German pharmaceutical firm Hoechst would be funding the establishment of a new department of molecular biology there, providing $70 million over ten years. In return for its large contribution, Hoechst would be able to send its employees to the department for research and training and would have first rights to exclusive licensing of any patents, though Mass General would own them. The department itself would report to a scientific advisory committee made up of two representatives of Mass General, two from Hoechst, and two others.[36] Again, the deal, which dwarfed previous university-industry partnerships, drew negative attention, this time notably in the form of hearings held by the House Committee on Science and Technology's Subcommittee on Investigations and Oversight.[37]

While other university-industry partnerships were not nearly this large, there were perhaps a dozen multiyear, multimillion-dollar industry grants to support academic biotech research between 1981 and 1983 at schools like Yale, Rockefeller, the University of California, MIT, Johns Hopkins, Cornell, and the University of Maryland.[38] Some of these, including the Hoechst–Mass General partnership, emerged out of preexisting relations between a specific faculty member and a firm.[39] Others, however, were initiated by university leaders. Monsanto and Washington University Medical School, for example, negotiated a $23.5 million contract in 1982 to help Monsanto expand its capacity in biomedical research. Though the two organizations were geographically close, they did not have strong preexisting ties.[40]

This spate of major partnerships, however, also turned out to be a passing phenomenon. As early as 1982, the apparently ubiquitous Robert Rosenzweig (then vice president for public affairs at Stanford) was noting that "very few people think that the very large and highly publicized contracts are likely to be duplicated very widely or become anything like the norm," and this did indeed prove to be the case.[41] While these agreements were short-run bonanzas for the universities who secured them, by 1985 *Science* was observing that "despite the enthusiasm of three to four years ago for joint research ventures between industry and academia, relatively few such arrangements materialized on a large scale."[42] Thus while the very visible rewards of biotech entrepreneurship encouraged university administrations to try to extend market logic in an effort to secure more resources for the institution as a whole, that turned out to be harder to do than many anticipated.

During the 1980s, then, the expansion and extension of market logic throughout academic science was significant, but uneven. The practices of biotech entrepreneurship, university patenting, and UIRCs continued to expand and develop. Older activities like research parks and industrial affiliates programs experienced a new wave of growth, though they did not always thrive. And several experiments with new activities, like direct university investment in startups and large-scale partnerships with industry, made some progress but on balance were less successful. But as market logic, originally deployed by individual faculty and administrators in response to specific opportunities, became visibly successful, administrations increasingly began using it strategically in an effort to harness its potential for the entire university. This took place partially through the kind of experimentation with new activities just described. But it also was reflected in the changing arguments universities used when making their case for the value of academic science to policymakers.

University Administrators and the Rhetoric of Innovation

By 1970, the postwar consensus between academic science and the federal government was already breaking down. But universities were slow to figure out how they should respond in order to regain policymakers' support. When testifying to Congress, for example, university presidents frequently did not bother to explain *why* academic science was worth funding, focusing instead on the terrible damage (as they saw it) that was being done to the academic enterprise by budget reductions.[43] This often involved hyperbole, as when one typical university leader said, "The scientific and educational structure on which America's future technical competence depends is in real and desperate jeopardy. And what I refer to is not a distant fear; collapse is already underway."[44]

When university representatives did specify why the federal government should support them, a couple of tactics were common. One was to argue that science was valuable for its own sake, rather than specifically as a means to economic (or other) ends. Thus in 1970 James Killian, chairman of the board of MIT, argued before Congress that

> there is urgent need for a reaffirmation by our national and institutional leaders of these values that have undergirded the high achievements and high purposes of our society. We must reaffirm those precious qualities of mind which lead man to scientific accomplishment—insatiable curiosity, the innate desire to explore, to understand and to create, and the unalterable capacity for wonder. In the end these qualities and values must be implicit in our national consensus and in all policies and arrangements designed to enable science to flourish and to serve man humanely.[45]

Another approach was emphasizing the role of science in meeting "national needs," a term that encapsulated everything from strengthening defense to improving health to solving social problems. But while administrators frequently appealed to national needs, they were often vague about the details of how, exactly, academic science was going to meet them.[46]

Yet by the early 1970s, it was becoming increasingly clear that not only did universities need explicit justifications for their ongoing support, but also that the kinds of arguments they had been using were no longer very effective. As one observer of the scientific community commented in 1973, "Crying in front of a Congressman is like bleeding in front of a shark. . . . It's self-defeating."[47] Another pointed out universities' strategic error in not focusing more explicitly on the contributions of academic science, noting that "relying purely on altruistic rationales for the financial support of science and technology would result in support that is comparable to what other endeavors of our Western cultural heritage are receiving, such as art, music, or philosophy."[48]

During the mid-to-late 1970s, policy interest in the economic role of technological innovation developed and strengthened, and by 1978 innovation arguments were clearly helping to shape policy decisions. Economists and industry leaders were the ones at the forefront in promoting the importance of innovation. But increasingly, particularly as the political effectiveness of innovation rhetoric became evident, university leaders also adopted the language of innovation to explain what academic science had to offer their states and the nation.

By the end of the 1970s, one still sometimes saw the language of national needs being used, as when University of California president David Saxon emphasized to Congress that his goal was "to secure for the people of the country the best possible responses to national needs for energy, for defense, for health, for economic progress, and for other major concerns."[49] But when Tulane president Sheldon Hackney testified in support of NSF in 1979, he took a different approach, explaining that "basic research is the spur to increased productivity and technological processes. It is a major contributor to our economic growth. Basic research, we believe, is an essential investment if we are going to retain our world markets and achieve continued growth without excessive inflation."[50]

Similarly, when Harvard proposed in 1980 that it help start a biotech company, it emphasized to the larger public that "there is widespread concern today over the flagging rate of economic growth and productivity in the country. . . . By involving the University in the technology transfer process, we believe that Harvard might contribute more effectively to these efforts and thereby benefit the public."[51] By the following year, the startup proposal had been abandoned, but president Derek Bok was reiterating the role of academic science in solving the "fatigue and sclerosis" and "surprising lag in productivity" of the American economy in *Harvard Magazine*.[52] MIT president Paul Gray picked up the theme that same year when he testified to Congress on behalf of the AAU in favor of an R&D tax credit for industry, noting that "as we look about us today we see that American industry faces a severe crisis brought about by rising costs, particularly with respect to energy; diminishing resources; declining productivity; and growing international competition," and emphasizing the need for university-industry cooperation in solving these problems.[53]

During the early 1980s, as market-oriented practices were taking off on campuses, this rhetoric became very common among university leaders. A dean at the University of Wisconsin, defending recent developments in university-industry relations, argued that "if there is a ferment, it is the expectations of our States and our Government and our industries that each wants and needs help to survive in a world economy."[54] The president of Dartmouth claimed that "the marriage [of business and universities] is fundamental to keeping U.S. companies competitive."[55] The chairman of the chemistry department at the University of Washington tied a proposed new instrumentation program at NSF to concerns about innovation and the economy:

> The immediate consequences of [inadequate instrumentation] is a decrease in the innovative capacity of industry. I think that is a very important consideration, because the economy is a concern for all of us, and the corporate members of CCR [the Council for Chemical Research, an industry consortium] have felt very strongly—strongly enough to create CCR—that this is becoming a serious problem in the country.[56]

And Robert Sproull, president of the University of Rochester and representative of the AAU, emphasized to Congress the "Federal Government responsibility . . . to maintain the basic research component, to help the universities work with industry, to bring on a new generation of young people who can participate strongly in raising the productivity of the country, to develop whole new industries, and to assure the basic economic strength of the country."[57]

Such arguments about the critical economic role of technological innovation had originated with other groups and initially focused on industrial, not academic, innovation. But universities picked up the language and ran with it, and by the mid-1980s university leaders had embraced these arguments wholeheartedly. They seemed to believe what they were saying, too. In 1986, the National Governors Association surveyed leaders of states, businesses, and universities about the role of academic science in economic development. A full 67% of university leaders thought that cooperative university-industry research was "critical" to U.S. economic competitiveness, while only 45% of business leaders did.[58] In fact, by the end of the decade universities had moved so far toward portraying themselves as economic engines that some industry leaders had begun to grumble that universities "exaggerate[d] their role in stimulating commercial innovations," and that "the limited role of universities in innovation has not been recognized."[59] But whatever the reality of universities' claims that their science drove American innovation, the rhetoric had become widespread.

Science Logic and Market Logic: An Uneasy Coexistence

By the second half of the 1980s, then, market logic had come to play a much larger role in academic science than it had a decade before. It was no longer unusual or, for most observers, problematic to think of science in terms of its economic value. Instead, people in various parts of the university had started to treat academic science as if its economic impact were one of its most important contributions. This was reflected both in the practices scientists and administrators engaged in, as they became more actively entrepreneurial, more collaborative with industry, and more interested in monetizing the results of scientific research, and in how they justified financial support for academic science to their government patrons.

To some extent the expansion of market logic displaced the use of science logic. The mission of technology transfer implied that science was *not* valuable for its own sake, or at least not nearly as valuable as it would be if it were applied in the outside world. And when university presidents argued their case to Congress in terms of the economic contribution of academic science, this replaced earlier claims that the pursuit of knowledge itself was a value worthy of generous support, or that universities met "national needs" of one sort or another.

But rather than saying that market logic replaced the logic of science, it would be more accurate to say that as market logic strengthened within the university, it became a more visible and legitimate alternative to the logic of science, coming to coexist uneasily with it rather than displace it. Vannevar Bush's argument that science should be done without regard to its practical value—that "applied science drives out pure"—became less widely heard, and while some faculty continued to disdain involvement with the commercialization of science, such views became less common.

Yet other elements of the logic of science remained strong. Academics continued to value scientifically interesting work, even when it had no obvious practical implications. Peer-reviewed publications remained the gold standard of scientific research, and while patents might have become secondary indicators of research productivity, they certainly did not supplant purely academic work. Externally, universities might justify themselves as economic engines. Internally, however, many scientists continued to be motivated, in Merton's terms, by the joy of discovery and the desire for the recognition of their peers, even as more of them became interested in pursuing the commercial implications of their work as well.[60]

Moreover, while policy decisions had changed the environment of academic science in ways that encouraged the spread of market-logic practices, the limits to the growth of market-logic experiments that were visible in the 1950s and 1960s did not disappear entirely during the 1970s and 1980s. The cultures of industrial science and academic science moved a bit closer to one another, but they were still quite different.[61] The advances of biotechnology created commercial opportunities in new fields of science, but not every field proved so easy to connect to the market. And government policies subsidized collaboration with industry and strengthened universities' intellectual property rights, but the old challenge of balancing the long-term, theoretical orientation of academic science with the short-term, practical perspective of commercial development continued to be challenging. Academic science did move toward the market. But it could only move so far.

CHAPTER 8

Conclusion

THIS BOOK BEGAN WITH A PUZZLE. In 1961, the governor of Illinois asked the University of Illinois to consider how it might strengthen its contribution to the state's economy. The university was not averse to playing an economic role. But its response—a vague committee report prescribing few real actions and presenting no strong vision of how to achieve the governor's goals—reflected the difficulty the university had in thinking about its role as an economic actor. By 1999, though, when the university faced a similar request, its response was radically different. It leapt into action, creating and expanding initiatives designed to maximize the economic impact of its scientific and technological innovations. What changed in the intervening decades that could explain this shift in behavior, itself part of a larger evolution of the relationship between academic science and the market?

I have argued that government decisions were the most important driver of this change, and that those decisions were made because a new way of thinking became politically important. In the late 1970s, the idea that technological innovation drives economic growth became increasingly influential among policymakers, giving a boost to policy proposals that could be framed as strengthening innovation. While academics had always experimented with activities that were oriented toward the market, such experiments had historically remained relatively local and small in scale. The policies that were compatible with innovation claims, however, collectively tended to encourage activities that focused on the specifically economic value of academic science. They did this in a variety of ways: sometimes by making the products of science more valuable (as the *Chakrabarty* decision and the creation of the Court of Appeals for the Federal Circuit [CAFC] did), sometimes by making it easier for universities to monetize their science (as Bayh-Dole did), and sometimes by subsidizing the science that industry might be interested in (as National Science Foundation [NSF] and state support for university-industry research centers [UIRCs] did). As the political effectiveness of innovation arguments became clear and market-oriented practices became visibly successful, more people in universities began drawing on market logic both as a basis for new activities and as a justification for existing ones. Academic science took on a new role, not just as a creator of knowledge or even a resource for industry, but as an economic engine.

This final chapter will reexamine the evidence for that argument and compare the explanation I propose with alternative possibilities. Then I will take a step back to consider some broader implications of the story I tell about the transformation of academic science, both for how we understand the changing role of the market in our society and for how we think about the university today.

How Academic Science Became an Economic Engine: Considering the Evidence

The starting point of this project was a comparison of the development of three specific practices in academic science that reflect a market orientation: biotech entrepreneurship, university patenting, and university-industry research centers. Looking at the origins and trajectories of these three should show what common factors, if any, led to their growth and spread. Any commonalities should help explain why academic science made its move toward the market at the time that it did. The first step toward an explanation, then, was identifying the historically specific reasons each practice became successful. To simplify comparison, I grouped these into necessary conditions and facilitating conditions. Of course, making such a distinction is a judgment call, not a science, but it was nonetheless useful to try to identify which elements were relatively more or less important in driving the development of different practices, even if dividing them into two groups was somewhat arbitrary. Table 6.2, on page 144, summarizes these observations.

Initially, the diversity of contributing factors stood out more than their commonalities. In the biotech case, the necessary conditions included scientific breakthroughs, the fact that industrially relevant expertise could be found only in universities, the organizational model of Genentech, and a generous venture capital environment shaped by changes in tax and pension policy. For patenting, the most important factors included the efforts of a network of government administrators to encourage the practice, the passage of the Bayh-Dole Act, and the emergence of the biotechnology industry. In the UIRC case, the most critical elements were NSF's Industry/University Cooperative Research Center (I/UCRC) program and state funding for UIRCs. While it was evident that government actions played an important role in the development of each practice, it was less obvious that policy decisions were absolutely critical, particularly in the biotech case.

A consideration of the *histories* of each of these cases, however, reinforced the key role played by government decisions. By the late 1970s, one could find people experimenting with each of these practices in academic science, but it was far from clear that any of them was about to become widespread. On the contrary, one could identify specific barriers that appeared likely to limit their development. For biotech entrepreneurship, as late as November 1977 most observers thought that Congress was about to restrict recombinant DNA (rDNA) research, and even after that became less likely, biotech startups were still struggling to raise funding in a decidedly chilly financial environment. For patenting, it was becoming evident that no more federal agencies were likely to adopt institutional patent agreements, and that without statutory support, universities' ability to patent would remain fragile, as Joseph Califano's abrupt reversal of National Institutes of Health (NIH) patent policy in 1977 made clear. And the handful of UIRCs that were established prior to 1980 were either struggling to maintain industry support, dependent on government support, having difficulty finding common ground between academia and industry, or all three.

Yet within a few years—by 1981 for biotech and patenting, and perhaps 1983 for UIRCs—the tide had turned, and while the three practices were not fully institutionalized, the most significant barriers to their development had been removed and the activities were spreading rapidly. In each case, it is hard to imagine how the practice could have taken off in the absence of key policy decisions. Even when the critical environmental change was only partially the result of government action, as when a wave of venture capital became available starting in late 1978, government policies appear to have been necessary for the creation of the favorable conditions.

But recognizing that policy decisions played an important role, and even recognizing that those decisions were made within a relatively narrow band of time, means little if the actions taken shared nothing but their government origins. And on the surface, policies as diverse as a regulation governing how pension funds could be invested, the creation of a special court to deal with patents, and state decisions to fund university-industry collaboration seem minimally—if at all—related.

A closer look at the histories of these policy decisions, however, showed that they did have something in common: they were each framed in terms of the economic importance of innovation, a frame that was newly and powerfully salient in the late-1970s political climate. In some cases, the decisions were a direct result of emerging political interest in strengthening innovation. NSF, for example, initiated its I/UCRC program to forestall Congress from requiring that it make grants available to industry as well as universities, which it appeared Congress might do because of concern with industrial innovation. And as states began adopting R&D-driven economic development strategies, they started funding UIRCs as part of that effort. In other cases, though, the policies in question had been promoted unsuccessfully in the past but were now given a political boost by being portrayed as helpful to innovation and thus the economy. Encouraging university patenting and creating a specialized patent court were both actions that specific groups had been promoting for years, but the new attitude toward innovation turned the tide in making them more broadly acceptable.

Of course, claims about innovation were not the only political factor leading to any of these policies. But of the ten decisions I examine, innovation arguments appear to have played a critical role in six.[1] In two more, the Employee Retirement Income Security Act (ERISA) clarification and the *Chakrabarty* decision, they were quite visible, but I could not find enough evidence to judge one way or the other their political significance. In one case, the capital gains tax cut, innovation arguments were used and were clearly helpful, but it seems possible—though not certain—that legislation might have passed even without the availability of the innovation frame. And in the one policy decision that predated the mid-1970s, that of federal administrators to create institutional patent agreements (IPAs), innovation arguments were not used, though supporters of IPAs would later adopt such arguments as they began working for the passage of Bayh-Dole.

This shift in the policy environment certainly did not mean that every proposal that could be framed in terms of its contributions to innovation would be successful. And some of the decisions examined here might have been made even if concern with innovation had not become widespread. Moreover, these innovation-oriented policy decisions were politically diverse and reflected a variety of philosophies about the appropriate economic role of government, from interventionist (the UIRC programs) to hands-off (the capital gains tax cut and Bayh-Dole). What they shared, however, was a focus on the economic value of science and technology, not its value as knowledge or even as a means to solve other social problems. That is, by definition innovation arguments were grounded in market logic. And so regardless of the political origins of these policy decisions or whether they were intended to push academic science toward the market, their collective effect was to encourage activity that emphasized science's economic contributions.

One final comparison reinforces the argument that government decisions made in a particular policy context were key to the changes that took place in academic science. In the 1950s and 1960s, one could find academics experimenting with market logic in universities, establishing industrial affiliates programs, industrial extension offices, and research parks, but while these activities spread modestly, none became very deeply rooted in this era. The most significant reason for this was financial: all of these practices had trouble securing the material resources needed to reproduce themselves and thrive in the long run. In a different policy environment, one could imagine forms of government intervention that might have made such activities work. Tax credits for companies participating in industrial affiliates programs or greater federal support for industrial extension could have helped these activities to expand further, for example. And indeed, in the 1980s, when interest in using science to drive economic development had become pervasive, government support did contribute to a second and much larger wave of growth for research parks.

But in the 1960s, policymakers did not pay much attention to the economic impact of science and were not creating policies with the intent of leveraging that impact. So while the limits encountered by the market-logic experiments of that era were not so different from those encountered by the experiments of the 1970s, government did not act to remove those limits, as it would a decade later. And to make the counterfactual comparison, if one imagines that biotech entrepreneurship, university patenting, or UIRCs had reached a critical moment in their development in the 1950s or 1960s, before innovation arguments had become influential, it is hard to imagine government taking the actions that, in reality, created such a favorable environment for their development in the late 1970s and early 1980s.

Reconsidering Alternative Arguments

With this evidence in mind, I will now revisit other possible explanations for academic science's move toward the market and consider the extent to which they are consistent with the historical record. While there are elements of truth in each of these explanations, none fits the overall story as well as the argument just presented.

Government Cut Resources, so Universities Turned toward the Market

One common assumption is that the commercialization of academic science was the direct result of government cutbacks. After federal funding for academic R&D peaked in 1968 and failed to recover over the next several years, universities, accustomed to rapid growth, began to look elsewhere for support. They turned to industry as a new source of funding and began trying to make money through activities like the patenting and licensing of their research.

The kernel of truth here is that government cutbacks *were* painful for academic science, and *did* make universities more open to activities outside their comfort zone. But if universities looked to the market primarily because of stagnating federal support, we would expect to see such activities initiated by those particularly affected by government cutbacks, or by upper-level administrators concerned with their institution's overall health.

This is not what happened, however. University leaders were relative latecomers to market logic, tending to adopt it only after it had proven successful or lucrative elsewhere within the university, or after its political appeal had become obvious. Biotech entrepreneurship was first initiated by venture capitalists looking for faculty partners and then, once the practice had become more familiar, by faculty themselves. Only once the revenue potential of biotech had become very clear did university administrations begin trying to secure a piece of it for their institutions. University patenting *was* driven by administrators, but by mid-level research administrators, not by heads of institutions. It was only after Bayh-Dole that presidents and provosts widely became interested in expanding patenting efforts. And with a few exceptions, early UIRCs were initiated by faculty and industry representatives, not by university administrations.[2] It was not until UIRCs had already begun to spread that many universities began to lobby actively for state programs to support them.

Furthermore, the market-oriented practices that began to take off in the late 1970s did not originate in the parts of academic science hardest hit by federal cutbacks. When Bruce Smith and Joseph Karlesky made their comprehensive survey of academic science in 1977, just as the period of federal retrenchment was ending, they found that funding cuts were having a significant impact on physics and many parts of chemistry, and to a lesser extent mathematics and some fields of engineering. But it was not in these areas of belt-tightening that market-logic activities were being initiated. The life sciences, where biotech entrepreneurship was taking place, were coming off a period of "dramatic growth," not cutbacks, and federal funding for rDNA research in particular was increasing exponentially.[3] And while UIRCs were formed in a variety of fields, microelectronics and materials science were the most commonly represented (see table 6.1). These were not areas that saw large reductions in federal support during the 1970s.[4] So while tighter budgets may have made universities more open to unconventional innovations in this period, these market-logic practices were not initiated because other funding sources dried up.

Industry Looked to Universities to Replace Its Own Basic Research

A second possible explanation would emphasize the role of industry in pulling universities toward the market. Firms that were reducing internal spending on R&D during the 1970s thought they could replace expensive company labs with government-subsidized academic science, and so they began seeking out collaborations with universities.

There is some limited truth to this argument as well. Certainly, industry R&D spending stagnated during the 1970s. In real terms, industry spending on basic research peaked in 1966 and had decreased 29% by 1975, and industry spending on applied research and development remained essentially flat during this period.[5] In the 1970s, representatives of R&D-intensive industries were becoming increasingly concerned about the state of industrial innovation, and by the second half of the decade they were pushing hard for Washington to pay attention to the issue as well. And one result was the formation of groups focused on strengthening university-industry relations, like the Business-Higher Education Forum and the National Commission on Research, both of which were established in 1978.[6]

But while industry was paying some attention to university collaboration as a means to solve its innovation problems, closer relations with academic science were pretty far down the industrial agenda. The industry-supported Domestic Policy Review for Industrial Innovation focused on areas like patent policy (though not university patent policy), antitrust policy, government regulation, capital formation, and federal procurement.[7] University relations were not entirely absent from the discussion, but they played a small role. Even an industry panel convened specifically to examine NSF-industry relations emphasized that while it would be beneficial for the agency to encourage university-industry collaboration, government efforts "to decrease current disincentives and to increase direct incentives"—the panel referred here to changes in federal regulations, antitrust laws, patent laws, tax rules and accounting practices—"far outweigh[ed]" the importance of strengthening ties with universities.[8]

On the university side, industry interest in academia as a new, cheap source of R&D does not seem to have played a significant role in the expansion of biotech entrepreneurship, university patenting, or UIRCs. In the biotech case, existing pharmaceutical and chemical companies were notably slow to appreciate and act on the new scientific breakthroughs being made in universities, which partly accounts for why the technology was developed in startup companies first. In the case of patenting, industry was hardly knocking down the door to gain access to faculty inventions. On the contrary, Stanford's success at licensing faculty inventions has often been attributed to its adoption of a "marketing" model of technology transfer, where the focus was on promoting the potential of university inventions to relatively indifferent firms.[9] Similarly, during this era UIRCs were more frequently started when university scientists approached industry counterparts than the reverse, and centers had to work hard to maintain industry support, particularly if they were not subsidized by government.[10] So while industry R&D cutbacks may have increased firms' interest in collaborating with universities to some extent, this renewed interest does not appear to have been the main driver of the expansion of market-logic practices in academic science.

The Advent of Biotech Gave Academic Science Something Valuable to Sell

A third story would attribute the changes in academic science to the invention of biotechnology. The practical, and potentially valuable, implications of scientific breakthroughs in the biosciences in the 1970s created large incentives for academics to become involved in commercializing their research. Universities' shift toward the market was thus the almost-inevitable consequence of a specific set of scientific advances.

This is a strong argument. The discoveries that led to biotechnology played a big role in the rise of market logic in academic science. Biotech entrepreneurship obviously would not have developed without them, and many of universities' most lucrative patents in the 1980s and 1990s were based on biotechnology and its products. But while advances in the biosciences clearly had practical implications, they are not a sufficient explanation for the changes that took place in academic science. Practical implications can be realized in a variety of ways, and not every potential path that biotechnology could have taken would have created the same financial incentives for academics to become involved in the commercialization process.

Much of the value of biotech, for example, depended on its techniques and products being patentable, which in turn depended on government decisions to expand the scope and strength of intellectual property rights in the early 1980s. Furthermore, if venture capital had remained scarce in the late 1970s and early 1980s, it is hard to see how biotech could have developed as an independent industrial sector.[11] In Britain, which had scientific leadership but much less venture capital, the biotech sector remained stunted in comparison to the one that developed in the United States. While biotechnology doubtless would have reached the market eventually even if venture capital had remained unavailable in the United States as well, alternative paths to commercialization, like the slower development of biotechnology in large multinationals, seem much less likely to have involved academic scientists in the integral, entrepreneurial role that they ended up taking.

Yet even if the advent of biotech was not a sufficient condition for the expansion of market logic in academic science, could it have been a necessary condition? It seems likely that market logic would have been limited somewhat in the absence of biotechnology. But while no biotechnology would have meant no biotech entrepreneurship, its absence would not have stopped the development of other market-oriented practices. University patenting might not have expanded quite as rapidly as it actually did, but patenting was already on a growth trajectory by the time the first biotech patent was issued in 1980, and there is no reason to think that it wouldn't have kept growing even without biotech. There were other lucrative university inventions not based on biotechnology that still could have tempted universities into patenting. The development of nonbiotech chemotherapy drugs cisplatin and carboplatin at Michigan State in the late 1970s, for example, earned $160 million for the university in the 1980s and 1990s.[12] Between examples like this and the impetus of the Bayh-Dole Act, patenting still would have appeared attractive to pursue even in the absence of biotechnology.

Beyond patenting, the absence of biotech seems even less likely to have had a significant impact on the spread of market-oriented activities. UIRCs were not typically located in biotech disciplines at all, particularly during the late 1970s and early 1980s. NSF's I/UCRC program, for example, did not fund a biotech center till 1985, at which point it had already supported twenty centers in other fields.[13] Nor did research parks, which experienced a period of rapid expansion in the 1980s, tend to emphasize biotechnology.[14] Biotechnology played an important and catalytic role in the expansion of market logic in academic science. But it seems likely that market logic would have expanded substantially in universities even in the absence of the biotech breakthroughs, and it seems unlikely that it would have had the effects on universities that it did without significant government intervention.

What about Legitimacy?

I approach the question of why market logic gained strength in academic science by comparing the development of three practices that reflect that logic, and I emphasize that changes in resource availability and, secondarily, the regulatory environment made that strengthening possible. But one of the basic assumptions of institutionalism is that existing institutional arrangements constrain action in part by establishing norms about what kind of behavior is and is not appropriate. Behavior that does not conform with those norms is seen as illegitimate, which makes it hard or impossible to sustain.

Clearly academic science's move toward the market was controversial when it began and remains somewhat controversial to the present. For the practices of biotech entrepreneurship, university patenting, and UIRCs to spread successfully and move toward institutionalization, they, and the market logic they were grounded in, needed to overcome perceptions of illegitimacy. But the story I have presented deemphasizes the role of legitimacy relative to resource availability in explaining why market-logic practices gained ground. Am I missing something here by minimizing illegitimacy as a barrier to the expansion of market-logic practices, either in the 1950s and 1960s or the 1970s and 1980s?

The process of overcoming illegitimacy may sometimes be central to explaining how a particular logic gains strength in a field. But in this specific case, I simply did not find evidence that the illegitimacy of market-logic practices was a significant barrier to their spread. Some people did resist market logic or find it problematic during each of these decades. But, as chapter 2 suggests, it was not as strongly opposed in the 1950s and 1960s as one might imagine. The University of Illinois committee's 1962 survey of universities' level of interest in industry partnership showed a level of enthusiasm that surprised even the committee members. Similarly, Kleinman, Habinek, and Vallas's recent survey of higher education publications, which begins in 1960, found market language present in the early years as well as later ones.[15] Market logic may have been less legitimate than the logic of science in these decades, but it was not rejected entirely.

If overcoming a lack of legitimacy were critical to explaining why market logic gained ground in academic science when it did, one would expect to see that illegitimacy created problems for the market-logic experiments of the 1950s and 1960s. But I did not find evidence that industrial affiliates programs, research parks, or industrial extension programs failed to thrive in this period because they were seen as illegitimate. If anything, the successful instances of such programs were held up as models for other universities to emulate before resource limitations put a halt to their spread. And while the market-logic practices that began to take off in the late 1970s certainly encountered resistance from those who disapproved of them—the hostile reaction of many of Herbert Boyer's UCSF colleagues to his founding of Genentech comes to mind—ultimately such reactions do not appear to have slowed their development very much.

Indeed, what is surprising is how rapidly the new practices spread *despite* outcries about the commercialization of the university. Maybe this is because market logic was never all that illegitimate in academic science. Maybe it was because the influx of resources for market-logic practices was so great that it simply overwhelmed concerns about their legitimacy. Either way, while figuring out how logics gain legitimacy is doubtless critical to a full understanding of how they gain strength in fields more generally, an increase in legitimacy does not appear to have been the factor that caused market-logic practices to spread in academic science at the moment that they did.

Speaking to Larger Conversations

The main goal of this project has simply been to understand empirically why academic science made its move toward the market. Academic science is an important social domain that has changed a great deal in the last few decades, and people continue to debate the meaning of those changes and how best to manage them. So understanding why those changes occurred in the first place seemed like a worthwhile endeavor.

But I also became interested in this topic because it speaks to a larger question—the question of how we decide what role markets and market ideals will play in our society. How do we decide when society is best served by relying on individual self-interest and exchange to allocate scarce resources efficiently, and when other means of organizing human activity are better, fairer, or more appropriate? It is possible to read the entire history of the industrial era as a story about the expansion of markets, and certainly that expansion has coincided with a massive increase in the average standard of living. But the last thirty years in particular have been marked by the extension of markets into more and more realms of life where they once saw little play, a development that has had negative as well as positive consequences. Looking at what led this to happen in one domain might, I hoped, shed some light on a broader trend. In this final section, I turn to some of these larger implications.

How Institutional Logics Gain Strength

At the most abstract level, this study tries to explain how institutional logics gain strength in fields. The empirical trend I just described—of the spread of market ideals into more domains of social life—can be recast as a question of why one institutional logic, the logic of the market, has become stronger relative to other institutional logics in a variety of fields. Academic science is one field where this shift has occurred, as market logic has become more common and the logic of science has, by comparison, weakened.

Research on how institutional logics shift within fields has been moving in directions similar to the one I take here. A lot of work on institutional change has, with good reason, focused on intentional efforts, either by institutional entrepreneurs or social-movement-like forms of collective action, to destabilize existing institutional arrangements and promote alternatives.[16] But some authors have criticized the "'hero' imagery" that can go along with institutional entrepreneurship explanations and worried that the institutional entrepreneur is being invoked "as a deus ex machina."[17] Such scholars have called for a more distributed, less heroic notion of institutional entrepreneurship, as well as greater attention to the coexistence of multiple logics in a field.[18] Others have reminded us that institutional logics do not exist only at the level of the field, but must be instantiated in specific practices, and have suggested a focus on the role of practice variation in creating institutional change.[19] These observations are consistent with studies that have found institutional change emerging not only from the top down but also from the bottom up, as individuals work "under the radar," rather than at the field level, to promote it.[20]

This book builds on such work. I start with the assumption that within a field, one can always find people experimenting with new practices as they pursue their goals. Drawing on Friedland and Alford's observation that society makes multiple institutional logics available for individuals to use, I assume that while most of these innovations will use whatever logic is strong within their field, some will be grounded in other socially available logics.[21] While the bulk of such innovations will remain local, or spread in a limited way, a few will disseminate widely and even become institutionalized practices. The question is, under what circumstances do practices based on a non-dominant logic begin to grow and spread?

Institutions, by definition, constrain behavior. If one institutional logic is dominant within a field, one would expect practices based on other logics to encounter challenges—to be seen as illegitimate, or even be prohibited by organizations within the field or by the state. One would imagine that a person innovating with an alternative logic might experience disapproval, or professional repercussions, or simply have trouble convincing other people to participate in or adopt the new practice.

What the story of academic science suggests, however, is three things. First, it serves as a reminder that reproducing and institutionalizing a new practice requires material resources as well as sufficient legitimacy. Innovations that cannot gain enough material support to sustain themselves will not persist, no matter how consistent they are with the dominant institutional logic. On the flip side, practices based on alternative logics that are only mildly or moderately illegitimate may begin to thrive if the resource environment changes in ways that favor them. While market-logic innovations like industrial affiliates programs and research parks gained only modest traction in the 1950s and 1960s, their 1970s counterparts grew rapidly after new resources to support them became available. This observation is consistent with Friedland and Alford's emphasis on institutional orders being material as well as symbolic, but the importance of resources is often overlooked in favor of an emphasis on the normative, cognitive, and regulatory effects of institutions.[22]

Second, it demonstrates that in the right resource environment, practices based on a nondominant logic can spread even in the absence of intentional efforts to promote them. Although I thought at the outset that the changes in academic science might be driven by a field-level project of institutional entrepreneurship, that turned out not to be the case. Even the individual practices I looked at did not show consistent evidence of entrepreneurial efforts to advance them. Some did. University patenting, for example, was actively promoted by NIH's Norman Latker and his colleagues. But others did not. Biotech entrepreneurship did not spread because someone evangelized on its behalf. It took off because a few individuals who experimented with the practice were extraordinarily successful and others decided to copy them. This diversity reinforces the point that while institutional entrepreneurship and social movement dynamics are undoubtedly important, and may sometimes be decisive, in instigating institutional change, they are not the only thing that can drive the spread of a new institutional logic.

Finally, it turns our attention back to the relationship between fields, not only to dynamics within fields. The resource environment did not change in ways that favored market-logic practices for completely arbitrary reasons. It changed because policymakers decided that they needed to strengthen technological innovation in the hope of improving the U.S. economy. This change was not specifically intended to transform the field of academic science, but it had that effect.[23] The effect was so significant partly because academic science is highly dependent on government for resources. But it was also significant because government has a unique capacity to create the rules that structure markets, a point I turn to in the next section.

Arguing that a change in one field is an unintended consequence of a change in another field is frustrating in a way. It implies that there are limits to our potential ability to predict or control the outcomes of our actions, which is often a hope, at least in the background, of social science. The social world is complex, and perhaps that hope is misguided. On the other hand, though, there is still the possibility that we can learn, even from the unintended consequences of past actions, lessons that make us act more thoughtfully in the future.

Government and the Market for Academic Science

As I use the concept, market logic in academic science involves treating science as an activity that is worthwhile because it, or what it produces, has specifically economic value. One can push this definition a step further, though, by actually thinking of academic science as constituting a sort of market, if a market that is far from perfectly competitive. Academics "sell" science, and industry representatives "buy" it, by licensing inventions, funding research projects, and supporting university-industry research centers.

Economic sociologists often talk about the embeddedness of markets, meaning that markets are nested within other sets of social relations that set the rules of those markets and shape the behavior of individuals participating in them.[24] One of the most important ways that markets are embedded is within states, which create rules governing what can be bought and sold and under what conditions. Shifting momentarily from considering how government action strengthened market *logic* to considering how it created an actual *market* can shed some light on both the question of how governments shape markets and the limits of their capacity to do so. It also suggests a possible explanation for why market logic apparently plateaued in academic science around the year 2000.

Universities have long been interested in realizing the economic value of their science. Fifty years ago, universities were trying to bring in revenues by establishing research parks.[25] *Ninety* years ago, universities were trying to convince industry that investing in academic science would pay off, as Roger Geiger and others have detailed.[26] Historically, though, these efforts had limited success. While the culture gap between academia and industry was always a challenge to manage, the larger problem was that the practical benefits of academic science were too unpredictable and the payoff period too long for it to make sense for industry to purchase academic science in the hopes of getting a financial return. In the postwar decades, this meant that universities struggled to sell companies on the idea that they should locate in research parks, or that they should pay $10,000 a year for privileged access to the latest research.

In the late 1970s and early 1980s, government changed the rules in ways that expanded this very limited market for academic science. It did this in at least three ways. Some policy decisions made the products of science more valuable for universities. The creation of the Court of Appeals for the Federal Circuit strengthened intellectual property rights, and decisions like *Chakrabarty* made more research results patentable. Other policy decisions removed restrictions on the selling of science. The Bayh-Dole Act, for example, gave universities the clear right to patent and license government-funded inventions, which they didn't have before. And still other policy decisions subsidized the kind of science that industry was interested in, making it cheaper for industry to buy, as when state governments and the National Science Foundation channeled a lot of money into industrially relevant research.

Even policy decisions less obviously related to the market for academic science can be seen in terms of government changing the way that market operates. In 1983, Stanford president Donald Kennedy noted that

> something very interesting is happening in the industrial sector . . . ; that is a new style of capitalization of high technology ventures. The new tax law changes four or five years ago have spawned a variety of new, high technology companies in which rapid and dramatic changes of value have been associated with the early possession of an idea.
>
> When that kind of financial incentive exists, you are going to perceive a migration of corporate interest to the earliest stages of this trajectory of innovation, because it is perceived that the great changes in the value of a corporate venture can take place if they are seen to possess important ideas.[27]

Kennedy was essentially arguing here that changed tax laws led to a perceived increase in the value of ideas, which in turn expanded the market for academic science.

Thinking of university-industry relations as constituting a market embedded in government rules can help to make sense of more recent developments. By the turn of the century, just as many observers had started to think that market logic might expand indefinitely in academic science, two indicators started to suggest that a peak had been reached.

First, the fraction of university R&D spending provided by industry, which had increased every year for several decades, suddenly began to decline. It dipped from 7.4% in 1988 to 5.1% in 2004, the lowest it had been since 1982. Real dollars spent by industry on academic R&D declined at a slower rate, but by 2003 had still dropped 8% from their 2000 peak. Since then, trends have reversed somewhat. But in 2008, the most recent year for which data are available, industry funding still accounted for only 5.7% of the university total—less than it did every year from 1985 to 2002.[28]

Second, the number of patents being issued to universities flattened. Universities were awarded the most utility patents, 3,698, in the year 1999. After that, the number fluctuated between 2,952 and 3,612, with no consistent pattern detectable.[29] Patenting has been frequently cited as indicating a more entrepreneurial, market-oriented university. But this leveling trend, now a decade old, raises questions about how much further market activities are going to expand.

There are several reasons these indicators peaked at the time that they did. Congress's initiative to double the budget of NIH between 1998 and 2003, for example, accounts for much of the decline in the *fraction* of university funding coming from industry.[30] And the bursting of the tech bubble in 2000, followed by a period of recession, doubtless explains some of the real decrease in industry funding between 2001 and 2004. It is also possible that this is a temporary, if relatively long, pause in a longer-term trend, or that universities' economic activities are expanding in areas not captured by these particular indicators.[31]

The story told in this book, however, suggests another explanation. Thinking of science's move toward the market as the consequence of a specific set of government interventions that expanded that market implies that the commercialization of academic science may prove more self-limiting than some hope and others fear.

Even if we assume, perhaps unreasonably, that universities are willing to sell any aspect of science for which they can find a buyer, they still cannot sell things for which buyers are unwilling to pay. There have been a number of instances in which universities have tried to turn to the market for revenue, but not found interested customers. In the early 1980s, for example, a number of large-scale university-industry partnerships in biotechnology were launched in a burst of enthusiasm. But these partnerships quickly demonstrated that they were not paying off for the firms supporting them, and while universities were clearly willing to engage in this type of partnership, it did not go on to become commonplace.

Thus while the last several decades saw significant expansion in what academic science has to offer that the private sector can rationalize paying for, there are also inherent limits to this expansion. Multiple kinds of government decisions made this market possible. But most restrictions on universities' ability to sell science are gone, and there aren't a lot of other obvious interventions for government to make. On intellectual property rights, for example, the pendulum appears to be swinging slightly toward weakening them, if anything. And it seems unlikely that government will step up the subsidy for industry-oriented science in the near future.[32] It is possible, of course, that a major scientific breakthrough might create new commercial value in academic science the way that biotechnology once did. But this is an unpredictable prospect. Nanotechnology, which has been hyped as similarly transformative, has thus far had trouble living up to promises about its commercial potential.[33] Even the biotech sector has had very limited profitability in the long run.[34]

It has been several decades since government decisions changed the market for academic science so substantially. Since then, an equilibrium of sorts has been reached: universities sell more science, and industry buys more. Government does hold the power to transform the market for academic science once again if it so chooses. But this seems unlikely to happen. And barring such unexpected intervention by government and major technological breakthroughs within the university itself, the level of interaction between academic science and the market is likely to remain fairly steady for the foreseeable future.

Academic Science, the Story of Neoliberalism, and Economic Rationalization

I have suggested that the changes that have taken place in academic science are just one instance of a broader shift toward markets in our society. Sociologists' response to this observation is often to ask, reasonably enough, Then isn't this just another story about neoliberalism? The developments described in this book are not unrelated to conventional accounts of the rise of neoliberalism. But the developments in academic science cannot be explained purely in terms of a political shift toward free-market ideals.

The neoliberalism argument is a tricky one to engage with. The term *neoliberalism* has become, to a considerable extent, a pejorative used by the left to critique a set of unwelcome trends rather than a word used neutrally to describe a particular political philosophy or set of policies. This is unfortunate, as the term does capture an important set of developments that deserve unpoliticized study.

The word can also be poorly defined. At times it is used so broadly that it becomes roughly synonymous with what I refer to here as *market logic*, that is, seeing the purpose of an activity in its capacity to create economic value. For the sake of this discussion, however, I will use a more precise definition: David Harvey's well-known formulation of neoliberalism as "a theory of political economic practices that proposes that human well-being can best be advanced by liberating individual entrepreneurial freedoms and skills within a institutional framework characterized by strong private property rights, free markets, and free trade."[35] To that, I would add that neoliberalism has generally been characterized by policies that include, but are not limited to, lower taxes, deregulation, privatization of state enterprises, reductions in welfare spending, and liberalization of trade policy.[36] Scholars have typically explained the rise of neoliberalism as the result of some combination of the influence of free-market economics (the Chicago school), conservative institution-building (through think tanks, magazines, etc.), the increasing political organization of business interests, the effects of globalization, and the structure of national political institutions.[37]

At first glance, it appears that the developments in academic science fit the label of neoliberalism pretty well. Property rights were strengthened, entrepreneurship was encouraged, and markets were expanded. And academic science today as well as the larger university has frequently been described as neoliberal in character.[38] But upon closer look, the story of academic science complicates the neoliberalism story in a couple of ways.

First, the policies that moved academic science toward the market were not uniformly free-market in orientation. Most of them—the capital gains tax cut, the strengthening of intellectual property rights, the relaxation of investment rules for pension funds—were. But state and federal support for UIRCs, as well as government subsidies for research parks, encouraged a market orientation but were clearly interventionist. State support for university-industry collaboration has even been called "probably as close to an industrial policy as we will see in the U.S."[39] While some might argue that UIRCs fall into a different category than biotech entrepreneurship and patenting because their relationship with the market is more mediated, they nevertheless encourage a focus on the economic value of science, and are a product of the same political concern with innovation that stimulated more obviously entrepreneurial practices.

Second, the developments that *led* to the popularization of the innovation frame were different from those that have been used to explain neoliberal policies. Most significantly, the intellectual source of the innovation framework was not the economics of Milton Friedman or George Stigler, but the work of scholars like Kenneth Arrow and Richard Nelson. These economists were interested in, among other things, the ways that markets left to themselves could lead to suboptimal investment in research and development. While they emphasized the role of technological innovation in driving economic growth, they had no prior commitment to the belief that minimizing government intervention was the best way to make that happen. Their ideas were promoted in part by industry groups that argued that deregulation and tax cuts were the best way to stimulate innovation, but free-market policy choices were not an inherent implication of these economists' work.

How then, to explain a set of developments that look broadly like neoliberalism, in that they imply that entrepreneurship, property rights, and markets are appropriate and desirable principles around which to organize academic science, but that do not map neatly onto conventional stories about neoliberalism's rise? I suggest that there are two strands that need to be untangled here. One strand does line up with conventional narratives about the rise of neoliberalism. But a second strand also comes into play. This second strand reflects a dynamic distinct from neoliberalism that has independently contributed to changing the relationship between society and the market in the last thirty years—one that I refer to, following Max Weber, as a process of economic rationalization.

Some elements of the shift in academic science do fit with the usual story told about the rise of neoliberalism. Industry groups made strong efforts in the 1970s to push the innovation frame, and those groups saw a particular set of solutions to the innovation problem—lower taxes, deregulation, stronger patent rights and looser antitrust enforcement—as appropriate. This is compatible with a neoliberalism narrative arguing that a conservative political movement, a free-market intellectual movement, and increasingly organized business interests came together to gain political influence during the 1970s. The policy outcomes I examine that were compatible with the preferences of innovation-focused industry groups, like the capital gains tax cut and the creation of the Federal Circuit, can be explained without having to challenge the broad outlines of this story.

But, as mentioned already, other elements of the shift in academic science, like the role of interventionist industrial policies and the less-than-neoliberal intellectual underpinnings of the new interest in innovation, do not fit a narrative about the idealization of free markets so well. I suggest that these developments make more sense if one thinks of them as part of a dynamic in which economic issues—and in particular "the economy," in the abstract—are placed at the heart of political life. As Mark Smith has amply documented, starting in the 1970s political issues in the United States increasingly came to be framed in economic terms, a development tied to the shaky state of the nation's economy as well as to rising levels of individual economic insecurity.[40] This shift toward making the health of the economy a central purpose of government action does not necessarily imply the embrace of free markets for their own sake.

What it does imply, however, is a specific kind of rationalization. In Weber's work, instrumentally rational action is action undertaken because it is seen as the most effective means to achieve a given end. It goes hand in hand with an increase in formal rationality, in which it becomes more possible to calculate what action will be most effective, as well as the development of a body of technical knowledge about how means and ends are connected. The advance of capitalism is itself bound up with the rationalization of the economic domain, as individuals come to see economic action as involving calculable decisions made with the intent to maximize financial gain.[41]

What I am calling *economic rationalization* here, however, is not the expansion of instrumental economic behavior among individuals, but rather a shift in substantive rationality—in the ends that are themselves seen as legitimate purposes of action. Here, government activities become the means to a particular end, economic growth, which can at least in theory be achieved through the application of a formal body of abstract knowledge about the economy.

The change in academic science, then, can be seen as resulting from the economic rationalization of political life as much as it resulted from the growing influence of neoliberalism. The rationale for supporting academic science shifted away from expanding knowledge or meeting national needs and toward strengthening innovation and thus economic productivity. It did not matter that the theoretical arguments for the importance of innovation came from economists who had no inherent problem with government intervention in the economy. By explaining the role of science in driving innovation and economic growth, they helped to redefine the purpose of academic science in economic terms. This, by definition, is market logic. Thus whatever action policymakers took to strengthen innovation, whether free-market or interventionist, it tended to encourage activity that treated science as an economic input.

Economic rationalization, then, is a move toward explaining a domain of life in terms of its economic role. It relies on the assumption that people of all political stripes share the goals of economic growth and increased productivity—of better standards of living—an assumption that has persistently remained safe in a political world characterized by sharply divergent beliefs about the purpose and capacities of government. It also has the advantage of turning policy decisions into technical questions with the potential to be solved using the tools of economics. If we can assume that growth and productivity are shared goals, and, for example, that they result from a workforce with high levels of education, then at least in theory there should be objective answers to the question of what the best education policies are, answers that are not merely about politics.

While in reality any attempt to answer such questions will be political as well as technical, debating which education policies will do the most to encourage economic growth is nonetheless easier than arguing over whether the purpose of education is to create good citizens, or to provide for social mobility, or to give people useful skills, as well as needing to figure out how best to achieve that goal.

While this process of economic rationalization has been particularly pronounced in academic science, it can be seen elsewhere as well. One reflection of the trend has been a proliferation of institutions, inventions, and human activities characterized as *economic engines*. A quick Google search on the term turns up a list that is startling in its range. On the first three pages one finds, in the following order, a public park, Moon Pies, the California Public Employees' Retirement System, an oil refinery, U.N. peace operations, "cleantech," 3G wireless, Stanford University, small businesses, hunting, race car testing, the University of Madison-Milwaukee, the Panama Canal, Honda imports, Westchester Community College, and the arts.[42] What is notable is how many of these things were not, presumably, created with the intent of stimulating the economy. This points to the problem with economic rationalization. While economic growth and productivity may be worthy goals, and we all presumably want to be wealthier, placing them at the center of political life makes it harder to legitimately consider, or choose to pursue, other goals that may be equally or even more worthy. Is economic stimulus really the best reason we can come up with to have public parks, arts, or a retirement system?

For universities in particular, the effects of economic rationalization extend well beyond the research laboratory. Even academic science has trouble living up to its promises to create jobs, launch industries, and revitalize economies. The humanities, too, can try to sell themselves in terms of the economic value they create by teaching students to think critically, to write, to be creative. But is this enough? As former Harvard president—and early proponent of academia's move toward the market—Derek Bok said in the *New York Times* in 2009, "There's a lot more to a liberal education than improving the economy. I think that is one of the worst mistakes that policy makers often make—not being able to see beyond that."[43]

However true Bok's observation may be, though, it is not clear that there is much space left in American political life for seeing beyond that. Nearly 150 years ago, the Morrill Act established the land-grant colleges in the United States. These were intended to "teach such branches of learning as are related to agriculture and the mechanic arts . . . in order to promote the liberal and practical education of the industrial classes in the several pursuits and professions in life."[44] The mission of the land-grant universities is a practical mission. It is a mission that embraces science and technology. And it is a mission with a distinctly American flavor. But while such a mission may have economic effects, it is not, on its face, an economic mission. And it is one that is hard to imagine the nation proposing today.

Ultimately, then, I find myself ending this book on an ambivalent note. The average human being today has much greater material well-being than—not to mention double the life span of—her historical counterpart, in no small part because of massive increases in economic productivity. Technological innovation and economic growth really do have the potential to improve people's lives in truly meaningful ways. But while the dynamics of economic rationalization are powerful, they are also constraining. As we come to understand activities as economic inputs, we lose some of our ability to treat them as having other, noneconomic values—to choose different substantive rationalities. Perhaps it has come to seem like a luxury to pursue activities like science or, still more, the humanities on grounds other than the economic. But if we choose to accept that belief as reality, we should be aware that we are losing as well as gaining something, adding bars to the iron cage as we try to provide ourselves with better material circumstances.

This inevitable tension is what makes economic rationalization poignant as well as powerful. Neoliberalism, in the sense of idealizing free markets, may come and go. In the wake of financial crisis, even some diehard proponents of the power of markets have reevaluated their stance toward laissez-faire capitalism.[45] Economic rationalization, however, shows no signs of weakening; if anything, our ability to make policy decisions on grounds other than economic ones seems to be increasingly constrained. And as this process gains momentum, it becomes easy to forget the real reason to value increasing productivity and an expanding economy: because they improve human well-being, not for their own sake. We should, however, resist this myopia. Because if we lose sight of the ultimate, human purpose of economic growth, we risk becoming servants of the economy, rather than allowing the economy to serve us.

Notes

Abbreviations

AAU	Association of American Universities
AUTM	Association of University Technology Managers
BIO	Biotechnology Industry Organization
CHF	Chemical Heritage Foundation
COGR	Council on Governmental Relations
ERC	Engineering Research Center
FCST	Federal Council for Science and Technology
GUIRR	Government-University-Industry Research Roundtable
IASC AC265	[Massachusetts] Institute [of Technology] Archives and Special Collections, Cambridge, MA, Archives Collections 265: Industrial Liaison Program, Records of Member Companies, 1948–
IBHE	Illinois Board of Higher Education
MIT	Massachusetts Institute of Technology
NAE	National Academy of Engineering
NAS	National Academy of Sciences
NBER	National Bureau of Economic Research
NGA	National Governors Association
NIH	National Institutes of Health
NRC	National Research Council
NSB	National Science Board
NSF	National Science Foundation
NVCA	National Venture Capital Association
SUA SC 160	Stanford University Archives, Stanford, CA, Special Collections 160: Frederick Emmons Terman Papers. See http://www-sul.stanford.edu/depts/spc/xml/sc0160.xml for a guide to these papers (last accessed 21 April 2011).
UIA 5/2/10	University of Illinois Archives, Urbana, IL, Record Series No. 5/2/10: Role of Universities in Regional Economic Growth File, 1961–1963. See www.library.illinois.edu/archives/uasfa/0502010.pdf for the contents of this record series (last accessed 21 April 2011).
U.S. BEA	U.S. Bureau of Economic Analysis
U.S. DOJ	U.S. Department of Justice
U.S. DOL	U.S. Department of Labor
U.S. GAO	U.S. General Accounting Office
U.S. OMB	U.S. Office of Management and Budget
U.S. OSTS	U.S. Office of State Technical Services
U.S. PTO	U.S. Patent and Trademark Office

Chapter 1. Academic Science as an Economic Engine

1. Otto Kerner to David Dodds Henry, 4 October 1961, "Correspondence—Industry, Research, Universities, 1962–63" folder, Box 1, UIA 5/2/10.

2. Top-ten engineering fields included chemical engineering, electrical engineering, and mechanical engineering. See Cartter (1966) for department rankings.

3. Final Report: Committee on the Role of Universities in Economic Growth, 6 February 1963, "Reports and Recommendations, 1962–63" folder, Box 1, UIA 5/2/10.

4. IBHE (1999).

5. University of Illinois (2002).

6. University of Illinois (1999).

7. University of Illinois (2002).

8. University of Illinois (2000).

9. See NSB (2010:appendix table 5-2). In 2008, the most recent year for which data are available, industry provided $2.9 billion in support for academic R&D. Industry funding peaked as a percentage of all university R&D spending in 1999, at 7.4%, but made up only 5.5% of the total in 2008. It increased 13% in real dollars during that period, but the 1998 to 2003 doubling of the NIH budget made industry funding a smaller percentage of the total.

10. For recent figures on patents issued and gross royalties, see NSB (2010:appendix table 5-47) as well as Blumenstyk (2010). For patents issued in 1980, see NSB (1996:appendix table 5-42). For patents issued prior to 1974, see Mowery et al. (2004:47). The number of patents issued to universities has remained roughly flat during the last decade, but royalty revenues, which trail patents by a number of years, have increased substantially.

11. E.g., Shane (2004), Stuart and Ding (2006).

12. See NSB (2010:appendix table 4-3) for historical data on federal funding of academic R&D.

13. Real industry spending on basic research peaked in 1966, then declined fairly steadily until 1975. The 1966 spending level was not regained until 1981. See NSB (2010:appendix table 4-4).

14. Federal expenditures on university R&D in 1966, the year that industry funding was lowest as a percentage of the total, were (in constant dollars) seven times what they had been in 1953, when NSF started publishing data. Industry expenditures increased 73% in real terms during that period (NSB 2010:appendix table 4-3).

15. The period when the percentage of industry funding was increasing most rapidly shows a similar trend, peaking between about 1980 and 1986. See NSB (2010:appendix table 4-3) for data underlying these figures.

16. Smith (1990b:338). The back-story Smith presents, however, also demonstrates the complexity of attitudes toward patenting, even in this era. The National Foundation for Infantile Paralysis, which sponsored the research, had actually considered applying for a patent on the vaccine but rejected the possibility because they thought the vaccine would not be patentable. However, the impetus did not come from Pitt, whose policy at the time was to handle inventions on a case-by-case basis, "with the understanding among faculty members and research workers that an individual would not benefit

personally from patentable discoveries or inventions arising from a University research program" (Palmer 1955b:58).

17. Archie Palmer, in conjunction with the National Research Council, conducted a number of surveys of university patenting policies between the 1940s and the 1960s. See, for example, Palmer (1948, 1955a, 1955b, 1962). See also Mowery and Sampat (2001b) and Metlay (2006) on the history of university patenting.

18. See Palmer (1955b, 1962). For examples of policies stating that the university will not profit from its research, see those of Princeton University, the State University of New York, and the University of Chicago (Palmer 1955b:60, 71, 79).

19. Palmer (1962:124).

20. AUTM (2008).

21. COGR (1996).

22. AUTM (2010).

23. Glenna et al. (2007:155).

24. Hammett (1953), cited in Shapin (2008).

25. Re Boyer's post-IPO wealth, see Cole (1980).

26. See, e.g., Lam (2010), Owen-Smith and Powell (2001).

27. Rutter (1998:58).

28. Kornberg (1997).

29. See, for various elements of these critiques, Bok (2003), Bekelman, Li, and Gross (2003), Heller and Eisenberg (1998), Krimsky (2003), Nelson (2006), and Washburn (2005).

30. See, e.g., AUTM (2007) and Vest (2004, 2007).

31. Heyneker (2002:148).

32. See, e.g., Etzkowitz (2002) and GUIRR (1999, 2000).

33. Vance (2007). The University of Illinois and Lawrence Berkeley National Laboratory were also participants in the partnership.

34. Hardin (2007) and Zachary (2007).

35. Culliton (1977:763).

36. I drew particularly on Etzkowitz (2002), Etzkowitz and Leydesdorff (2000), Geiger (2004), Kleinman and Vallas (2001), Krimsky (2003), Slaughter and Leslie (1997), Slaughter and Rhoades (2004), and Washburn (2005) in formulating the project. Although I do not review here the large literature on university-industry relations in general or on the practices this book examines in particular, see Bercovitz and Feldman (2008), Colyvas (2006), Colyvas and Powell (2006, 2007), Evans (2010a, 2010b), Hong and Walsh (2009), Jones (2009), Murray (2004, 2010), Owen-Smith (2003, 2005), Rudy et al. (2007), Siegel, Wright, and Lockett (2007), Valdivia (2011), Walsh, Cohen, and Cho (2007), Welsh and Glenna (2006), and Welsh et al. (2008) for some useful points of entry.

37. Friedland and Alford (1991:248). Other scholars have developed concepts similar to "institutional logic," including Fligstein's (1990) "conception of control" and Boltanski and Thévenot's (2006 [1991]) "orders of worth." For a thorough review of the literature on institutional logics and related concepts, see Thornton and Ocasio (2008); for a review of institutional theory more generally, see Scott (2007).

38. I use the term "field" here in the organizational sense, meaning a group of individual and collective actors who orient their behavior to one another and see themselves as playing the same game. The field of academic science would include individual

scientists, universities, professional organizations, funding agencies, policymakers, and others, all of whom share some general sense of what it means to do academic science and some expectations of how participants in the field are supposed to act.

39. Most research on institutional logics has focused on explaining the effects of changes in logic, not the causes. Several studies, however, have examined the question of how logics change. While Scott et al. (2000) is first and foremost interested in measuring changes in logic, it also contains historical analysis of political and resource changes that caused the shifts. Rao, Monin, and Durand's (2003) study of how French cuisine shifted from the logic of classical cuisine to the logic of nouvelle cuisine identifies number of prior adopters, their professional legitimacy, and their subsequent success as predictors of the logic's further diffusion. Much explanation of why logics change has focused on the role of institutional entrepreneurship, which plays a relatively limited role in the case of academic science. See Hardy and Maguire (2008) for a review of the literature on institutional entrepreneurship.

40. Friedland and Alford (1991); see also Thornton and Ocasio (2008).

Chapter 2
Market Logic in the Era of Pure Science

1. National Resources Committee (1938:177). This is, after controlling for inflation, about one-third of what NSF found was being spent in 1953, the first year it began publishing figures (NSB 2010:appendix table 4-3).

2. Heilbron and Seidel (1989).

3. Brookings Institution (2002). This estimate is based on current, not inflation-adjusted, dollars. See also Hughes (2003) on pre–Manhattan Project antecedents to big science.

4. See Dupree (1957) and Geiger (1986) on the relative insignificance of federal funding to university research before 1940.

5. NIH (2010). NSF was founded in 1950.

6. Geiger (1986:chapter 4).

7. See Etzkowitz (2002:chapter 4) and Servos (1980) on MIT, and Mowery and Sampat (2001a) on Cottrell. See also Geiger (1986:174–191) on university-industry relations in the 1920s and 1930s.

8. Kevles (1978:308).

9. Geiger (1993:31).

10. National Resources Committee (1938:190).

11. See Geiger (1993:44) on voluntary support.

12. NSB (2010:appendix table 4-3).

13. See England (1983), Hart (1998), Kevles (1977), and Kleinman (1995) for various takes on this episode.

14. Hart (1998).

15. Bush (1960 [1945]:18).

16. Bush (1960 [1945]:83); italics in original.

17. Bush (1960 [1945]).

18. Geiger (1993:18). See also Smith (1990a:48–49).

19. See Kleinman (1995) for a complete account of the legislative battle leading up to the creation of NSF.

20. Hart (1998:162–163).

21. Peer review may have been transferred to NSF from the Office of Naval Research, where it was used informally, by NSF's first director, Alan Waterman. See Chubin and Hackett (1990:20), England (1983:165) and Roy (1985:74).

22. NSF provided 5% of all federal R&D funding obligated to universities in 1955, a proportion that increased to 15% by 1968 (NSF 2003:table B).

23. Geiger (1993:32).

24. Geiger (1993:19).

25. NSF (2003:table B). The 1955 figure actually represents the National Advisory Committee for Aeronautics, NASA's predecessor organization. Data prior to 1955 are not available.

26. NSF (2003:table B).

27. Mandel (1996:46–47), Strickland (1989:25); see also Swain (1962:1236).

28. Endicott and Allen (1953:341).

29. The phrase is David Guston's (1993).

30. NSB (2010:appendix table 4-3).

31. Lowen (1997:14).

32. Roy (1972:955).

33. Kleinman, Habinek, and Vallas (2011).

34. John W. Daly, "Results of Survey to Determine Characteristics of Existing University Related Research/Industrial Park Programs," "Reports, Photocopies, Clippings on Industry, Research, Locations, Etc., 1961–1963" folder, Box 1, UIA 5/2/10.

35. John Clair Thompson to J. D. Ryder, 24 August 1962, "Progress Reports & Research Plans, 1962" folder, Box 1, UIA 5/2/10.

36. "Statistical Appendix for Questionnaires on Industry-University Relationships," "Reports and Recommendations, 1962–63" folder, Box 1, UIA 5/2/10.

37. "Notes on University Letters," "Reports and Recommendations, 1962–63" folder, Box 1, UIA 5/2/10.

38. Because of the way responses were categorized, this misses some positive answers; it is likely that another ten or so also expressed interest in contract awards. See "Notes on University Letters," tables 6 and 7.

39. "Notes on University Letters."

40. Geiger (1993:64); History of the MIT Industrial Liaison Program, Finding Aid, MIT IASC AC265.

41. MIT (1955:214, 342). That year, thirteen symposia were held with an average attendance of forty-eight, 546 publications were sent to companies, and 515 visits were paid to the Industrial Liaison Office (MIT 1955:342–343).

42. Lenoir et al. (2003:13).

43. Leslie (1993:127–128). See also Folder 1, Box 18, Series III, SUA SC 160 for archival material on Stanford's industrial affiliates programs.

44. Caltech's program was established in 1949. See "News and Notes" (1952a:470), "Scientists in the News"(1957).

45. References to programs other than MIT's and Stanford's were found through a search of the journal *Science* using the terms *industrial liaison*, *industry liaison*, *industrial affiliates*, *industry affiliates*, *industrial associates*, and *industry associates*. Mount Holyoke's program was discussed as being new in 1952, Buffalo's was mentioned in 1953, and Penn's in 1956. See "Scientists in the News" (1957), "News and Notes" (1952b:683), "News and Notes" (1953), and "Scientific Meetings" (1956).

46. MIT (1969:692, 717–718).

47. Berg (1997:132–134), Mosher (2001:44), and Frederick E. Terman, "The Development of an Engineering College Program," 18 May 1968, Folder 8, Box 3, Series VIII, SUA SC 160.

48. "Announcements" (1963), "Calendar of Events" (1967:1506).

49. MIT (1969:717).

50. A report summarized the seventy-eight university responses to the letter. Many universities referred the electronics firm to specific individuals within the university, most frequently a head of engineering extension or chair of electrical engineering. Fifteen universities referred the firm to an "other university administrator" than a research director or faculty member; "this group included graduate deans, placement officers, research and/or business vice-presidents, and even industrial liaison personnel." While the number of industrial liaison personnel is not specified, the language used suggests that they were mentioned quite infrequently. See "Notes on University Letters" and "Statistical Appendix for Letters on Industry-University Relationships," "Reports and Recommendations, 1962–63" folder, Box 1, UIA 5/2/10.

51. "Notes on University Letters" and "Statistical Appendix for Letters on Industry-University Relationships."

52. Roy (1972:956–957). Industrial affiliates programs are also rarely mentioned in other places one might expect to see references. For example, the magazine *Industrial Research* published a special issue on university research each April for several years in the mid-1960s, but while these include articles on university-industry relations there is little on industrial affiliates programs. Brodsky, Kaufman, and Tooker also mention only MIT, Caltech, Penn State, Stanford, and Lehigh by name in their discussion of industrial liaison programs (1980:45).

53. O'Mara (2005:chapter 3). See also Luger and Goldstein (1991:chapter 7).

54. Dates of founding are often difficult to identify, since early parks developed gradually. While most sources list the University of Oklahoma Research Park (also known as Swearingen Research Park) as being founded in 1957 ("First Annual Survey" 1962:35, Link and Link 2003:82), at least one source dates it to 1950 (Luger and Goldstein 1991:190), which would make it older than Stanford's park. Cornell's park is sometimes cited as being established in 1951 (Cornell University 2007, Luger and Goldstein 1991:190) or 1952 (Link and Link 2003:82, Link and Scott 2003:79), but until 1958 it involved only one firm, General Electric (Cornell University 2007), so 1958 is probably more appropriate as a starting date (see also "First Annual Survey" 1962:35). Research Triangle Park, involving Duke, the University of North Carolina, and North Carolina State, is generally dated to 1959 ("First Annual Survey" 1962:85, Link and Link 2003:82, Luger and Goldstein 1991:189). On Research Triangle Park generally, see Link (1995, 2002) and Luger and Goldstein (1991:chapter 5).

55. The magazine *Industrial Development and Manufacturers Record* identified existing parks affiliated with Illinois Institute of Technology, Pomona, Purdue, and the University of Missouri, as well as the four established before 1960. It cited Colorado State, the Graduate Institute of Technology (Little Rock, AR), the University of Connecticut, the University of Miami, the University of Wyoming, and Wayne State as planning parks ("First Annual Survey" 1962). A survey conducted by the Albuquerque Industrial Development Service for its own use added to that list existing parks at Indiana and the University of Colorado, and mentioned MIT, Northwestern, Ohio State,

the University of Alabama, the University of Kansas, the University of Minnesota, and the University of Nebraska as also actively planning parks, as well as another seven considering the possibility. See Daly, "Results of Survey to Determine Characteristics of Existing University Related Research/Industrial Park Programs." The University of Pennsylvania was also planning a park by this point (O'Mara 2005:chapter 4).

56. Daly, "Results of Survey to Determine Characteristics of Existing University Related Research/Industrial Park Programs," Schwitter (1965).

57. "First Annual Survey" (1962), Luger and Goldstein (1991:78).

58. Schwitter (1965); see also "Site Selector's Guide" (1966) for a list of parks, sixteen of which are clearly university-affiliated (including one in Canada).

59. Danilov (1971:45). In 1966, of fourteen university research parks listing occupancy rates, only four had rates of 50% or higher ("Site Selector's Guide" 1966). On MIT's Technology Square, see Simha (2003:78–83).

60. Danilov (1971:47).

61. These programs typically were started in close conjunction with agricultural extension programs in the early decades of the twentieth century. For thumbnail histories of several engineering extension programs, all started before World War II, see Georgia Tech Archives (2011); Hitchcock (1925), Iowa State University (2010), Texas A&M (2010), University of Illinois (1995), and University of Utah Archives (2010).

62. On passage of the Act, see Carter (1965).

63. U.S. OSTS (1968:1). See Nelkin (1971) on Hollomon, especially chapter 2.

64. Located, respectively, at the University of Arkansas, the University of Delaware, the University System of Georgia, and the University of Iowa. See U.S. OSTS (1968:51–80) for a list of the offices managing each state's program as of 1968.

65. The report is reprinted in U.S. House (1971b:201–349).

66. Hamilton (1969); see also Carter (1965). See Nelkin (1971) on the politics of the Civilian Industrial Technology Program, which was in many ways the antecedent to the State Technical Services Act.

67. For example, in Vermont the state technical services agency prevented a number of cheese producers from going bankrupt after environmental regulation required them to stop dumping their excess whey into streams by demonstrating the feasibility of converting the whey to a dried, edible product. This was estimated to save 51 jobs, to directly create 82 more, and to indirectly create another 119 (U.S. House 1971b:216–218).

68. U.S. House (1971b:146).

69. Hamilton (1969:1606). The exceptions were the few programs that developed state-level support for such efforts, such as PennTAP in Pennsylvania—see, e.g., "Boosting Small Business" (1982)—but these were relatively rare.

70. There are affinities between what I am describing as a shift from a science-as-resource to a science-as-engine model and Peter Eisinger's (1988) description of the rise of a supply-side model of state economic development at the end of the 1970s. Before that point, Eisinger argues, states almost universally thought about economic development in terms of luring industry to locate in them rather than in terms of stimulating the growth of small and local businesses to create a broader economic base. The shift toward the latter strategy, which Eisinger calls a "supply-side strategy," is closely tied to ideas about technological innovation as a source of economic growth and development. Chapter 6 will return to this theme in a discussion of the role of state economic development policy in encouraging the growth of university-industry research centers in the 1980s.

71. Frederick Emmons Terman, "Education—A Basic Component of the New Electronics," speech given to the National Electronics Conference in Chicago, 11 October 1960, "Reports, Photocopies, Clippings on Industry, Research, Location, Etc., 1961–1963" folder, Box 1, UIA 5/2/10.

72. W. L. Everitt, "Panel on the Future of Chicago Area Electronics," unpublished speech given to the National Electronics Conference in Chicago, October 1961, "Reports, Photocopies, Clippings on Industry, Research, Location, Etc., 1961–1963" folder, Box 1, UIA 5/2/10; Albert H. Rubenstein and Dawson E. Brewer, "Preliminary Report: A Study of Research and Development in the Chicago Area Electronics Industry," paper presented to the National Electronics Conference in Chicago, 11 October 1960, "Reports, Photocopies, Clippings on Industry, Research, Location, Etc., 1961–1963" folder, Box 1, UIA 5/2/10.

73. See, e.g., "Midwest Finds" (1961).

74. Otto Kerner to David Dodds Henry, 4 October 1961, "Correspondence—Industry, Research, Universities, 1962-63" folder, Box 1, UIA 5/2/10.

75. Thompson to Ryder, 24 August 1962.

76. The survey was sent to a random sample of 1,154 firms in five Census categories: pharmaceuticals, computers, radio and television transmission equipment, telephone and telegraph apparatus, and scientific instruments. It had fourteen pages and sixty-four questions, and 236 usable replies were received. The original survey responses can be found in the committee's archival records. See Box 2, UIA 5/2/10.

77. Lyle Lanier to the Committee, 14 June 1962, "Reports and Recommendations, 1962–63" folder, Box 1, UIA 5/2/10; Lyle H. Lanier to Deans and Directors of Academic Divisions, 13 June 1962, "Correspondence—Industry, Research, Universities, 1962–63" folder, Box 1, UIA 5/2/10. See Berman (2007:51–92) for more details on all of the committee's activities.

78. The Committee to Lyle Lanier, 14 June 1962, "Reports and Recommendations, 1962–63" folder, Box 1, UIA 5/2/10.

79. "Final Report," 6 February 1963, "Reports and Recommendations, 1962–63" folder, Box 1, UIA 5/2/10.

80. Joseph M. Heikoff to the Committee, 28 January 1963, "Reports and Recommendations, 1962–63" folder, Box 1, UIA 5/2/10.

81. Carl W. Larsen and Sheldon Garber, "The Attraction of University-Oriented Research and Development Programs to the Middlewest," 7 March 1962, "Correspondence—Industry, Research, Universities, 1962–63" folder, Box 1, UIA 5/2/10.

82. Daly, "Results of Survey to Determine Characteristics of Existing University Related Research/Industrial Park Programs."

83. Heikoff to the Committee, 28 January 1963.

84. F. E. Terman to David S. Jacobson, 20 June 1958, Folder 1, Box 18, Series VIII, SUA SC 160.

85. Adams (2005). This figure is from 1959; by 1965, only two of seventeen affiliates were local, and none of the top three additional prospects were local either.

86. NSF (2003:table B). Total federal spending, in contrast, increased only an average of 2.6% per year in real terms during this period, and GDP increased an average of 3.8% per year in real terms. See U.S. OMB (2008:table 1.3) and U.S. BEA (2010:table 1.1.1).

87. See NAS (1965) for such statements, and Greenberg (1967a) for a mention of this estimate in the press.

88. See Swazey and Reeds (1978:5–8) for a fascinating discussion of how the concept of the serendipity of basic research developed.

89. During the 1950–1969 period, GDP grew an average of 4.3% per year, and federal spending increased even faster, at 5.5% per year (both figures adjusted for inflation). Real GDP growth has not broken 3.3% for any decade since then (U.S. BEA 2011:table 1.1.1).

90. Inflation was under 2% for most of the 1950s and 1960s but over 5% by the end of the 1960s (U.S. DOL 2010d). The trade balance was hovering around zero by 1968 and became negative shortly thereafter (U.S. Census Bureau 2010). For recession dates, see NBER (2010).

91. Greenberg (1965).

92. Boffey (1967); see also Boffey (1968b), Walsh (1966b).

93. See Geiger (1993:230–242) on student protest in the late 1960s. There were also, for example, proposals in Wisconsin to eliminate tenure and threats of reduced appropriations in Pennsylvania in response to campus unrest. See Boffey (1969), Walsh (1969).

94. Gruchow (1970), Jamison (1968). NSF also rescinded a research grant to a Berkeley math professor who was a prominent critic of the war (Greenberg 1967b).

95. See Public Law 85-568 for the statutory requirement.

96. See Doctors (1969: 68–70) on NASA and its response to these criticisms.

97. Quoted in Walsh (1966a). See also Semple (1966).

98. Langer (1967), Walsh (1966a).

99. For contemporary conversations on technology transfer, see NASA (1964) and Rosenbloom (1965) regarding space and defense. On the biomedical sciences, see U.S. NIH Study Committee (1965) and U.S. Senate (1966, 1967a). On technology transfer and small business, see U.S. Senate (1967b, 1967c, 1968, 1970). Bibliographies on technology transfer include Clearinghouse (1966), Defense Documentation Center (1968), and Sovel (1969). The most notable studies of the role of basic science in technological innovation were Project Hindsight, sponsored by the Defense Department, and TRACES ("Technology in Retrospect and Critical Advances in Science"), funded by NSF. See Coillet (1971), Sherwin and Isenson (1966, 1967), and U.S. Office of the Director (1969) on Project Hindsight, and Illinois Institute of Technology (1969) on TRACES.

100. NSB (2010:appendix table 4-3).

101. Public Law 91-121.

102. Richard J. Barber Associates (1975:VIII-22).

103. Richard J. Barber Associates (1975:VIII-20). Several accounts of the Mansfield amendment are inaccurate with respect to dates and details; Richard J. Barber Associates (1975:VIII-19–24), though not easy to acquire, is the most definitive I have found.

104. Belanger (1998:chapter 3), Mazuzan (1988), U.S. House (1980:143–145).

105. Belanger (1998:chapter 3), Green and Lepkowski (2006), Semas (1973:1). RANN was preceded by the smaller IRRPOS, Interdisciplinary Research Relevant to Problems of Our Society.

106. Strickland (1972:271).

107. Strickland (1972:289). See also Rettig (1977) for the story of the War on Cancer.

108. NSB (2010:appendix table 4-3).

109. Geiger (1993).

110. Boffey (1968a:340), Boffey (1970b:555). See also Schmeck (1970) for a gloomy view of the state of science.

111. Bazell (1971:878).

112. See, e.g., Boffey (1970b), Smith and Karlesky (1977:5).

113. In 1969, 54% of all doctoral institutions were running deficits (Jellema 1973:9), and in 1971, Earl Cheit categorized only three of the seventeen doctoral institutions he studied as "not in financial trouble" (1971:131). See Cheit (1973) and Jellema (1970, 1971) for additional studies of the financial condition of higher education in this period, and Boffey (1970b) and Semas (1973) for press accounts of a "recession" in science.

114. Smith and Karlesky (1977:87, 121, 150) identified these fields as ones impacted by the Mansfield amendment based on interviews with university scientists. One ARPA director later recalled, "the most tragic part of the Mansfield amendment was what happened to the professors, not what happened to Defense. Defense got its work done—hell, it just simply went someplace else. But the poor guys who were out in the universities were caught in the middle and cruelly so" (Richard J. Barber Associates 1975:VIII-22).

115. Geiger (1993:245), citing NSF data.

116. Boffey (1970b); see also Smith and Karlesky (1977:5).

117. U.S. Senate (1967a:8–9).

118. The quotation is of Murray Weidenbaum, assistant secretary of the treasury for economic affairs (Boffey 1970a:512, 515).

119. Semas (1973).

Chapter 3
Innovation Drives the Economy—an Old Idea with New Implications

1. For example, Adam Smith notes the importance of technology in his pin factory example (2000 [1776]:9–11), and Karl Marx of course makes technology a driver of history (e.g., 2005 [1847]:119).

2. See Warsh (2006) for an excellent explanation of the concept of increasing returns in economics from Adam Smith to the present and of the effort to make ideas and technological change endogenous to theories of economic growth. However, while new growth theory, which finally succeeded in solving this technical problem, did not develop until the late 1980s, a serious concern with technological innovation began to develop much earlier among economists; see, for example, Nelson (1997) for a review of this earlier work. The growing interest of economists in technological change in the 1960s and 1970s was picked up and amplified by policymakers and the media in the mid-to-late 1970s, well before Warsh's story reaches its climax.

3. Schumpeter, while well-known, was writing nonmathematical economics at a time when formalization was rapidly becoming dominant within the discipline. While his ideas resonated with many, they had limited short-term influence on academic economics (Warsh 2006:121–125).

4. The fraction of federal R&D spending at universities that came from the defense-related agencies (the Department of Defense, the Atomic Energy Commission, and NASA) decreased from 44% in 1960 to 30% in 1970, while the fraction of *all* federal R&D spending that came from the defense agencies was 91% in 1960, declining only to 82% by 1970. NSF (2003:table B).

5. U.S. Senate (1963b:2). This statement was part of Senator Hubert Humphrey's opening remarks in a six-volume set of Congressional hearings on the *Role and Effect of Technology in the Nation's Economy*, convened on behalf of a subcommittee of the Select Committee on Small Business. These hearings use a language very similar to that which became common fifteen years later, but they seem to have garnered little attention. Indeed, Humphrey appears to have been the only senator present for much of the proceedings.

6. See, for example, Davis (1988), on economic policy during the Kennedy administration.

7. U.S. President (1947:24). The report continues, "But we do need Nation-wide concerted action to remove the fear that demand will periodically be inadequate to absorb maximum production. This is what puts brakes on inventiveness and initiative."

8. U.S. President (1962:123–127).

9. Graham (1978a), "The 'Innovation Recession'" (1978), "The Right Way" (1978), "Vanishing Innovation" (1978).

10. "Innovation: Some Positive Steps" (1979).

11. Based on a search of the *Congressional Record* on HeinOnline conducted 28 July 2010 using the terms *technological innovation* and *"innovation economy"~20 OR "innovation economic"~20*. The trend holds across a variety of searches on technology, innovation, and the economy. Numbers are corrected for the increasing length of the *Congressional Record* during this period and reflect the number of pages that contain the search term, not the total number of times the term is found.

12. Griliches (1996) gives a brief history of the discovery of the residual and Nelson (1997) reviews these developments as well.

13. Solow (1957). Solow and others did not, however, assume these estimates were accurate: "All of the pioneers of this subject were quite clear about the tenuousness of such calculations and that it may be misleading to identify the results as 'pure' measures of technical progress" (Griliches 1996:1328). See Abramowitz (1956) and Fabricant (1954) for other early important work in this area.

14. See Denison (1962) and Griliches (1964) for examples of work attempting to sort out factors contributing to the residual. See Nelson (1959) and Arrow (1962) for examples of work looking at levels of investment in invention and scientific research.

15. In 1971, for example, Richard Nelson commented "that while a handful of economists have, for the past decade or so, been studying the impact of technology on international trade, their work is still only trickling into the main line literature. 'I don't feel my confreres realize how important [technology] is. . . . It's very important'" (Boffey 1971:41). See Mansfield (1972) for a useful review of the state of the literature by the early 1970s.

16. See Collins (2000) on growth policy and Stein (1991) and Davis (1988) on economic policy during the Kennedy administration.

17. Nelkin (1971:19).

18. Nelkin (1971:21). Note that the term *civilian technology* was used in contrast to the default assumption that government supported technology for defense purposes.

19. Solow (2000) provides an interesting perspective on the CEA's thinking about how to increase economic growth in the long run.

20. Nelkin (1971:30–31).

21. Nelkin (1971) is entirely devoted to this political episode; see also Katz (1978:138–142).

22. Carter (1965), Hamilton (1969), Katz (1978:168–171).

23. See Greenberg (1963) for the comparison with NSF. It is also worth noting that President Johnson appointed a Task Force on Innovation and Economic Growth, chaired by Bureau of the Budget director Charles Zwick, that was meant to review existing recommendations in this area. The report of the task force, which was completed in November 1966, is available from the Johnson presidential library, but as these reports were confidential, it was not published.

24. NAE (1992:124).

25. U.S. Senate (1979c:511).

26. U.S. House (1979b:160).

27. Charpie himself had earlier chaired the housing subpanel of the civilian technology panel (Nelkin 1971:21).

28. U.S. Senate (1979c:568). The entire Charpie report is reprinted within these Senate hearings.

29. Peterson would go on to found the Blackstone Group in the 1980s. See NAE (1992:204–208) for a short biography of Morse.

30. U.S. Senate (1979c:504–593). The panel recommended against an R&D tax credit, suggesting only some special considerations for small high-tech businesses and individual inventors. It saw no need for additional federal support of venture capital, but suggested that more information about regional venture capital availability be provided. And it recommended no changes in antitrust and regulatory laws, other than a consideration of innovation, as well as competition, effects going forward.

31. See, e.g., Gilpin (1968), Wolfle (1968).

32. NBER (2010), U.S. DOL (2010a, 2010e).

33. U.S. Census Bureau (2010).

34. Boffey (1971). Boretsky did not publish extensively on the issue, but his chapter in NAE (1971) provides a good summary of his argument.

35. Boffey (1971:41).

36. Shapley (1973a:881).

37. Numbers are inflation-adjusted. See NSB (2010:appendix table 4-7), NSF (2003:table 8). Between 1967 and 1975, real year-over-year change in industry-performed R&D averaged –1%. Government funding of industrial R&D has never again reached its 1967 level.

38. The American Presidency Project (2008a), Wade (1971).

39. Boffey (1971). See NAE (1971) for the proceedings of the symposium and U.S. House (1971c:3–31) for Stans' testimony to Congress on the issue. Branscomb (1973) also provides a nice retrospective on this debate.

40. Wade (1971).

41. Shapley (1971:387).

42. Shapley (1971:388, 1972a:279).

43. Shapley (1972a).

44. Shapley (1972b:1343).

45. See Britan (1981) on ETIP, and chapter 6 of this book on ERDIP. ERDIP had been "practically shelved" by 1975 (Carey 1975); ETIP dragged on a little longer (Britan 1981).

46. See U.S. House (1971c) for an example of Nelson's testimony, U.S. House (1972, 1976a) for Mansfield's and U.S. Senate (1974) for Arrow's. Economists' writings are also included in U.S. House (1971d) and (1976b), among others. The quotation is from Walsh (1976:1101).

47. The report, "The Role of New Technical Enterprises in the U.S. Economy," by John O. Flender and Richard S. Morse, can be found reprinted in U.S. Senate (1979c:594–606). Morse had been a member of the Charpie panel. Among other things, the report would play a significant role in the National Venture Capital Association's effort to cut the capital gains tax, as discussed in chapter 4.

48. Quoted in Walsh (1976:1103).

49. See NRC (1978:143–145) for a short discussion and summary of Boretsky's data as well as an alternative analysis of the same data showing a general improvement of the high-tech trade balance since 1967 to 1975, with only a modest one-year decline between 1971 and 1972. A 1976 NSF report also showed a large, favorable, and increasing trade balance in products from R&D-intensive industries, with the positive balance doubling between 1970 and 1974 alone. The only real caveat was Japan, where a deficit had developed in the mid-1960s and continued to persist as of 1974 (Ford 1976:25–26).

50. Ford (1976:82).

51. Ford (1976:154). Japan was catching up, but had not yet reached U.S. levels of R&D spending.

52. Ford (1976:18–19, 165). The fraction of U.S. innovations classified as "radical innovations" also declined by nearly 50% between the 1953–1959 and 1967–1973 periods (Ford 1976:20).

53. "American Ingenuity" (1976).

54. McCurdy (1976).

55. "The Breakdown of U.S. Innovation" (1976).

56. Several industry representatives, including Texas Instruments' Patrick Haggerty, General Electric's Arthur Bueche, and Ford's Michael Ference, also served on a President's Science Advisory Committee panel on the economic impact of R&D; see Boffey (1971). And NTOP leader Magruder was from the aerospace industry (Shapley 1971).

57. See Katz (1978:chapter 9) on Nixon's approach to science policy, which was more partisan than his predecessors', and in which he took little personal interest.

58. Arthur D. Little and the Industrial Research Institute (1973).

59. Haggerty (1974), Abelson (1974), U.S. Senate (1974), U.S. Congress (1975).

60. NAE (1976). Discussion of industry innovation concerns had taken place within NAE earlier as well, notably at a 1970 symposium on technology and international trade (NAE 1971).

61. NAS (1976:77), NRC (1978).

62. U.S. House (1976a:3–38).

63. "The Breakdown of U.S. Innovation" (1976), "The Silent Crisis in R&D" (1976). Walsh (1976:1102) refers to "a survey of company-sponsored R&D by 730

firms in the 28 July issue of *Business Week*"; however, I was not able to find the article to which he refers.

64. Dickson (1984:35), NSF (1976).

65. Lewis Branscomb, for example, suggested in early 1973 that "An improving economy, a gradual but steady reduction in unemployment, and the passage of an election year may have lessened the sense of urgency in Washington"; similarly, *Science* editor Philip Abelson noted, in an editorial on threats to the Experimental Technology Incentives Program, that "1973 has brought new political realities. The economy is more robust. Talk of unemployment of scientists and engineers has abated. The President has won reelection. The big push in Washington is now to hold federal expenditures to $250 billion" (Abelson 1973, Branscomb 1973:145). See also Shapley (1973b) on the tight link between economic conditions and support for these programs.

66. NBER (2010), U.S. DOL (2010c, 2010d).

67. NRC (1978:143–145), U.S. Census Bureau (2010), U.S. DOL (2010e). The overall balance of trade was slightly positive in 1973 and 1975, but its trend was in the negative direction (U.S. Census Bureau 2010).

68. Carey (1975).

69. U.S. House (1976a), "New NSF Advisory Groups" (1976), NRC (1978), NSF (1976).

70. Walsh (1976:1101).

71. U.S. House (1976b:123–127), Carey (1977).

72. Carey (1977).

73. "Vanishing Innovation" (1978), "Federal Aid" (1977).

74. In his 1978 State of the Union address, Carter said, "I am recommending a program of real growth of scientific research and other steps that will strengthen the Nation's research centers and encourage a new surge of technological innovation by American industry" (Greenberg 1978). On the Domestic Policy Review, see "The Right Way" (1978), "Research: No More" (1978), "Vanishing Innovation" (1978).

75. Dickson (1984:275–276). See Turner (2006) for a participant's account; he writes that about "500 private-sector participants and 250 representatives from twenty-eight federal agencies" were involved (p. 124).

76. "On the Hill, a Dud" (1979), "Innovation: Some Positive Steps" (1979), "A Policy for Industry" (1980).

77. "Vanishing Innovation" (1978). See also "America's Technological Lag" (1979), "Digging a Spur into Innovation" (1979), "The 'Innovation Recession'" (1978), "Research: No More" (1978), "The Sad State of Innovation" (1979) for other examples of this rhetoric.

78. Turner (2006) also argues that the DPR had significant indirect effects.

79. "Innovation: Some Positive Steps" (1979).

80. "Innovation: Some Positive Steps" (1979), "A Policy for Industry" (1980). This level of attention continued—if not increased—for the next several years. Dickson (1984:12) noted that between January and March 1983, over 200 bills were introduced that purported to improve technological innovation.

81. Based on a HeinOnline search conducted 28 July 2010 of the *Congressional Record* for the term *innovation* within 20 words of the terms *economy* or *economic*. This could be found on 0.55 pages per thousand in 1973 (n = 24), 1.16 pages per thousand in 1976 (n = 40), 2.09 pages per thousand in 1979 (n = 79), and 3.42 pages per

thousand in 1981 (n = 111). The value ranged from 1.10 to 1.46 from 1983 to 1988, and dropped back below 1.00 in 1989. Related phrases like *industrial innovation*, *technology policy*, *technological innovation*, and *technology* near *economy* or *economic* show similar trends, with peaks in 1979, 1980, 1981, or 1982, depending on the exact term. My perception is that references on the floor of Congress may have slightly trailed discussions in more specialized policy circles. The innovation debate was distinct from the competitiveness debate, which was emerging by the end of the 1970s but peaked significantly later, from about 1987 to 1993 (based on uses of the term *competitiveness* per thousand pages of the *Congressional Record*).

82. "A Policy for Industry" (1980).

83. Walsh (1976:1102).

84. "The Sad State" (1979), Manners and Nason (1978:10), NSB (1979:table 4.1). Figures are in current dollars. See also Dickson (1984:chapter 6) on the connections the business community made between excessive regulation and innovation problems.

85. "A Policy for Industry" (1980).

86. U.S. Senate (1978a:87).

87. "Digging a Spur" (1979).

88. Walsh (1981).

89. For examples of university scientists discussing the economic role of academic research, see Roy (1972) and Walker and Hampel (1974).

90. For example, at the National Research Council's Woods Hole conference in 1976, while a number of professors of economics or law were in attendance, no university scientists, university leaders, or representatives of university organizations (like the Association of American Universities) were listed (NRC 1978).

91. NSF (1976:5–6).

92. NSF (1976:5).

Chapter 4
Faculty Entrepreneurship in the Biosciences

1. Cohen et al. (1973).

2. See BIO (2008) re industry size.

3. Lecuyer (2005), Murmann (2004).

4. Quittmeyer (1960), Teague (1982).

5. See also Trow (1972), Roizen, Fulton, and Trow (1978), Boyer and Lewis (1984, 1986), and Rebne (1989) on faculty consulting practices.

6. Cape (2003).

7. Berg (1997).

8. Kornberg (1997).

9. There were a very few exceptions to this, one of which—the firm Cetus, founded in 1971—will be discussed later in the chapter.

10. NIH (2010). The 1966 appropriation of $1.1 billion was 9.32 times the 1956 appropriations in inflation-adjusted dollars.

11. See Abir-Am (1982), Bud (1993), Kay (1996), Morange (1998) on the history of molecular biology.

12. Judson (1996) is an excellent account of the discovery of the structure of DNA.

13. Although biochemistry is now closely tied to molecular biology, it has a distinct intellectual tradition rooted in medical schools; see Gilbert (1982), Kohler (1982), van Helvoort (2002).

14. See Creager (1996) on an early attempt to establish a biochemistry department at Berkeley. For a history of the reorganization of Berkeley's biological sciences, see Trow (1984, 1999). For a firsthand account, see Koshland, Park, and Taylor (2003).

15. On Terman and Stanford, see Gillmore (2004), Leslie (1993), Lowen (1997).

16. Vettel (2004:103).

17. In 1966, Stanford's graduate faculty in biochemistry were ranked third nationally, after Harvard and Berkeley (Cartter 1966:46).

18. Rutter (1998). UCSF was not ranked among the top 53 biochemistry departments in 1966 (Cartter 1966:46).

19. Goulian, Kornberg, and Sinsheimer (1967).

20. "Synthetic Version" (1967), "Uncovering Life's Secrets" (1967), Bengelsdorf (1967), U.S. Senate (1968).

21. See Jackson, Symons, and Berg (1972). Arthur Kornberg also emphasized the early contributions of another Stanford postdoc, Peter Lobban, whose 1972 thesis, Kornberg said, was "clearly the first report on recombinant DNA technology" (Kornberg 1997). See also Berg (1997), Kornberg (1995:275–281), Lear (1978) on Lobban.

22. Berg (1997).

23. Many scientists were shifting from work on bacteria to tumor viruses in response to NIH's growing interest in funding research relevant to cancer. For contemporary discussions of fears around recombinant DNA research, see Lear (1978), Wade (1977).

24. Lear (1978:59–60). See Boyer (1994:31–35) for Herbert Boyer's account of this meeting.

25. On the work ethic in the UCSF biochemistry department and its diffusion into the early biotech companies, see Edward Penhoet's statement in D'Andrade, Holveck, and Penhoet (2001:77–78).

26. Cohen et al. (1973); see also Hughes (2001:542).

27. Berg (1997:70–71).

28. The debate over the safety of recombinant DNA technology has received a great deal of attention. Wright (1994) is the definitive account. Also see Krimsky (1982) for a critical perspective and Fredrickson (2001) for an insider's account. A large collection of oral histories on the rDNA controversy is available at the MIT Archives.

29. Berg (1997:120). The small group of attendees included, in addition to Berg, David Baltimore, Hermann Lewis, Daniel Nathans, Richard Roblin, James Watson, Sherman Weissman, and Norton Zinder (Wright 1994:137).

30. See Berg et al. (1974) for the *Science* version of the letter.

31. Wright (1994:140).

32. Wright (1994:144–148). Berg's lab's 1972 paper had already led to a first Asilomar conference on biohazards in 1973. See Hellman, Oxman, and Pollack (1973) for the proceedings of Asilomar 1.

33. Wright (1994:144–157).

34. U.S. Senate (1975).

35. Wright (1994).

36. McElheny (1974), Bylinsky (1974:96).

37. This is a paraphrase of Cetus founder Ron Cape's (2003) statement about biotech prior to rDNA: "You can look at the stars all you want; you can't move them around."

38. Wright (1986:324).

39. While there may be examples of other early bioscience firms founded by academics, the only other one I know of is Collaborative Research. It was founded in 1961 by Brandeis chemistry professor Orrie Friedman, who left his faculty position to start the company (Baker 2007, Friedman 2004). Another contender for the label of first biotech firm is Bio-Rad, founded in 1952 by Berkeley graduates to sell tobacco mosaic virus to researchers (CHF 2010). Bio-Rad's founders were never professors, though.

40. Vettel (2006:chapter 8). As Paul Berg (1997) later recalled, Berkeley professor and Cetus founder Donald Glaser came to Stanford in the early 1970s "and gave a seminar and got a big yawn. He was a very bright guy, very dynamic. But nobody that I recall ever said, 'Hey, that's the wave of the future.'" Other academics involved in Cetus included Joshua Lederberg, chair of the genetics department at Stanford, and Arnold Demain, a professor of microbiology at MIT. In addition to Vettel (2006), see the oral histories of founders Ronald Cape (2003) and Donald Glaser (2004).

41. See Hughes (2001:562) re Cohen's sign-on. The quotation, from an unpublished Cetus Corporation "Special Report" written in the second half of 1975, is from Wright (1986:324).

42. Cohen may have been reluctant for multiple reasons, including a view of patents as covering devices, rather than techniques, and discomfort with the fact that the patent would credit only himself and Boyer, and not their co-authors. He was not, however, opposed to protecting intellectual property in general; he himself had received a patent as a postdoc, and he had previously worked with Reimers on a software copyright (Hughes 2001:548–550, Reimers 1997).

43. See Hughes (2001) for a comprehensive account of the patenting of recombinant DNA, and Reimers (1995 [1987], 1997) for firsthand accounts.

44. Wright (1986:325) notes six by late 1976: Hoffman-La Roche, Upjohn, Eli Lilly, SmithKline Corporation, Merck, and Miles Laboratories. See Robertson (1974) re ICI's collaboration.

45. Wright (1994:87–92).

46. Imperial Chemical Industries memorandum, 2 July 1976, cited in Wright (1986:325).

47. Cohn (1977).

48. Perkins (2001:3).

49. See Swanson (1997:9–15) for a personal account of these events, as well as the oral histories of Boyer (1994), Perkins (2001), Byers (2006), and Cape (2003). Kleiner & Perkins was already becoming disillusioned with Cetus by this point, and Cape has noted that he thought it was "sort of weird" that Robert Swanson was coming to him looking for a job in 1975 when "Kleiner Perkins had given us some indication . . . that they didn't think we were running the company right" (2003:80).

50. Swanson (1997:16).

51. Boyer (1994:71).

52. Perkins (2001:6), Swanson (1997:19, 21).

53. On the second project, see Boyer (1994:71–78).

54. See Itakura (2006), Riggs (2006).

55. Itakura (2006), Riggs (2006). Itakura later recalled that "unconsciously maybe I have some hesitation. I think I never expressed, so that's just my own thoughts" (Itakura 2006:29).

56. Swanson (1997:27).

57. Swanson (1997:25).

58. The phrase "viciously attacked" is from Swanson (1997:30). See Betlach (1994:31–33), Boyer (1994:96–99), D'Andrade, Holveck, and Penhoet (2001), Heyneker (2002:39–41), Rutter (1998:102–107), Ullrich (2006:22–23) for various takes on the internal environment at UCSF when Genentech was founded.

59. See Boyer (1994:96–98).

60. Wright (1994:274).

61. Cooke (1978:12). The chair, University of Michigan professor David Jackson, had done a postdoc with Paul Berg and coauthored the 1972 paper that had recombined DNA using the technically difficult method.

62. Georges Köhler and César Milstein first created hybridomas that could produce antibodies at the Medical Research Council's Laboratory of Molecular Biology in Cambridge, England (Köhler and Milstein 1975). These hybridomas fused together tumor cells and antibody-producing cells; they could live indefinitely, like tumor cells, but also steadily produce pure antibodies (called *monoclonal antibodies*). Unlike recombinant DNA, hybridoma technology was not patented; as the *Economist* colorfully put it, "The Cambridge boffins did not think to take out a patent on it" ("Invented in Britain" 1979). That statement is not quite accurate, however. While in general Milstein (Köhler was his postdoc) preferred that academic work not be patented, he did contact a government official to suggest patenting the technology; the official told him it was not possible (Mackenzie, Keating, and Cambrosio 1990, Wade 1980d). Hybritech, the first hybridoma startup, would be started in 1978.

63. Itakura (2006), Riggs (2006).

64. Wright (1994:224), Norman (1977:2).

65. Berg (1997), Cohen (1995).

66. Wright (1994:187–190).

67. "The Maddening Struggle" (1975).

68. U.S. Senate (1979c:606).

69. Reiner (1989).

70. See Perez (1986:30), citing Venture Economics, Inc. The total pool of venture capital remained relatively stable during the years 1969 to 1977, fluctuating from $2.5 to $3.5 billion, but as IPOs dried up in the bear market much of that money remained tied up in existing investments. See "The Tax Cut" (1978) on the effects of the poor market for IPOs on the availability of new venture capital.

71. Lerner (2002:37).

72. See Vettel (2006:192–193) on Cetus, Swanson (1997) and Boyer (1994) on Genentech, Reinhold (1980) on Genex, and Hall (1987:191–195) on Biogen.

73. Wright (1986:352). The first hybridoma product, introduced in December 1979, actually beat it (Wade 1980c).

74. U.S. Congress (1988b:81).

75. Wade (1979, 1980a).

76. "Industry Starts" (1978).

77. See Wright (1986:330–331) for a list of early investments by multinationals in biotech firms.

78. Cape (2003).

79. Glaser (2004:104). For dates on Cetus's acquiring funding, see Wright (1994:88).

80. Hilts (1982:185), cited in Etzkowitz (1983:201). While entrepreneurship was

certainly no longer unusual by 1982, the question of just how common it had become is more debatable, and I will return to it later in this chapter.

81. Wright (1994:186–191,221–224).

82. Wright (1994:263).

83. In addition to Norman (1977:2), see "Administration to Seek" (1977).

84. "Academy Opposes" (1977).

85. "Set for Biology's" (1977). See also Eli Lilly's Irving Johnson: "It appears inevitable that there will be legislation in this area" (Hall 1987:133).

86. Norman (1977:2), Wright (1994:264–271).

87. Wright (1994:187–190).

88. Hall (1987:212–213), Ullrich (2006:20). See also Johnson (2006:18–20) and Rathmann (2004:13–14) on the effects of rDNA restrictions on early commercial development.

89. "Federal Aid" (1977).

90. U.S. Senate (1977d); see also U.S. House (1977a).

91. U.S. Senate (1977a:13–14).

92. "A Commercial Debut" (1977).

93. See U.S. Senate (1977a:206, 290, 341, 368). Note that each of these statements was made by a different speaker; this was not the rhetorical strategy of a single individual.

94. Hughes (2001:566), Wright (1994:278).

95. Wright (1994:275–276).

96. U.S. House (1978b).

97. See Gompers (1994) and Gompers and Lerner (1998) for economic analyses of the factors affecting investment in venture capital during this period. See Reiner (1989), especially chapter 6, for a historical account.

98. U.S. Congress (1988a). From 1954 to 1967, the maximum marginal tax rate on capital gains was 25%. A surtax was in effect from 1968 to 1970 to help finance the Vietnam War, raising the rate to 26.9% in 1968 and 27.5% in 1969. In 1969, the Tax Reform Act raised the maximum rate to 35% by 1972, but changes in the alternative tax, the introduction of an add-on minimum tax on some tax preference income, and a 50-cent reduction in the new maximum tax for every dollar of tax preference income meant that some taxpayers could pay as much as a 45.5% marginal tax rate on capital gains. The Tax Reform Act of 1976 further increased effective maximum marginal rates to 49.125%, though few taxpayers were actually taxed at this rate. See U.S. Congress (1988a:30–40).

99. Longstreth (1986:33).

100. See Ross (1977a, 1977b) and Thomas and Segall (1977) for news accounts of the problem. See "ERISA Amendments" (1977) and "Witnesses Support Bill" (1977) for the perspective of fund managers. See Board of Governors (2007:67) for data on pension fund holdings. Gompers (1994) and Gompers and Lerner (1998) actually argue that relaxing the ERISA restrictions was a more significant factor than cutting the capital gains tax in stimulating investment in venture capital. Robert Swanson, incidentally, later noted that Kleiner & Perkins initially looked into Cetus because an institutional investor had to pull out due to the prudent man rule (1997:12).

101. Reiner (1989). Bancroft (2010:54) recalls thirty-seven original members.

102. Johnson (1980:41).

103. See Johnson (1980:41–44) for the history. The Department of Commerce report (by John O. Flender and Richard S. Morse, and also mentioned in chapter 3) can be found reprinted in U.S. Senate (1979c:594–606).

104. The NVCA report can be found reprinted in U.S. House (1977e:123–134). Quotations are from p. 123.

105. U.S. House (1977e:133–134).

106. "The Business Stakes" (1977). At the time, the top rate on earned income was 70%.

107. Dennis (2009:33).

108. The American Electronics Association was actually called the Western Electronics Manufacturers' Association until 1978 (Johnson 1980:59).

109. Johnson (1980:45–51).

110. See Johnson (1980:51–127) on this phase of the campaign. The American Council for Capital Formation was formed by timber interests, who were particularly affected by the capital gains tax (Martin 1991:117), and led by a former vice president of the American Banking Association (p. 62). The ACCF would go on to play a key role in the supply-side revolution; see, e.g., Martin (1991:chapter 5). The American Electronics Association, on the other hand, primarily represented the interests of small to midsized electronics firms, though it had a few large members (Johnson 1980:46).

111. See U.S. Congress (1977), U.S. House (1977e), U.S. Senate (1977b, 1977c, 1977e, 1977f). While NVCA and AEA knew that ERISA was a problem (see Johnson 1980:56–57, NVCA 1977:133–134), they chose to focus their efforts on the capital gains tax (Johnson 1980:70). Nevertheless, representatives of the venture capital and small business communities were well represented at ERISA hearings as well (U.S. House 1977e, U.S. Senate 1977c).

112. See Crawford (1982:5–15) on the proposed bills. One, for example, a bill introduced by Senator Lloyd Bentsen (S. 285), would have explicitly allowed pension fund managers to invest up to 2% of their funds in small businesses or venture capital that supported small businesses (U.S. Senate 1977c:1–17). See "Carter Pulls Back" (1978) on the administration's actions.

113. "Partial Text" (1977), "Prudent Man Rule" (1977).

114. "Investment Work Group of the Advisory Council on Employee Welfare and Pension Benefit Plans Position Paper" (24 January 1978), National Archives, General Records of the Department of Labor, Records of the Office of the Assistant Secretary for Labor-Management Relations, Records of the Advisory Council on Employee Welfare and Pension Benefit Plans, record group 174.4.3.

115. "Rules and Regulations" (1978). It is difficult to say how much impact the NVCA had on the DOL decision, but Reiner (1989:387–388) notes that NVCA cofounder Charles "Lea and other NVCA leaders lobbied for language [in the ERISA guidelines] that would let pension fund managers invest in venture capital without being held personally liable."

116. Letter of the National Venture Capital Association to the Office of Regulatory Standards and Exceptions, Pension and Welfare Benefit Programs, U.S. Department of Labor (22 June 1978), cited in Crawford (1982:5–18); see also Letter of the U.S. Small Business Administration to the Office of Regulatory Standards and Exceptions, Pension and Welfare Benefit Programs, U.S. Department of Labor (10 May 1978). See "Rules and Regulations" (1979) for the final version of the new regulations.

117. It averaged 39% throughout the 1980s. See Gompers and Lerner (1998:165).

118. See Johnson (1980:45–126) for a detailed account of this effort.

119. Egan (1977).

120. "American Venture Capital" (1978).

121. Johnson (1980:82–83). See also Lardner (1978) for another account of Zschau prompting Steiger's interest.

122. U.S. House (1978c:1310–1311).

123. U.S. House (1978c:1307).

124. Cowan (1978).

125. Wanniski (1978).

126. Pine (1978a, 1978c).

127. Proposition 13 capped (and dramatically reduced) property taxes in California; see Martin (2008).

128. Pine (1978c). See also Johnson (1980:161–304) for a detailed account of the legislative battle.

129. Fraker, Hubbard, and Witherspoon (1978).

130. U.S. Senate (1979c:1–2).

131. Lea (2008:89). The report "The Role of New Technical Enterprises in the U.S. Economy" was commissioned by the Department of Commerce and conducted by John O. Flender and Richard S. Morse, then both at MIT. Coincidentally (or perhaps not), Morse was Robert Swanson's mentor as an undergraduate at MIT. See MIT Entrepreneurship Center (2010).

132. Pine (1978b), Graham (1978c).

133. Johnson (1980:298).

134. The $600 million figure is from Perez (1986:30), citing Venture Economics, Inc. A December 1979 *U.S. News & World Report* article, citing *Venture Capital Journal*, said that more than half of funds raised in 1978 were raised in the last quarter, but that article gives a much lower estimate for total new investment in 1978 ($216 million) ("Wallets Open Up" 1979).

135. Bethesda Research Labs was founded in 1975 to produce restriction enzymes, but it did not move into the rDNA field until 1978 (Cooke 1978).

136. Scherer (1980).

137. U.S. Congress (1984a:93, 1988b:78–79), Crawford (1986:13).

138. See Hall (1987) for an account of the competition among these labs.

139. Hall (1987:191–192).

140. Hall (1987:191–195, 209–210).

141. Swanson (1997:31); see also Kleid (2002:101) and Hall (1987:192–194).

142. See Hall (1987) on the formation of Biogen.

143. See Villa-Komaroff et al. (1978) for the paper and Hall (1987) for the story behind it.

144. See Boyer (1994), Goeddel (2002), Hall (1987), Itakura (2006), Johnson (2006), Riggs (2006), Swanson (1997) for various accounts of these events.

145. See Cooke (1978) re the 150 employees at Cetus and Lewin (1978) on the five PhDs at Cetus. Lewin also notes that Cetus had about three times that number in technical support for genetic engineering, while Genentech had five total working on rDNA.

146. Cooke (1978).

147. See an earlier note in this chapter re the production of monoclonal antibodies by Köhler and Milstein in 1975.

148. Byers (2006:15). In an indication of the importance of Silicon Valley social networks to the early development of biotech, the reason Royston knew to call Byers was because Royston, who had studied at Stanford, was dating a woman (later to become his wife) who had previously dated Byers (Powell and Sandholtz forthcoming).

149. The exact founding date of IPRI is hard to determine. U.S. Congress (1984a:69) dates it to 1978, while "On the Front Lines" (1980) suggests it was founded in 1976. The article "On the Front Lines" (published August 1980) contains the earliest reference to it I have found. It is not clear that IPRI was as solidly grounded a startup as the others discussed so far. William Rutter (1998:59), of UCSF's biochemistry department, has said, "Some of the early biotechnology companies were based almost purely on hucksterism. There was a young faculty person in pharmacology named Martin Apple who started IPRI. . . . Apple had a strong imagination and a flair for selling. . . . For a relatively poor scientist, there was the vision of sudden riches. . . . When it came to science, he stretched the truth, he was not rigorous. In fact he was a phony. . . . But he had a strong entrepreneurial instinct and was savvy about many aspects of science."

150. I am counting here Cetus, Genentech, Genex, Biogen, Hybritech, and IPRI, but it is not totally clear that IPRI was actually active in 1978; alternatively, one might argue that Bethesda Research Laboratories should be included in this count. Enzo Biochem, founded in 1976, is sometimes mentioned as an early biotech company, but it was founded to produce enzymes, not to work on rDNA. The best description of Enzo's history I have been able to find is at Funding Universe (2010).

151. Pisano (2006:85).

152. Pisano (2006:87).

153. Glaser (2004:104). See "A Commercial Debut" (1977) and "Set for Biology's" (1977).

154. See Wright (1994:88–89) for a list of early investors in Genentech and other firms.

155. Swanson (1997:48), Kiley (2002:19).

156. See Pisano (2006:86–87) on the importance of the Genentech–Lilly deal as a model for financing biotech R&D.

157. Hall (1987). See also Johnson (2006) for an account from Lilly's perspective.

158. Hall (1987:309).

159. U.S. Congress (1984a:93); U.S. Congress (1988b:78–79) gives higher numbers of total firms founded each year, but the proportions are similar. My sense, however, is that U.S. Congress (1988b) uses a definition of biotech firms that is more expansive than I use here, and that the 1984 report better reflects the number of firms specifically focusing on recombinant DNA and hybridoma technologies.

160. Wade (1979).

161. Perez (1986:30), citing Venture Economics, Inc.

162. The quotations come from venture capitalists; the first two refer to the capital gains tax cut and the third to ERISA (Bancroft 2010:61, Dennis 2009:45, Lea 2008:90).

163. Gompers and Lerner (1998, 2004:chapter 3).

164. "Wallets Open Up" (1979).

165. "More Firms Join" (1979).

166. "Gene Splicing" (1979).

167. "Where Genetic Engineering" (1979).

168. "DNA Is" (1979), Crittenden (1981). To be fair to IPRI founder Martin Apple, who made the statement, he meant not that they would literally make pork chops grow on trees, but that they might create genetically engineered plants with the nutritive value of a pork chop. See Charles (2001:12) for one account of the story.

169. Wade (1980c). Centocor went on to relative success and was acquired by Johnson & Johnson in 1999 (Powell and Sandholtz forthcoming:81–84). I have seen few other references to Clonal Research, but it is still on a list of biotech firms in U.S. Congress (1984a:543). Monoclonal Antibodies, which made diagnostics, went public in 1981 and in 1984 was sued by Hybritech for patent infringement, a suit that was ultimately dismissed (Hoovers 2010).

170. On Molecular Genetics, see Kenney (1986:98, 104). On Collaborative Genetics, see Wade (1980e). Collaborative Genetics was set up by Collaborative Research, a company that was founded in 1962 and sold tissue culture.

171. Powell and Sandholtz (forthcoming:81–82). See O'Mara (2005:chapter 4) on the University City Science Center, where Centocor was initially located. See Vaughan (2000) on Centocor founder and Wistar Institute director Hilary Koprowski.

172. Wade (1979).

173. "Research Teams Use" (1979).

174. Wade (1980c).

175. Wade (1979:665).

176. Wright (1986:352).

177. Wright (1994:97–98); see Andreopoulos (1980) for the original criticism.

178. Hughes (2001); see also Yi (2008).

179. Kevles (1994); see Bugos and Kevles (1992) on the history of the 1970 Plant Variety Protection Act.

180. Press et al. (1980).

181. Clark, Begley, and Hager (1980).

182. "DNA Is" (1979).

183. Kleid (2002:101). Similarly, a lawyer who worked for Genentech in the early 1980s later recalled that "the management of Genentech, when I worked there, was convinced that, were it not for patents, they could not survive as a company. It was always considered an essential part of the business plan" (Charles 2001:10–11). And Thomas Kiley (2002:22), Genentech's legal counsel and vice president, said that "had the Court gone the other way, I think we would have been significantly wounded."

184. Dennis (2009:35).

185. Kiley (2002:21).

186. Wade (1980a).

187. Wade (1980a:691).

188. Kevles (1994).

189. D'Andrade, Holveck, and Penhoet (2001). The quotation is of Edward Penhoet, Berkeley professor and cofounder of Chiron.

190. Kevles (1994:130), paraphrasing the amicus briefs of Genentech and the Pharmaceutical Manufacturers Association.

191. Kiley (2002:21).

192. Hughes (2001:569).

193. Scherer (1980).

194. Kenney (1986:156–157).

195. U.S. Congress (1984a:93).

196. Hughes (2001:541–542).

197. Hughes (2001:570).

198. Wade (1980c:692–693).

199. Cole (1980).

200. Gannes (1987:9), quoted in Powell and Sandholtz (forthcoming:88).

201. Kenney (1986:136–138).

202. Bowes (2008:21–22). Bowes was familiar with the industry in part because he had previously served on the board of Cetus (pp. 16–19).

203. Bowes (2008:22–25).

204. Rathmann (2004:16).

205. See also Robbins-Roth (2000:chapter 3), on the Amgen story.

206. Berg (1997).

207. Cape (2003:14).

208. See Berg (1997) and Kornberg (1995, 1997) for different accounts of this story.

209. Berg (1997:138).

210. D'Andrade, Holveck, and Penhoet (2001:99).

211. D'Andrade, Holveck, and Penhoet (2001:100–109).

212. U.S. Congress (1984a:93). This compares to 26 firms founded in 1980 and 13 founded before 1980. A later OTA report (U.S. Congress 1988b:78–79), which gives higher numbers (see note 159 of this chapter for a brief discussion), still clearly shows 1981 as the peak year, with more than twice as many firms founded that year as any other.

213. Crawford (1986:13).

214. Hall (1987:301). This would be the only recombinant product on the market until 1985, when Genentech's human growth hormone was approved.

215. Kenney (1986:157).

216. U.S. Congress (1984a:282–283).

217. Kenney (1986:157).

218. Perez (1986:30), citing Venture Economics, Inc.

219. U.S. Congress (1988b:84).

220. U.S. Congress (1984a:275–276).

221. See U.S. Congress (1984a:95) for references to a coming shakeout in 1981 and 1982, as well as U.S. House (1982:104).

222. U.S. Congress (1984a:93, 1988b:78–79).

223. U.S. Congress (1984a:95).

224. U.S. Congress (1988b:82). The most successful class of products were not therapeutics but monoclonal antibody diagnostics, with $150 million in sales in 1985.

225. Crawford (1986:13).

226. U.S. Congress (1988b:78).

227. Crawford (1986:13).

228. See Crawford (1986:13) for another prediction of a shakeout, and U.S. Congress (1988b:92) on the lack thereof.

229. Kenney (1986:149–154).

230. Kenney (1986:101–103).

231. Again, this is based on OTA's 1984 numbers (U.S. Congress 1984a:93); its 1988 numbers (U.S. Congress 1988b:78–79) report substantially higher figures for firm foundings in the 1970s and early 1980s.

232. The quote, which refers to those working with monoclonal antibodies, comes from Wade (1980c:692–693). See also Hilts (1982:185), cited in Etzkowitz (1983:201). Etzkowitz also quotes *Science* reporter Barbara Culliton, who makes a more modest claim: "A majority of the country's leading researchers in molecular genetics and related disciplines are known to have affiliations with . . . [the] new, highly competitive [biotechnology] companies" (Culliton 1982a:961).

233. Etzkowitz (1983:201).

234. Blumenthal et al. (1986).

235. Byers (2006:19).

236. Boly (1982), reprinted in U.S. House (1982:171–178).

237. Culliton (1982a:960).

238. See, for example, Culliton (1982b) and Langfitt et al. (1983).

239. Boyer (1994), Swanson (1997), Hall (1987).

240. Pisano (2006:85, 198–199).

241. Wade (1977:70).

242. Hall (1987:254–259).

243. Boyer (1994), Swanson (1997).

244. Pisano (2006:86–87).

245. Bowes (2008:19–20).

246. Ullrich (2006:22). David Jackson, founding chair of Genex's scientific advisory board, later decided that Genex's more restrictive approach to publication was misguided, saying, "I have come to think Genentech's way is the right way. I think it does help one recruit to let people who you're trying to hire know that they will be able to continue to publish" (Powell and Sandholtz forthcoming:35). See also Boyer (1994:87): "I insisted that we have the scientists publish their research in journals. Any proprietary information would have to be covered by patents. I felt this was extremely important for attracting outstanding young scientists in the community that were interested in doing research in an industrial setting."

247. Powell and Sandholtz (forthcoming:78). Cetus had similar issues; see Vettel (2006:chapter 8).

248. Goeddel (2002:24).

249. "American Venture Capital" (1978).

250. Reiner (1989:381). The final ERISA regulations were published in June 1979, but pension funds started to respond before as it became clear that the rules would be clarified to permit investment in venture capital.

251. See, for example, Graham (1978c), Pauly (1979), "The Tax Cut" (1978), "Venture Capital" (1979), and "Wallets Open Up" (1979).

252. Reiner (1989:389).

253. Gompers and Lerner (1998, 2004:chapter 3).

254. Köhler and Milstein (1975).

255. "Where Are Britain's" (1977).

256. U.S. Congress (1984a:287).

257. Wright (1994).

258. "Biotechnology in Britain" (1983), "Bugging Britain" (1980). For comparison, Britain had one-fifth the population of the U.S. in the early 1980s.

259. "The Bugs Business" (1980). See also "A Fast but Bumpy Track" (1980), "National Enterprise Board" (1980).

260. Aisenberg (1982).

261. A similar, though not identical, argument with respect to Germany is made by Loeppky (2005).

Chapter 5
Patenting University Inventions

1. Hughes (2001:541).

2. See Public Law 98-517.

3. Feldman, Colaianni, and Liu (2007), Hughes (2001:570).

4. Curtis (2000), Demenet (2002). The patent had brought in this amount by 2000, when Yale sold 80% of its rights in exchange for up-front income.

5. Blumenstyk (1999, 2005).

6. AUTM (2008). Not every university responded to AUTM's survey, and not every respondent allowed its data to be published, but Yale University, Scripps Research Institute, and North Carolina State University are the only schools among the fifty with the highest R&D expenditures (NSB 2010:table 27) whose 2007 licensing incomes are not listed.

7. Mowery et al. (2004:47).

8. NSB (1996:appendix table 5-42, 2006:appendix table 5-68).

9. See Article I, Section 8.

10. See Metlay (2006) for a comparison of patent policy debates in the early twentieth century with those in the Bayh-Dole era.

11. Cottrell (1932:222), cited in Mowery and Sampat (2001a:321).

12. Weick (1967:1237) cites multiple studies showing that rickets was, almost unbelievably, present among 95–100% of U.S. infants in the 1920s. See also Rajakumar (2003) on the history of rickets.

13. Apple (1989). While Steenbock does not appear to have been interested in profiting from his invention, his motives were not entirely driven by public health concerns. He also wanted to keep vitamin D out of the hands of margarine producers. He was afraid that if margarine producers could add vitamin D to their product, they would be able to claim it was nutritionally equivalent to butter and thus harm Wisconsin's dairy industry.

14. Cottrell (1912:865), cited in Mowery and Sampat (2001a:320).

15. Metlay (2006).

16. Palmer (1934) presents an early review of university patent policies. He describes the policies of seventeen institutions, and identifies another seven that handle the matter on a case-by-case basis. Only a couple of dozen universities had active research agendas in the 1930s (Geiger 1986), so this may be a relatively complete review of extant policies.

17. U.S. House (1982:217).

18. Apple (1989).

19. U.S. House (1982:221); Apple (1989:390), citing Palmer (1956).

20. Metlay (2006:570).

21. See Etzkowitz (2002:60–73) on the development of MIT's patent policy in the 1930s.

22. Mowery and Sampat (2001a:330). Mowery and Sampat note that many university research foundations eventually entered into invention administration agreements with the Research Corporation rather than manage patents directly (p. 329).

23. Palmer (1955b:55–59,75–79,84–88).

24. Palmer (1962:iv–v).

25. Mowery et al. (2004:47), Mowery and Sampat (2001a:331).

26. Bremer (2004).

27. See Metlay (2006) on the debates of the 1930s.

28. See Dupree (1957) and Geiger (1986) on the historical role of federal research funding in universities.

29. NSB (2004:appendix table 4-6). As Howard Bremer said in 1974, "At most universities there is so much federal agency funding that it is almost impossible today to find an invention that isn't touched by, or contaminated, if you want to use the word, by some federal agency funding." See National Conference (1974:134).

30. Eisenberg (1996) is the most complete short history of federal patent policy from 1941 to 1980.

31. Guston (1999:93).

32. Although in *Science—The Endless Frontier*, Bush made the fairly modest argument that the National Research Foundation should have discretion over what kind of patent arrangements to make, in general he took a stronger stance against a government-title approach.

33. Kleinman (1995:76). See also Maddox (1979) on Kilgore.

34. Kevles (1977:24). See Kleinman (1995) for an extensive discussion of the struggle between Bush and Kilgore over postwar science policy, including the issue of patents. The government-title position can also be seen in the three-volume study published by the Attorney General's office in 1947, which recommended that government should take all rights to patents (U.S. DOJ 1947). The Department of Justice historically tended to take a government-title position on patents because of its general antitrust orientation.

35. Kleinman (1995), Eisenberg (1996).

36. FCST (1976:414–457).

37. FCST (1968:1).

38. For reviews, see U.S. DOJ (1947), U.S. Senate (1959), FCST (1976).

39. U.S. Senate (1965).

40. See Mowery et al. (2004:47), NSB (1996:appendix table 5-42). Exact numbers vary somewhat depending on who is counting, but all estimates are similar. The number of patents issued to Research Corporation did not rise significantly from their 1950 to early 1960s levels; see Mowery and Sampat (2001a:331).

41. See Henderson, Jaffe, and Trajtenberg (1998:120) for a chart of university patents/university research dollars from 1965 to 1988.

42. Mowery and Sampat (2001a).

43. NSF (2003:table B).

44. Shannon (1964:1).

45. He also believed exclusive licenses, then completely banned, should be permitted (Latker and Wylie 1965).

46. These paragraphs draw on interviews with Norman Latker (2005).

47. Harbridge House (1968), U.S. GAO (1968).

48. IPAs had been used at HEW in the 1950s, but were not uniform and pursued no consistent principles or goals. See Berman (2008b) for more on IPAs and patent policy at HEW in this era more generally.

49. Latker (1971:2).

50. Latker (1976:14–15).

51. Lasken (2005), Latker (2005).

52. NSF (2003:table B).

53. DOD, again, had historically been generous with the rights to inventions resulting from the R&D it funded. Since 1964, DOD had maintained a list of institutions, published in Defense Procurement Circular No. 65, to which it would routinely waive title upon request (National Conference 1974:39).

54. Latker (2005).

55. Bremer (2001:50).

56. Bremer (2004).

57. Ancker-Johnson (2005).

58. Hammersla, Weeks, and Innes (2004). Bremer (2004) also said that Ancker-Johnson "fomented" the Case Western meeting.

59. National Conference (1974:197–204). Ancker-Johnson was the keynote speaker.

60. National Conference (1974).

61. Bremer (2001:178).

62. Sandelin (2003).

63. Kraemer (1999).

64. Latker (2005).

65. National Conference (1974:40).

66. Later to become the Department of Energy.

67. Eden (2005), Latker (2005). See FCST (1976:414–457) on AEC's policy.

68. Latker (2005).

69. Smith (1978).

70. Latker (1977:2).

71. Latker (2005).

72. Broad (1979:476).

73. Leshowitz (1979:1).

74. For the text, see Commission on Government Procurement (1972:139–146). Also see Latker (1971) and Berman (2008a).

75. For the text, see FCST (1976:82–133).

76. The bill was introduced as 95 H.R. 6249 in April 1977, and as 95 H.R. 8596 in July. See U.S. House (1976c, 1977d) for hearings. The account of why the bills died is from Latker (2005).

77. Lovell (1978:1666).

78. These included Admiral Hyman Rickover and Senator Russell Long (U.S. Senate 1978b).

79. Lasken (2005).

80. Latker (2005). Provisions of the Act were indeed extended to large businesses by executive memorandum in 1983 (Eisenberg 1996:1665).

81. See, e.g., U.S. Senate (1959, 1960, 1963a). It was the Senate Select Committee on Small Business where Senator Nelson's hearings opposing a government license patent policy were held (U.S. Senate 1978b).

82. Latker (2005).

83. U.S. House (1977d:1–2).

84. U.S. House (1977d:821–913).

85. U.S. Senate (1978c:978).

86. For more details, see Stevens (2004).

87. Berman (2008b), Stevens (2004).

88. The bill was introduced as 95 S. 3496 in 1978, and reintroduced as 96 S. 414 in 1979.

89. U.S. Senate (1979b:1, 3).

90. Graham (1979).

91. Eisenberg (1996), Stevens (2004).

92. Jaffe (2000), Jaffe and Lerner (2004).

93. In 1987 the Board of Patent Appeals and Interferences of the U.S. PTO issued *Ex Parte Allen*, which found that patents could be granted on other nonhuman animals as well as microorganisms (Kevles 2002).

94. Kevles (2002). The patent was on a mouse genetically engineered to be susceptible to cancer.

95. Kevles (2002:80).

96. Abramson (2007:12). In addition to Bayh-Dole, *Chakrabarty*, and the creation of the Court of Appeals for the Federal Circuit (which I will discuss shortly), Abramson includes the Hatch-Waxman Act, which allowed drug companies to extend their patents to compensate for regulatory reviews as well as making it easier for generic products to be launched after patent protection ended, and the Semiconductor Chip Protection Act of 1984, which made it illegal to copy the layout of a computer chip. He also refers to a Supreme Court case determining that "algorithms encoded as software" were patentable and here cites *Gottschalk v. Benson*, but I believe he intends to refer to the 1981 ruling *Diamond v. Diehr*, the effect of which was to open the door to patenting software. These last three decisions are less directly relevant to universities.

97. According to Janicke (2002:645), patent-friendly circuits "held contested patents valid approximately half the time, while most other appellate courts found patents valid far less frequently, in some as few as 12 percent of contested patents being found valid." See also Jaffe and Lerner (2004:100).

98. See Jaffe and Lerner (2004), Janicke (2002), U.S. Judicial Conference Committee (1991) on the history of the Court of Appeals for the Federal Circuit generally. See Abramson (2007:1–18) for a more popular history of CAFC.

99. Dunner, Jakes, and Karceski (1995:154), Henry and Turner (2006), Merz and Pace (1994). For other observations of the changes resulting from CAFC, see Harmon (1992), Jaffe (2000), Jaffe and Lerner (2004), Kastriner (1991).

100. See Hall (2005), Hall and Ziedonis (2001), Kim and Marschke (2004), Turner (2005). Kortum and Lerner (1998) makes a fairly strong argument that CAFC is *not* responsible for increased patenting, but Lerner, at least, has since reversed that position (Jaffe and Lerner 2004). The CAFC is certainly not the only source of increased patenting; increased investment in R&D almost definitely plays an important role (Kim and Marschke 2004, Kortum and Lerner 1998).

101. Janicke (2002:651–653).

102. See U.S. House (1977b:226–229) for a summary of the recommendations of the Hruska Commission. The Hruska Commission proposed a general court of appeals, not a specialist patent court, but did recommend that if a national court of appeals was not created, a special court of patent appeals should be considered (U.S. Senate 1981:202).

103. Meador (1992). At the outset, it was imagined the court would also hear tax appeals, but that part of the proposal was eventually dropped for political reasons.

104. Meador (1992).

105. Meador (1992:615–616).

106. Meador (1992:615).

107. Dunner (2001:546).

108. Newman (2001:543).

109. U.S. House (1981b), U.S. Senate (1981).

110. U.S. House (1981b:208).

111. Jaffe and Lerner (2004:12).

112. NSB (1983a:134–135, 2004:figure O-13).

113. NSB (1996:appendix table 5-42, 2006:appendix table 5-67).

114. Mowery et al. (2001:114).

115. Mowery et al. (2001:105, 108).

116. AAU (1986:7).

117. Matkin (1990:74).

118. AUTM (2004:12). This is based on start dates of tech transfer offices still in existence in 2003, but few offices were shut down once they opened.

119. NSB (1985:110). SUPA was later renamed AUTM, the Association of University Technology Managers, later in the decade.

120. U.S. PTO (2010).

121. Hughes (2001:541).

122. Hughes (2001:569–570).

123. Colaianni and Cook-Deegan (2009).

124. NSB (2006:567), AUTM (2004:12). Again, the number is based on the start dates of tech transfer offices still in existence in 2003.

125. Henderson, Jaffe, and Trajtenberg (1998:120–121).

126. NSB (1989:123). This figure is from 1988 as well.

127. E.g., Rosenzweig (1985); see also a special section on "Private Appropriation of Public Research" in *Science, Technology & Human Values* 12(1).

128. Matkin (1990:53). An even larger 47% thought that university-industry research relations were among the four most critical issues.

129. Matkin (1990:159).

130. AUTM (1996:19). Note that equity in lieu of royalties is, in addition to being a way for universities to license technologies to small companies without revenues, also a way of investing in startups created by their faculty. A proposal by Harvard to invest directly in faculty startups was shot down in 1980 after a national uproar, but by the time MIT started doing it in the patent context the issue generated much less heat. See Matkin (1990:148–177) as well as chapter 7 of this book.

131. In 1983, the NSB surveyed the thirty-six universities thought to receive the largest amounts of royalty income. These numbers are based on the twenty-five universities that responded. Fewer than ten universities earned at least $500,000 in a

given year. It is possible that this figure is a substantial underestimate if the survey missed one or more "hit" patents, but there is no particular reason to think that they did. See NSB (1983b:105). Matkin (1990:127) contains licensing revenue data for the four universities he studied during this period. In FY 1981, MIT earned $1.6 million and the University of California earned $1.3 million. His data for Stanford begin in FY 1983, when the university earned $2.1 million, and his data for Penn State begin in FY 1986, when the university earned $457,000. These numbers seem to be in accordance with the NSB figures, since Stanford, UC, and MIT were three of the most active patenters as of 1980.

132. AUTM (1996).

133. NSB (2008:appendix table 5-42).

134. Berman (2008b).

Chapter 6
Creating University-Industry Research Centers

1. Brody (1985).

2. Cohen, Florida, and Goe (1994:9).

3. Roy (1972:955–956).

4. Roy (1972:956). The university-industry coupling program of ARPA, the Advanced Research Projects Agency, in the field of materials science, is the best-known of the latter type. See NAS (1975a:270–271), Radcliffe (1969), Richard J. Barber Associates (1975), Sproull (2002), Test (1966).

5. Roy (1972:956).

6. Ikenberry (1970:2). See also Geiger (1990), Ikenberry (1970), Ikenberry and Friedman (1972) on the history of ORUs.

7. Ikenberry and Friedman (1972).

8. On the Materials Research Centers, see Hartman (1992), Leslie (1993:chapter 8), Radcliffe (1969), Richard J. Barber Associates (1975), Test (1966). It was in part this lack of interaction that led ARPA to develop its university-industry coupling program.

9. For an ethnography of the NBS program, the Experimental Technology Incentives Program (ETIP), see Britan (1981).

10. Shapley (1973b:1105–1106). See also Branscomb (1973) for a criticism of the ERDIP approach.

11. Robbins, Burke, and Milliken (1973).

12. Shapley (1973b:1106).

13. See Block (1977:22–23) for a list of all ten experiments and Colton (1982) for a post hoc review of the five programs that focused on the private sector. ERDIP left a dense paper trail; see Cunningham, Craig, and Schlie (1977:441–494) for a bibliography of the 100-plus reports that had resulted from the program by that point.

14. Sometimes referred to as the Cooperative Research & Development Experiment.

15. Colton (1982).

16. Burger, Cole, and Burnett (1982:73).

17. Burger, Cole, and Burnett (1982:85–101).

18. Burger, Cole, and Burnett (1982:85–95). See also Baer (1976:6–7).

19. Burger, Cole, and Burnett (1982:100).

20. See also U.S. House (1979b:69–90, and particularly 72–74) for the testimony of Richard Atkinson, Director of NSF, on lessons learned from ERDIP's UIRC-building experiments.

21. Shapley (1973b:1107).

22. Carey (1975).

23. See Baer (1978:90–91), NAS (1975a:269).

24. Keller (1996:28), Mead (1996:10–14); see also Gilder (1990:186–188), "Joining Hands" (1980). See also Mead (1991) for more background on Mead himself. In the 1960s, Sutherland was director of ARPA's Information Processing Techniques Office; see Sutherland (1989) on Sutherland's time at ARPA.

25. Gilder (1990:186).

26. "Joining Hands" (1980), Mead (1996:12).

27. "Joining Hands" (1980), Mead (1996:12), Norman (1982:514).

28. Norman (1982:514).

29. Mead (1996:12).

30. NSB (1983b:246).

31. Mead (1996:12).

32. NSB (1983b:249).

33. NSB (1983b:249), U.S. Congress (1985:178).

34. Cibuzar (1993:170), "Joining Hands" (1980); see also NSB (1983b:249).

35. "Joining Hands" (1980).

36. NSB (1983b:249).

37. U.S. Congress (1984b:30).

38. NSB (1983b:249), U.S. Congress (1985:178–179).

39. Cibuzar (1993:170).

40. Cibuzar (1993:170–171); see also Cibuzar, Polla, and McGlennen (1997:146). The center continues to exist, though it has gone through additional name changes. In the 1990s, it was called the Microtechnology Laboratory (Cibuzar, Polla, and McGlennen 1997:145), and as of mid-2011 it is the Nanofabrication Center, supported in part by NSF as part of the National Nanotechnology Infrastructure Network.

41. On Low's reputation at NASA, see Leslie (2001:242), citing Chaikin (1998 57–62).

42. Leslie (2001:242–245).

43. U.S. GAO (1983:8).

44. U.S. Congress (1985:181).

45. Leslie (2001:245–248). See Norman (1982:512) on the cost of the electronic beam lithography system.

46. Norman (1982:512).

47. Leslie (2001:248).

48. Leslie (2001:249–253).

49. Brown (1988).

50. Leslie (2001:260–264).

51. Le Maistre (1989:207), U.S. Congress (1985:180–181).

52. Smith and Karlesky (1977:76).

53. See Belanger (1998) on the evolution of the role of applied science (particularly engineering) at NSF. The applied science effort was housed in the RANN (Research Applied to National Needs) program. For a more recent reflection on RANN, see Green and Lepkowski (2006).

54. See NSF (1976:1) on the creation of the NSF-Industry Relations Committee. See U.S. House (1983c:130–131) on the 1975 reaffirmation of NSF's policy regarding industry funding.

55. U.S. Senate (1976).

56. See NSF (1976) for the resultant report; see U.S. House (1983c:135) on NSB's blocking the change.

57. "House, Senate Split" (1977).

58. U.S. House (1983c:135).

59. U.S. House (1977c:968–1006); see also U.S. House (1983c:447).

60. U.S. House (1978a:4).

61. See Atkinson testimony in U.S. House (1978a).

62. "Digging a Spur" (1979).

63. U.S. GAO (1983:33).

64. U.S. Senate and U.S. House (1979:19–20).

65. Public Law 96-480.

66. "A Shred" (1981).

67. U.S. GAO (1983:32); see also Walsh (1981).

68. Eveland, Hetzner, and Tornatzky (1984); see also Eveland and Hetzner (1982).

69. Hetzner, Gidley, and Gray (1989:337–338). The I/UCRC program is still in existence.

70. Cohen, Florida, and Goe (1994).

71. Baer (1980:19, 21).

72. See Eveland and Hetzner (1982), Eveland, Hetzner, and Tornatzky (1984) for early reflections on the success and problems of I/UCRC centers.

73. McGowen (2008).

74. U.S. GAO (1983:v).

75. Hersman (1974:2567), Plosila (2004:114). For example, the State Technical Services Program of the Department of Commerce, which was the source of industrial extension efforts, also funded state-level S&T advisory boards in the late 1960s (Coburn and Berglund 1994:50), and in 1969 NSF established an Office of Intergovernmental Science, which worked with state government organizations to encourage states to develop resources for applying S&T to their problems (NSF 1971:101–102).

76. See, for example, Nixon's historic 1972 Science and Technology Message to Congress, which called for greater partnership between the federal, state, and local levels (American Presidency Project 2008b).

77. Hersman (1974:2567).

78. The State Science, Engineering, and Technology program gave planning grants to forty-nine governors and forty-two state legislators, but the planning stage ended in 1979 and further funds did not materialize (Carnegie Commission 1992).

79. See, e.g., Plosila (2004:115).

80. Eisinger (1988:10–11).

81. Eisinger (1988).

82. Eisinger (1988:11).

83. Osborne (1988), Plosila (2004). California was a notable exception to this geographic pattern. Jerry Brown's gubernatorial administration (1975 to 1983) pushed the state in an entrepreneurial direction early, but this effort was blunted for political reasons and as a result the shift was not as decisive as in many of the other states (Osborne 1988).

84. U.S. DOL (2010b).

85. See Birch (1979) on the role of small business in job creation. See Hollister, Lee, and Cummings (1979), Kieschnick (1981), Peirce, Hagstrom, and Steinbach (1979), Vaughan (1979) for examples of CSPA publications.

86. Osborne (1988:33–34).

87. See Muchmore (1983) on the political and organizational reasons that NSF's late-1970s approach to encouraging states to adopt a more active science policy generally failed.

88. Eisinger (1988:241–265, 281). See also Fosler (1988) for a number of case studies of state approaches to economic development strategy in the 1970s and 1980s, though not with a particular focus on innovation.

89. See, e.g., Plosila (2004:116–117).

90. Landry (1988:259–260). See Barnhill (2001), Lambright (1999), Lippmann (1981), Norman (1982), Osborne (1988:135–136) for other accounts, some of which credit Babbitt with taking more of the initiative in pushing the effort on the university.

91. Estimates of initial budget proposals vary slightly; see Landry (1988:260), Lippman (1981), and Osborne (1988:135).

92. Osborne (1988:135).

93. Landry (1988:260), Osborne (1988:134–135).

94. Landry (1988:260–261), Osborne (1988:136).

95. NSB (1983b:248).

96. "California's Own" (1981), NSB (1983b:248).

97. "California's Own" (1981), NSB (1983b:248), Walker (1982).

98. NSB (1983b:249), U.S. Congress (1985:184), Walker (1982). The universities included Duke, NC State, UNC-Chapel Hill, UNC-Charlotte, and North Carolina A&T State.

99. U.S. Congress (1985:186–188).

100. NSB (1983b:249).

101. U.S. Congress (1985:189).

102. U.S. Congress (1985:184).

103. "California's Own" (1981).

104. "California's Own" (1981), Henton and Waldhorn (1988:229), Terry (1981).

105. Atkinson (2007).

106. Osborne (1988:37–38), Terry (1981); see Kieschnick (1981) for a CSPA report.

107. Henton and Waldhorn (1988:238), NSB (1983b:246).

108. "Boosting Small Business" (1982), Pennsylvania Bureau (1974); see also NAS (1975b:271–272) on PSEF's efforts in materials science.

109. Thornburgh (2003:126), Osborne (1988:47).

110. Osborne (1988:48), Thornburgh (2003:134–137).

111. See Osborne (1988:48–60) for a detailed analysis of the Ben Franklin Partnership and some of the Advanced Technology Centers created under its auspices.

112. "Boosting Small Business" (1982), Eisinger (1988:285).

113. Osborne (1988:48–60).

114. Eisinger (1988:285).

115. See Osborne (1988) and Plosila (2004) on the general trend. See NSB (1983b:109), Osborne (1988:145–174), Potts (1983), Rees (1991) on these particular states and state programs more generally. On the order in which states moved toward

entrepreneurship-oriented economic development policies and the reasons for that movement, see Clarke and Gaile (1989), Grant, Wallace, and Pitney (1995), Jenkins, Leicht, and Wendt (2006), Leicht and Jenkins (1994, 1998).

116. De Laski (1985:24–25). Similarly, an OTA survey of "'dedicated' high-technology development" programs identified eight programs in eight states in 1979, but thirty-five in twenty-two states in 1983 (U.S. Congress 1983:7–8), and another survey found forty-three "high tech development programs" in thirty-three states in 1985 (Brody 1985). See also NGA (1982, 1983) for surveys of such activities.

117. Feller (1984).

118. Coburn and Berglund (1994:17). Similarly, Plosila (2004:116–117) has written that university research centers and university matching grant programs were "clearly the dominant mode by which states exercised their technology-based economic development practices" by the late 1980s.

119. Herzik (1985). The analysis covered speeches from 1976 to 1985.

120. Brody (1985:20–23), Minnesota (1988:2). This figure does not, however, exclude centers with little or no university involvement. Another study focusing specifically on microelectronics and computer-aided manufacturing found four states with such centers in 1980, sixteen in 1984, and thirty-one in 1988 (Rees 1991:5). This figure also includes both university and nonuniversity centers.

121. Belanger (1998).

122. Walsh (1981). See Belanger (1998:211–234) for a history of the origins of the ERC program, as well as NRC (1986). Notably, participants singled out RPI's George Low as playing a catalytic role in encouraging this vision (NRC 1986:vi).

123. Keyworth (1984:11), Belanger (1998:214). See also Bloch (1986), Keyworth (1986) for other examples of "competitiveness" language.

124. Belanger (1998:216).

125. See, e.g., Norman (1985b), Walsh (1987).

126. Belanger (1998:216), Norman (1985a).

127. Norman (1985b). Suh had been involved with the ERC program from its conception; see Belanger (1998:211–234), NSF ERC (1998), Suh (1986) on his role. Erich Bloch, NSF director and another champion of the ERCs, has claimed that the they were not modeled after the I/UCRCs, saying in an interview that "The ERCs are a different animal. They are much more research oriented. They are also broader in scope. I/UCRCs drilled down to very specific topics. To me it was an entirely different program. Also, ERCs got a lot more money than I/UCRCs. The two programs were not in conflict nor was one a continuation of the other" (Bozeman and Boardman 2004:371). Nevertheless, while there were significant differences between the two programs, it is hard not to see ERCs as a continuation of the I/UCRC goal—strengthening university-industry interaction in order to encourage industrial innovation—not least because of Suh's role.

128. Belanger (1998:219), Gray, Gidley, and Koester (1987), Walsh (1986, 1987:18).

129. Feller, Ailes, and Roessner (2002:459).

130. Walsh (1987).

131. American Presidency Project (2008c).

132. Fitzsimmons, Grad, and Lal (1996:10, 21–23). Another smaller center program, the State/Industry University Cooperative Research Centers (S/IUCRC) program, was started in 1991; closer to the I/UCRCs in scope and design, the S/IUCRCs

were intended to create centers that would facilitate federal/state cooperation and help states meet their economic development needs (Roessner 2000).

133. Gray and Baneth (1992), Feller, Ailes, and Roessner (2002:459), Fitzsimmons, Grad, and Lal (1996:10). The estimate for NSF funding is based on the number of I/UCRCs, ERCs, and STCs created during the 1980s and the amount of support they were typically given.

134. Arvind, Dahbura, and Caro (2000), Coburn and Berglund (1994:505–510).

135. See, e.g., Coburn and Berglund (1994:523).

136. Amato (1992), "Commercial Development" (1994).

137. Ikenberry and Friedman (1972), Smith and Karlesky (1977:chapter 3).

138. NSB (1983b:11,16).

139. NSB (1983b:11).

140. Cohen, Florida, and Goe (1994:6).

141. NSB (1983b:83) defines cooperative research centers as "Centers having associated industrial affiliate programs where member companies serve in an advisory capacity regarding the direction of research." This did not include industrial affiliate programs connected with departments rather than centers, such as those at Stanford and MIT. Cohen, Florida, and Goe (1994:5) define them as "(1) university-affiliated research centers, institutes, laboratories, facilities, or other organizations; that (2) conducted research and development in science and engineering fields; (3) had a total 1990 budget of at least $100,000, with (4) part of the budget consisting of industry-sponsored funds."

142. NSF (2007:table 1), Cohen, Florida, and Goe (1994:9).

143. Smith and Karlesky (1977:65, 76). In addition to Smith and Karlesky's observations, see a special May 1976 issue of *Research Management* on universities and industry, Baer (1976, 1978), and articles like David (1979), Drucker (1979), "Industry R&D" (1979), and Magarrell (1979).

144. "Midland Meeting Aim" (1979). The conference led to the creation of the Council for Chemical Research, an industry organization that would fund academic R&D. See "The Chemical Industry Heads Back" (1980), "Firms Launch a Group" (1980), King (2007).

145. This is an extrapolation based on the state of Minnesota's 1988 survey that found states spending more than $225 million on "technology or research centers" that year. Since such programs had already spread widely by 1985, it is possible that states spent $1 billion just in the last half of the decade.

146. Cohen, Florida, and Goe (1994:8), NSF (2007:table 1).

147. Osborne (1988:50).

148. Gray and Walters (1998:9–15).

149. Eveland and Hetzner (1982), Eveland, Hetzner, and Tornatzky (1984), Tornatzky et al. (1982). See I/UCRCs Program Evaluation Project (2011) for a bibliography of publications on the I/UCRC program, including many from the 1980s.

150. U.S. GAO (1983:v).

151. Public Law 96-480.

152. For example, in the case of Arizona State's Center for Excellence in Engineering. See Landry (1988:257–261), Lippman (1981), Norman (1982).

153. See, for example, Bloch (1986).

Chapter 7
The Spread of Market Logic

1. Rosenzweig (1985:41).

2. Rosenzweig (1985:47).

3. U.S. Congress (1984a:93); this is a low estimate. See also note 159 of chapter 4 on estimates of firm formation.

4. U.S. Congress (1988b:78) counts over 400, but this study seems relatively expansive in the way it defines a dedicated biotechnology firm.

5. Bouton (1983), but see Etzkowitz (1983).

6. See U.S. Congress (1984a:67–70) for a list of early biotech firms and their product areas.

7. AUTM (2004:12).

8. NSB (1996:appendix table 5-42, 2006:appendix table 5-67).

9. NSB (2010:appendix table 4-3).

10. Cohen, Florida, and Goe (1994:6), NSB (1983b:11, 16).

11. Cohen, Florida, and Goe (1994:8)

12. For example, an influential 1978 *Business Week* article, "Vanishing Innovation," mentioned a role for universities only once, in passing, in its six pages (1978). The article was cited five times in Congressional hearings and twice reprinted into the *Congressional Record.* See also Graham (1978a, 1978b), "The 'Innovation Recession'" (1978) for examples of media discussion of the innovation issue that barely mentions universities. Academic science was similarly missing in the spate of media coverage of innovation in 1979 and 1980, prompted by Carter's Domestic Policy Review for Industrial Innovation; see, e.g., "America's Technological Lag" (1979), "Digging a Spur" (1979), "A Policy for Industry" (1980), "The Sad State" (1979).

13. Steinbach (2005).

14. Danilov (1971).

15. U.S. GAO (1983). Similarly, a 2003 study of then-existing university-related research parks identified nine that had been founded between 1951 to 1970, but only three established between 1971 and 1979, and noted that "even though by the 1970s there was general acceptance of the concept of a park benefiting both research organizations and universities, park creation slowed at this time because a number of park ventures failed and an uncertain economic climate led to a decline in total R&D activity" (Link 2003:79).

16. Savoye (1983), "Attracting the Research Dollar" (1985). See also Luger and Goldstein (1991) on the development of research parks in the 1980s.

17. Pieretti (1982).

18. U.S. Congress (1983:29–30); the site became Chicago Technology Park.

19. "Attracting the Research Dollar" (1985).

20. Powers et al. (1988:79).

21. See U.S. Congress (1984b) for a compendium of state high-tech development programs, including research parks.

22. Battelle Memorial Institute (2007:vii, 19). The estimate of park failure is based on the Battelle report's statement that about 62% of the parks that responded to its survey were founded since 1990, which would suggest that somewhere on the order

of sixty-six parks had been established before then. Already by 1990, observers were noticing the "economic pitfalls" of research parks and "increasingly frequent accounts of park failures." See Blumenstyk (1990).

23. Peters and Fusfeld (1983), Matkin (1990:179).

24. Matkin (1990:178), for example, notes that their diversity makes even defining them difficult.

25. A list of high-value university patents published in *Business Week* in 1981, for example, listed only three from the 1970s. These had collectively earned just $3.61 million in licensing fees to date, though an eventual $34 million in revenues was anticipated. See "The Colleges Discover" (1981) for the list and Wade (1979:663) on the "enjoyable hoopla."

26. Cole (1980), Scherer (1980).

27. Wade (1980a).

28. "Harvard Considers" (1980), Steiner (1980:208).

29. "Harvard Considers" (1980), Hilts (1980); see also Sheils (1980).

30. "Harvard Considers" (1980). Stanford, Yale, and Johns Hopkins, at least, were actively considering similar plans; see Berg (1997:144–145), Dickson (1980b:6), Sheils (1980).

31. "Harvard Finally Backs Off" (1980). Re Harvard's proposal, see also Bauer (1981), Dickson (1980a, 1980b), "Harvard Backs Off" (1980), Jablin (1980), "Of Professors and Money" (1980), "Sharing the Wealth" (1980), Wade (1980b).

32. The intent of Engenics was to commercialize bioprocessing research being done at Berkeley and Stanford. The investing corporations received 35% of Engenics' shares, and "founders and key professionals, including Professors Channing Robertson of chemical engineering at Stanford and Harvey Blanch of chemical engineering at UCB," received another 35% (Kenney 1986:48). At the same time, an independent nonprofit group, the Center for Biotechnology Research, was formed with the mission of financing basic research at Stanford and the University of California. The Center for Biotechnology Research was given 30% of the equity in Engenics, as well as $2.4 million in funding up front. If the Center for Biotechnology Research were to sell its share of Engenics, proceeds would go to Berkeley and Stanford (Culliton 1982a:960–961, U.S. Library of Congress 1982:7).

33. Kenney (1986:83), Sanger (1982).

34. See, e.g., Grassmuck (1990), Desruisseaux (2000).

35. See Matkin (1990:chapter 8) for a review of university investments in venture capital.

36. See U.S. House (1981a:87–96) for a summary and discussion of the Mass General–Hoechst agreement. While this describes the contract as providing $50 million over ten years, later sources suggest the agreement was for $70 million; see Bouton (1983) and U.S. Congress (1984a:575).

37. U.S. House (1981a).

38. Kenney's (1986:56) list of these is very comprehensive; I have not encountered more than passing mentions of additional contracts signed during this period. Also see U.S. Library of Congress (1982) and GUIRR (1986) for discussions of some of these.

39. The Mass General agreement was tied to Howard Goodman, who brought Hoechst's interest with him from UCSF to Harvard.

40. Bouton (1983), "Business and Universities" (1982), GUIRR (1986:83–87). See also U.S. House (1982:48) on the Washington University–Monsanto agreement.

41. U.S. House (1982:107).

42. Barnes (1985:1255).

43. Parts of this section are based on a collection of the 122 instances between 1965 to 1985 in which presidents of AAU member institutions testified to Congress on matters related to academic science. This material is available from the author upon request.

44. Case Western Reserve University president Robert W. Morse in U.S. House (1970a:830).

45. U.S. House (1970b:354). Also see these rest of these hearings and Boffey (1970b) for coverage of them.

46. For example, Berkeley chancellor Roger Heyns claimed that universities were the "centers for the analysis of the problems that confront the nation" (U.S. House 1971a:17). Debates around NSF's Research Applied to National Needs program (RANN) also frequently touch on this theme; see Greenberg (1970) and Green and Lepkowski (2006) for descriptions of RANN. See also chapter 2 of this book for other examples of arguments from this era.

47. Semas (1973), quoting Bruce L. R. Smith, professor of government at Columbia and future author of Smith and Karlesky (1977).

48. Semas (1973), quoting Gabor Strasser, director of planning for Battelle Memorial Institute.

49. U.S. Senate (1979a:35).

50. U.S. House (1979a:615).

51. Steiner (1980:204).

52. Bok (1981:24).

53. U.S. House (1981c:2059).

54. U.S. House (1982:126).

55. "Business and Universities" (1982:58).

56. U.S. House (1983b:438).

57. U.S. House (1983a:8).

58. NGA and The Conference Board (1987:21). The survey was of "senior research and development officers of technology-based companies," "university leaders," and "senior state officials responsible for science and technology policy." Notably, given the role of government policy in facilitating such ties, the percentage of state leaders who agreed with this statement was highest of all, at 83%. Related questions, such as on the "significance of increasing industry support for university-based research," showed similar patterns (59% of university representatives and 62% of state officials said it was critical, but only 34% of business leaders).

59. See "Industry Said to Be Primary Innovator" (1991) and "Universities Exaggerate Their Innovations" (1991). Both of these newspaper articles are based on GUIRR (1991).

60. Merton (1973 [1957]).

61. See Kleinman and Vallas (2001) and Vallas and Kleinman (2007) on the "asymmetrical convergence" of the cultures of academic and industrial science.

Chapter 8
Conclusion

1. The six were Congress's decision not to regulate rDNA research, the passage of the Bayh-Dole Act, the establishment of CAFC, the creation of the I/UCRC program, state funding for UIRCs, and expansion of NSF support for UIRCs in the 1980s.

2. The exceptions that come to mind are RPI's UIRCs, which President George Low strongly supported, and to some extent Arizona State's Center for Engineering Excellence, which was led by the dean of its engineering school. However, at least some accounts attribute the initiative for the latter center to the business community, not to the university. See Landry (1988:259–261), Lippman (1981).

3. Smith and Karlesky (1977:136). NIH support for rDNA research increased from essentially nothing in the mid-1970s to $103 million in 1979 and $185 million in 1982. See Wright (1994:78).

4. Materials science, in fact, was a field that had largely been created by the federal government; see Bensaude-Vincent (2001), NAS (1975b), Schwartz (1987), Test (1966). The ARPA-funded Materials Research Centers, which helped hold the young field together, did experience some uncertainty during the Mansfield Amendment era. But their transfer to NSF beginning in 1972 meant that they did not suffer from the sharp cuts that some other research areas did. While Bensaude-Vincent notes that Materials Research Center faculty numbers decreased significantly during the 1970s, Schwartz makes clear that NSF was shifting some of its materials science funding from the large centers to smaller research groups, and that materials science as a field was not suffering from cutbacks.

5. Data available from NSF's Industrial Research & Development Information System (IRIS) database at http://www.nsf.gov/statistics/iris/ (last accessed 21 April 2011).

6. National Commission on Research (1980), Stauffer (1980).

7. U.S. Senate (1979c:47–111).

8. NSF (1976:3, 10, attachment A-3).

9. See, e.g., Wiesendanger (2000).

10. NSB (1983b).

11. As Stanford president Donald Kennedy noted at the time, "Sudden increases in value have come to be associated much more with research ideas in the new biomedical technology than has been customary in earlier scientific developments. In part, this relates to the swiftness with which new research opportunities have developed. But in part also, it is due to a new environment for the capital support of research ventures" (U.S. House 1981a:12).

12. Blumenstyk (1999). The patents on cisplatin and carboplatin were managed, however, by Research Corporation and not by Michigan State itself.

13. Eveland and Hetzner (1982), Eveland, Hetzner, and Tornatzky (1984), Gray, Gidley, and Koester (1987).

14. Luger and Goldstein's 1991 book on research parks, for example, makes only passing mention of biotech firms.

15. Kleinman, Habinek, and Vallas (2011).

16. See Fligstein (2001b), Rao (1998), Suddaby and Greenwood (2005) for examples of work taking an entrepreneurship approach to explaining institutional change, and Hardy and Maguire (2008) for a review of the literature on institutional entrepreneur-

ship. Hargrave and Van de Ven (2006), Lounsbury, Ventresca, and Hirsch (2003), Rao, Monin, and Durand (2003), Swaminathan and Wade (2001) all take a social movements approach to institutional change; see Schneiberg and Lounsbury (2008) for a review.

17. See, e.g., Lounsbury and Crumley (2007:993), Powell and Colyvas (2008), Thornton and Ocasio (2008:1006) for critiques of the institutional entrepreneurship literature.

18. See Lounsbury (2007), Nelson (2005), Scott et al. (2000) on multiple logics. See also Glynn and Lounsbury (2005) on "blending" logics and Schneiberg (2007) on rejected logics as an ongoing resources for field transformation. Heimer (1999) also looks at how multiple logics compete in a particular organizational setting.

19. See Friedland (2009), Lounsbury (2008), Lounsbury and Crumley (2007), Miettinen, Samra-Fredericks, and Yanow (2009), Purdy and Gray (2009), for example.

20. Maguire, Hardy, and Lawrence (2004), Reay, Golden-Biddle, and Germann (2006). The phrase *under the radar* is borrowed from Reay and Hinings (2009:632).

21. Friedland and Alford (1991:232).

22. Friedland and Alford (1991:232). It is also consistent with empirical work on how institutional logics change, as in Thornton (2004:chapter 2) and Scott et al. (2000).

23. I think of the relationship between these fields in terms similar to Abbott's (2005) conceptualization of "linked ecologies," although avatars and hinges do not play a key role in this story.

24. See Burt (1992), Granovetter (1985), Uzzi (1997), for example, on the embeddedness of markets in social networks, and Block and Evans (2005), Fligstein (2001a), Vogel (1998) on the embeddedness of markets in state rules. For a comparison of the two approaches to embeddedness, see Krippner and Alvarez (2007).

25. See chapter 2 of this book.

26. See, for example, Etzkowitz (2002), Geiger (1986:95–101), Newfield (2003).

27. U.S. Senate (1983:80).

28. NSB (2010:appendix table 4-3).

29. NSB (2010:appendix table 5-45); data end in 2008. These data are from NSF and the Patent Board, but AUTM figures show a similar trend. 2003 was the high point for patents issued, with 3,450, but between 1999 to 2007 (the last year available) the number of patents awarded ranged from 2,944 (in 2005) to 3,450 (in 2003). See NSB (2010:appendix table 5-47).

30. See NIH (2010) for NIH appropriations figures. By 2003, NIH represented 63.2% of all federal obligations for academic R&D (NSB 2010:appendix table 5-3), and federal support represented 61.8% of the total (NSB 2010:appendix table 5-2).

31. For example, Geiger and Sá (2008) recently argue that while there has been leveling in certain trends, other kinds of university interaction with the market, like university spin-off firms and a new wave of state-supported economic development initiatives, suggest that the move toward the market continues.

32. Rhetoric about academic science as an economic engine seems, if anything, to be increasing, but questions about the effectiveness of policies meant to leverage science for regional economic development have been asked repeatedly. See, e.g., Feller, Ailes, and Roessner (2002), Florida and Cohen (1999), Mowery and Sampat (2006:226). Irwin Feller, in particular, has been making the point about the tendency to overstate the economic impact of state technology-driven economic development programs for some time (e.g., Feller 1997, 2004).

33. See, e.g., Ebeling (2008), Selin (2007). Berger (2007) debunks the claim—first set forth by NSF in 2001—that nanotechnology will be a $1 trillion market by 2015.

34. Pisano (2006:114–115), surveying all publicly held biotech companies in existence between 1975 and 2004, claims that the biotech sector has had a profitability level of close to zero (where profitability is measured as net operating income before depreciation), and that if the firm Amgen is removed, "the industry has sustained steady losses throughout its history."

35. Harvey (2005:2). Campbell and Pedersen (2001:1) define it as "market deregulation, state decentralization, and reduced state intervention into economic affairs," and call it "a political project," integral to which has been "a shift away from Keynesian economic ideas, which emphasized the political management of aggregate demand, to a more conservative discourse based on monetarist, supply-side, and rational expectations theories." Mudge (2008:706), following Bourdieu, similarly calls it "an ideological system that holds the 'market' sacred, born within the 'human' or social sciences and refined in a network of Anglo-American-centric knowledge producers, expressed in different ways within the institutions of the postwar nation-state and their political fields."

36. This is a somewhat arbitrary list. Prasad (2006:4–5) defines neoliberalism as involving tax policies that favor capital accumulation, industrial policies that minimize the role of the state, and reductions in welfare spending. The ten policy prescriptions of the "Washington Consensus" are also commonly associated with neoliberalism (see Williamson 2004). Vogel (1998) was among the first to emphasize the positive role of the state (reregulation) rather than its withdrawal from the market (deregulation).

37. See Prasad (2006:15–22), who herself emphasizes the structure of political institutions in causing neoliberal policies, for a review of the major perspectives.

38. For example, see Canaan and Shumar (2008), Feller (2008), Giroux (2002), Lave, Mirowski, and Randalls (2010), Moore et al. (2010), Slaughter and Rhoades (2004).

39. Carnegie Commission (1992:21).

40. Smith (2007).

41. Weber (1978 [1922], 2002 [1904–1905]). See Brubaker (1984) on Weber's use of the concepts of rationality and rationalization.

42. This is a complete list based on a search of "economic engine" conducted on 30 December 2010. I omitted instances where the site was not referring to something specific acting as an economic engine.

43. Cohen (2009).

44. Morrill Act of 1862, 7 U.S.C. § 304.

45. Most prominently, perhaps, legal scholar and judge Richard Posner (2009).

Bibliography

Abbott, Andrew. 2005. "Linked Ecologies: States and Universities as Environments for Professions." *Sociological Theory* 23:245–274.

Abelson, Philip. 1973. "Technological Initiatives and Political Realities." *Science* 179:333.

———. 1974. "Academic Science and Industry." *Science* 183:1251.

Abir-Am, Pnina. 1982. "The Discourse of Physical Power and Biological Knowledge in the 1930s: A Reappraisal of the Rockefeller Foundation's 'Policy' in Molecular Biology." *Social Studies of Science* 12:341–382.

Abramowitz, Moses. 1956. "Resource and Output Trends in the United States since 1870." *American Economic Review* 46:5–23.

Abramson, Bruce D. 2007. *The Secret Circuit: The Little-Known Court Where the Rules of the Information Age Unfold*. Lanham, MD: Rowman & Littlefield Publishers.

"Academy Opposes Local DNA Research Rules." 1977. *Science & Government Report*, 15 May, 8.

Adams, Stephen B. 2005. "Stanford and Silicon Valley: Lessons on Becoming a High-Tech Region." *California Management Review* 48:29–51.

"Administration to Seek Wide DNA Guidelines." 1977. *Science & Government Report*, 1 March, 8.

Aisenberg, James. 1982. "Commercialization of Research: So Far . . ." *Nature* 297:617.

Amato, Ivan. 1992. "Microgravity Materials Science Strives to Stay in Orbit." *Science* 257:882–883.

"American Ingenuity: Still Going Strong." 1976. *Time*, 5 July.

The American Presidency Project. 2008a. "Richard Nixon: Address to the Nation Outlining a New Economic Policy: 'The Challenge of Peace.'" Available at http://www.presidency.ucsb.edu/ws/index.php?pid=3115. Last accessed 21 April 2011.

———. 2008b. "Richard Nixon: Special Message to the Congress on Science and Technology." Available at http://www.presidency.ucsb.edu/ws/index.php?pid=3773. Last accessed 21 April 2011.

———. 2008c. "Ronald Reagan: Address before a Joint Session of Congress on the State of the Union." Available at http://www.presidency.ucsb.edu/ws/index.php?pid=34430. Last accessed 21 April 2011.

"American Venture Capital: Fun No More." 1978. *Economist*, 25 February, 98.

"America's Technological Lag." 1979. *New York Times*, 24 April.

Ancker-Johnson, Betsy. 2005. Interview by author. Tape recording of phone interview. Austin, TX, 22 April.

Andreopoulos, Spyros. 1980. "Sounding Board: Gene Cloning by Press Conference." *New England Journal of Medicine* 302:743–746.

"Announcements." 1963. *Science* 141:415–418.

Apple, Rima D. 1989. "Patenting University Research: Harry Steenbock and the Wisconsin Alumni Research Foundation." *Isis* 80:375–394.

Arrow, Kenneth. 1962. "Economic Welfare and the Allocation of Resources for Invention." Pages 609–626 in *The Rate and Direction of Inventive Activity*, edited by Richard R. Nelson. Princeton, NJ: Princeton University Press.

Arthur D. Little, Inc., and Industrial Research Institute. 1973. *Barriers to Innovation in Industry: Opportunities for Public Policy Changes*. Washington, DC: National Science Foundation.

Arvind, Anton T. Dahbura, and Alejandro Caro. 2000. "From Monsoon to StarT-Voyager: University-Industry Collaboration in Research." *IEEE Micro* 20:75–84.

Association of American Universities. 1986. *Trends in Technology Transfer at Universities: Report of the Clearinghouse on University-Industry Relations*. Washington, DC: American Association of Universities.

Association of University Technology Managers. 1996. *AUTM Licensing Survey FY 1991–FY 1995: Five-Year Survey Summary*. Northbrook, IL: Association of University Technology Managers.

———. 2004. *AUTM U.S. Licensing Survey: FY 2003: Survey Summary*. Northbrook, IL: Association of University Technology Managers.

———. 2007. *AUTM U.S. Licensing Activity Survey: FY 2006 (Survey Summary)*. Northbrook, IL: Association of University Technology Managers.

———. 2008. *AUTM U.S. Licensing Activity Survey: FY 2007: Survey Summary*. Northbrook, IL: Association of University Technology Managers.

———. 2010. "About Technology Transfer." Available at http://www.autm.net/Tech_transfer.htm. Last accessed 21 April 2011.

Atkinson, Richard C. 2007. "Curriculum Vitae." Available at http://www.rca.ucsd.edu/docs/RCAvita.pdf. Last accessed 21 April 2011.

"Attracting the Research Dollar." 1985. *New York Times*, 9 March.

Baer, Walter S. 1976. "University-Industry Interactions in Civil Sector R&D." Report No. P-5724. Santa Monica, CA: RAND Corporation. Available at www.rand.org/pubs/papers/2009/P5724.pdf. Last accessed 21 April 2011.

———. 1978. "The Changing Relationship: Universities and Other R&D Performers." Pages 61–103 in *The State of Academic Science: Background Papers*, edited by Bruce L. R. Smith and Joseph J. Karlesky. New York: Change Magazine Press.

———. 1980. "Strengthening University-Industry Interactions." Report No. P-6438. Santa Monica, CA: RAND Corporation. Available at www.rand.org/pubs/papers/2009/P5724.pdf. Last accessed 21 April 2011.

Baker, Billy. 2007. "He Wants to Use Biotech against Alzheimer's." *Boston Globe*, 23 July.

Bancroft III, Paul. 2010. "Paul Bancroft III: Early Bay Area Venture Capitalists: Shaping the Economic and Business Landscape." Oral history conducted by Sally Smith Hughes. Berkeley: Regional Oral History Office, Bancroft Library, University of California.

Barnes, Deborah M. 1985. "New University-Industry Pact Signed." *Science* 230:1255–1256.

Barnhill, Robert E. 2001. *Evaluating Research Productivity*. Lawrence: Merrill Center, University of Kansas. Available at http://merrill.ku.edu/publications/2001whitepaper/barnhilltext.html. Last accessed 21 April 2011.

Battelle Memorial Institute. 2007. *Characteristics and Trends in North American Research Parks: 21st Century Directions*. Columbus, OH: Battelle Memorial Institute.

Bauer, Nancy F. 1981. "'The Ptashne Fiasco.'" *Harvard Crimson*, 4 June.

Bazell, Robert J. 1971. "Cancer Research Proposals: New Money, Old Conflicts." *Science* 171:877–879.

Bekelman, Justin E., Yan Li, and Cary P. Gross. 2003. "Scope and Impact of Financial Conflicts of Interest in Biomedical Research: A Systematic Review." *Journal of the American Medical Association* 289:454–465.

Belanger, Dian Olson. 1998. *Enabling American Innovation: Engineering and the National Science Foundation*. West Lafayette, IN: Purdue University Press.

Bengelsdorf, Irving. 1967. "Caltech and Stanford Join in Achievement: First Biologically Active DNA Made in Lab." *Los Angeles Times*, 15 December.

Bensaude-Vincent, Bernadette. 2001. "The Construction of a Discipline: Materials Science in the United States." *Historical Studies in the Physical and Biological Sciences* 31:223–248.

Bercovitz, Janet, and Maryann Feldman. 2008. "Academic Entrepreneurs: Organizational Change at the Individual Level." *Organization Science* 19:69–89.

Berg, Paul. 1997. "Paul Berg." Oral history conducted by Sally Smith Hughes. Berkeley: Regional Oral History Office, Bancroft Library, University of California.

Berg, Paul, David Baltimore, Herbert W. Boyer, Stanley N. Cohen, Ronald W. Davis, David S. Hogness, Daniel Nathans, Richard Roblin, James D. Watson, Sherman Weissman, and Norton D. Zinder. 1974. "Potential Biohazards of Recombinant DNA Molecules." *Science* 185:303.

Berger, Michael. 2007. "Debunking the Trillion Dollar Nanotechnology Market Size Hype." Available at http://www.nanowerk.com/spotlight/spotid=1792.php. Last accessed 21 April 2011.

Berman, Elizabeth Popp. 2007. "Creating the Market University: Science, the State, and the Economy, 1965–1985." PhD dissertation, University of California, Berkeley.

———. 2008a. "The Politics of Patent Law and Its Material Effects: The Changing Relationship between Universities and the Marketplace." Pages 191–213 in *Living in a Material World: Economic Sociology Meets Science and Technology Studies*, edited by Trevor Pinch and Richard Swedberg. Cambridge, MA: MIT Press.

———. 2008b. "Why Did Universities Start Patenting? Institution-Building and the Road to the Bayh-Dole Act." *Social Studies of Science* 38:835–871.

Betlach, Mary C. 1994. "Early Cloning and Recombinant DNA Technology at Herbert W. Boyer's UCSF Laboratory in the 1970s." Oral history conducted by Sally Smith Hughes. Berkeley: Regional Oral History Office, Bancroft Library, University of California.

"Biotechnology in Britain: Growing Pains." 1983. *Economist*, 30 July.

Biotechnology Industry Organization. 2008. *Guide to Biotechnology 2008*. Available at http://www.bio.org/speeches/pubs/er/BiotechGuide2008.pdf. Last accessed 21 April 2011.

Birch, David. 1979. *The Job Generation Process*. Cambridge, MA: MIT Program on Neighborhood and Regional Change.

Bloch, Erich. 1986. "Basic Research and Economic Health: The Coming Challenge." *Science* 232:595–599.

Block, Fred, and Peter Evans. 2005. "The State and the Economy." Pages 505–526 in *The Handbook of Economic Sociology*, edited by Neil J. Smelser and Richard Swedberg. Princeton, NJ: Princeton University Press.

Block, Richard B. 1977. "The Experimental R&D Incentives Program: Past and Present." Pages 16–24 in *Technological Innovation: The Experimental R&D Incentives Program*, edited by Donald E. Cunningham, John R. Craig, and Theodore W. Schlie. Boulder, CO: Westview Press.

Blumenstyk, Goldie. 1990. "Pitfalls of Research Parks Lead Universities and States to Reassess Their Expectations." *Chronicle of Higher Education*, 4 July.

———. 1999. "How One University Pursued Profit from Science—And Won." *Chronicle of Higher Education*, 12 February.

———. 2005. "Bad Chemistry: Scientist Sues Florida State U., Saying It Reneged on Gift Deal." *Chronicle of Higher Education*, 18 November.

———. 2010. "University Inventions Sparked Record Number of Companies in 2008." *Chronicle of Higher Education*, 15 February.

Blumenthal, David, Michael Gluck, Karen Seashore Louis, Michael A. Stoto, and David Wise. 1986. "University-Industry Research Relationships in Biotechnology: Implications for the University." *Science* 232:1361–1366.

Board of Governors of the Federal Reserve System. 2007. *Flow of Funds Accounts of the United States: Annual Flows and Outstandings, 1975–1984*. Washington, DC: Federal Reserve.

Boffey, Philip M. 1967. "Federal Research Funds: Science Gets Caught in a Budget Squeeze." *Science* 158:1286–1288.

———. 1968a. "Budget Paradox: Spending Holds Even, Yet Researchers Are Hurt." *Science* 162:340–342.

———. 1968b. "LBJ's New Budget: Another Tight Year for Research and Development." *Science* 159:509–511.

———. 1969. "Campus Unrest: Riots Bring Danger of Punitive Backlash." *Science* 164:161–165.

———. 1970a. "R&D Funding: Top Treasury Aide Decries Blind Faith Approach." *Science* 170:512–516.

———. 1970b. "Recession in Science: Ex-Advisors Warn of Long-Term Effects." *Science* 168:555–557.

———. 1971. "Technology and World Trade: Is There Cause for Alarm?" *Science* 172:37–41.

Bok, Derek. 1981. "Business and the Academy." Pages 23–35 in *Harvard Magazine*.

———. 2003. *Universities in the Marketplace: The Commercialization of Higher Education*. Princeton, NJ: Princeton University Press.

Boltanski, Luc, and Laurent Thévenot. 2006 [1991]. *On Justification: Economies of Worth*. Princeton, NJ: Princeton University Press.

Boly, William. 1982. "The Gene Merchants." *California Monthly*, September, 76–78, 170–171.

"Boosting Small Business." 1982. *Inc.*, October, 100.

Bouton, Katherine. 1983. "Academic Researchers and Big Business: A Delicate Balance." *New York Times Magazine*, 11 September, 63.

Bowes, Jr., William K. 2008. "William K. Bowes, Jr.: Bay Area Venture Capitalists: Shaping the Economic and Business Landscape." Oral history conducted by Sally Smith Hughes. Berkeley: Regional Oral History Office, Bancroft Library, University of California.

Boyer, Carol M., and Darrell R. Lewis. 1984. "Faculty Consulting: Responsibility or Promiscuity?" *Journal of Higher Education* 55:637–659.

———. 1986. *And on the Seventh Day: Faculty Consulting and Supplemental Income*. Washington, DC: Association for the Study of Higher Education.

Boyer, Herbert W. 1994. "Recombinant DNA Research at UCSF and Commercial Application at Genentech." Oral history conducted by Sally Smith Hughes. Berkeley: Regional Oral History Office, Bancroft Library, University of California.

Bozeman, Barry, and Craig Boardman. 2004. "The NSF Engineering Research Centers and the University-Industry Research Revolution: A Brief History Featuring an Interview with Erich Bloch." *Journal of Technology Transfer* 29:365–375.

Branscomb, Lewis M. 1973. "Federal Support of Commercially Relevant R&D." *American Scientist* 61:144–151.

"The Breakdown of U.S. Innovation." 1976. *Business Week*, 16 February, 56.

Bremer, Howard W. 2001. "Oral History No. 565." Oral history conducted by Barry Teicher. Madison, WI: University of Wisconsin Oral History Program.

———. 2004. Interview by author. Tape recording of phone interview. Madison, WI, 21 December.

Britan, Gerald M. 1981. *Bureaucracy and Innovation: An Ethnography of Policy Change.* Beverly Hills, CA: SAGE Publications.

Broad, William J. 1979. "Whistle Blower Reinstated at HEW." *Science* 205:476.

Brodsky, Neal H., Harold G. Kaufman, and John D. Tooker. 1980. "University/Industry Cooperation: A Preliminary Analysis of Existing Mechanisms and Their Relationship to the Innovation Process." New York: New York University Graduate School of Public Administration Center for Science and Technology Policy.

Brody, Herb. 1985. "States Vie for a Slice of the Pie." *High Technology*, January, 16–28.

Brookings Institution. 2002. "U.S. Nuclear Weapons Cost Study Project." Available at http://www.brookings.edu/projects/archive/nucweapons/manhattan.aspx. Last accessed 21 April 2011.

Brown, Sylvia K. 1988. "George M. Low." Available at http://www.lib.rpi.edu/dept/library/html/Archives/history/presidents/low,gm.html. Last accessed 21 April 2011.

Brubaker, Rogers. 1984. *The Limits of Rationality: An Essay on the Social and Moral Thought of Max Weber*. London: George Allen & Unwin.

Bud, Robert. 1993. *The Uses of Life: A History of Biotechnology*. Cambridge, UK: Cambridge University Press.

"Bugging Britain." 1980. *Economist*, 19 January, 72.

Bugos, Glenn E., and Daniel Kevles. 1992. "Plants as Intellectual Property: American Practice, Law, and Policy in World Context." *Osiris* 7:74–104.

"The Bugs Business." 1980. *Economist*, 19 April, 14.

Burger, Robert M., S. H. Cole, and C. H. Burnett. 1982. "An Analysis of the National Science Foundation's University-Industry Cooperative Research Centers Experiment: An Effort to Stimulate University-Industry Cooperative Research in Solving R&D Problems in American Industry." Pages 71–107 in *Analyses of Five National Science Foundation Experiments to Stimulate Increases Technological Innovation in the Private Sector*, edited by Robert M. Colton. Washington, DC: National Science Foundation.

Burt, Ronald S. 1992. *Structural Holes: The Social Structure of Competition*. Cambridge, MA: Harvard University Press.

Bush, Vannevar. 1960 [1945]. *Science—The Endless Frontier: A Report to the Presidentn a Program for Postwar Scientific Research*. Washington, DC: National Science Foundation.

"Business and Universities: A New Partnership." 1982. *Business Week*, 20 December, 58.

"The Business Stakes." 1977. *Business Week*, 29 August, 53.

Byers, Brook. 2006. "Brook Byers: Biotechnology Venture Capitalist, 1970–2006." Oral history conducted by Thomas D. Kiley. Berkeley: Regional Oral History Office, Bancroft Library, University of California.

Bylinsky, Gene. 1974. "Industry Is Finding More Jobs for Microbes." *Fortune*, February, 96–102.

"Calendar of Events—January." 1967. *Science* 158:1502, 1505–1506, 1508.

"California's Own Industrialization Program." 1981. *Business Week*, 26 January, 40.

Campbell, John L., and Ove K. Pedersen, eds. 2001. *The Rise of Neoliberalism and Institutional Analysis*. Princeton, NJ: Princeton University Press.

Canaan, Joyce, E., and Wesley Shumar, eds. 2008. *Structure and Agency in the Neoliberal University*. New York: Routledge.

Cape, Ronald. 2003. "Biotech Pioneer and Co-Founder of Cetus." Oral history conducted by Sally Smith Hughes. Berkeley: Regional Oral History Office, Bancroft Library, University of California.

Carey, William D. 1975. "Muddling Through: Government and Technology." *Science* 188:13.

———. 1977. "The Blind Side of Science Policy." *Science* 196:1045.

Carnegie Commission on Science, Technology, and Government. 1992. *Science, Technology, and the States in America's Third Century*. Available at http://www.ccstg.org/pdfs/States0992.pdf. Last accessed 21 April 2011.

Carter, Luther J. 1965. "Technical Services Act: Industry to Benefit from New State Programs Paralleling Farm Extension Service." *Science* 149:1485–1486, 1547–1550.

"Carter Pulls Back on Reorganization." 1978. *Business Week*, 20 February, 33.

Cartter, Allan M. 1966. *An Assessment of Quality in Graduate Education*. Washington, DC: American Council on Education.

Chaikin, Andrew. 1998. *A Man on the Moon*. New York: Penguin.

Charles, Daniel. 2001. *Lords of the Harvest: Biotech, Big Money, and the Future of Food*. Washington, DC: Perseus Books.

Cheit, Earl. 1971. *The New Depression in Higher Education: A Study of Financial Conditions at 41 Colleges and Universities*. New York: McGraw-Hill.

———. 1973. *The New Depression in Higher Education—Two Years Later*. Berkeley, CA: The Carnegie Commission on Higher Education.

Chemical Heritage Foundation. 2010. "David Schwartz." Available at http://www.chemicalheritage.org/visit/events/awards/affiliate-partnership-awards/pittcon-hof-schwartz.aspx. Last accessed 21 April 2011.

"The Chemical Industry Heads Back to College." 1980. *Chemical Week*, 17 September, 54.

Chubin, Daryl E., and Edward J. Hackett. 1990. *Peerless Science: Peer Review and U.S. Science Policy*. Albany: SUNY Press.

Cibuzar, Gregory T. 1993. "Microelectronics at the University of Minnesota." Pages 170–173 in *Proceedings of the Tenth Biennial University/Government/Industry Microelectronics Symposium, 1993*. Research Triangle Park, NC: IEEE.

Cibuzar, Gregory T., D. Polla, and R. McGlennen. 1997. "Biomedical MEMS Research at the University of Minnesota." Pages 145–149 in *University/Government/Industry Microelectronics Symposium, 1997, Proceedings of the Twelfth Biennial*. Rochester, NY: IEEE.

Clark, Matt, Sharon Begley, and Mary Hager. 1980. "The Miracles of Spliced Genes." *Newsweek*, 17 March, 62.

Clarke, Susan E., and Gary L. Gaile. 1989. "Moving toward Entrepreneurial Economic Development Policies: Opportunities and Barriers." *Policy Studies Journal* 17:574–598.

Clearinghouse for Federal Scientific and Technical Information. 1966. *Technology Transfer and Innovation: A Guide to the Literature*. Springfield, VA: U.S. Department of Commerce, Office of State Technical Services.

Coburn, Christopher, and Dan Berglund. 1994. *Partnerships: A Compendium of State and Federal Cooperative Technology Programs*. Columbus, OH: Battelle Press.

Cohen, Patricia. 2009. "In Tough Times, the Humanities Must Justify Their Worth." *New York Times*, 25 February.

Cohen, Stanley N. 1995. "Science, Biotechnology, and Recombinant DNA: A Personal History." Oral history conducted by Sally Smith Hughes. Berkeley: Regional Oral History Office, Bancroft Library, University of California.

Cohen, Stanley N., Annie C. Y. Chang, Herbert W. Boyer, and Robert B. Helling. 1973. "Construction of Biologically Functional Bacterial Plasmids *In Vitro*." *Proceedings of the National Academy of Sciences* 70:3240–3244.

Cohen, Wesley M., Richard Florida, and W. Richard Goe. 1994. *University-Industry Research Centers in the United States*. Pittsburgh: Carnegie Mellon University.

Cohn, Victor. 1977. "'Products' of Genetic Engineering Seen Less Than Five Years Away." *Washington Post*, 11 November.

Coillet, Dudley W. 1971. *The Management of Mission-Oriented Research: An Independent Study of Project Hindsight Data Base*. Cambridge, MA: MIT Sloan School of Management.

Colaianni, C. Alessandra, and Robert M. Cook-Deegan. 2009. "Columbia University's Axel Patents: Technology Transfer and Implications for the Bayh-Dole Act." *Milbank Quarterly* 87:683–715.

Cole, Robert J. 1980. "Genentech, New Issue, Up Sharply." *New York Times*, 15 October.

"The Colleges Discover a Profit in Patents." 1981. *Business Week*, 12 January, 86.

Collins, Robert M. 2000. *More: The Politics of Economic Growth in Postwar America*. Oxford, UK: Oxford University Press.

Colton, Robert M., ed. 1982. *Analyses of Five National Science Foundation Experiments to Stimulate Increases Technological Innovation in the Private Sector*. Washington, DC: National Science Foundation.

Colyvas, Jeannette A. 2007. "From Divergent Meanings to Common Practices: The Early Institutionalization of Technology Transfer in the Life Sciences at Stanford University." *Research Policy* 36:456–476.

Colyvas, Jeannette A., and Walter W. Powell. 2006. "Roads to Institutionalization: The Remaking of Boundaries between Public and Private Science." *Research in Organizational Behavior* 27:305–353.

———. 2007. "From Vulnerable to Venerated: The Institutionalization of Academic Entrepreneurship in the Life Sciences." *Research in the Sociology of Organizations* 25:219–259.

"A Commercial Debut for DNA Technology." 1977. *Business Week*, 12 December, 128.

"Commercial Development: NASA Centers for the Commercial Development of Space." 1995. *Space Technology Innovation*, May/June.

Commission on Government Procurement. 1972. *Report of the Commission on Government Procurement*. Washington, DC: U.S. Government Printing Office.

Cooke, Robert. 1978. "Clone Business: It's Growing Fast It's Growing Fast." *Boston Globe*, 25 June.

Cornell University. 2007. "Cornell Business & Technology Park: Park History." Available at http://cure.compguard.net/history.htm. Last accessed 21 April 2011.

Cottrell, Frederick. 1912. "The Research Corporation, an Experiment in Public Administration of Patent Rights." *Journal of Industrial and Engineering Chemistry* 4:864–867.

———. 1932. "Patent Experience of the Research Corporation." *Transactions of the American Institute of Chemical Engineers* 29:222–225.

Council on Governmental Relations. 1996. "University Technology Transfer—Questions and Answers." Available at http://www.ucop.edu/ott/faculty/tech.html. Last accessed 21 April 2011.

Cowan, Edward. 1978. "President and House Democrats Discuss Tax Cut without Reform." *New York Times*, 22 April.

Crawford, Jr., J. Hamilton. 1982. "Prudent Investments for Plan Fiduciaries and Plan Administrators." *Proceedings of the New York University Institute on Federal Taxation [ERISA Supplement]* 40:5-1–5-55.

Crawford, Mark. 1986. "Biotech Market Changing Rapidly." *Science* 231:12–14.

Creager, Angela N. H. 1996. "Wendell Stanley's Dream of a Free-Standing Biochemistry Department at the University of California, Berkeley." *Journal of the History of Biology* 29:331–360.

Crittenden, Ann. 1981. "The Gene Machine Hits the Farm." *New York Times*, 28 June.

Culliton, Barbara J. 1977. "Harvard and Monsanto: The $23-Million Alliance." *Science* 195:960–962.

———. 1982a. "The Academic-Industrial Complex." *Science* 216:960–962.

———. 1982b. "Pajaro Dunes: The Search for Consensus." *Science* 216:155–156, 158.

Cunningham, Donald E., John R. Craig, and Theodore W. Schlie, eds. 1977. *Technological Innovation: The Experimental R&D Incentives Program*. Boulder, CO: Westview Press.

Curtis, John. 2000. "A Lifetime Making Mischief with DNA." New Haven, CT: Yale School of Medicine.

D'Andrade, Hugh A., David P. Holveck, and Edward E. Penhoet. 2001. "Regional Characteristics of Biotechnology in the United States: Perspectives of Three Industry Insiders." Oral history conducted by Sally Smith Hughes. Berkeley: Regional Oral History Office, Bancroft Library, University of California.

Danilov, Victor J. 1971. "The Research Park Shake-Out." *Industrial Research* 13:1–4.

David, Edward. 1979. "Science Futures: The Industrial Connection." *Science* 203:837–840.

Davis, Amy Elisabeth. 1988. "Politics of Prosperity: The Kennedy Presidency and Economic Policy." PhD dissertation, Columbia University.

Defense Documentation Center. 1968. "A DDC Bibliography on Cost/Benefits of Technical Information Services and Technology Transfer." Alexandria, VA: Defense Documentation Center.

de Laski, Kathleen. 1985. "Trouble in Mecca: New Programs Threaten Established Strongholds." *High Technology*, January, 24–25.

Demenet, Philippe. 2002. "Yale University Shares Profits from AIDS Drug." *Le Monde Diplomatique*, 12 February.

Denison, Edward F. 1962. *The Sources of Economic Growth in the United States and the Alternatives Before Us*. New York: Committee for Economic Development.

Dennis, Reid. 2009. "Reid Dennis: Early Bay Area Venture Capitalists: Shaping the Economic and Business Landscape." Oral history conducted by Sally Smith Hughes. Berkeley: Regional Oral History Office, Bancroft Library, University of California.

Desruisseaux, Paul. 2000. "Universities Venture into Venture Capitalism." *Chronicle of Higher Education*, 26 May.

Dickson, David. 1980a. "Backlash against DNA Ventures?" *Nature* 288:203–204.

———. 1980b. "Gene-Splicing Riches Stir Academic Debate." *Science & Government Report*, 15 November, 6–7.

———. 1984. *The New Politics of Science*. New York: Pantheon.

"Digging a Spur into Innovation." 1979. *Business Week*, 12 February, 94.

"DNA Is on the Way to Chemicals." 1979. *Chemical Week*, 26 September, 34.

Doctors, Samuel I. 1969. *The Role of Federal Agencies in Technology Transfer*. Cambridge, MA: MIT Press.

Drucker, Peter F. 1979. "Science and Industry, Challenges of Antagonistic Interdependence." *Science* 204:806–810.

Dunner, Donald R. 2001. "Reflections on the Founding of the Federal Circuit." *Federal Circuit Bar Journal* 11:545–546.

Dunner, Donald R., J. Michael Jakes, and Jeffrey D. Karceski. 1995. "A Statistical Look at the Federal Circuit's Patent Decisions: 1982–1994." *Federal Circuit Bar Journal* 5:151–179.

Dupree, A. Hunter. 1957. *Science in the Federal Government: A History of Policies and Activities to 1940*. Cambridge, MA: Belknap Press of Harvard University Press.

Ebeling, Mary. 2008. "Mediating Uncertainty: Communicating the Financial Risks of Nanotechnologies." *Science Communication* 29:335–361.

Eden, David. 2005. Telephone conversation with the author. 21 February.

Egan, Jack. 1977. "Carter Won't Push End of Preference on Capital Gains." *Washington Post*, 21 November.

Eisenberg, Rebecca S. 1996. "Public Research and Private Development: Patents and Technology Transfer in Government-Sponsored Research." *Virginia Law Review* 82:1663–1727.

Eisinger, Peter. 1988. *The Rise of the Entrepreneurial State: State and Local Economic Development Policy in the U.S.* Madison, WI: University of Wisconsin Press.

Endicott, Kenneth M., and Ernest M. Allen. 1953. "The Growth of Medical Research 1941–1953 and the Role of Public Health Service Research Grants." *Science* 118:337–343.

England, J. Merton. 1983. *A Patron for Pure Science: The National Science Foundation's Formative Years*. Washington, DC: National Science Foundation.

"ERISA Amendments: Possible Litigation Main Bar to Plan Investment in Small Firms, Senate Panel Told." 1977. *BNA Pension Reporter*, 25 July, A-12–A-13.

Etzkowitz, Henry. 1983. "Entrepreneurial Scientists and Entrepreneurial Universities in American Academic Science." *Minerva* 21:1–21.

———. 2002. *MIT and the Rise of Entrepreneurial Science*. London: Routledge.

Etzkowitz, Henry, and Loet Leydesdorff. 2000. "The Dynamics of Innovation: From National Systems and 'Mode 2' to a Triple Helix of University-Industry-Government Relations." *Research Policy* 29:109–123.

Evans, James A. 2010a. "Industry Collaboration, Scientific Sharing, and the Dissemination of Knowledge." *Social Studies of Science* 40:757–791.

Evans, James A. 2010b. "Industry Induces Academic Science to Know Less about More." *American Journal of Sociology* 116:389–452.

Eveland, J. D., and William Hetzner, eds. 1982. *Development of University-Industry Cooperative Research Centers: Historical Profiles*. Washington, DC: National Science Foundation.

Eveland, J. D., William A. Hetzner, and L. G. Tornatzky, eds. 1984. *Development of University-Industry Cooperative Research Centers: Historical Profiles*. Washington, DC: National Science Foundation.

Fabricant, Solomon. 1954. *Economic Progress and Economic Change*. Cambridge, MA: National Bureau of Economic Research.

"A Fast but Bumpy Track for Biotechnology." 1980. *Economist*, 5 April, 73.

"Federal Aid for Industrial R&D Under Study." 1977. *Science & Government Report*, 15 December, 7.

Federal Council for Science and Technology. 1968. *Annual Report on Government Patent Policy*. Washington, DC: U.S. Government Printing Office.

———. 1976. *Report on Government Patent Policy, 1973–1976*. Washington, DC: U.S. Government Printing Office.

Feldman, Maryann P., Alessandra Colaianni, and Connie Kang Liu. 2007. "Lessons from the Commercialization of the Cohen-Boyer Patents: The Stanford University Licensing Program." Pages 1797–1807 in *Intellectual Property Management in Health & Agricultural Innovation: A Handbook of Best Practices*, edited by Anatole F. Krattiger, Richard T. Mahoney, Lita Nelsen, Jennifer A. Thompson, Alan B. Bennett, Kanikaram Satyanarayana, Gregory D. Graff, Carlos Fernandez, and Stanley P. Kowalsky. Davis, CA: PIPRA.

Feller, Irwin. 1984. "Political and Administrative Aspects of State High Technology Programs." *Policy Studies Review* 3:460–466.

———. 1997. "Federal and State Government Roles in Science and Technology." *Economic Development Quarterly* 11:283–295.

———. 2004. "Virtuous and Vicious Cycles in the Contributions of Public Research Universities to State Economic Development Objectives." *Economic Development Quarterly* 18:138–150.

———. 2008. "Neoliberalism, Performance Measurement, and the Governance of Academic Science." Report No. CSHE.13.08. Berkeley: Center for Studies in Higher Education, University of California, Berkeley. Available at http://cshe.berkeley.edu/publications/docs/ROPS-Feller-Neoliberalism-9-24-08.pdf. Last accessed 21 April 2011.

Feller, Irwin, Catherine P. Ailes, and J. David Roessner. 2002. "Impacts of Research Universities on Technological Innovation in Industry: Evidence from Engineering Research Centers." *Research Policy* 31:457–474.

"Firms Launch a Group to Spur Basic Research." 1980. *Chemical Week*, 24 September, 15.

"First Annual Survey of Research Parks." 1962. *Industrial Development and Manufacturers Record*, August, 32–43.

Fitzsimmons, Stephen J., Oren Grad, and Bhavya Lal. 1996. *An Evaluation of the NSF Science and Technology Centers Program*. Cambridge, MA: Abt Associates, Inc.

Fligstein, Neil. 1990. *The Transformation of Corporate Control*. Cambridge, MA: Harvard University Press.

———. 2001a. *The Architecture of Markets: An Economic Sociology of Twenty-First-Century Capitalist Societies*. Princeton, NJ: Princeton University Press.

———. 2001b. "Institutional Entrepreneurs and Cultural Frames: The Case of the European Union's Single Market Program." *European Societies* 3:261–287.

Florida, Richard, and Wesley M. Cohen. 1999. "Engine or Infrastructure? The University Role in Economic Development." Pages 589–610 in *Industrializing Knowledge: University-Industry Linkages in Japan and the United States*, edited by Lewis M. Branscomb, Fumio Kodama, and Richard L. Florida. Cambridge, MA: MIT Press.

Ford, Gerald R. 1976. *Science Indicators 1974, Message from the President*. Washington, DC: U.S. Government Printing Office.

Fosler, R. Scott, ed. 1988. *The New Economic Role of American States: Strategies in a Competitive World Economy*. Oxford, UK: Oxford University Press.

Fraker, Susan, with Henry W. Hubbard and Deborah Witherspoon. 1978. "Congress's Own Tax Revolt." *Newsweek*, 10 July, 33.

Fredrickson, Donald S. 2001. *The Recombinant DNA Controversy: A Memoir: Science, Politics, and the Public Interest, 1974–1981*. Washington, DC: American Society for Microbiology Press.

Friedland, Roger. 2009. "Institution, Practice, and Ontology: Toward a Religious Sociology." *Research in the Sociology of Organizations*, 27:45–83.

Friedland, Roger, and Robert R. Alford. 1991. "Bringing Society Back In: Symbols, Practices, and Institutional Contradictions." Pages 232–263 in *The New Institutionalism in Organizational Analysis*, edited by Walter W. Powell and Paul J. DiMaggio. Chicago: The University of Chicago Press.

Friedman, Orrie M. 2004. "The Original, Original Biotech." *Scientist* 18:10.

Funding Universe. 2010. "Enzo Biochem, Inc." Available at http://www.fundinguniverse.com/company-histories/Enzo-Biochem-Inc-Company-History.html. Last accessed 21 April 2011.

Gannes, Stuart. 1987. "Striking It Rich in Biotech." *Fortune*, 9 November, 9.

Geiger, Roger L. 1986. *To Advance Knowledge: The Growth of American Research Universities, 1900–1940*. New York: Oxford University Press.

———. 1990. "Organized Research Units—Their Role in the Development of University Research." *Journal of Higher Education* 61:1–19.

———. 1993. *Research and Relevant Knowledge: American Research Universities since World War II*. New York: Oxford University Press.

———. 2004. *Knowledge and Money: Research Universities and the Paradox of the Marketplace*. Stanford, CA: Stanford University Press.

Geiger, Roger L., and Creso M. Sá. 2008. *Tapping the Riches of Science: Universities and the Promise of Economic Growth*. Cambridge, MA: Harvard University Press.

"Gene Splicing: Key to Miracles in Science?" 1979. *U.S. News & World Report*, 31 December, 48.

Georgia Tech Archives and Records Management. 2011. "The Research Engineer Photograph Collection." Available at http://www.library.gatech.edu/archives/finding-aids/view?docId=ead/VAC300-ead/VAC300-ead.xml&anchor.id=0;query=vac300#1. Last accessed 21 April 2011.

Gilbert, Scott. 1982. "Intellectual Traditions in the Life Sciences: Molecular Biology and Biochemistry." *Perspectives in Biology and Medicine* 26:151–162.

Gilder, George. 1990. *Microcosm: The Quantum Revolution in Economics and Technology*. New York: Free Press.

Gillmore, C. Stewart. 2004. *Fred Terman at Stanford: Building a Discipline, a University, and Silicon Valley*. Stanford, CA: Stanford University Press.

Gilpin, Robert. 1968. "The Technology Gap: Causes and Consequences." *Science* 161:559–560.

Giroux, Henry A. 2002. "Neoliberalism, Corporate Culture, and the Promise of Higher Education: The University as a Democratic Public Sphere." *Harvard Educational Review* 4:425–463.

Glaser, Donald. 2004. "The Bubble Chamber, Bioengineering, Business Consulting, and Neurobiology." Oral history conducted by Eric Vettel. Berkeley: Regional Oral History Office, Bancroft Library, University of California.

Glenna, Leland L., William B. Lacy, Rick Welsh, and Dina Biscotti. 2007. "University Administrators, Agricultural Biotechnology, and Academic Capitalism: Defining the Public Good to Promote University-Industry Relationships." *Sociological Quarterly* 48:141–163.

Glynn, Mary Ann, and Michael Lounsbury. 2005. "From the Critics' Corner: Logic Blending, Discursive Change and Authenticity in a Cultural Production System." *Journal of Management Studies* 42:1031–1055.

Goeddel, David V. 2002. "Scientist at Genentech, CEO at Tularik." Oral history conducted by Sally Smith Hughes. Berkeley: Regional Oral History Office, Bancroft Library, University of California.

Gompers, Paul A. 1994. "The Rise and Fall of Venture Capital." *Business and Economic History* 23:1–26.

Gompers, Paul A., and Josh Lerner. 1998. "What Drives Venture Capital Fundraising?" *Brookings Papers on Economic Activity, Microeconomics* 1998:149–192.

———. 2004. *The Venture Capital Cycle*. Cambridge, MA: MIT Press.

Goulian, Mehran, Arthur Kornberg, and Robert L. Sinsheimer. 1967. "Enzymatic Synthesis of DNA, XXIV: Synthesis of Infectious Phage Phi-X174 DNA." *Proceedings of the National Academy of Sciences* 58:2321–2328.

Government-University-Industry Research Roundtable. 1986. *New Alliances and Partnerships in Science and Engineering*. Washington, DC: National Academy Press.

———. 1991. *Industrial Perspectives on Innovation and Interactions with Universities: Summary of Interviews with Senior Industrial Officials*. Washington, DC: National Academies of Science.

———. 1999. *Overcoming Barriers to Collaborative Research: Report of a Workshop*. Washington, DC: National Academy of Sciences.

———. 2000. *Industry-University Research Partnerships: What Are the Limits of Intimacy?* Washington, DC: National Academy of Sciences.

Graham, Bradley. 1978a. "Something's Happened to Yankee Ingenuity." *Washington Post*, 3 September.

———. 1978b. "Waning of Innovation Is Seen." *Washington Post*, 16 November.

———. 1978c. "World of Venture Capitalists Becomes More Complicated; Endless Variations on a Lending Theme." *Washington Post*, 1 October.

———. 1979. "Patent Bill Seeks Shift to Bolster Innovation." *Washington Post*, 8 April.

Granovetter, Mark. 1985. "Economic Action and Social Structure: The Problem of Embeddedness." *American Journal of Sociology* 91:481–510.

Grant II, Don Sherman, Michael Wallace, and William D. Pitney. 1995. "Measuring State-Level Economic Development Programs, 1970–1992." *Economic Development Quarterly* 9:134–145.

Grassmuck, Karen. 1990. "Boston U. Says It Will Write Off $16.4-Million of Its Investment in Biotechnology Company." *Chronicle of Higher Education*, 10 January.

Gray, Denis O., and R. C. Baneth. 1992. "1990–1991 Structural Information." Available at http://www.ncsu.edu/iucrc/PDFs/scanned%20CD%20reports/CD%2090-91.pdf. Last accessed 21 April 2011.

Gray, Denis O., Teresa Gidley, and Nancy Koester. 1987. "1986–1987 Center Director Report." Available at http://www.ncsu.edu/iucrc/PDFs/scanned%20CD%20reports/CD%2086-87.pdf. Last accessed 21 April 2011.

Gray, Denis O., and S. George Walters. 1998. *Managing the Industry/University Cooperative Research Center*. Columbus, OH: Battelle Press.

Green, Richard J., and Wil Lepkowski. 2006. "A Forgotten Model for Purposeful Science." *Issues in Science and Technology*, Winter.

Greenberg, Daniel S. 1963. "Civilian Technology: Concern over Pace of Growth Inspires Program for Research and Development Effort." *Science* 139:576–577.

——— 1965. "Money for Science: Budget Faces Pressure from Vietnam Conflict." *Science* 150:1790.

———. 1967a. "LBJ's Budget: Lean Fare Set Forth for Research and Development." *Science* 155:434–435.

———. 1967b. "Smale and NSF: A New Dispute Erupts." *Science* 157:1285.

———. 1970. "Research Priorities: New Program at NSF Reflects Shift in Values." *Science* 170:144–146.

———. 1978. "Washington Focuses on Industrial R&D Lag." *Science & Government Report*, 1 March, 1–3.

Griliches, Zvi. 1964. "Research Expenditures, Education, and the Aggregate Agricultural Production Function." *American Economic Review* 54:961–974.

———. 1996. "The Discovery of the Residual: A Historical Note." *Journal of Economic Literature* 34:1324–1330.

Gruchow, Nancy. 1970. "House Bill Hits Campus Unrest." *Science* 168:807.

Guston, David H. 1993. "The Social Contract for Science: Congress, the National Institutes of Health, and the Boundary between Politics and Science." PhD dissertation, Massachusetts Institute of Technology.

———. 1999. "Stabilizing the Boundary between U.S. Politics and Science: The Role of the Office of Technology Transfer as a Boundary Organization." *Social Studies of Science* 29:87–111.

Haggerty, Patrick. 1974. "Science and National Policy." *Science* 184:1348–1350.

Hall, Bronwyn H. 2005. "Exploring the Patent Explosion." *Journal of Technology Transfer* 30:35–48.

Hall, Bronwyn H., and Rosemary Ham Ziedonis. 2001. "The Patent Paradox Revisited: An Empirical Study of Patenting in the U.S. Semiconductor Industry, 1979–1995." *RAND Journal of Economics* 32:101–128.

Hall, Stephen S. 1987. *Invisible Frontiers: The Race to Synthesize a Human Gene*. Redmond, WA: Tempus Books.

Hamilton, Andrew. 1969. "State Technical Services: Congress Swings the Axe." *Science* 166:1606–1608.

Hammersla, Ann, Patricia Harshe Weeks, and Catherine Innes. 2004. *Recollections: Celebrating the History of AUTM and the Legacy of Bayh-Dole*. Northbrook, IL: Association of University Technology Managers.

Hammett, Frederick J. 1953. "Uncommitted Researchers." *Science* 117:64.

Harbridge House, Inc. 1968. *Government Patent Policy Study: Final Report*. Washington, DC: U.S. Government Printing Office.

Hardin, Angela Y. 2007. "Lawrence Berkeley Lab to House Facility for $500-Million BP Bioscience Program." *Inside Energy*, 5 February.

Hardy, Cynthia, and Steve Maguire. 2008. "Institutional Entrepreneurship." Pages 198–217 in *The SAGE Handbook of Organizational Institutionalism*, edited by Royston Greenwood, Christine Oliver, Roy Suddaby, and Kerstin Sahlin-Andersson. Thousand Oaks, CA: SAGE Publishers, Ltd.

Hargrave, Timothy, and Andrew H. Van de Ven. 2006. "A Collective Action Model of Institutional Innovation." *Academy of Management Review* 31:864–888.

Harmon, Robert L. 1992. "Seven New Rules of Thumb: How the Federal Circuit Has Changed the Way Patent Lawyers Advise Clients." *George Mason University Law Review* 14:573–584.

Hart, David M. 1998. *Forged Consensus: Science, Technology, and Economic Policy in the United States, 1921–1953*. Princeton, NJ: Princeton University Press.

Hartman, Paul L. 1992. "MSC Decade & a Half: A Brief History of the Formative First Decade and a Half of the Materials Science Center at Cornell University." Available at http://authors.library.caltech.edu/5456/1/hrst.mit.edu/hrs/materials/public/CCMR/Hartman1960-1975.htm. Last accessed 21 April 2011.

"Harvard Backs Off Recombinant DNA." 1980. *Nature* 288:423–424.

"Harvard Considers Commercial Role in DNA Research." 1980. *New York Times*, 27 October.

"Harvard Finally Backs Off Gene Venture." 1980. *Nature* 288:311.

Harvey, David. 2005. *A Brief History of Neoliberalism*. Oxford, UK: Oxford University Press.

Heilbron, John, and Robert Seidel. 1989. *Lawrence and His Laboratory: A History of the Lawrence Berkeley Laboratory, Volume I*. Berkeley: University of California Press.

Heimer, Carol A. 1999. "Competing Institutions: Law, Medicine, and Family in Neonatal Intensive Care." *Law and Society Review* 33:17–66.

Heller, Michael A., and Rebecca S. Eisenberg. 1998. "Can Patents Deter Innovation? The Anticommons in Biomedical Research." *Science* 280:698–701.

Hellman, Alfred, M. N. Oxman, and Robert Pollack, eds. 1973. *Biohazards in Biological Research: Proceedings of a Conference Held at the Asilomar Conference Center, Pacific Grove, California, January 22–24, 1973*. Cold Spring Harbor, NY: Cold Spring Harbor Laboratory.

Henderson, Rebecca, Adam B. Jaffe, and Manuel Trajtenberg. 1998. "Universities as a Source of Commercial Technology: A Detailed Analysis of University Patenting, 1965–1988." *Review of Economics and Statistics* 80:119–127.

Henry, Matthew D., and John L. Turner. 2006. "The Court of Appeals for the Federal Circuit's Impact on Patent Litigation." *Journal of Legal Studies* 35:85–117.

Henton, Douglas, and Steven A. Waldhorn. 1988. "California: The Megastate Economy." Pages 201–247 in *The New Economic Role of American States: Strategies in a Competitive World Economy*, edited by R. Scott Fosler. Oxford, UK: Oxford University Press.

Hersman, M. Frank. 1974. "Science and the Public Sector: A National Policy Overview." *Proceedings of the National Academy of Sciences* 71:2565–2570.

Herzik, Eric B. 1985. "The Governors' State-of-the-State Addresses: A Focus on Higher Education." *State Government* 58:65–66.

Hetzner, William A., Teresa R. Gidley, and Denis O. Gray. 1989. "Cooperative Research and Rising Expectations: Lessons from NSF's Industry/University Cooperative Research Centers." *Technology in Society* 11:335–345.

Heyneker, Herbert L. 2002. "Molecular Geneticist at UCSF and Genentech, Entrepreneur in Biotechnology." Oral history conducted by Sally Smith Hughes. Berkeley: Regional Oral History Office, Bancroft Library, University of California.

Hilts, Philip J. 1980. "Ivy-Covered Capitalism: Colleges Weigh Spinoffs to Plug the Profits Leak." *Washington Post*, 10 November.

———. 1982. *Scientific Temperaments: Three Lives in Contemporary Science*. New York: Simon & Schuster.

Hitchcock, E. M. 1925. "The Engineering Experiment Station: The Latest Step in the Quadrangle Development." *Ohio State Engineer* 9:9–10.

Hollister, Robert M., Tunney Lee, and Katina Cummings. 1979. *Development Politics: Private Development and the Public Interest*. Washington, DC: Council of State Planning Agencies.

Hong, Wei, and John P. Walsh. 2009. "For Money or Glory? Commercialization, Competition, and Secrecy in the Entrepreneurial University." *Sociological Quarterly* 50:145–171.

Hoovers. 2010. "Quidel Corporation." Available at http://www.hoovers.com/company/Quidel_Corporation/ryjytil.html. Last accessed 21 April 2011.

"House, Senate Split on Authorization for NSF." 1977. *Science & Government Report*, 15 May, 5.

Hughes, Jeff. 2003. *The Manhattan Project: Big Science and the Atom Bomb*. New York: Columbia University Press.

Hughes, Sally Smith. 2001. "Making Dollars out of DNA: The First Major Patent in Biotechnology and the Commercialization of Molecular Biology, 1974–1980." *Isis* 92:541–575.

Ikenberry, Stanley O. 1970. *A Profile of Proliferating Institutes: A Study of Selected Characteristics of Institutes and Centers in 51 Land-Grant Universities*. University Park, PA: The Pennsylvania State University Center for the Study of Higher Education.

Ikenberry, Stanley O., and Renee C. Friedman. 1972. *Beyond Academic Departments: The Story of Institutes and Centers*. San Francisco: Jossey-Bass.

Illinois Board of Higher Education. 1999. *The Illinois Commitment: Partnerships, Opportunities, and Excellence*. Springfield: Illinois Board of Higher Education.

Illinois Institute of Technology Research Institute. 1969. *Technology in Retrospect and Critical Events in Science (TRACES)*. Chicago: IIT (Illinois Institute of Technology) Research Institute.

"Industry R&D Renews the Old Campus Ties." 1979. *Chemical Week*, February 21, 38.

"Industry Said to Be Primary Innovator." 1991. *Chronicle of Higher Education*, 15 May.

"Industry Starts to Do Biology with Its Eyes Open." 1978. *Economist*, 2 December, 95.

Industry/University Cooperative Research Centers Program Evaluation Project. 2011. "Publications." Available at http://www.ncsu.edu/iucrc/NatReports.htm#pubs. Last accessed 21 April 2011.

"The 'Innovation Recession.'" 1978. *Time*, 2 October.
"Innovation: Some Positive Steps." 1979. *Business Week*, 26 November, 96.
"Invented in Britain, Made in America." 1979. *Economist*, 21 April, 124.
Iowa State University, University Extension. 2010. "Center for Industrial Research and Service (CIRAS): History." Available at http://www.ciras.iastate.edu/history.asp. Last accessed 21 April 2011.
Itakura, Keiichi. 2006. "Keiichi Itakura: DNA Synthesis at City of Hope for Genentech." Oral history conducted by Sally Smith Hughes. Berkeley: Regional Oral History Office, Bancroft Library, University of California.
Jablin, Burton F. 1980. "Making Research Pay." *Harvard Crimson*, 25 October.
Jackson, David A., Robert H. Symons, and Paul Berg. 1972. "Biochemical Methods for Inserting New Genetic Information into DNA of Simian Virus 40: Circular SV40 DNA Molecules Containing Lambda Phage Genes and the Galactose Operon of Escherichia Coli." *Proceedings of the National Academy of Sciences* 69:2904–2909.
Jaffe, Adam B. 2000. "The U.S. Patent System in Transition: Policy Innovation and the Innovation Process." *Research Policy* 29:531–557.
Jaffe, Adam B., and Josh Lerner. 2004. *Innovation and Its Discontents: How Our Broken Patent System Is Endangering Innovation and Progress, and What to Do About It.* Princeton, NJ: Princeton University Press.
Jamison, Andrew. 1968. "Senate Aims Blow at Colleges That Bar Recruiters." *Science* 160:1320.
Janicke, Paul M. 2002. "To Be or Not To Be: The Long Gestation of the U.S. Court of Appeals for the Federal Circuit (1887–1982)." *Antitrust Law Journal* 69:645–667.
Jellema, William W. 1970. *The Red and the Black.* Washington, DC: Association of American Colleges.
———. 1971. *Redder and Much Redder: A Follow-Up Study to "The Red and the Black."* Washington, DC: Association of American Colleges.
———. 1973. *From Red to Black?* San Francisco: Jossey-Bass.
Jenkins, J. Craig, Kevin T. Leicht, and Heather Wendt. 2006. "Class Forces, Political Institutions, and State Intervention: Subnational Economic Development Policy in the United States, 1971–1990." *American Journal of Sociology* 111:1122–1180.
Johnson, Irving S. 2006. "Eli Lilly and the Rise of Biotechnology." Oral history conducted by Sally Smith Hughes. Berkeley: Regional Oral History Office, Bancroft Library, University of California.
Johnson, Robert Wolcott. 1980. "The Passage of the Investment Incentive Act of 1978: A Case Study of Business Influencing Public Policy." PhD dissertation, Harvard University.
"Joining Hands against Japan." 1980. *Business Week*, 10 November, 108.
Jones, Mark Peter. 2009. "Entrepreneurial Science: The Rules of the Game." *Social Studies of Science* 39:821–851.
Judson, Horace Freeland. 1996. *The Eighth Day of Creation: Makers of the Revolution in Biology*. Cold Spring Harbor, NY: Cold Spring Harbor Laboratory.
Kastriner, Lawrence G. 1991. "The Revival of Confidence in the Patent System." *Journal of the Patent and Trademark Office Society* 73:5–23.
Katz, James Everett. 1978. *Presidential Politics and Science Policy*. New York: Praeger Publishers.

Kay, Lily E. 1996. *The Molecular Vision of Life: Caltech, the Rockefeller Foundation, and the Rise of the New Biology*. Oxford, UK: Oxford University Press.

Keller, Herbert B. 1996. "Interview with Herbert B. Keller." Oral history conducted by Shirley K. Cohen. Pasadena, CA: California Institute of Technology Archives.

Kenney, Martin. 1986. *Biotechnology: The University-Industrial Complex*. New Haven, CT: Yale University Press.

Kevles, Daniel J.. 1994. "Ananda Chakrabarty Wins a Patent: Biotechnology, Law, and Society: 1972–1980." *Historical Studies in the Physical and Biological Sciences* 25:111–135.

———. 1977. "The National Science Foundation and the Debate over Postwar Research Policy, 1942–1945." *Isis* 68:4–26.

———. 1978. *The Physicists: The History of Scientific Community in Modern America*. Cambridge, MA: Harvard University Press.

———. 2002. "Of Mice & Money: The Story of the World's First Animal Patent." *Daedalus* 131:78–88.

Keyworth, II, George A. 1984. "Four Years of Reagan Science Policy: Notable Shifts in Priorities." *Science* 224:9–13.

———. 1986. "Improving the U.S. Position in International Industrial Competitiveness." Pages 11–18 in *The New Engineering Research Centers: Purposes, Goals, and Expectations*, edited by the Commission on Engineering and Technical Systems Cross-Disciplinary Engineering Research Committee of the National Research Council. Washington, DC: National Academy Press.

Kieschnick, Michael. 1981. *Taxes and Growth: Business Incentives and Economic Development*. Washington, DC: Council of State Planning Agencies.

Kiley, Thomas D. 2002. "Genentech Legal Counsel and Vice President, 1976–1988, and Entrepreneur." Oral history conducted by Sally Smith Hughes. Berkeley: Regional Oral History Office, Bancroft Library, University of California.

Kim, Jinyoung, and Gerald Marschke. 2004. "Accounting for the Recent Surge in U.S. Patenting: Changes in R&D Expenditures, Patent Yields, and the High Tech Sector." *Economics of Innovation and New Technology* 13:543–558.

King, C. Judson. 2007. Interview by author. Digital recording. Berkeley, 8 January.

Kleid, Dennis G. 2002. "Scientist and Patent Agent at Genentech." Oral history conducted by Sally Smith Hughes. Berkeley: Regional Oral History Office, Bancroft Library, University of California.

Kleinman, Daniel L. 1995. *Politics on the Endless Frontier: Postwar Research Policy in the United States*. Durham, NC: Duke University Press.

Kleinman, Daniel L., Jacob Habinek, and Steven P. Vallas. 2011. "Codes of Commerce: The Uses of Business Rhetoric in the American Academy, 1960–2000." In *The American Academic Profession: Transformation in Contemporary Higher Education*, edited by Joseph Hermanowicz. Baltimore: Johns Hopkins University Press.

Kleinman, Daniel L., and Steven P. Vallas. 2001. "Science, Capitalism, and the Rise of the 'Knowledge Worker': The Changing Structure of Knowledge Production in the United States." *Theory and Society* 30:451–492.

Köhler, Georges, and César Milstein. 1975. "Continuous Cultures of Fused Cells Secreting Antibody of Predefined Specificity." *Nature* 256:495–497.

Kohler, Robert E. 1982. *From Medical Chemistry to Biochemistry: The Making of a Biomedical Discipline*. Cambridge, UK: Cambridge University Press.

Kornberg, Arthur. 1995. *The Golden Helix: Inside Biotech Ventures*. Sausalito, CA: University Science Books.

———. 1997. "Biochemistry at Stanford, Biotechnology at DNAX." Oral history conducted by Sally Smith Hughes. Berkeley: Regional Oral History Office, Bancroft Library, University of California.

Kortum, Samuel, and Josh Lerner. 1998. "Stronger Protection or Technological Revolution: What Is behind the Recent Surge in Patenting?" *Carnegie-Rochester Conference Series on Public Policy* 48:247–304.

Koshland, Jr., Daniel E., Roderic B. Park, and Louise Taylor. 2003. "The Reorganization of Biology at the University of California, Berkeley." Oral history conducted by Sally Smith Hughes. Berkeley: Regional Oral History Office, Bancroft Library, University of California.

Kraemer, Sylvia Katharine. 1999. "NASA, Monopolies, and the Cold War: The Origins and Consequences of NASA Patent Policy, 1958–1996." Paper presented at the Annual Meeting of the Society for the History of Technology, October. Available at http://www.hq.nasa.gov/office/codez/plans/R&D/SHOTOCT99.html. Last accessed 21 April 2011.

Krimsky, Sheldon. 1982. *Genetic Alchemy: The Social History of the Recombinant DNA Controversy*. Cambridge, MA: The MIT Press.

———. 2003. *Science in the Private Interest: Has the Lure of Profits Corrupted Biomedical Research?* Lanham, MD: Rowman & Littlefield Publishers, Inc.

Krippner, Greta R. 2007. "The Making of U.S. Monetary Policy: Central Bank Transparency and the Neoliberal Dilemma." *Theory and Society* 36:477–513.

Krippner, Greta R., and Anthony S. Alvarez. 2007. "Embeddedness and the Intellectual Projects of Economic Sociology." *Annual Review of Sociology* 33:219–240.

Lam, Alice. 2010. "From 'Ivory Tower Traditionalists' to 'Entrepreneurial Scientists'?" *Social Studies of Science* 40:307–340.

Lambright, W. Henry. 1999. "Building State Science: The EPSCoR Experience." Coeur d'Alene, ID: American Association for the Advancement of Science Workshop on Academic Research Competitiveness.

Landry, Larry. 1988. "Arizona: Diversifying a Natural Resource-Based Economy." Pages 250–268 in *The New Economic Role of American States: Strategies in a Competitive World Economy*, edited by R. Scott Fosler. Oxford, UK: Oxford University Press.

Langer, Elinor. 1967. "LBJ at NIH: President Offers Kind Words for Basic Research." *Science* 157:403–405.

Langfitt, Thomas W., Sheldon Hackney, Alfred P. Fishman, and Albert V. Glowasky, eds. 1983. *Partners in the Research Enterprise: University-Corporate Relationships*. Philadelphia: University of Pennsylvania Press.

Lardner, Jr., George. 1978. "Tax Cuts on the Hill; Conservatives Celebrate, Liberals Struggle against Further Slashes." *Washington Post*, 31 July.

Lasken, Jesse E. 2005. Interview by author. Tape recording of phone interview. Potomac, MD, 7 March.

Latker, Norman J. 1971. "Presentation of Norman J. Latker before the Commission on Government Procurement, July 29, 1971." Bethesda, MD. Document from the personal files of Norman J. Latker. (Photocopy available from the author.)

———. 1976. "Statement of Norman J. Latker, Patent Counsel, Department of Health, Education, and Welfare Before the Subcommittee on Domestic and International

Scientific Planning and Analysis, Committee on Science and Technology, House of Representatives. September 29, 1976." Report No. ED144429. Washington, DC: Education Resources Information Center.

———. 1977. "Current Trends in Government Patent Policy." Report No. ED144428. Washington, DC: Education Resources Information Center.

———. 2005. Interviews by author. Tape recording of telephone and in-person interviews. Bethesda, MD, 21, 24, and 28 January, 6 April.

Latker, Norman J., and Ronald J. Wylie. 1965. "Utilization of Government-Owned Health and Welfare Inventions." *Journal of the Patent Office Society* 47:868–879.

Lave, Rebecca, Philip Mirowski, and Samuel Randalls. 2010. "Introduction: STS and Neoliberal Science." *Social Studies of Science* 40:659–675.

Lea, Charles L. 2008. "Charles L. Lea, Jr." Oral history conducted by Carole Kolker. Easton, MD: National Venture Capital Association.

Lear, John. 1978. *Recombinant DNA: The Untold Story*. New York: Crown Publishers, Inc.

Lecuyer, Christophe. 2005. *Making Silicon Valley: Innovation and the Growth of High Tech, 1930–1970*. Cambridge, MA: MIT Press.

Leicht, Kevin T., and J. Craig Jenkins. 1994. "Three Strategies of State Economic Development: Entrepreneurial, Industrial Recruitment, and Deregulation Policies in the American States." *Economic Development Quarterly* 8:256–269.

———. 1998. "Political Resources and Direct State Intervention: The Adoption of Public Venture Capital Programs in the American States, 1974–1990." *Social Forces* 76:1323–1345.

Le Maistre, C. W. 1989. "Academia Linking with Industry—The R.P.I. Model." *Sixth IEEE/CHMT International Electronic Manufacturing Technology Symposium*: 207–208.

Lenoir, Timothy, Nathan Rosenberg, Henry Rowen, Christophe Lécuyer, Jeannette A. Colyvas, and Brent Goldfarb. 2003. "Inventing the Entrepreneurial University." Available at http://replay.web.archive.org/20070609174912/http://siepr.stanford.edu/programs/SST_Seminars/Lenoir.doc. Last accessed 21 April 2011.

Lerner, Josh. 2002. "Boom and Bust in the Venture Capital Industry and the Impact on Innovation." *Federal Reserve Bank of Atlanta Economic Review* 87(4):25–39.

Leshowitz, Barry. 1979. "The Demise of Technology Transfer in DHEW." Bethesda, MD. Unpublished paper from the personal files of Norman J. Latker. (Photocopy available from the author).

Leslie, Stuart W. 1993. *The Cold War and American Science: The Military-Industrial-Academic Complex at MIT and Stanford*. New York: Columbia University Press.

———. 2001. "Regional Disadvantage: Replicating Silicon Valley in New York's Capital Region." *Technology and Culture* 42:236–264.

Lewin, Roger. 1978. "Modern Biology at the Industrial Threshold." *New Scientist*, 5 October, 18–19.

Link, Albert N. 1995. *A Generosity of Spirit: The Early History of the Research Triangle Park*. Research Triangle Park, NC: Research Triangle Foundation.

———. 2002. *From Seed to Harvest: The History of the Growth of the Research Triangle Park*. Research Triangle Park, NC: Research Triangle Foundation.

———. 2003. "University-Related Research Parks." *Issues in Science and Technology* 20:79–81.

Link, Albert N., and Kevin R. Link. 2003. "On the Growth of U.S. Science Parks." *Journal of Technology Transfer* 28:81–85.

Link, Albert N., and John T. Scott. 2003. "U.S. Science Parks: The Diffusion of an Innovation and Its Effects on the Academic Mission of Universities." *International Journal of Industrial Organization* 21:1323–1356.

Lippman, Thomas W. 1981. "Government-Industry-Academia: Engineer Shortage Sparks a Once-Unlikely Merger." *Washington Post*, 27 December.

Loeppky, Rodney. 2005. "History, Technology, and the Capitalist State: The Comparative Political Economy of Biotechnology and Genomics." *Review of International Political Economy* 12:264–286.

Longstreth, Bevis. 1986. *Modern Investment Management and the Prudent Man Rule.* New York: Oxford University Press.

Lounsbury, Michael. 2007. "A Tale of Two Cities: Competing Logics and Practice Variation in the Professionalizing of Mutual Funds." *Academy of Management Journal* 50:289–307.

———. 2008. "Institutional Rationality and Practice Variation: New Directions in the Institutional Analysis of Practice." *Accounting, Organizations, and Society* 33:349–361.

Lounsbury, Michael, and Ellen T. Crumley. 2007. "New Practice Creation: An Institutional Perspective on Innovation." *Organization Studies* 28:993–1012.

Lounsbury, Michael, Marc Ventresca, and Paul M. Hirsch. 2003. "Social Movements, Field Frames and Industry Emergence: A Cultural-Political Perspective on U.S. Recycling." *Socio-Economic Review* 1:71–104.

Lovell, D. J. 1978. "Patents Patter." *Journal of Applied Optics* 17:1666–1667.

Lowen, Rebecca S. 1997. *Creating the Cold War University: The Transformation of Stanford.* Berkeley: University of California Press.

Luger, Michael I., and Harvey A. Goldstein. 1991. *Technology in the Garden: Research Parks and Regional Economic Development.* Chapel Hill: University of North Carolina Press.

Mackenzie, Michael, Peter Keating, and Alberto Cambrosio. 1990. "Patents and Free Scientific Information in Biotechnology: Making Monoclonal Antibodies Proprietary." *Science, Technology and Human Values* 15:65–83.

"The Maddening Struggle to Survive." 1975. *Business Week*, 30 June, 96.

Maddox, Robert F. 1979. "The Politics of World War II Science: Senator Harley M. Kilgore and the Legislative Origins of the National Science Foundation." *West Virginia History* 41:20–39.

Magarrell, Jack. 1979. "Academe and Industry Weigh a New Alliance." *Chronicle of Higher Education*, 5 February.

Maguire, Steve, Cynthia Hardy, and Thomas B. Lawrence. 2004. "Institutional Entrepreneurship in Emerging Fields: HIV/AIDS Treatment Advocacy in Canada." *Academy of Management Journal* 47:657–679.

Mandel, Richard. 1996. *A Half Century of Peer Review, 1946–1996.* Bethesda, MD: National Institutes of Health, Division of Research Grants.

Manners, George E., and Howard K. Nason. 1978. "The Decline in Industrial Research—Causes and Cures." *Research Management* 21:8–11.

Mansfield, Edwin. 1972. "Contribution of R&D to Economic Growth in the United States." *Science* 175:477–486.

Martin, Cathie Jo. 1991. *Shifting the Burden: The Struggle over Growth and Corporate Taxation.* Chicago: University of Chicago Press.

Martin, Isaac William. 2008. *The Permanent Tax Revolt: How the Property Tax Transformed American Politics*. Stanford, CA: Stanford University Press.

Marx, Karl. 2005 [1847]. *The Poverty of Philosophy: Being a Translation of the Misère de la Philosophie*. Chestnut Hill, MA: Adamant Media Corporation.

Massachusetts Institute of Technology. 1955. *President's Report Issue of the Bulletin of the Massachusetts Institute of Technology*. Cambridge, MA: Massachusetts Institute of Technology. Available at http://libraries.mit.edu/archives/mithistory/presidents-reports/1955.pdf. Last accessed 21 April 2011.

———. 1969. *Massachusetts Institute of Technology Bulletin: Report of the President*. Cambridge, MA: Massachusetts Institute of Technology. Available at http://libraries.mit.edu/archives/mithistory/presidents-reports/1969.pdf. Last accessed 21 April 2011.

Matkin, Gary W. 1990. *Technology Transfer and the University*. New York: American Council on Education in collaboration with MacMillan Publishing Company.

Mazuzan, George T. 1988. "The National Science Foundation: A Brief History." Report No. NSF 88-16. Washington, DC: National Science Foundation.

McCurdy, Patrick P. 1976. "Needed: More Entrepreneurial Sparks." *Chemical Week*, 2 June, 5.

McElheny, Victor K. 1974. "Gene Transplants Seen Helping Farmers and Doctors." *New York Times*, 20 May.

McGowen, Lindsey. 2008. "Predictors of Cooperative Rsearch Centers Post-Graduation Success: Update." Available at http://www.ncsu.edu/iucrc/Jan'08/McGowenNSF%201-9-08denis.pdf. Last accessed 21 April 2011.

Mead, Carver. 1991. "Carver Mead." Oral history conducted by Loren Butler. New Brunswick, NJ: Center for the History of Electrical Engineering, IEEE.

———. 1996. "Interview with Carver A. Mead." Oral history conducted by Shirley K. Cohen. Pasadena, CA: California Institute of Technology Archives.

Meador, Daniel J. 1992. "Origin of the Federal Circuit: A Personal Account." *American University Law Review* 41:581–620.

Merton, Robert K. 1973 [1957]. "Priorities in Scientific Discovery." Pages 286–324 in *The Sociology of Science: Theoretical and Empirical Investigations*, edited by Norman W. Storer. Chicago: University of Chicago Press.

Merz, Jon, and Nicholas M. Pace. 1994. "Trends in Patent Litigation: The Apparent Influence of Strengthened Patents Attributable to the Court of Appeals for the Federal Circuit." *Journal of the Patent and Trademark Office Society* 76:579–590.

Metlay, Grischa. 2006. "Reconsidering Renormalization: Stability and Change in 20th-Century Views on University Patents." *Social Studies of Science* 36:565–597.

"Midland Meeting Aim: Tilting R&D Upward." 1979. *Chemical Week*, 31 October, 29.

"Midwest Finds Itself Guilty." 1961. *Business Week*, 21 October.

Miettinen, Reijo, Dalvir Samra-Fredericks, and Dvora Yanow. 2009. "Re-Turn to Practice: An Introductory Essay." *Organization Studies* 30:1309–1327.

Minnesota Department of Trade and Economic Development. 1988. *State Technology Programs in the United States: 1988*. St. Paul, MN: Minnesota Department of Trade and Economic Development.

MIT Entrepreneurship Center. 2010. "Legendary Leaders and Memorials." Available at http://replay.web.archive.org/20100601185135/http://entrepreneurship.mit.edu/legendary_leaders_memorials.php. Last accessed 21 April 2011.

Moore, Kelly, Daniel L. Kleinman, David Hess, and Scott Frickel. 2010. "Science and Neoliberal Globalization: A Political Sociological Approach." Available at http://www.davidjhess.org/SciNeolGlobaliz.pdf. Last accessed 21 April 2011.

Morange, Michel. 1998. *A History of Molecular Biology*. Cambridge, MA: Harvard University Press.

"More Firms Join the DNA Race." 1979. *Chemical Week*, 27 June, 32.

Mosher, Harry S. 2001. "Stanford Chemistry Department History 1977 to 2000." Available at http://www-sul.stanford.edu/depts/swain/history/mosher/pdf_index.html. Last accessed 21 April 2011.

Mowery, David C., Richard R. Nelson, Bhaven N. Sampat, and Arvids A. Ziedonis. 2001. "The Growth of Patenting and Licensing by U.S. Universities: An Assessment of the Effects of the Bayh-Dole Act of 1980." *Research Policy* 30:99–119.

———. 2004. *Ivory Tower and Industrial Innovation: University-Industry Technology Transfer before and after the Bayh-Dole Act*. Stanford, CA: Stanford University Press.

Mowery, David C., and Bhaven N. Sampat. 2001a. "Patenting and Licensing University Inventions: Lessons from the History of the Research Corporation." *Industrial and Corporate Change* 10:317–355.

———. 2001b. "University Patents and Patent Policy Debates in the USA, 1925–1980." *Industrial and Corporate Change* 10:781–814.

———. 2006. "Universities in National Innovation Systems." Pages 209–239 in *The Oxford Handbook of Innovation*, edited by Jan Fagerberg, David C. Mowery, and Richard R. Nelson. Oxford, UK: Oxford University Press.

Muchmore, Lynn. 1983. "Science Advice to Governors: Non-Politics in the Policy Process." Pages 182–191 in *Being Governor: The View from the Office*, edited by Thad L. Beyle and Lynn R. Muchmore. Durham, NC: Duke University Press.

Mudge, Stephanie Lee. 2008. "What Is Neoliberalism?" *Socio-Economic Review* 6:703–731.

Murmann, Johann Peter. 2004. *Knowledge and Competitive Advantage: The Coevolution of Firms, Technology, and National Institutions*. Cambridge, UK: Cambridge University Press.

Murray, Fiona. 2004. "The Role of Academic Inventors in Entrepreneurial Firms: Sharing the Laboratory Life." *Research Policy* 33:643–659.

———. 2010. "The Oncomouse That Roared: Hybrid Exchange Strategies as a Source of Distinction at the Boundary of Overlapping Institutions." *American Journal of Sociology* 116:341–388.

National Academy of Engineering. 1971. *Technology and International Trade: Proceedings of the Symposium*. Washington, DC: National Academy of Engineering.

———. 1976. *U.S. Technology and International Trade: Proceedings of the Technical Session at the Eleventh Annual Meeting, April 23–24, 1975*. Washington, DC: National Academy of Engineering.

———. 1992. *Memorial Tributes: National Academy of Engineering, Volume 5*. Washington, DC: National Academies Press.

National Academy of Sciences, Committee on Science, Engineering, and Public Policy. 1975a. *Materials and Man's Needs: Materials Science and Engineering—Volume I, The History, Scope, and Nature of Materials Science and Engineering*. Washington, DC: National Academy of Sciences.

———. 1975b. *Materials and Man's Needs: Materials Science and Engineering—Volume III, The Institutional Framework for Materials Science and Engineering*. Washington, DC: National Academy of Sciences.

National Academy of Sciences, Committee on Science and Public Policy, and U.S. House Committee on Science and Astronautics. 1965. *Basic Research and National Goals: A Report to the Committee on Science and Astronautics, U.S. House of Representatives*. Washington, DC: U.S. Government Printing Office.

National Academy of Sciences, National Academy of Engineering, Institute of Medicine, and National Research Council. 1976. *Annual Report: Fiscal Year 1975–76*. Washington, DC: National Academy Press.

National Aeronautics and Space Administration. 1964. *Transforming and Using Space-Research Knowledge (Ten Diversified Views)*. Los Angeles: NASA-UCLA Symposium and Workshop.

National Bureau of Economic Research. 2010. "U.S. Business Cycle Expansions and Contractions." Available at http://www.nber.org/cycles/cyclesmain.html. Last accessed 21 April 2011.

National Commission on Research. 1980. *Industry and the Universities: Developing Cooperative Research Relationships in the National Interest*. Pasadena, CA: National Commission on Research.

National Conference on the Management of University Technology Resources. 1974. *Technology Transfer: University Opportunities and Responsibilities*. Cleveland, OH: Case Western Reserve University.

"National Enterprise Board: Biogenic Business." 1980. *Economist*, 26 July, 60.

National Governors Association. 1982. *State Activities to Encourage Technological Innovation: An Update*. Springfield, VA: National Technical Information Service.

———. 1983. *Technology and Growth: State Initiatives in Technological Innovation*. Washington, DC: National Governors Association.

National Governors Association, Center for Policy Research and Analysis, and The Conference Board. 1987. *The Role of Science and Technology in Economic Competitiveness*. Washington, DC: National Governors Association.

National Institutes of Health, Office of Budget. 2010. "Appropriations History by Institute/Center (1938 to Present)." Available at http://officeofbudget.od.nih.gov/approp_hist.html. Last accessed 21 April 2011.

National Research Council. 1978. *Technology, Trade, and the U.S. Economy: Report of a Workshop Held at Woods Hole, Massachusetts, August 22–31, 1976*. Washington, DC: National Academy of Sciences.

National Research Council, Commission on Engineering and Technical Systems, Cross-Disciplinary Engineering Research Committee. 1986. *The New Engineering Research Centers: Purposes, Goals, and Expectations*. Washington, DC: National Academy Press.

National Resources Committee. 1938. *Research—A National Resource*. Washington, DC: U.S. Government Printing Office.

National Science Board. 1979. *Science Indicators, 1978*. Washington, DC: U.S. Government Printing Office.

———. 1983a. *Science Indicators, 1982: Report of the National Science Board, 1983*. Washington, DC: U.S. Government Printing Office.

———. 1983b. *University-Industry Research Relationships: Selected Studies*. Washington, DC: National Science Foundation.

National Science Board. 1985. *Science Indicators: The 1985 Report*. Washington, DC: U.S. Government Printing Office.

———. 1989. *Science and Engineering Indicators—1989*. Washington, DC: National Science Board.

———. 1996. *Science and Engineering Indicators—1996*. Washington, DC: U.S. Government Printing Office. Available at http://www.nsf.gov/statistics/seind96/. Last accessed 21 April 2011.

———. 2004. *Science and Engineering Indicators—2004*. Arlington, VA: National Science Foundation. Available at http://www.nsf.gov/statistics/seind04/. Last accessed 21 April 2011.

———. 2006. *Science and Engineering Indicators—2006*. Arlington, VA: National Science Foundation. Available at http://www.nsf.gov/statistics/seind06/. Last accessed 21 April 2011.

———. 2008. *Science and Engineering Indicators 2008*. Arlington, VA: National Science Foundation. Available at http://www.nsf.gov/statistics/seind08/. Last accessed 21 April 2011.

———. 2010. *Science and Engineering Indicators 2010*. Arlington, VA: National Science Foundation. Available at http://www.nsf.gov/statistics/seind10/. Last accessed 21 April 2011.

National Science Foundation. 1971. "National Science Foundation: Twentieth Annual Report for the Fiscal Year Ended June 30, 1970." Report No. NSF 71-1. Washington, DC: National Science Foundation.

———. 1976. *Research in Industry: Roles of the Government and the National Science Foundation*. Washington, DC: National Science Foundation.

National Science Foundation, Division of Science Resources Statistics. 2003. *Federal Funds for Research and Development, Detailed Historical Tables: Fiscal Years 1951–2002*. Arlington, VA: National Science Foundation. Available at http://www.nsf.gov/statistics/nsf03325/. Last accessed 21 April 2011.

———. 2007. *Academic Research and Development Expenditures: Fiscal Year 2005*. Arlington, VA: National Science Foundation. Available at http://www.nsf.gov/statistics/nsf07318/. Last accessed 21 April 2011.

National Science Foundation, Engineering Research Centers. 1998. *ERC Best Practices Manual*. Available at http://erc-assoc.org/manual/bp_acknowl.htm. Last accessed 21 April 2011.

National Venture Capital Association. 1977. "A Program of Tax Revision Proposals to Enhance Capital Formation for Growth Businesses." Pages 135–147 in *Small Business Access to Equity and Venture Capital*, U.S. House, Committee on Small Business, Subcommittee on Capital, Investment and Business Opportunities. Washington, DC: U.S. Government Printing Office.

Nelkin, Dorothy. 1971. *The Politics of Housing Innovation: The Fate of the Civilian Industrial Technology Program*. Ithaca, NY: Cornell University Press.

Nelson, Andrew J. 2005. "Cacophony or Harmony? Multivocal Logics and Technology Licensing by the Stanford University Department of Music." *Industrial and Corporate Change* 14:93–118.

Nelson, Richard R. 1959. "The Simple Economics of Basic Scientific Research." *Journal of Political Economy* 67:297–306.

———. 1997. "How New Is New Growth Theory?" *Challenge* 40:29–58.

———. 2006. "Reflections on 'The Simple Economics of Basic Scientific Research': Looking Back and Looking Forward." *Industrial and Corporate Change* 15:903–918.

"New NSF Advisory Groups." 1976. *Computer*, January, 14.

Newfield, Christopher. 2003. *Ivy and Industry: Business and the Making of the American University, 1880–1980*. Durham, NC: Duke University Press.

Newman, Pauline. 2001. "Origins of the Federal Circuit: The Role of Industry." *Federal Circuit Bar Journal* 11:541–543.

"News and Notes." 1952a. *Science* 116:469–473.

———. 1952b. *Science* 116:681–684.

———. 1953. *Science* 118:509–514.

Norman, Colin. 1977. "Recombinant DNA Pioneers Lower the Alarm." *Science & Government Report*, 1 July, 1–3.

———. 1982. "Electronics Firms Plug into Universities." *Science* 217:511–514.

———. 1985a. "NSF Names Engineering Centers." *Science* 228:304.

———. 1985b. "NSF Readies New Engineering Program." *Science* 227:38–39.

"Of Professors and Money." 1980. *Harvard Crimson*, 26 November.

O'Mara, Margaret Pugh. 2005. *Cities of Knowledge: Cold War Science and the Search for the Next Silicon Valley*. Princeton, NJ: Princeton University Press.

"On the Front Lines of the New Plant Research." 1980. *Business Week*, 25 August, 92.

"On the Hill, a Dud." 1979. *Business Week*, 12 November, 50.

Osborne, David. 1988. *Laboratories of Democracy*. Boston: Harvard Business School Press.

Owen-Smith, Jason. 2003. "From Separate Systems to Hybrid Order: Accumulative Advantage across Public and Private Science at Research One Universities." *Research Policy* 32:1081–1104.

———. 2005. "Dockets, Deals, and Sagas: Commensuration and the Rationalization of Experience in University Licensing." *Social Studies of Science* 35:69–97.

Owen-Smith, Jason, and Walter W. Powell. 2001. "Careers and Contradictions: Faculty Responses to the Transformation of Knowledge." *Research in the Sociology of Work* 10:109–140.

Palmer, Archie M. 1934. "University Patent Policies and Procedures." *Journal of the Patent Office Society* 16:96–131.

———. 1948. *Survey of University Patent Policies, Preliminary Report*. Washington, DC: National Academy of Sciences–National Research Council.

———. 1955a. *Administration of Medical and Pharmaceutical Patents*. Washington, DC: National Academy of Sciences–National Research Council.

———. 1955b. *Supplement to University Patent Policies and Practices*. Washington, DC: National Academy of Sciences–National Research Council.

———. 1956. *Nonprofit Research and Patent Management in the United States*. Washington, DC: National Academy of Sciences–National Research Council.

———. 1962. *University Research and Patent Policies, Practices, and Procedures*. Washington, DC: National Academy of Sciences–National Research Council.

"Partial Text of Address by Ian D. Lanoff, Labor Department Administrator of Pension and Welfare Benefit Programs, before ABA Annual Meeting, August 10, 1977." 1977. *BNA Pension Reporter*, 15 August, R-4–R-6.

Pauly, David. 1979. "Venture Capital Comes Back." *Newsweek*, 4 June, 67.

Peirce, Neal R., Jerry Hagstrom, and Carol Steinbach. 1979. *Economic Development: The Challenges of the 1980s*. Washington, DC: Council of State Planning Agencies.

Pennsylvania Bureau of Scientific and Technological Development. 1974. *The Pennsylvania Science and Engineering Foundation: A Summary Report of Its Accomplishments (1967–73) and Its Impact on Pennsylvania*. Harrisburg, PA: The Bureau.

Perez, Robert C. 1986. *Inside Venture Capital: Past, Present, and Future*. New York: Praeger.

Perkins, Thomas J. 2001. "Kleiner Perkins, Venture Capital, and the Chairmanship of Genentech, 1976–1995." Oral history conducted by Glenn E. Bugos. Berkeley: Regional Oral History Office, Bancroft Library, University of California.

Peters, Lois S., and Herbert I. Fusfeld. 1983. "Current U.S. University/Industry Research Connections." Pages 1–162 in *University-Industry Research Relationships: Selected Studies*, edited by the National Science Board. Washington, DC: National Science Foundation.

Pieretti, Nancy. 1982. "Dartmouth Ventures into Real Estate." *New York Times*, 21 May.

Pine, Art. 1978a. "Capital Gains Rollback Might Revive President's Long-Dormant Tax Cuts." *Washington Post*, 27 May.

———. 1978b. "Liberal Chances 'Dim' for Capital Gains Bill." *Washington Post*, 21 July.

———. 1978c. "A Tax Break for the Rich in Election Year?" *Washington Post*, 21 May.

Pisano, Gary P. 2006. *Science Business: The Promise, the Reality, and the Future of Biotech*. Boston: Harvard Business Review.

Plosila, Walter H. 2004. "State Science- and Technology-Based Economic Development Policy: History, Trends and Developments, and Future Directions." *Economic Development Quarterly* 18:113–126.

"A Policy for Industry: What It Takes to Spur Innovation." 1980. *Business Week*, 30 June, 122.

Posner, Richard A. 2009. *A Failure of Capitalism: The Crisis of '08 and the Descent into Depression*. Cambridge, MA: Harvard University Press.

Potts, Mark. 1983. "The Regions of America in the Grip of Recession: North Central Region." *Washington Post*, 9 January.

Powell, Walter W., and Jeannette A. Colyvas. 2008. "Microfoundations of Institutional Theory." Pages 276–298 in *The SAGE Handbook of Organizational Institutionalism*, edited by Royston Greenwood, Christine Oliver, Roy Suddaby, and Kerstin Sahlin-Andersson. Thousand Oaks, CA: SAGE Publishers.

Powell, Walter W., and Kurt Sandholtz. Forthcoming. "Chance, Necessité, et Naïveté: Ingredients to Create a New Organizational Form." In *The Emergence of Organizations and Markets*, edited by John Padgett and Walter W. Powell. Princeton, NJ: Princeton University Press.

Powers, David R., Mary F. Powers, Frederick Betz, and Carol B. Aslanian. 1988. *Higher Education in Partnership with Industry: Opportunities and Strategies for Training, Research, and Economic Development*. San Francisco: Jossey-Bass Publishers.

Prasad, Monica. 2006. *The Politics of Free Markets: The Rise of Neoliberal Economic Policies in Britain, France, Germany, and the United States*. Chicago: University of Chicago Press.

Press, Aric, Diane Camper, Mary Hager, Susan Dentzer, and Mitchel Zoler. 1980. "The Right to Patent Life." *Newsweek*, 30 June, 74.

"Prudent Man Rule Sufficiently Flexible for Investments." 1977. *BNA Pension Reporter*, 15 August, A-18–A-20.

Purdy, Jill M., and Barbara Gray. 2009. "Conflicting Logics, Mechanisms of Diffusion, and Multilevel Dynamics in Emerging Institutional Fields." *Academy of Management Journal* 52:355–380.

Quittmeyer, Charles L. 1960. "Faculty Consulting Practices." *Journal of the Academy of Management* 3:41–50.

Radcliffe, S. Victor. 1969. "Two Decades of Change in Graduate Education in Metallurgy/Materials." *Journal of Metals* 21:29–35.

Rajakumar, Kumaravel. 2003. "Vitamin D, Cod-Liver Oil, Sunlight, and Rickets: A Historical Perspective." *Pediatrics* 112:132–135.

Rao, Hayagreeva. 1998. "Caveat Emptor: The Construction of Nonprofit Consumer Watchdog Organizations." *American Journal of Sociology* 103:912–961.

Rao, Hayagreeva, Philippe Monin, and Rodolphe Durand. 2003. "Institutional Change in Toque Ville: Nouvelle Cuisine as an Identity Movement in French Gastronomy." *American Journal of Sociology* 108:795–843.

Rathmann, George B. 2004. "Chairman, CEO, and President of Amgen, 1980–1988." Oral history conducted by Sally Smith Hughes. Berkeley: Regional Oral History Office, Bancroft Library, University of California.

Reay, Trish, Karen Golden-Biddle, and Kathy Germann. 2006. "Legitimizing a New Role: Small Wins and Microprocesses of Change." *Academy of Management Journal* 49:977–998.

Reay, Trish, and C. R. Hinings. 2009. "Managing the Rivalry of Competing Institutional Logics." *Organization Studies* 30:629–652.

Rebne, Douglas. 1989. "Faculty Consulting and Scientific Knowledge: A Traditional University-Industry Linkage." *Educational Administration Quarterly* 25:338–357.

Rees, John. 1991. "Universities and State Technology Research Centers." *Economic Development Commentary* 15(Spring):4–11.

Reimers, Niels. 1995 [1987]. "Tiger by the Tail." *Journal of the Association of University Technology Managers 7:25–47.*

———. 1997. "Niels Reimers." Oral history conducted by Sally Smith Hughes. Berkeley: Regional Oral History Office, Bancroft Library, University of California.

Reiner, Martha Louise. 1989. "The Transformation of Venture Capital: A History of Venture Capital Organizations in the United States." PhD dissertation, University of California, Berkeley.

Reinhold, Robert. 1980. "Bacteria Tycoons Start a Real Growth Industry; Marketing Microorganisms." *New York Times*, 3 February.

"Research: No More." 1978. *Economist*, 25 March, 39.

"Research Teams Use Recombinant DNA to Make Growth Hormone." 1979. *Chemical Week*, 18 July, 25.

Rettig, Richard. 1977. *Cancer Crusade: The Story of the National Cancer Act of 1971*. Princeton, NJ: Princeton University Press.

Richard J. Barber Associates, Inc. 1975. "The Advanced Research Projects Agency, 1958–1974." Springfield, VA: Defense Technical Information Center.

Riggs, Arthur D. 2006. "Arthur D. Riggs: City of Hope's Contribution to Early Genentech Research." Oral history conducted by Sally Smith Hughes. Berkeley: Regional Oral History Office, Bancroft Library, University of California.

"The Right Way to Spur R & D." 1978. *Business Week*, 3 July, 112.

Robbins, Martin D., Colleen A. Burke, and J. Gordon Milliken. 1973. *Federal Incentives for Innovation: A Discussion of the Technological Innovation Process and a Presentation of Possible Federal Policy Options for the Stimulation of Innovation in the Private and Public Sectors, Final Report*. Denver: Denver Research Institute, University of Denver.

Robbins-Roth, Cynthia. 2000. *From Alchemy to IPO: The Business of Biotechnology*. Cambridge, MA: Perseus.

Robertson, Miranda. 1974. "ICI Puts Money on Genetic Engineering." *Nature* 251:564–565.

Roessner, David. 2000. "Outcomes and Impacts of the State/Industry-University Cooperative Research Centers (S/IUCRC) Program." Available at http://www.nsf.gov/pubs/2001/nsf01110/nsf01110.html. Last accessed 21 April 2011.

Roizen, Judy, Oliver Fulton, and Martin Trow. 1978. *Technical Report: 1975 Carnegie Council National Surveys of Higher Education*. Berkeley: University of California, Center for Studies in Higher Education.

Rosenbloom, Richard S. 1965. *Technology Transfer—Process and Policy: An Analysis of the Utilization of Technological By-products of Military and Space R & D*. Washington, DC: National Planning Association.

Rosenzweig, Robert M. 1985. "Research as Intellectual Property: Influences within the University." *Science, Technology & Human Values* 10:41–48.

Ross, Nancy L. 1977a. "3-Year-Old ERISA Faces Serious Problems." *Washington Post*, 4 September.

———. 1977b. "Widening Pensions' Investing; Concentration of Pension Assets Hit; Source of Capital Dries Up for New Firms." *Washington Post*, 15 May.

Roy, Rustum. 1972. "University-Industry Interaction Patterns." *Science* 178:955–960.

———. 1985. "Funding Science: The *Real* Defects of Peer Review and an Alternative to It." *Science, Technology & Human Values* 10:73–81.

Rudy, Alan P., Dawn Coppin, Jason Konefal, Bradley T. Shaw, Toby Ten Eyck, Craig Harris, and Lawrence Busch. 2007. *Universities in the Age of Corporate Science: The UC Berkeley-Novartis Controversy*. Philadelphia: Temple University Press.

"Rules and Regulations for Fiduciary Responsibility." 1978. *Federal Register* 43:17480–17482.

"Rules and Regulations for Fiduciary Responsibility; Investment of Plan Assets Under the 'Prudence' Rule." 1979. *Federal Register* 44:37221–37225.

Rutter, William J. 1998. "William J. Rutter." Oral history conducted by Sally Smith Hughes. Berkeley: Regional Oral History Office, Bancroft Library, University of California.

"The Sad State of Innovation." 1979. *Time*, 22 October.

Sandelin, Jon. 2003. "30 Years of AUTM: Planning Begins." *AUTM Newsletter*, September/October.

Sanger, David E. 1982. "Corporate Links Worry Scholars." *New York Times*, 17 October.

Savoye, Craig. 1983. "Companies Hungry for Ideas, Talent Snuggle Up to Universities." *Christian Science Monitor*, 8 July.

Scherer, Ron. 1980. "Wall Street's Wild Fling with 'Hot' High Tech." *Christian Science Monitor*, 17 October.

Schmeck, Jr., Harold M. 1970. "Scientists Find Cutbacks Reaching a Critical Point." *New York Times*, 27 April.

Schneiberg, Marc. 2007. "What's on the Path? Path Dependence, Organizational Diversity and the Problem of Institutional Change in the U.S. Economy, 1900–1950." *Socio-Economic Review* 5:47–80.

Schneiberg, Marc, and Michael Lounsbury. 2008. "Social Movements and Institutional Analysis." Pages 648–670 in *The SAGE Handbook of Organizational Institutionalism*,

edited by Royston Greenwood, Christine Oliver, Roy Suddaby, and Kerstin Sahlin-Andersson. Thousand Oaks, CA: SAGE Publications Ltd.
Schwartz, Lyle H. 1987. "Materials Research Laboratories: Reviewing the First Twenty-Five Years." Pages 35–48 in *Advancing Materials Research*, edited by A. Peter Psaras and H. Dale Langford. Washington, DC: National Academy Press.
Schwitter, J. P. 1965. "Universities as Research Park Developers." *Industrial Research* 7:73–78.
"Scientific Meetings." 1956. *Science* 123:1088–1091.
"Scientists in the News." 1957. *Science* 125:593–594.
Scott, W. Richard. 2007. *Institutions and Organizations: Ideas and Interests*. Thousand Oaks, CA: SAGE Publications, Inc.
Scott, W. Richard, Martin Ruef, Peter J. Mendle, and Carol A. Caronna. 2000. *Institutional Change and Healthcare Organizations: From Professional Dominance to Managed Care*. Chicago: University of Chicago Press.
Selin, Cynthia. 2007. "Expectations and the Emergence of Nanotechnology." *Science, Technology & Human Values* 32:196–220.
Semas, Philip W. 1973. "'Deep Recession' Is Seen Hitting Basic Research." *Chronicle of Higher Education*, 8 January.
Semple, Robert B. 1966. "President Orders a Medical Review: Calls on Top Federal Aides to Restudy Priorities." *New York Times*, 28 June.
Servos, John W. 1980. "The Industrial Relations of Science: Chemical Engineering at MIT, 1900–1939." *Isis* 71:531–549.
"Set for Biology's New Revolution." 1977. *Business Week*, 17 January, 76.
Shane, Scott. 2004. *Academic Entrepreneurship: University Spinoffs and Wealth Creation*. Cheltenham, UK: Edward Elgar Publishing Limited.
Shannon, James A. 1964. "Memo to the Surgeon General from James A. Shannon, Director, NIH." Bethesda, MD, 14 August. Unpublished memorandum from the personal files of Norman J. Latker. (Photocopy available from the author.)
Shapin, Steven. 2008. "I'm a Surfer." *London Review of Books*, 20 March.
Shapley, Deborah. 1971. "Magruder in White House: SST Man Plans New Technology Take-Off." *Science* 174:386–388.
———. 1972a. "Technology Initiatives: Hints on the Magruder Effort." *Science* 175:279–281.
———. 1972b. "White House Presents Vapid Technology Plan." *Science* 175:1343.
———. 1973a. "Technology and the Trade Crisis: Salvation through a New Policy?" *Science* 179:881–883.
———. 1973b. "Technology Incentives: NSF Gropes for Relevance." *Science* 179:1105–1107.
"Sharing the Wealth." 1980. *Harvard Crimson*, 8 September.
Sheils, Nerrill. 1980. "Harvard as Entrepreneur." *Newsweek*, 10 November, 93.
Sherwin, Chalmers W., and Raymond S. Isenson. 1966. "First Interim Report on Project Hindsight." Washington, DC: Office of the Director of Defense Research and Engineering.
———. 1967. "Project Hindsight: A Defense Department Study of the Utility of Research." *Science* 156:1571–1577.
"A Shred of Carter Innovation Plan Survives." 1981. *Science & Government Report*, 15 August, 3.

Siegel, Donald S., Mike Wright, and Andy Lockett. 2007. "The Rise of Entrepreneurial Activity at Universities: Organizational and Societal Implications." *Industrial and Corporate Change* 16:487–504.

"The Silent Crisis in R&D." 1976. *Business Week*, 8 March, 90.

Simha, O. Robert. 2003. *MIT Campus Planning 1960–2000*. Cambridge, MA: MIT Press.

"Site Selector's Guide to Sites for Science." 1966. *Industrial Development*, August, 22–30.

Slaughter, Sheila, and Larry L. Leslie. 1997. *Academic Capitalism: Politics, Policies, and the Entrepreneurial University*. Baltimore: Johns Hopkins University Press.

Slaughter, Sheila, and Gary Rhoades. 2004. *Academic Capitalism and the New Economy: Markets, State, and Higher Education*. Baltimore: Johns Hopkins University Press.

Smith, Adam. 2000 [1776]. *An Inquiry into the Nature and Causes of the Wealth of Nations*. New York: Modern Library.

Smith, Bruce L. R. 1990a. *American Science Policy since World War II*. Washington, DC: Brookings Institution.

Smith, Bruce L. R., and Joseph J. Karlesky. 1977. *The State of Academic Science: The Universities in the Nation's Research Effort*. New York: Change Magazine Press.

Smith, Jane S. 1990b. *Patenting the Sun: Polio and the Salk Vaccine*. New York: Morrow.

Smith, Mark A. 2007. *The Right Talk: How Conservatives Transformed the Great Society into the Economic Society*. Princeton, NJ: Princeton University Press.

Smith, R. Jeffrey. 1978. "Patent Policy Changes Stir Concern." *Science* 199:1190.

Solow, Robert M. 1957. "Technical Change and the Aggregate Production Function." *Review of Economics and Statistics* 39:214–231.

———. 2000. "The Kennedy Council and the Long Run." Pages 111–124 in *Economic Events, Ideas, and Policies: The 1960s and After*, edited by George L. Perry and James Tobin. Washington, DC: Brookings Institution Press.

Sovel, M. Terry. 1969. "Technology Transfer: A Selected Bibliography." Report No. NASA CR-1355. Washington, DC: National Aeronautics and Space Administration.

Sproull, Robert Lamb. 2002. "Robert Lamb Sproull Interview." Oral history conducted by Arne Hessenbruch. Cambridge, MA: Dibner Institute for the History of Science and Technology, Massachusetts Institute of Technology.

Stauffer, Thomas M., ed. 1980. *Agenda for Business and Higher Education: Business-Higher Education Forum*. Washington, DC: American Council on Education.

Stein, Herbert. 1991. *The Fiscal Revolution in America*. Washington, DC: AEI Press.

Steinbach, Sheldon. 2005. Interview by author. Tape recording of phone interview. Washington, DC, 31 March.

Steiner, Daniel. 1980. "Technology Transfer at Harvard University." *Bioethics Quarterly* 2:203–211.

Stevens, Ashley J. 2004. "The Enactment of Bayh-Dole." *Journal of Technology Transfer* 29:93–99.

Strickland, Stephen P. 1972. *Politics, Science, and Dread Disease*. Cambridge, MA: Harvard University Press.

———. 1989. *The Story of the NIH Grants Program*. Lanham, MD: University Press of America.

Stuart, Toby E., and Waverly W. Ding. 2006. "When Do Scientists Become Entrepreneurs? The Social Structural Antecedents of Commercial Activity in the Academic Life Sciences." *American Journal of Sociology* 112:97–144.

Suddaby, Roy, and Royston Greenwood. 2005. "Rhetorical Strategies of Legitimacy." *Administrative Science Quarterly* 50:35–67.
Suh, Nam P. 1986. "The Concept and Goals of the Engineering Research Centers." Pages 37–43 in *The New Engineering Research Centers: Purposes, Goals, and Expectations*, edited by the Cross-Disciplinary Engineering Research Committee of the National Research Council Commission on Engineering and Technical Systems. Washington, DC: National Academy Press.
Sutherland, Ivan. 1989. "An Interview with Ivan Sutherland." Oral history conducted by William Aspray. Minneapolis: Charles Babbage Institute, Center for the History of Information Processing, University of Minnesota.
Swain, Donald C. 1962. "The Rise of a Research Empire: NIH, 1930 to 1950." *Science* 138:1233–1237.
Swaminathan, Anand, and James B. Wade. 2001. "Social Movement Theory and the Evolution of New Organizational Forms." Pages 286–313 in *The Entrepreneurship Dynamic in Industry Evolution*, edited by Claudia Bird Schoonhoven and Elaine Romanelli. Stanford, CA: Stanford University Press.
Swanson, Robert A. 1997. "Co-Founder, CEO, and Chairman of Genentech, Inc., 1976–1996." Oral history conducted by Sally Smith Hughes. Berkeley: Regional Oral History Office, Bancroft Library, University of California.
Swazey, Judith P., and Karen Reeds. 1978. "Today's Medicine, Tomorrow's Science: Essays on Paths of Discovery in the Biomedical Sciences." Washington, DC: U.S. Department of Health, Education, and Welfare.
"Synthetic Version of Chemical Controlling Growth, Heredity Produced by Scientist." 1967. *Wall Street Journal*, 15 December.
"The Tax Cut Spurs Venture Capital." 1978. *Business Week*, 30 October, 164.
Teague, Gerald V. 1982. "Faculty Consulting: Do Universities Have 'Control'?" *Research in Higher Education* 17:179–186.
Terry, Sara. 1981. "How Jerry Brown Envisions 'Investing in the Future.'" *Christian Science Monitor*, 12 February.
Test, Herbert H. 1966. "The Materials Research Centers." *Industrial Research* 8:41–47.
The Texas A&M University System. 2010. "A&M System History." Available at http://www.tamus.edu/about/history/. Last accessed 21 April 2011.
Thomas, Tony, and Anne Segall. 1977. "In Whom Do We Trust?" *Economist*, 22 January, 52.
Thornburgh, Dick. 2003. *Where the Evidence Leads*. Pittsburgh: University of Pittsburgh Press.
Thornton, Patricia H. 2004. *Markets from Culture: Institutional Logics and Organizational Decisions in Higher Education Publishing*. Stanford, CA: Stanford University Press.
Thornton, Patricia H., and William Ocasio. 2008. "Institutional Logics." Pages 99–129 in *The SAGE Handbook of Organizational Institutionalism*, edited by Royston Greenwood, Christine Oliver, Roy Suddaby, and Kerstin Sahlin-Andersson. Thousand Oaks, CA: SAGE Publications Ltd.
Tornatzky, L. G., W. A. Hetzner, J. D. Eveland, A. Schwartzkopf, and R. M. Colton. 1982. *University-Industry Cooperative Research Centers: A Practice Manual*. Washington, DC: National Science Foundation.
Trow, Martin. 1972. *Technical Report: National Survey of Higher Education*. Berkeley, CA: Carnegie Commission on Higher Education.

Trow, Martin. 1984. "Leadership and Organization: The Case of Biology at Berkeley." Pages 148–178 in *Higher Education Organization*, edited by Rune Premfors. Stockholm: Almqvist and Wiksell International.

———. 1999. "Biology at Berkeley: A Case Study of Reorganization and Its Costs and Benefits." Report No. CSHE.1.99. Berkeley: Center for the Study of Higher Education, University of California. Available at http://cshe.berkeley.edu/publications/docs/PP.Trow.Biology.1.99.pdf. Last accessed 21 April 2011.

Turner, James. 2006. "The Next Innovation Revolution: Laying the Groundwork for the United States." *Innovations: Technology, Governance, Globalization* 1:123–144.

Turner, John L. 2005. "In Defense of the Patent Friendly Court Hypothesis: Theory and Evidence." Available at http://ssrn.com/paper=713601. Last accessed 21 April 2011.

"Uncovering Life's Secrets." 1967. *New York Times*, 15 December.

"Universities Exaggerate Their Innovations." 1991. *Chronicle of Higher Education*, 15 May.

U.S. Bureau of Economic Analysis. 2011. "National Economic Accounts." Available at http://www.bea.gov/national/nipaweb/Index.asp. Last accessed 21 April 2011.

U.S. Census Bureau. 2010. "U.S. Trade in Goods and Services—Balance of Payments (BOP) Basis." Available at http://www.census.gov/foreign-trade/statistics/historical/gands.pdf. Last accessed 21 April 2011.

U.S. Congress, Congressional Budget Office. 1988a. *How Capital Gains Tax Rates Affect Revenues: The Historical Evidence*. Washington, DC: U.S. Government Printing Office. Available at http://www.cbo.gov/ftpdocs/84xx/doc8449/88-CBO-007.pdf. Last accessed 20 April 2011.

U.S. Congress, Joint Economic Committee. 1977. *Role of Federal Tax Policy in Stimulating Capital Formation and Economic Growth*. Washington, DC: U.S. Government Printing Office.

U.S. Congress, Joint Economic Committee, Subcommittee on Economic Growth. 1975. *Technology and Economic Growth*. Washington, DC: U.S. Government Printing Office.

U.S. Congress, Office of Technology Assessment. 1983. "Census of State Government Initiatives for High-Technology Industrial Development." Washington, DC: Office of Technology Assessment.

———. 1984a. *Commercial Biotechnology: An International Analysis*. New York: Pergamon Press.

———. 1984b. "Technology, Innovation and Regional Economic Development: Encouraging High-Technology Development." Report No. OTA-BP-STI-25. Washington, DC: Office of Technology Assessment.

———. 1985. *Information Technology R&D: Critical Trends and Issues*. Washington, DC: U.S. Government Printing Office.

———. 1988b. *New Developments in Biotechnology: U.S. Investment in Biotechnology*. Washington, DC: U.S. Government Printing Office.

U.S. Department of Justice. 1947. *Investigation of Government Patent Practices and Policies: Report and Recommendations of the Attorney General to the President*. Washington, DC: U.S. Government Printing Office.

U.S. Department of Labor, Bureau of Labor Statistics. 2010a. "Consumer Price Index (CPI): Historical Data." Available at http://www.bls.gov. Last accessed 21 April 2011.

———. 2010b. "Current Unemployment Rates for States and Historical Highs/Lows." Bureau of Labor Statistics. Available at http://www.bls.gov/web/lauhsthl.htm. Last accessed 21 April 2011.
———. 2010c. "Employment Status of the Civilian Noninstitutional Population, 1940 to Date." Available at http://www.bls.gov/cps/cpsaat1.pdf. Last accessed 21 April 2011.
———. 2010d. "History of CPI-U U.S. All Items Indexes and Annual Percent Changes from 1913 to Present." Available at ftp://ftp.bls.gov/pub/special.requests/cpi/cpiai.txt .Last accessed 21 April 2011.
———. 2010e. "Labor Productivity and Costs." Available at http://www.bls.gov/lpc/. Last accessed 21 April 2011.
U.S. General Accounting Office. 1968. *Problem Areas Affecting Usefulness of Results of Government-Sponsored Research in Medicinal Chemistry: A Report to the Congress.* Washington, DC: U.S. Government Printing Office.
———. 1983. *The Federal Role in Fostering University-Industry Cooperation.* Washington, DC: General Accounting Office.
U.S. House, Committee on Appropriations, Subcommittee on HUD-Independent Agencies. 1979a. *Department of Housing and Urban Development—Independent Agencies Appropriations for 1980.* Washington, DC: U.S. Government Printing Office.
U.S. House, Committee on Appropriations, Subcommittee on HUD-Space-Science Appropriations. 1971a. *HUD-Space-Science Appropriations for 1972.* Washington, DC: U.S. Government Printing Office.
U.S. House, Committee on Appropriations, Subcommittee on Independent Offices and Department of Housing and Urban Development. 1970a. *Independent Offices and Department of Housing and Urban Development Appropriations for 1971.* Washington, DC: U.S. Government Printing Office.
U.S. House, Committee on Budget. 1983a. *Higher Education and Innovation in the U.S. Economy and President's FY84 Budget: Perspective from the States.* Washington, DC: U.S. Government Printing Office.
U.S. House, Committee on Interstate and Foreign Commerce, Subcommittee on Commerce and Finance. 1971b. *State Technical Services Act Amendments.* Washington, DC: U.S. Government Printing Office.
U.S. House, Committee on Interstate and Foreign Commerce, Subcommittee on Health and Environment. 1977a. *Recombinant DNA Research Act of 1977.* Washington, DC: U.S. Government Printing Office.
U.S. House, Committee on Judiciary, Subcommittee on Courts, Civil Liberties, and Administration of Justice. 1977b. *State of the Judiciary and Access to Justice.* Washington, DC: U.S. Government Printing Office.
U.S. House, Committee on Science and Astronautics, Subcommittee on Science, Research, and Development. 1970b. *National Science Policy.* Washington, DC: U.S. Government Printing Office.
U.S. House, Committee on Science and Technology. 1980. *Toward the Endless Frontier: History of the Committee on Science and Technology, 1959–1979.* Washington, DC: U.S. Government Printing Office.
U.S. House, Committee on Science and Technology, Subcommittee on Domestic and International Scientific Planning and Analysis. 1976a. *Federal Research and Development Expenditures and the National Economy.* Washington, DC: U.S. Government Printing Office.

U.S. House, Committee on Science and Technology, Subcommittee on Domestic and International Scientific Planning and Analysis. 1976b. *Selected Readings on Research and Development Expenditures and the National Economy*. Washington, DC: U.S. Government Printing Office.

U.S. House, Committee on Science and Technology, Subcommittee on Investigations and Oversight and Subcommittee on Science, Research, and Technology. 1981a. *Commercialization of Academic Biomedical Research*. Washington, DC: U.S. Government Printing Office.

———. 1982. *University/Industry Cooperation in Biotechnology*. Washington, DC: U.S. Government Printing Office.

U.S. House, Committee on Science and Technology, Subcommittee on Science, Research, and Technology. 1977c. *1978 National Science Foundation Authorization*. Washington, DC: U.S. Government Printing Office.

———. 1978a. *1979 National Science Foundation Authorization*. Washington, DC: U.S. Government Printing Office.

———. 1978b. *Science Policy Implications of DNA Recombinant Molecule Research [report]*. Washington, DC: U.S. Government Printing Office.

———. 1979b. *Government and Innovation: University-Industry Relations*. Washington, DC: U.S. Government Printing Office.

———. 1983b. *1984 National Science Foundation Authorization*. Washington, DC: U.S. Government Printing Office.

———. 1983c. *The National Science Board: Science Policy and Management for the National Science Foundation 1968–1980*. Washington, DC: U.S. Government Printing Office.

U.S. House, Committee on Science, Space, and Technology. 1971c. *Science, Technology, and the Economy*. Washington, DC: U.S. Government Printing Office.

———. 1971d. *Selected Readings on Science, Technology, and the Economy*. Washington, DC: U.S. Government Printing Office.

———. 1972. *Science, Technology, and the Economy [hearings]*. Washington, DC: U.S. Government Printing Office.

U.S. House, Committee on Science, Space and Technology, Subcommittee on Domestic and International Scientific Planning and Analysis. 1976c. *Background Materials on Government Patent Policies: The Ownership of Inventions Resulting from Federally Funded Research and Development*. Washington, DC: U.S. Government Printing Office.

———. 1977d. *Government Patent Policy: The Ownership of Inventions Resulting from Federally Funded R&D*. Washington, DC: U.S. Government Printing Office.

U.S. House, Committee on Small Business. 1977e. *Small Business Access to Equity and Venture Capital*. Washington, DC: U.S. Government Printing Office.

U.S. House, Committee on the Judiciary, Subcommittee on Courts, Civil Liberties, and the Administration of Justice. 1981b. *Court of Appeals for the Federal Circuit, 1981*. Washington, DC: U.S. Government Printing Office.

U.S. House, Committee on Ways and Means. 1978c. *President's 1978 Tax Reduction and Reform Proposals, Part 3*. Washington, DC: U.S. Government Printing Office.

———. 1981c. *Tax Aspects of the President's Economic Program, Part 3*. Washington, DC: U.S. Government Printing Office.

U.S. Judicial Conference, Committee on the Bicentennial of the Constitution of the United States. 1991. *The United States Court of Appeals for the Federal Circuit: A History, 1982–1990*. Washington, DC: Court of Appeals for the Federal Circuit.

U.S. Library of Congress, Congressional Research Service. 1982. *Biotechnology: Commercialization of Academic Research*. Washington, DC: U.S. Government Printing Office. Available at http://digital.library.unt.edu/govdocs/crs/permalink/meta-crs-8589:1. Last accessed 21 April 2011.

U.S. NIH Study Committee. 1965. *Biomedical Science and Its Administration: A Study of the National Institutes of Health*. Washington, DC: United States Government Printing Office.

U.S. Office of Management and Budget. 2008. "Budget of the United States Government: Fiscal Year 2009: Historical Tables." Available at http://www.whitehouse.gov/sites/default/files/omb/budget/fy2009/pdf/hist.pdf. Last accessed 21 April 2011.

U.S. Office of State Technical Services. 1968. "Annual Report—Office of State Technical Services, Fiscal Year 1968." Clearinghouse No. AC00379. Washington, DC: U.S. Government Printing Office.

U.S. Office of the Director of Defense Research and Engineering. 1969. *Project Hindsight: Final Report*. Washington, DC: Office of the Director of Defense Research and Engineering.

U.S. Patent and Trademark Office, Patent Technology Monitoring Team. 2010. "U.S. Patent Activity: Calendar Years 1790 to the Present." Available at http://www.uspto.gov/web/offices/ac/ido/oeip/taf/h_counts.htm. Last accessed 21 April 2011.

U.S. President. 1947. *The Economic Report of the President*. Washington, DC: U.S. Government Printing Office.

———. 1962. *The Economic Report of the President*. Washington, DC: U.S. Government Printing Office.

U.S. Senate, Committee on Commerce, Science, and Transportation and Select Committee on Small Business, and U.S. House Committee on Small Business and Committee on Science and Technology. 1979. *Industrial Innovation*. Washington, DC: U.S. Government Printing Office.

U.S. Senate, Committee on Commerce, Science, and Transportation, Subcommittee on Science, Technology, and Space. 1977a. *Regulation of Recombinant DNA Research*. Washington, DC: U.S. Government Printing Office.

———. 1979a. *Oversight on OSTP*. Washington, DC: U.S. Government Printing Office.

———. 1983. *National Science Foundation Authorization*. Washington, DC: U.S. Government Printing Office.

U.S. Senate, Committee on Commerce, Special Subcommittee on Science, Technology, and Commerce. 1974. *Federal Incentives for Innovation*. Washington, DC: U.S. Government Printing Office.

U.S. Senate, Committee on Finance. 1977b. *Incentives for Economic Growth*. Washington, DC: U.S. Government Printing Office.

U.S. Senate, Committee on Finance, Subcommittee on Private Pension Plans and Employee Fringe Benefits. 1977c. *Pension Simplification and Investment Rules*. Washington, DC: U.S. Government Printing Office.

U.S. Senate, Committee on Finance, Subcommittee on Taxation and Debt Management Generally. 1978a. *Capital Gains Tax Bills*. Washington, DC: U.S. Government Printing Office.

U.S. Senate, Committee on Government Operations, Subcommittee on Government Research. 1966. *Research in the Service of Man: Biomedical Knowledge, Development, and Use*. Washington, DC: U.S. Government Printing Office.

U.S. Senate, Committee on Government Operations, Subcommittee on Government Research. 1967a. *Research in the Service of Man*. Washington, DC: U.S. Government Printing Office.

———. 1968. *National Commission on Health Science and Society*. Washington, DC: U.S. Government Printing Office.

U.S. Senate, Committee on Human Resources, Subcommittee on Health and Scientific Research. 1977d. *Recombinant DNA Regulation Act, 1977*. Washington, DC: U.S. Government Printing Office.

U.S. Senate, Committee on Human Resources, Subcommittee on Labor. 1977e. *Oversight of ERISA, 1977*. Washington, DC: U.S. Government Printing Office.

U.S. Senate, Committee on Labor and Human Resources, Subcommittee on Health. 1975. *Genetic Engineering, 1975*. Washington, DC: U.S. Government Printing Office.

———. 1976. *National Science Foundation Authorization Act, 1977*. Washington, DC: U.S. Government Printing Office.

U.S. Senate, Committee on the Judiciary. 1979b. *University and Small Business Patent Procedures Act*. Washington, DC: U.S. Government Printing Office.

U.S. Senate, Committee on the Judiciary, Subcommittee on Courts. 1981. *Federal Courts Improvement Act of 1981: S. 21, and State Justice Institute Act of 1981: S. 537*. Washington, DC: U.S. Government Printing Office.

U.S. Senate, Committee on the Judiciary, Subcommittee on Patents, Trademarks, and Copyrights. 1965. *Government Patent Policy*. Washington, DC: U.S. Government Printing Office.

U.S. Senate, Select Committee on Small Business. 1963a. *Economic Aspects of Government Patent Policies: Impact of Government Patent Policies on Economic Growth, Scientific and Technological Progress, Competition, Monopoly, and Opportunities for Small Business*. Washington, DC: U.S. Government Printing Office.

———. 1977f. *Small Business Issues and Priorities, 1977*. Washington, DC: U.S. Government Printing Office.

U.S. Senate, Select Committee on Small Business, Subcommittee on Antitrust, Consumers, and Employment. 1979c. *Small Business and Innovation*. Washington, DC: U.S. Government Printing Office.

U.S. Senate, Select Committee on Small Business, Subcommittee on Monopoly. 1959. *Patent Policies of Departments and Agencies of the Federal Government*. Washington, DC: U.S. Government Printing Office.

———. 1960. *Patent Policies of Government Departments and Agencies: Conference on Federal Patent Policies*. Washington, DC: U.S. Government Printing Office.

U.S. Senate, Select Committee on Small Business, Subcommittee on Monopoly and Anticompetitive Activities. 1978b. *Government Patent Policies*. Washington, DC: U.S. Government Printing Office.

———. 1978c. *Government Patent Policies: Institutional Patent Agreements*. Washington, DC: U.S. Government Printing Office.

U.S. Senate, Select Committee on Small Business, Subcommittee on Science and Technology. 1963b. *The Role and Effect of Technology in the Nation's Economy*. Washington, DC: U.S. Government Printing Office.

———. 1967b. *Policy Planning for Technology Transfer*. Washington, DC: U.S. Government Printing Office.

———. 1967c. *Technology Transfer*. Washington, DC: U.S. Government Printing Office.

———. 1970. *Technology Transfer, Part 1*. Washington, DC: U.S. Government Printing Office.

Ullrich, Axel. 2006. "Molecular Biologist at UCSF and Genentech." Oral history conducted by Sally Smith Hughes. Berkeley: Regional Oral History Office, Bancroft Library, University of California.

University of Illinois. 1999. *The University of Illinois: Engine of Economic Development*. Urbana-Champaign: University of Illinois.

———. 2000. *At the Crossroads: The State, the University, and Tomorrow's Technology*. Urbana-Champaign: University of Illinois.

University of Illinois, Department of Theoretical and Applied Mechanics. 1995. "The Engineering Experiment Station." Available at http://uihistoriesproject.chass.illinois.edu/TAMHistory/Talbot/history5.html. Last accessed 21 April 2011.

University of Illinois, Office of the Vice President for Economic Development and Corporate Relations. 2002. *Technology Commercialization at the University of Illinois: Growing the Illinois High Technology Economy*. Urbana-Champaign: University of Illinois.

University of Utah Archives. 2010. "Utah Engineering Experiment Station Records, 1936–1964." Available at http://content.lib.utah.edu/cdm4/item_viewer.php?CISOROOT=/UU_EAD&CISOPTR=212. Last accessed 21 April 2011.

Uzzi, Brian. 1997. "Networks and the Paradox of Embeddedness." *Administrative Science Quarterly* 42:35–67.

Valdivia, Walter. 2011. "The Stakes in Bayh-Dole: Public Values beyond the Pace of Innovation." *Minerva* 49:25–46.

Vallas, Steven Peter, and Daniel Lee Kleinman. 2008. "Contradiction, Convergence and the Knowledge Economy: The Confluence of Academic and Commercial Biotechnology." *Socio-Economic Review* 6:283–311.

Vance, Erik. 2007. "Energy Company Gives $500-Million Research Grant to Universities." *Chronicle of Higher Education*, 16 February.

van Helvoort, Ton. 2002. "Institutionalizing Biochemistry: The Enzyme Institute at the University of Wisconsin." *Journal of the History of Medicine and Allied Sciences* 57:449–479.

"Vanishing Innovation: A Hostile Climate for New Ideas and Products Is Threatening the Technological Superiority of the U.S." 1978. *Business Week*, 3 July, 46–54.

Vaughan, Roger. 1979. *Inflation and Unemployment: Surviving the 1980s*. Washington, DC: Council of State Planning Agencies.

———. 2000. *Listen to the Music: The Life of Hilary Koprowski*. New York: Springer.

"Venture Capital: Technology Can Pay." 1979. *Economist*, 21 April, 124.

Vest, Charles M. 2004. *Pursuing the Endless Frontier: Essays on MIT and the Role of Research Universities*. Cambridge, MA: MIT Press.

———. 2007. *The American Research University from World War II to World Wide Web: Governments, the Private Sector, and the Emerging Meta-University*. Berkeley: University of California Press.

Vettel, Eric J. 2004. "The Protean Nature of Stanford's Biological Sciences, 1946–1972." *Historical Studies in the Physical and Biological Sciences* 35:95–113.

———. 2006. *Biotech: The Countercultural Origins of an Industry*. Philadelphia: University of Pennsylvania Press.

Villa-Komaroff, Lydia, Argiris Efstratiadis, Stephanie Broome, Peter Lomedico, Richard Tizard, Stephen P. Naber, William L. Chick, and Walter Gilbert. 1978. "A Bacterial

Clone Synthesizing Proinsulin." *Proceedings of the National Academy of Sciences* 75:3727–3731.

Vogel, Steven K. 1998. *Freer Markets, More Rules: Regulatory Reform in Advanced Industrial Economies*. Ithaca, NY: Cornell University Press.

Wade, Nicholas. 1971. "Nixon's New Economic Policy: Hints of a Resurgence for R & D." *Science* 173:794–796.

———. 1977. *The Ultimate Experiment: Man-Made Evolution*. New York: Walker and Co.

———. 1979. "Recombinant DNA: Warming Up for Big Payoff." *Science* 206:663–665.

———. 1980a. "Cloning Gold Rush Turns Basic Biology into Big Business." *Science* 208:688–692.

———. 1980b. "Gene Goldrush Splits Harvard, Worries Brokers." *Science* 210:878–879.

———. 1980c. "Hybridomas: A Potent New Biotechnology." *Science* 208:692–693.

———. 1980d. "Inventor of Hybridoma Technology Failed to File for Patent." *Science* 208:693.

———. 1980e. "Three New Entrants in Gene Splicing Derby." *Science* 208:690.

Walker, Eric A., and Robert G. Hampel. 1974. "Improving Industrial R&D: University Relations." *Research Management* 17:23–28.

Walker, Ruth. 1982. "Gov. Hunt Tries to Balance the Future on Computer Chip." *Christian Science Monitor*, 15 June.

"Wallets Open Up for Risky Ventures." 1979. *U.S. News & World Report*, 24 December, 75.

Walsh, John. 1966a. "NIH: Demand Increases for Applications of Research." *Science* 153:149–152.

———. 1966b. "R & D Funds Show Effects of a Tough Budget Year." *Science* 151:425–428.

———. 1969. "Campus Unrest: Congress Ponders Federal Sanctions on Universities." *Science* 165:46–49.

———. 1976. "R & D and Economic Growth: Renewed Interest in Federal Role." *Science* 193:1101–1103.

———. 1981. "Innovation Act after the Fall." *Science* 213:627.

———. 1986. "NSF Designates Five New Engineering Centers." *Science* 232:18.

———. 1987. "NSF Puts Big Stake on Research Centers." *Science* 236:18–19.

Walsh, John P., Wesley M. Cohen, and Charlene Cho. 2007. "Where Excludability Matters: Material versus Intellectual Property in Academic Biomedical Research." *Research Policy* 36:1184–1203.

Wanniski, Jude. 1978. "Stupendous Steiger." *Wall Street Journal*, 26 April.

Warsh, David. 2006. *Knowledge and the Wealth of Nations: A Story of Economic Discovery*. New York: W.W. Norton & Company, Inc.

Washburn, Jennifer. 2005. *University, Inc.: The Corporate Corruption of American Higher Education*. New York: Basic Books.

Weber, Max. 1978 [1922]. *Economy and Society: An Outline of Interpretive Sociology*. Berkeley: University of California Press.

———. 2002 [1904–1905]. *The Protestant Ethic and the Spirit of Capitalism*. Los Angeles: Roxbury Publishing Company.

Weick, Sister Mary Theodora. 1967. "A History of Rickets in the United States." *American Journal of Clinical Nutrition* 20:1234–1241.

Welsh, Rick, and Leland Glenna. 2006. "Considering the Role of the University in Conducting Research on Agri-Biotechnologies." *Social Studies of Science* 36:929–942.
Welsh, Rick, Leland Glenna, William Lacy, and Dina Biscotti. 2008. "Close Enough but Not Too Far: Assessing the Rise of University-Industry Research Relationships and the Rise of Academic Capitalism." *Research Policy* 37:1854–1864.
"Where Are Britain's Capital Ventures?" 1977. *Economist*, 23 July, 72.
"Where Genetic Engineering Will Change Industry." 1979. *Business Week*, 22 October, 160.
Wiesendanger, Hans. 2000. "A History of OTL." Available at http://otl.stanford.edu/about/about_history.html. Last accessed 21 April 2011.
Williamson, John. 2004. "A Short History of the Washington Consensus." Paper presented at a conference, "From the Washington Consensus towards a New Global Governance," 24–25 September. Available at http://www.iie.com/publications/papers/williamson0904-2.pdf. Last accessed 21 April 2011.
"Witnesses Support Bill to Encourage Investment in Small Firms." 1977. *BNA Pension Reporter*, 4 July, A-1–A-4.
Wolfle, Dael. 1968. "Universities and the Technology Gap." *Science* 160:381.
Wright, Susan. 1986. "Recombinant DNA Technology and Its Social Transformation, 1972–1982." *Osiris* 2:303–360.
———. 1994. *Molecular Politics: Developing American and British Regulatory Policy for Genetic Engineering, 1972–1982*. Chicago: University of Chicago Press.
Yi, Doogab. 2008. "Who Owns What? Private Ownership and the Public Interest in Recombinant DNA Technology in the 1970s." Bethesda, MD. Unpublished paper from the NIH History Office Work-in-Progress Seminar.
Zachary, G. Pascal. 2007. "Bell Labs Is Gone. Academia Steps In." *New York Times*, 16 December.

Index